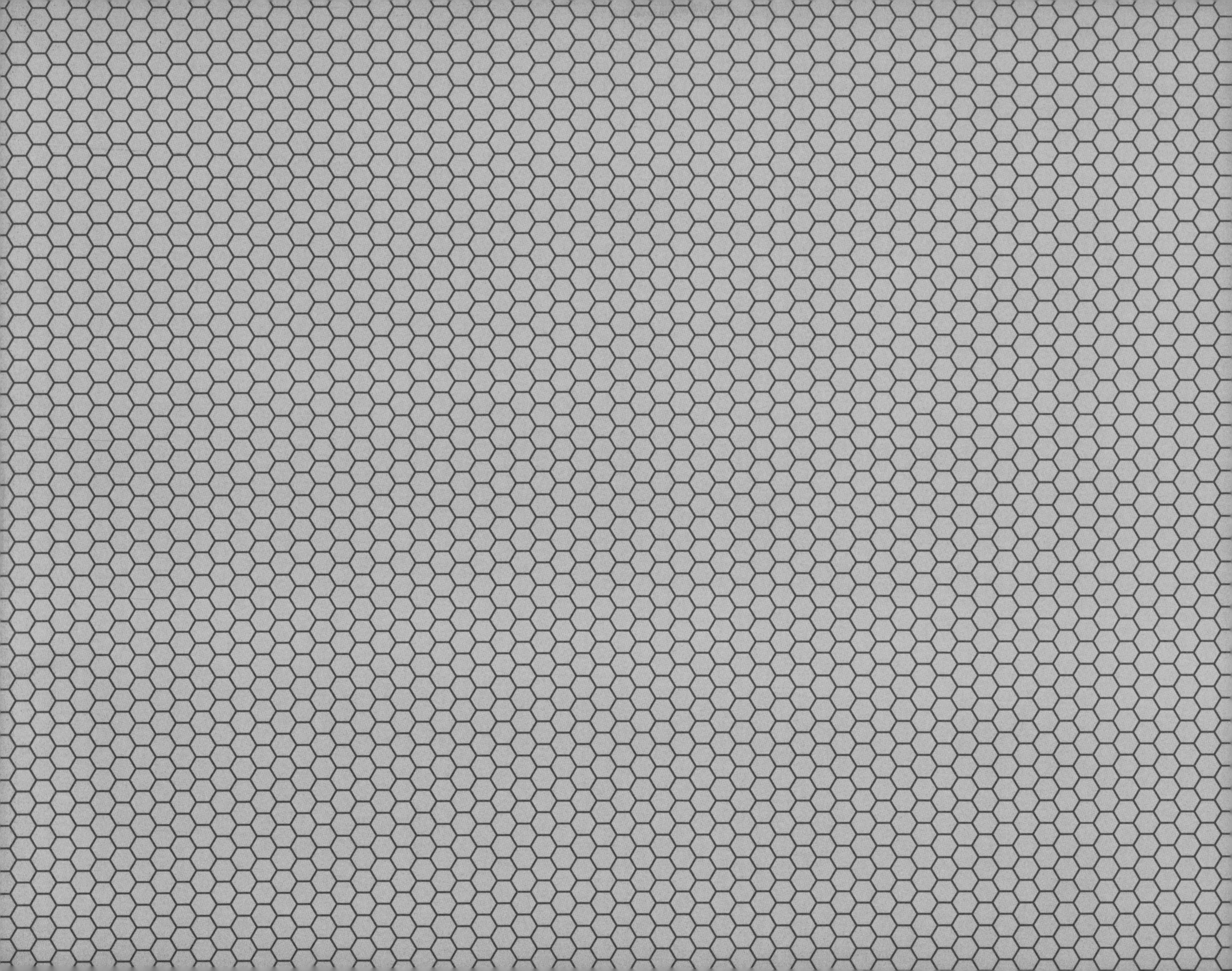

THE ART OF

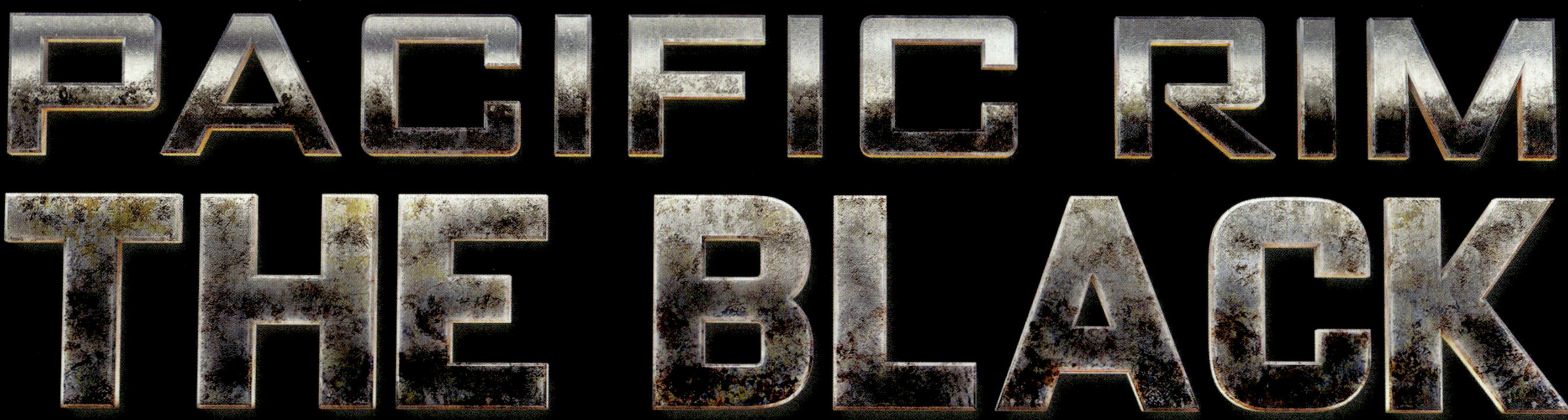

THE ART OF

PACIFIC RIM THE BLACK

ISBN: 9781789099454
Ebook ISBN: 9781803361024

Published by
Titan Books
A division of Titan Publishing Group Ltd
144 Southwark St
London
SE1 0UP

www.titanbooks.com

First edition: October 2022

2 4 6 8 10 9 7 5 3 1

Did you enjoy this book? We love to hear from our readers.
Please e-mail us at: readerfeedback@titanemail.com or
write to Reader Feedback at the above address.

To receive advance information, news, competitions, and exclusive offers online, please sign up for the Titan newsletter on our website:
www.titanbooks.com

A CIP catalogue record for this title is available from the British Library.

Printed and bound in China.

THE ART OF

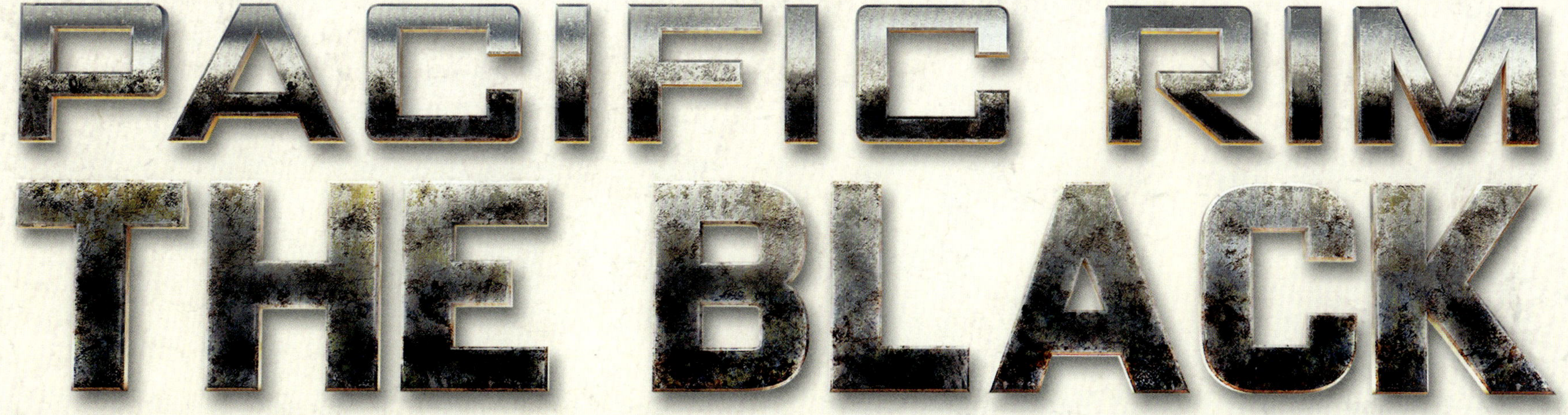

ANDREW OSMOND

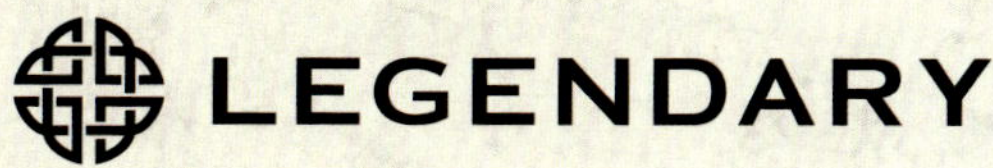

LEGENDARY

CONTENTS

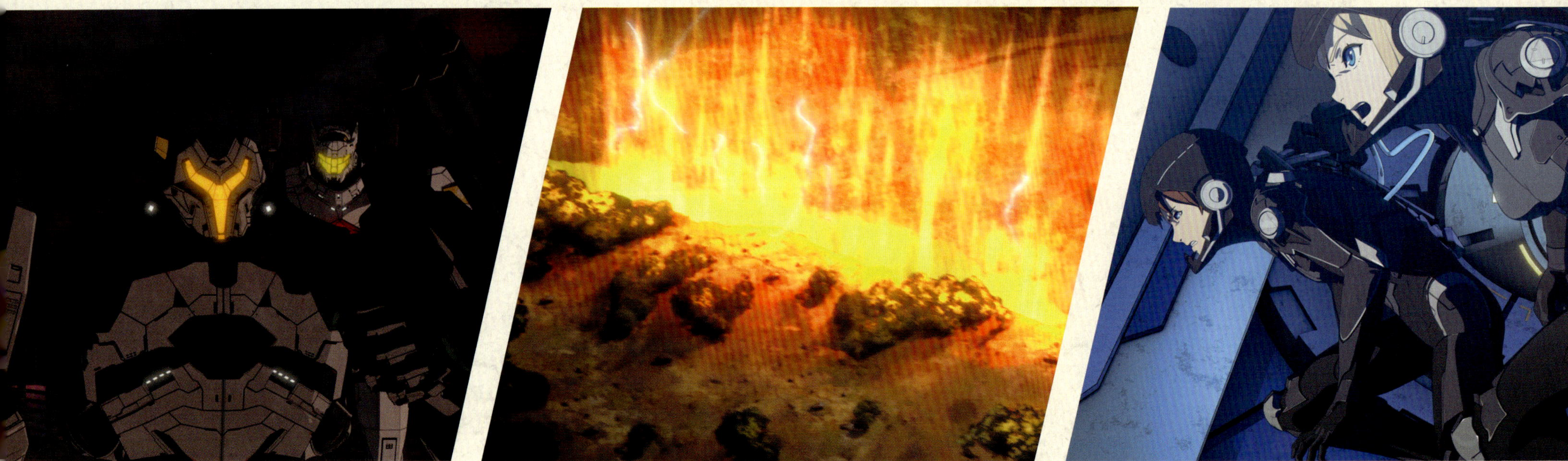

114 SEASON 2

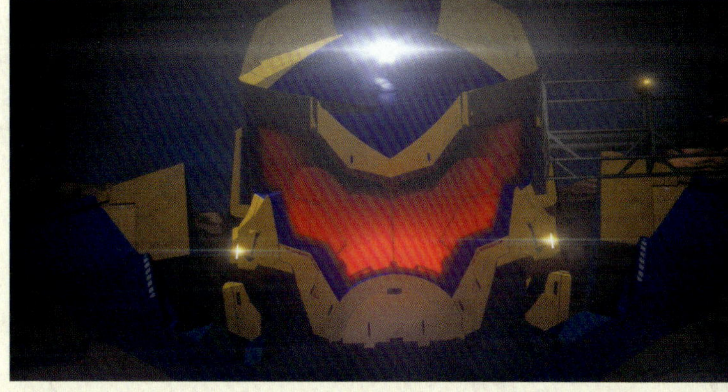

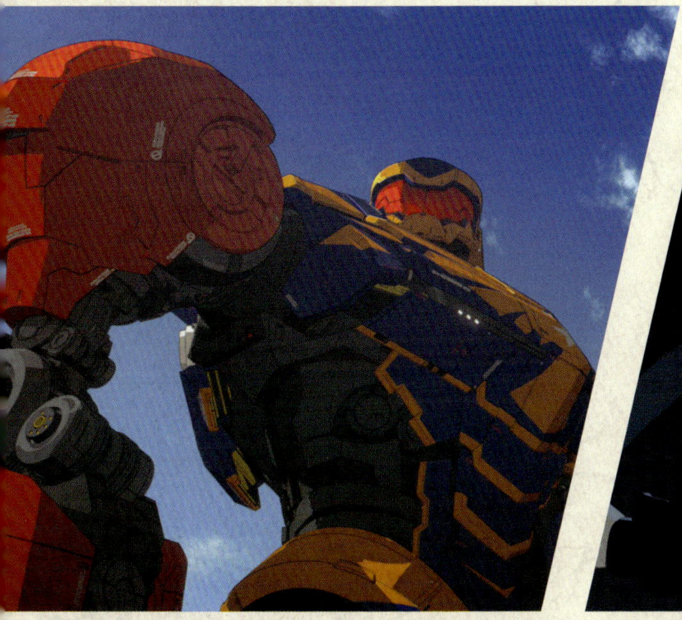

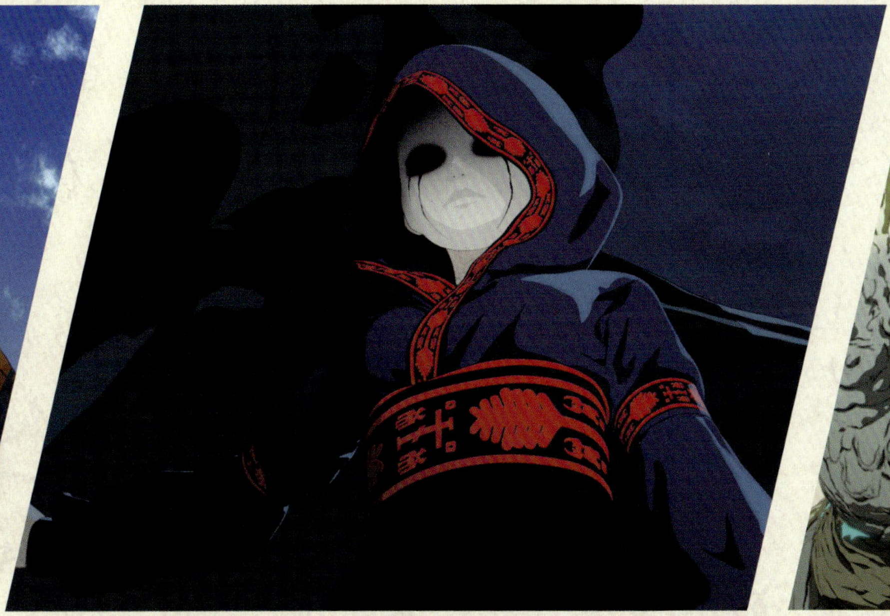

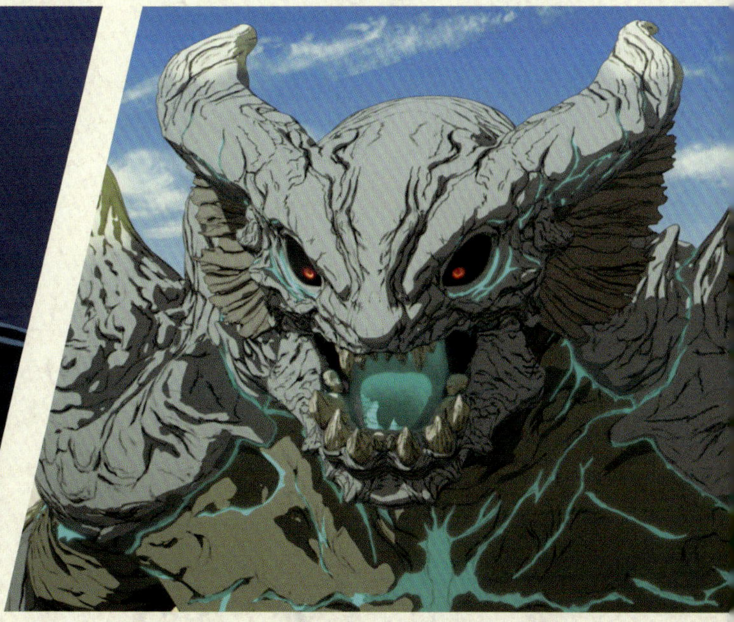

FOREWORD

I knew full well the kind of movie I was about to watch when the house lights dimmed. Giant robots against giant monsters. Jaegers vs Kaiju. Not a new idea in the annals of sci-fi storytelling, but this would be a new approach from a gifted filmmaker. As the movie opened, a battle-weary voice began describing the world; the breach on the ocean floor, monsters making landfall, tanks, jets, and missiles, cities destroyed, lives lost, and the rise of a new weapon.

2013's *Pacific Rim* reframed a familiar concept into a visually exciting, emotionally moving joyride. And 2018's *Pacific Rim: Uprising* showed us the messy aftermath once the apocalypse was successfully canceled and the cheers had long since faded. What remained was the wrecked landscape, the damaged lives, carcasses of both monster and robot being stripped for parts, a profiteering subculture, and even a devout Kaiju following. I fell in love with those movies for many reasons, but the world-building within them is what really made an impact. Normalcy trying to maintain itself amidst grand-scale ruin. The adaptability of the human race in shouldering an impossible burden while trying to rise above it. We understand that existence.

The durability of a story's world is essential when considering whether it would have legs as a series. Is the environment still interesting without the original plot? Can other characters inhabit it with goals and complications that are different from the source material? In regard to *Pacific Rim*, yes. Yes, it can. But it would take a village of artisans to get us there.

Descriptions on a page created by a solitary mind or through passionate collaboration are likely where such worlds begin, but it isn't until they evolve within the minds, hearts, and hands of artists that they finally gain form and become real. Layer upon layer of exciting ideas is added to the process until the creation emerges with its own unique identity, one that couldn't exist if not for every individual who touched it.

What I love about this book is that it shines a much-deserved klieg light on the magic of its visual art. But it also offers a peek at what goes into creating such a vibrant and fascinating world, as told by the passionate souls who devoted years to making it happen.

The Art of Pacific Rim: The Black is bursting with visual delight. Looking through these pages, I feel less like a contributor and more like that breathless movie-going fan settling into his seat, witnessing the unfolding of a world that is both mysterious and familiar. If the viewer can believe that such giants roam the same earth we walk on, that the people, places, monsters, and robots feel tangible, then the art has done its job. It has made that world real.

GREG JOHNSON
(PACIFIC RIM: THE BLACK SHOWRUNNER, EXECUTIVE PRODUCER, AND HEAD WRITER)

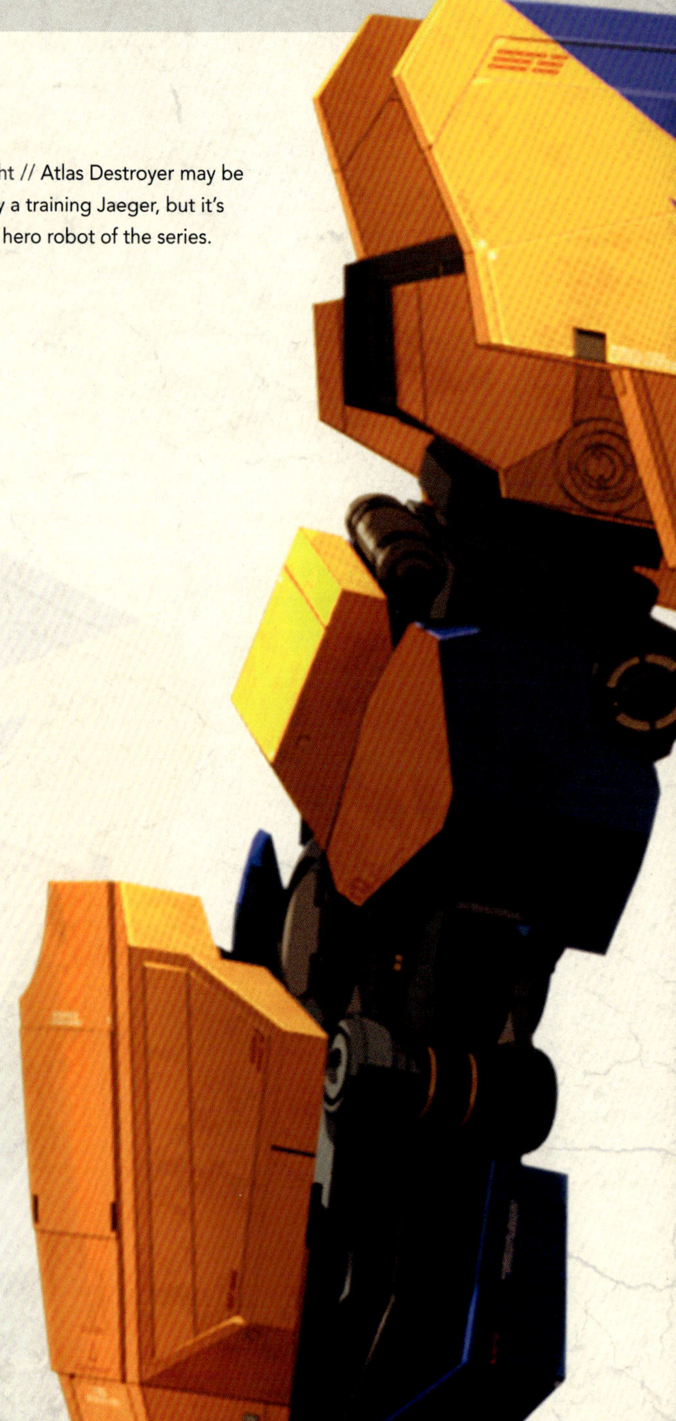

Right // Atlas Destroyer may be only a training Jaeger, but it's the hero robot of the series.

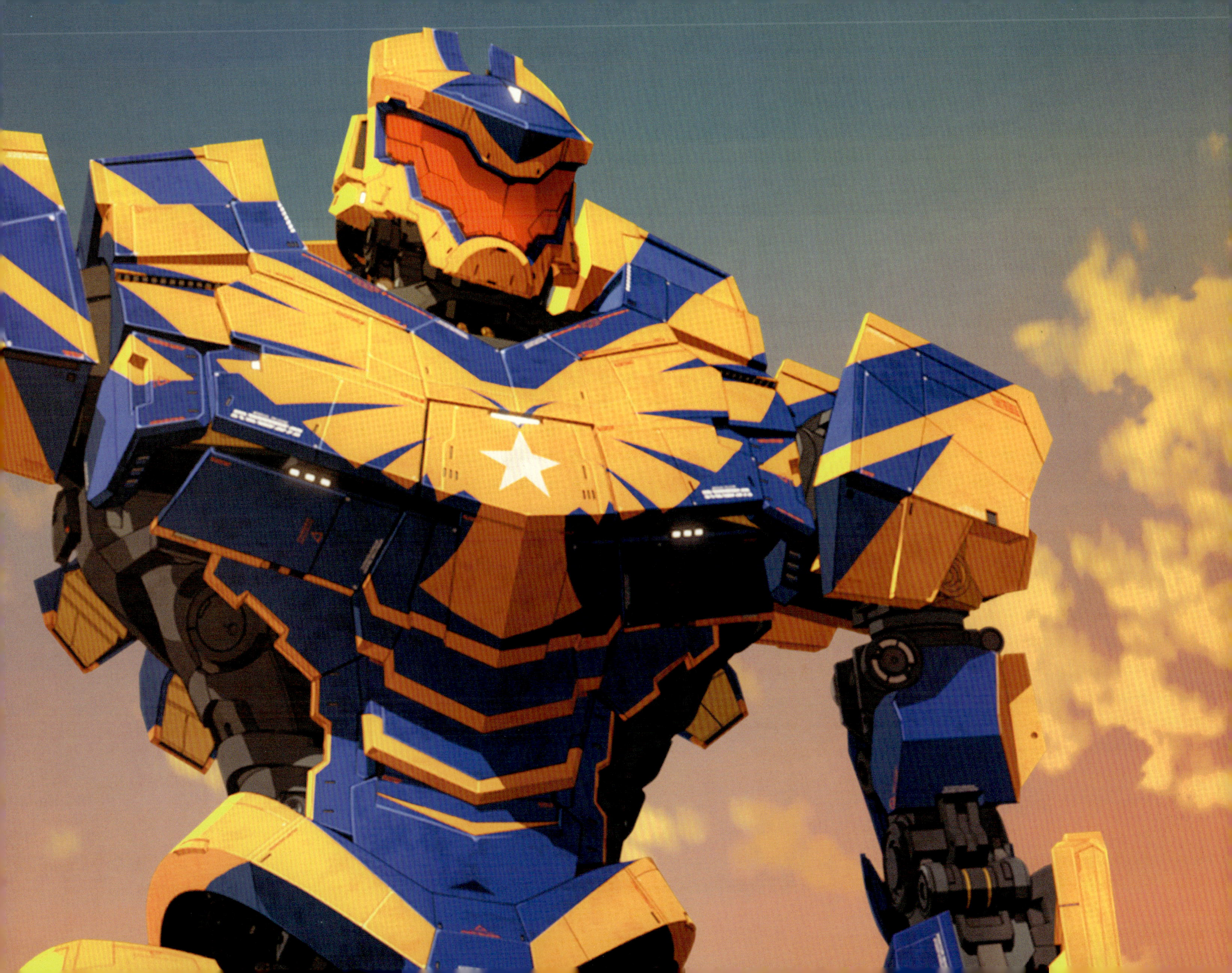

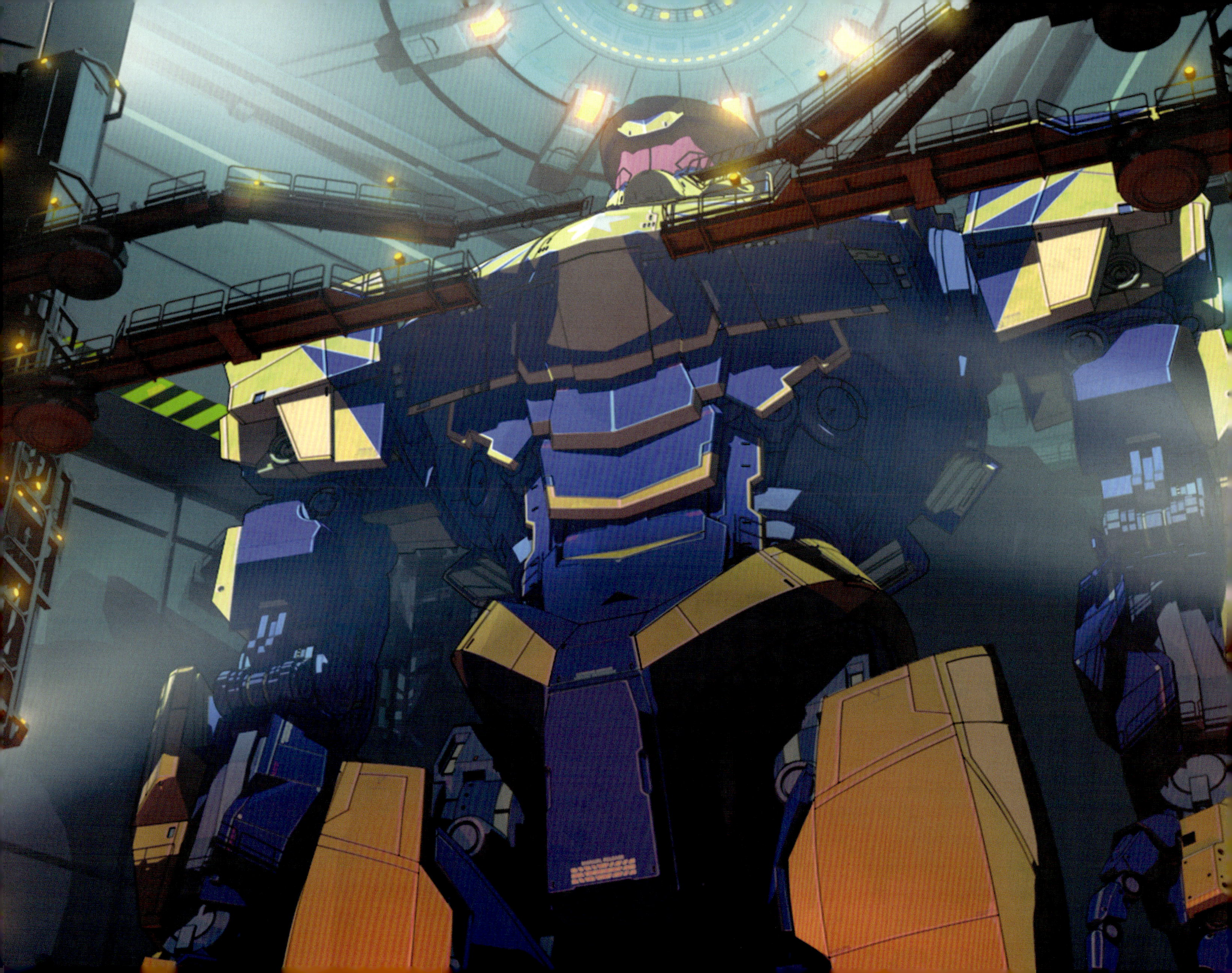

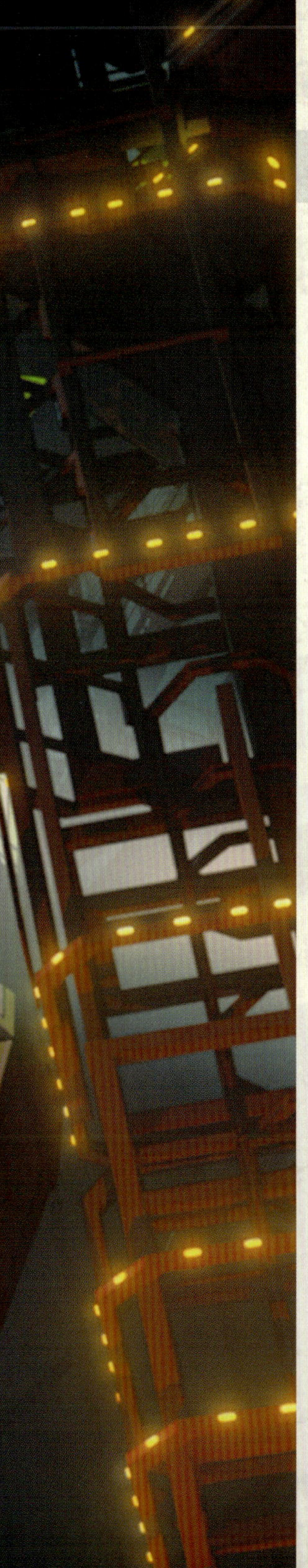

INTRODUCTION

The invasion began in summer 2013. That was when Legendary Pictures released the titanic spectacular *Pacific Rim* upon startled cinema audiences. Directed by Guillermo Del Toro, the film showed a world in which humanity is threatened by massive beast-monsters, huge enough to smash cities. They emerge from chasms under the Pacific Ocean, hence the film's title. Our defenders are young pilots who steer big robots, metal giants as great as the invaders.

The upshot: earthshaking widescreen slugfests between machines and monstrosities, fighting it out in the ocean waves or between shattered skyscrapers. The beasts are called Kaiju, a Japanese word for 'monster'. The robots are Jaegers, borrowing a German word for 'hunter'.

The first *Pacific Rim* film was a hit, leading to a cinema sequel in 2018, *Pacific Rim: Uprising*. Directed by Steven S. DeKnight, the second film continued the Kaiju-Jaeger conflict ten years further on, with mostly new characters. However, the third screen iteration of *Pacific Rim* wouldn't be a cinema film. Rather it would be an online animated series, streamed internationally by Netflix from 2021. Called *Pacific Rim: The Black*, it's set in the world established by the live-action films (chronologically the series is set some time after *Pacific Rim: Uprising*). However, this series tells a different kind of story from the films, and it takes a new perspective.

Whereas the earlier films featured soldiers trained to fight the Kaiju, the animated series focuses on children left on the battlefield. This particular battlefield is a ruined, post-civilization Australia (the 'Black' of the title), where Kaiju prowl unchallenged. Two of the children are a brother and sister, whose missing parents were Jaeger pilots. The siblings discover a third child, a mute boy in a laboratory tank whose origin is a mystery. Together, they'll learn that while Australia is roamed by monsters of all shapes and sizes—the show's bestiary of Kaiju goes far beyond the original films—the children's most dangerous enemy may be human.

Left // Our first sight of Atlas Destroyer, sealed underground until its inadvertent discovery in Episode One.

Below // The child protagonists of *Pacific Rim: The Black* are far removed from the pro pilots of the *Pacific Rim* films.

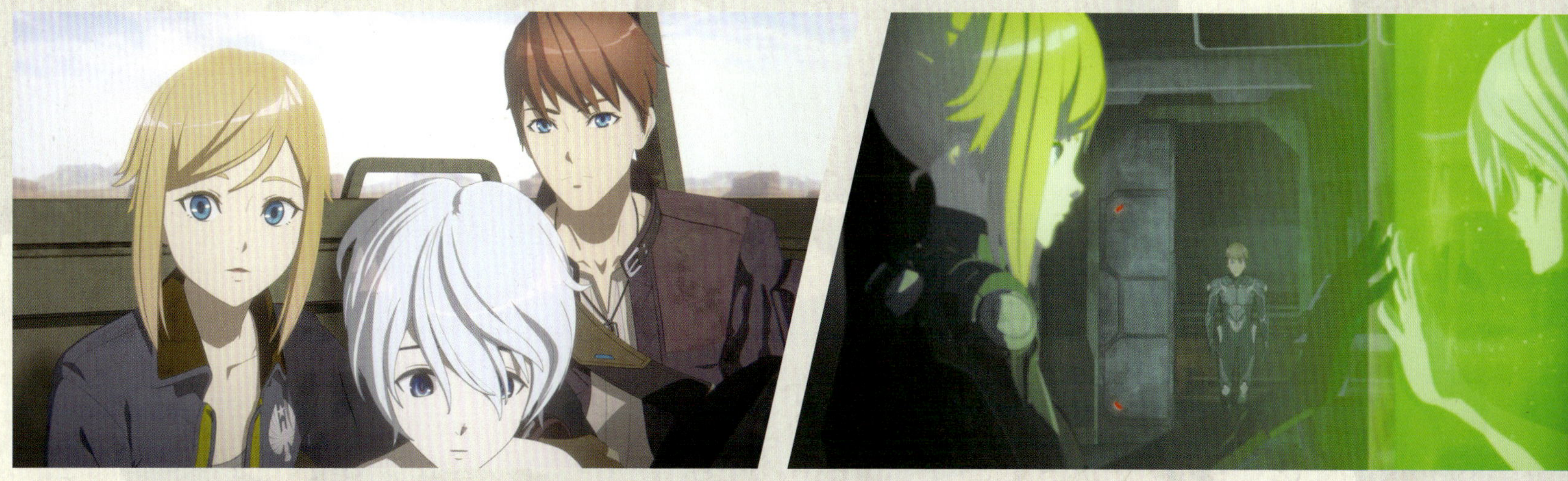

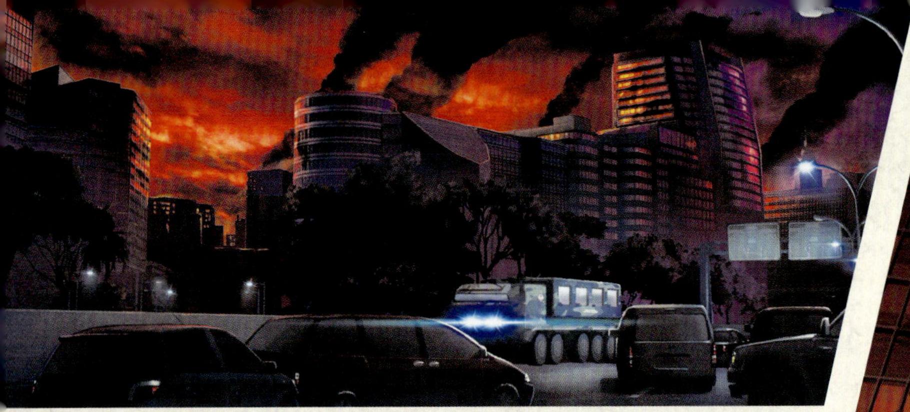

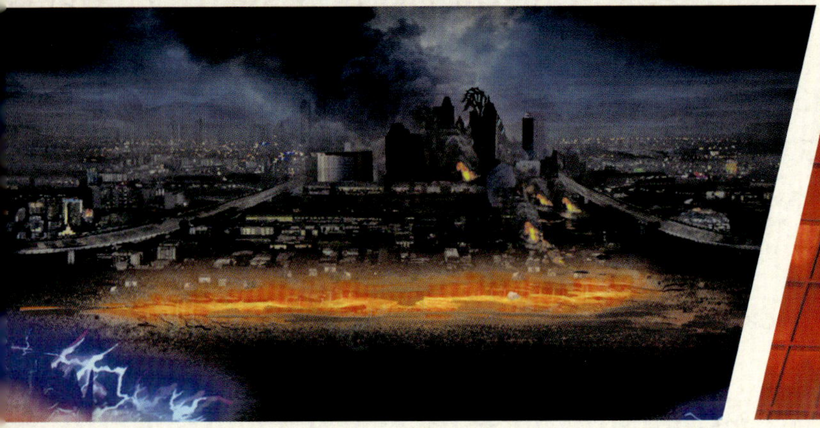

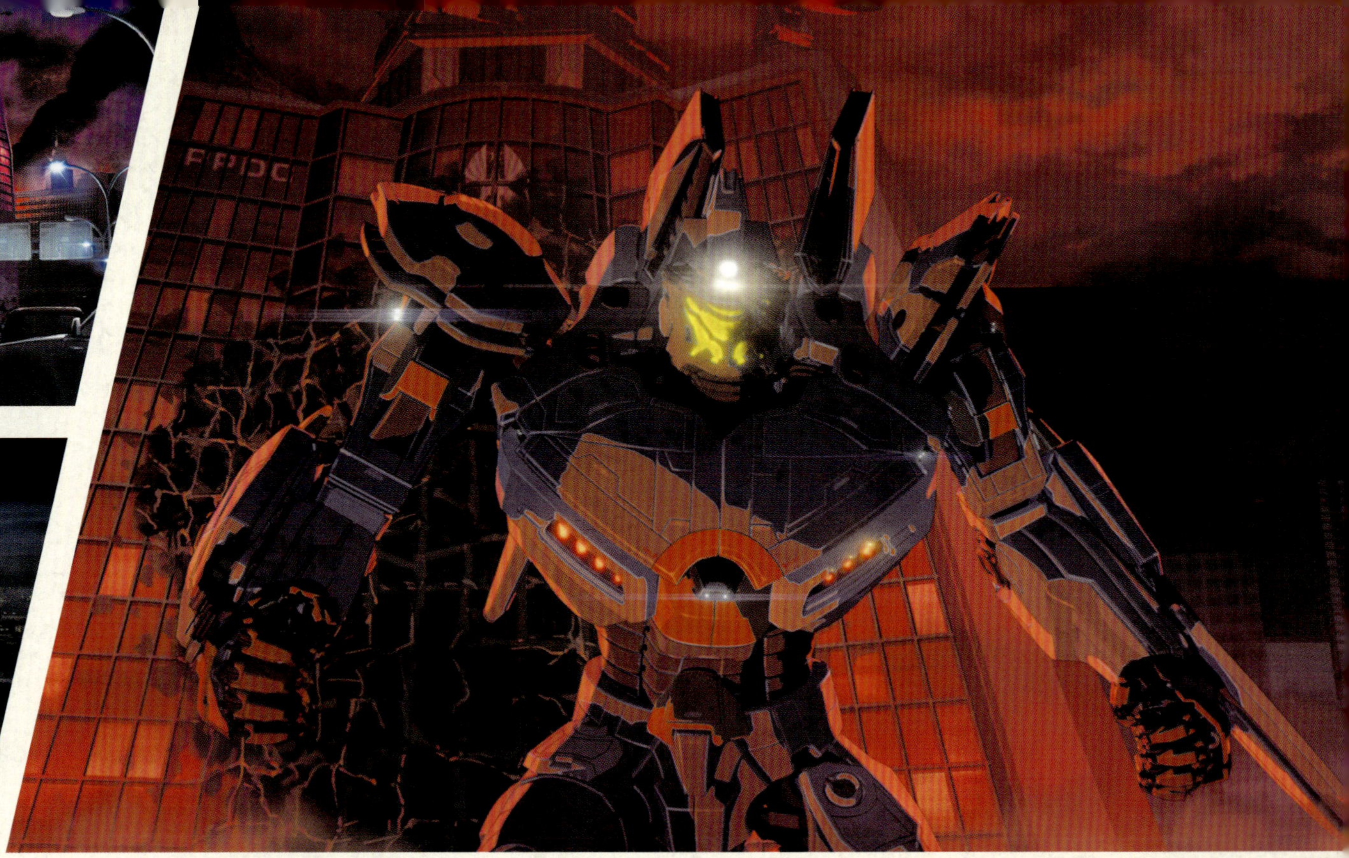

It's a new path for the *Pacific Rim* franchise, stemming from a pitch presented to Legendary Pictures by Greg Johnson and Craig Kyle. They would be the showrunners on *Pacific Rim: The Black*. Both have decades of experience in screen fantasy. Among other things, Johnson wrote the animated film adaptation of *Planet Hulk*, while Kyle was one of the writers on the live-action Marvel film *Thor: Ragnarok*. They teamed up to pitch one of several competing proposals for a *Pacific Rim* animated series.

Johnson stresses how he and Kyle felt that the series needed to be different from the films. "When Craig and I discussed partnering on a *Pacific Rim* idea to pitch to Legendary," Johnson says, "we first defined what we shouldn't do. And that was to present a series that depended on constant Kaiju and Jaeger battles in densely populated cities. One: it would cease to be interesting around the third episode. And two: it would be prohibitively expensive, even in animation."

Johnson and Kyle ruled out other approaches; for example, a *Pacific Rim* show about rookie Jaeger cadets learning the ropes within the PPDC, the military organization seen in the films (something like a *Jaeger Junior High*). The writers suspected some of the rival pitches would take that approach. "Not that it's a bad idea," Johnson says, "but we'd kind of seen it in the second movie." In *Pacific Rim: Uprising*, cadets are being trained at a pilot academy in China.

Instead, the writers wanted to make their own space in the franchise, one that wouldn't tread on the toes of potential future *Pacific Rim* stories. "Craig and I liked the idea of answering the question; what would happen if the Kaiju won?" Johnson says. "We couldn't do that worldwide, but we could do it on a continent that could be severed from the rest of the world. Australia fit perfectly."

With the standalone setting decided, who should the protagonists be? Johnson and Kyle began developing their leads, a teen brother and sister called Taylor and Hayley.

Above // The city battle which opens the first episode would be typical in the films, but not in the series.

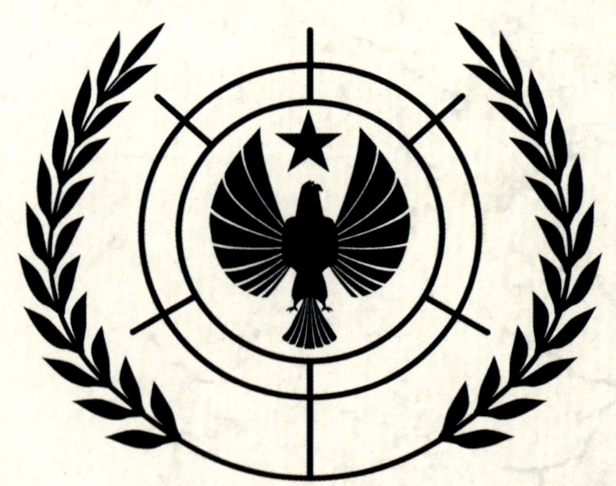

PAN PACIFIC DEFENSE CORPS

"They have enough emotional baggage to make our journey with them worth sticking around for," Johnson says. "Guilt, responsibility, uncertainty, desperation and love... They all become exposed."

Taylor and Hayley are the viewers' surrogates. "The siblings would serve as the eyes of the audience as they set out into unknown territory that's been under the control of Kaiju for five years," says Johnson. "We knew instinctively that our characters needed to be on the move for this series, trying to get out, trying to find answers about their missing parents. The stories needed momentum to drive us forward. As such, the series became what is termed a road picture."

Several reviewers describe *Pacific Rim: The Black* as more "serious" than the films. While the characters in the *Pacific Rim* movies face anguish and tragedy, the films tend to be upbeat and triumphalist. One of the first film's best-remembered lines, delivered by the patriarchal commander played by Idris Elba, is, "We are cancelling the apocalypse!" That wasn't what Johnson and Kyle wanted. "The concept of the series really dictated the tone," Johnson says. "The movies were more about what it takes to fight back and win. This series is not about winning, it's about surviving."

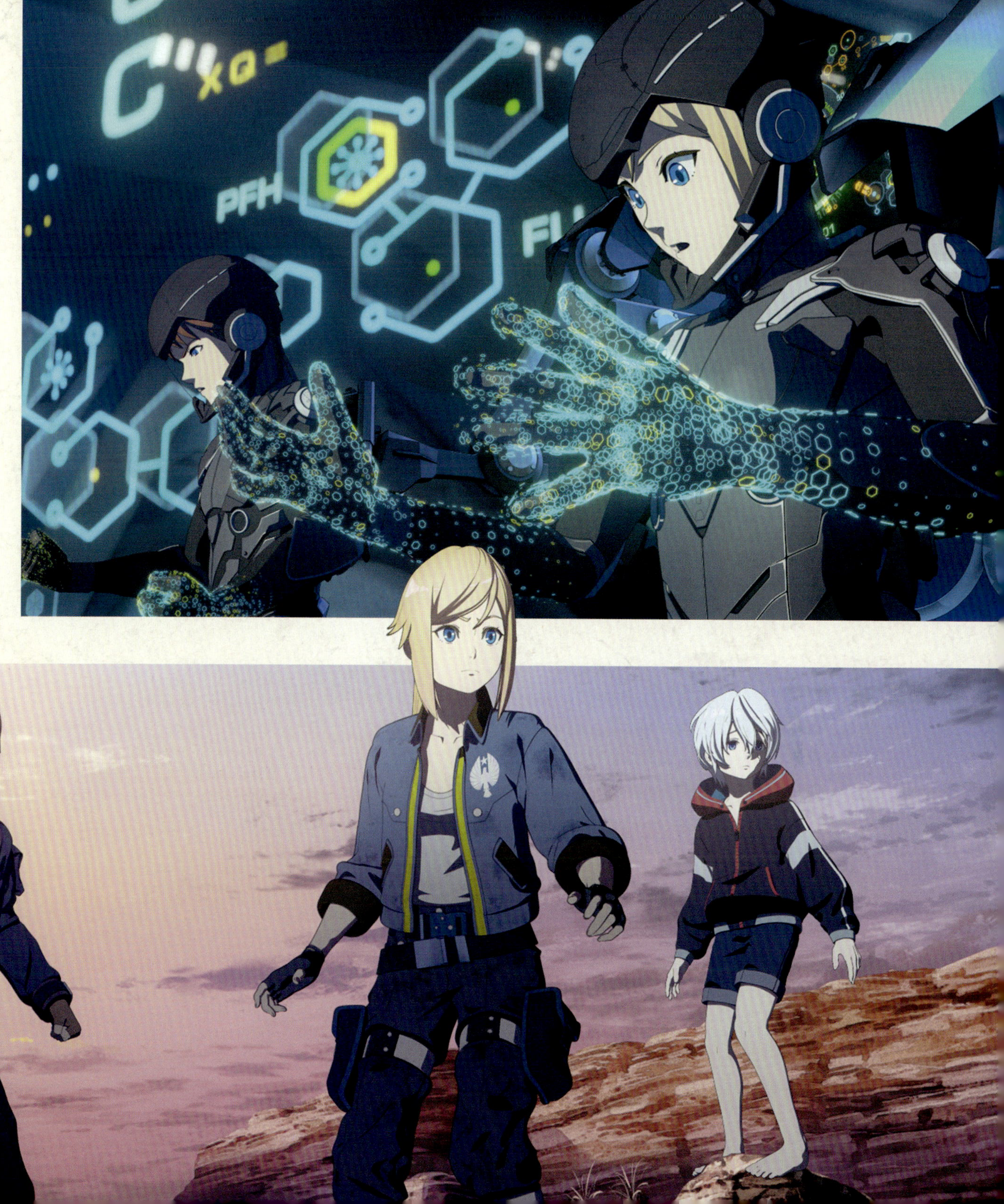

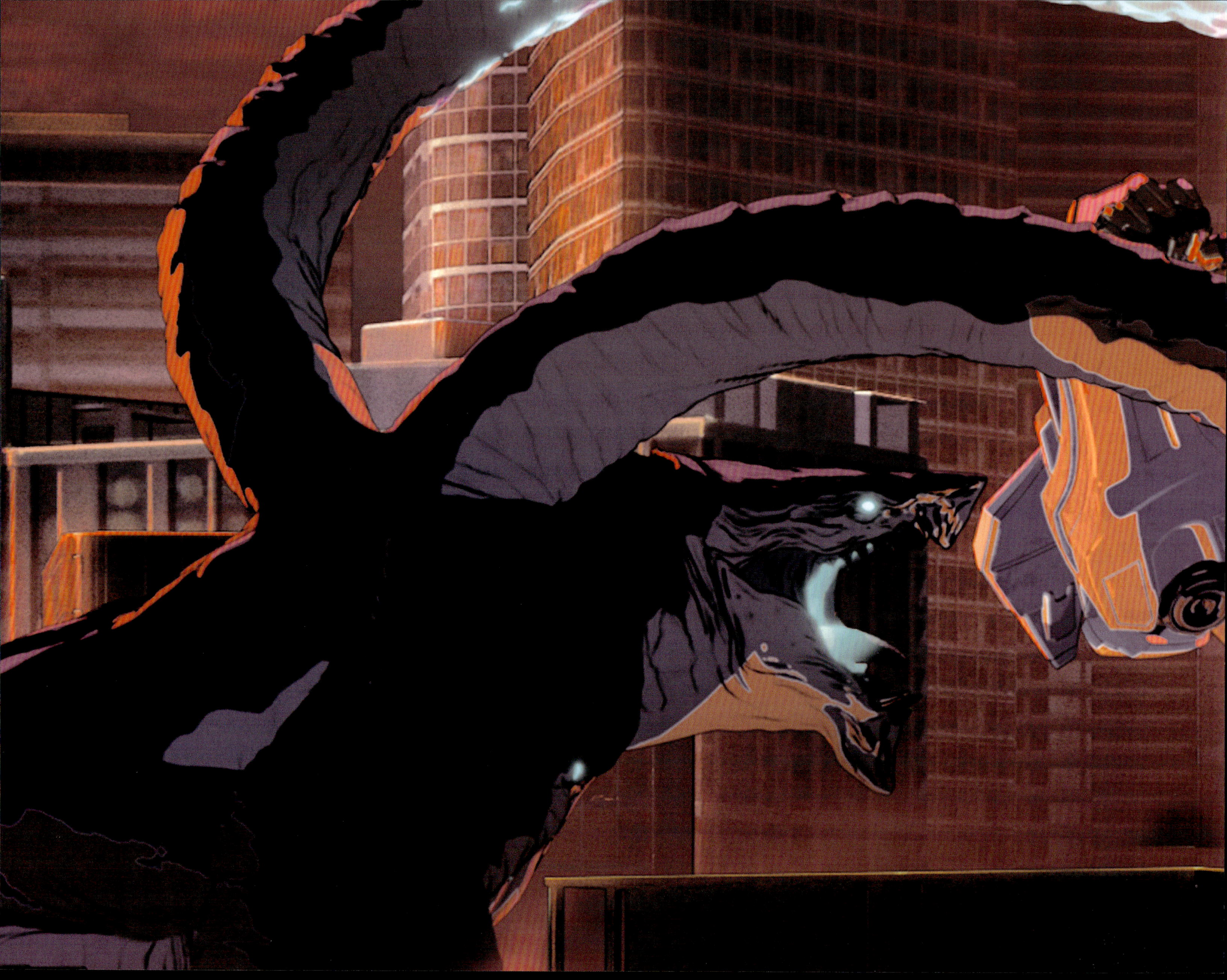

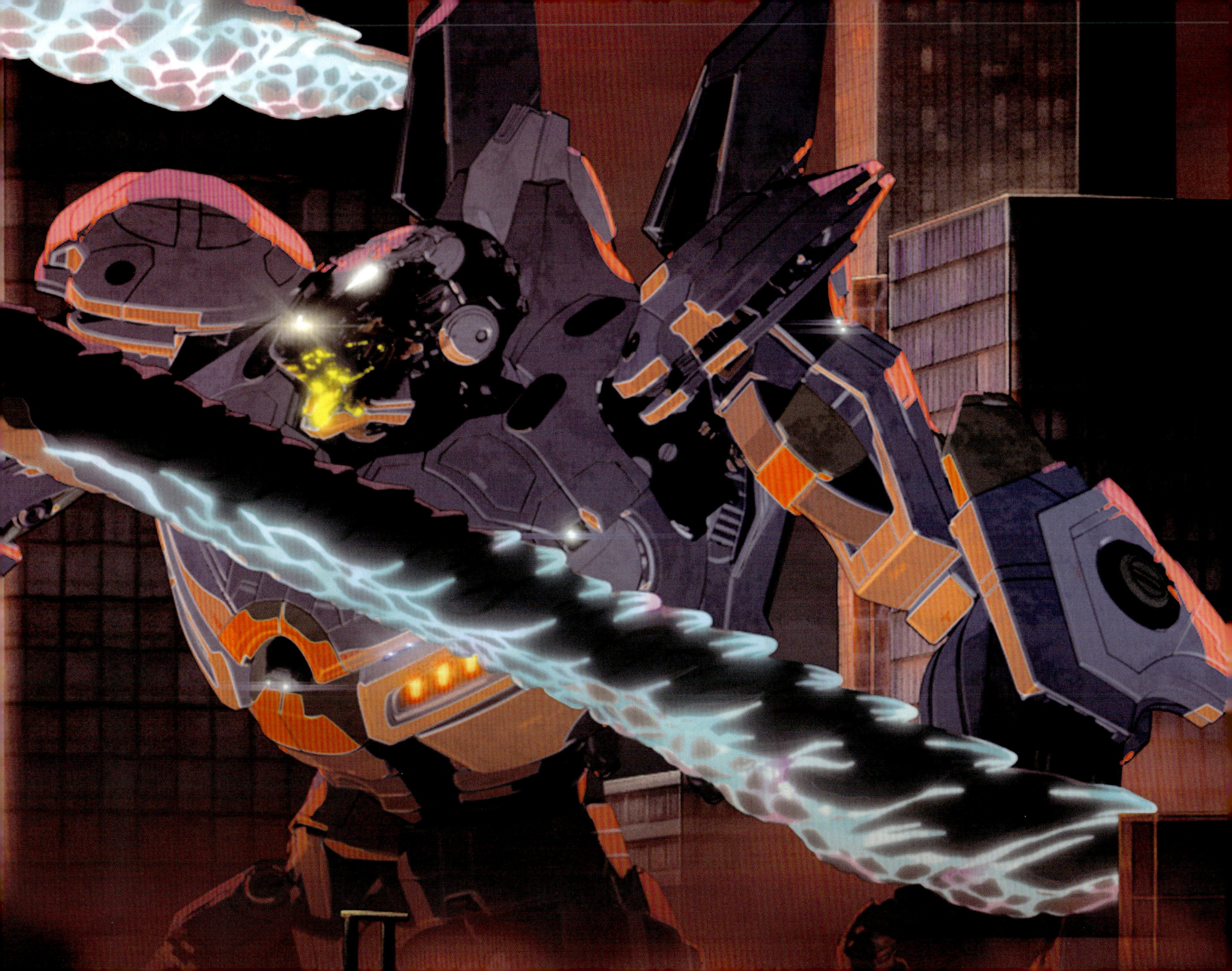

THE JAPANESE CONNECTION

Ken Duer is the co-producer of *Pacific Rim: The Black*. He has decades of experience in adapting properties to animation, ranging from his work on the 1980s cartoon *The Real Ghostbusters* to handling superhero titles. He says, "I think with any existing property, especially the successful ones like *Pacific Rim*, you don't want to do anything that would turn off the fans."

However, Duer agrees with Johnson that *Pacific Rim: The Black* had to take the franchise in a new direction. "I think inside Legendary, they were thinking how we could revive *Pacific Rim*, and bring in new fans and do spinoffs. Legendary made the right decision, I think, and they were very accommodating of the ideas from Greg and Craig."

The *Pacific Rim* films were new spins on a genre imported from Japan. "The 'Kaiju' monster genre has been around in Japan for years and years," Duer says, "and then *Pacific Rim* came out with its own way to handle the Kaiju. We wanted to do something different that would bring the *Pacific Rim* property forward into the future, bringing in not just the established fans, but also bringing new fans into this genre."

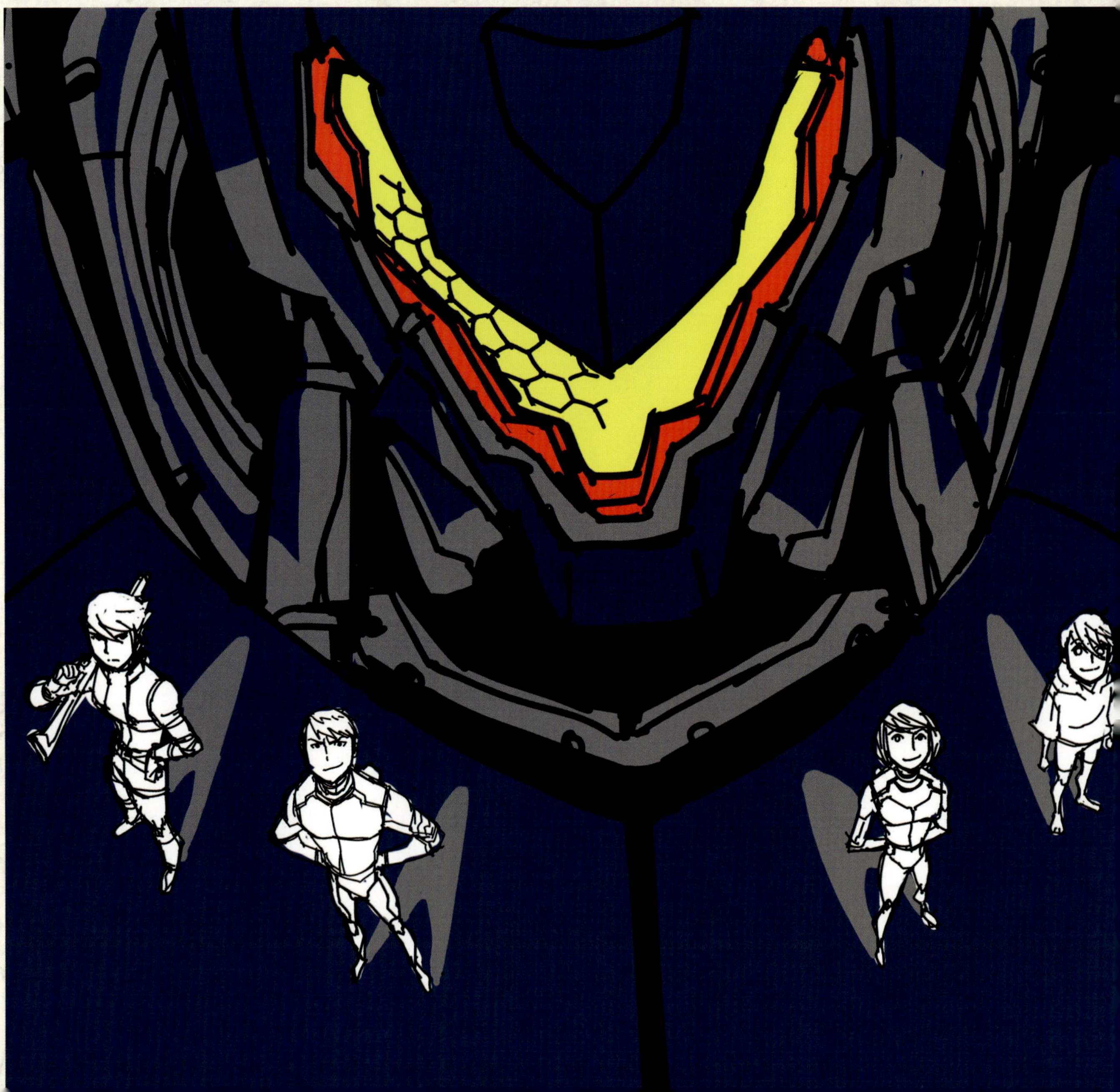

Right // Much of the final series revolves around a trio of characters, but the early concept sketches suggested a four-strong team.

Japan has made giant monsters for decades. You can go back to the first *Godzilla* live-action film in 1954, a response to the horrors of World War II. Since then, there have been scores of Japanese monster films for successive generations, as well as TV series. But many of these spectacles didn't just have giant monsters. They also had giant-sized heroes fighting the monsters and other menaces to save humanity.

Not all these saviors were mechanical. The live-action *Ultraman*, who stomped across Japanese TV screens in 1966, was a red-and-white-suited giant superhero, a combo of human and alien. But many of these monster-fighter titans were robots, often created in animation. Talking about his inspirations for *Pacific Rim*, Guillermo del Toro cited *Ultraman* and its sequel *Ultraseven*. But he also talked about giant robot anime such as 1963's *Tetsujin-28* (called *Gigantor* in America), and 1972's *Mazinger Z*.

These shows were made when Japan's burgeoning animation was little-known internationally. Often, the Japanese origins of cartoon exports were hidden in foreign territories. Of course, by the time *Pacific Rim* opened in 2013, all that had changed. Anime had fans worldwide, and multinational corporations were looking to invest.

A year after *Pacific Rim*'s release, in 2014, Netflix streamed a Japan-animated space opera called *Knights of*

"WE WANTED TO DO SOMETHING DIFFERENT THAT WOULD BRING THE *PACIFIC RIM* PROPERTY FORWARD INTO THE FUTURE."
Ken Duer, co-producer

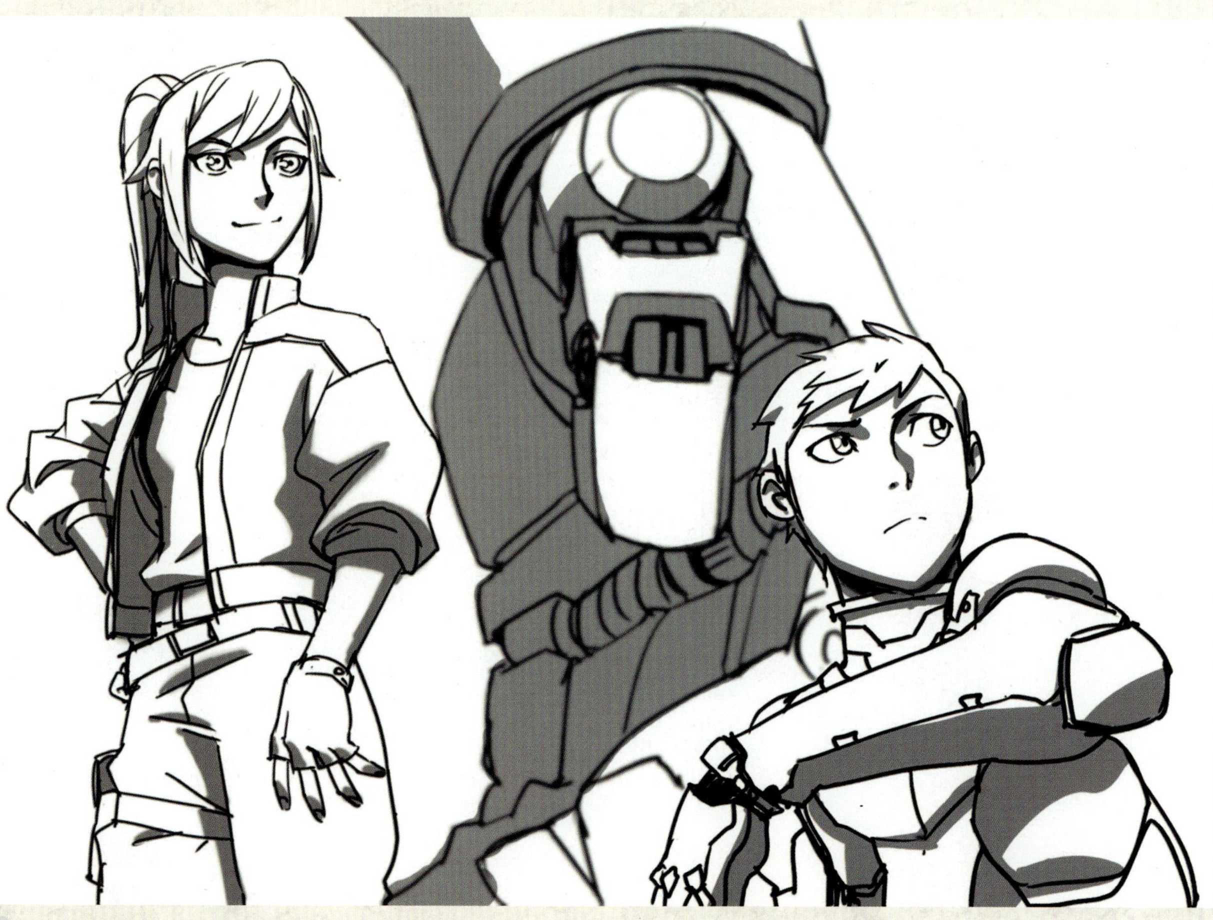

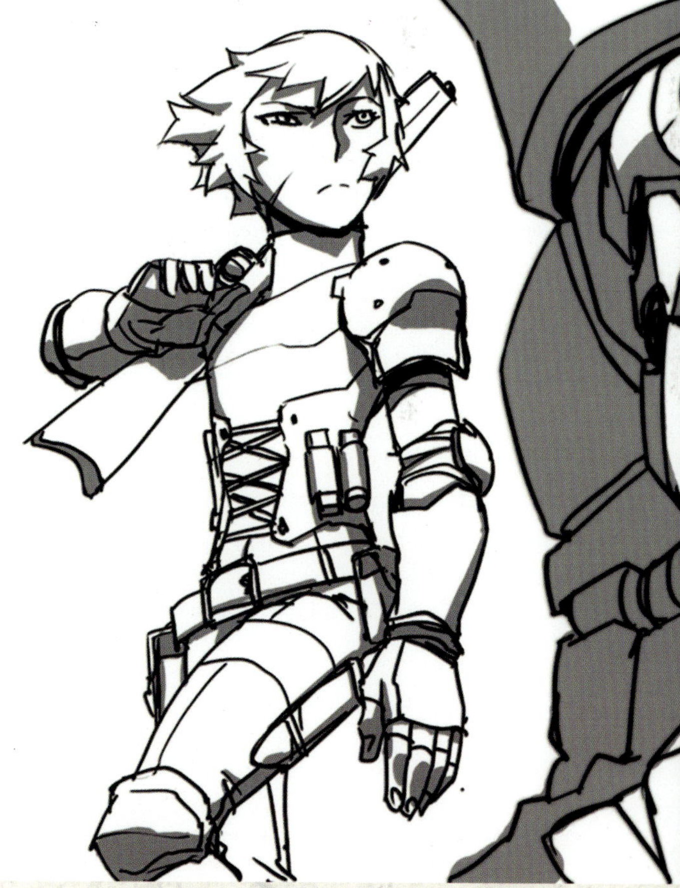

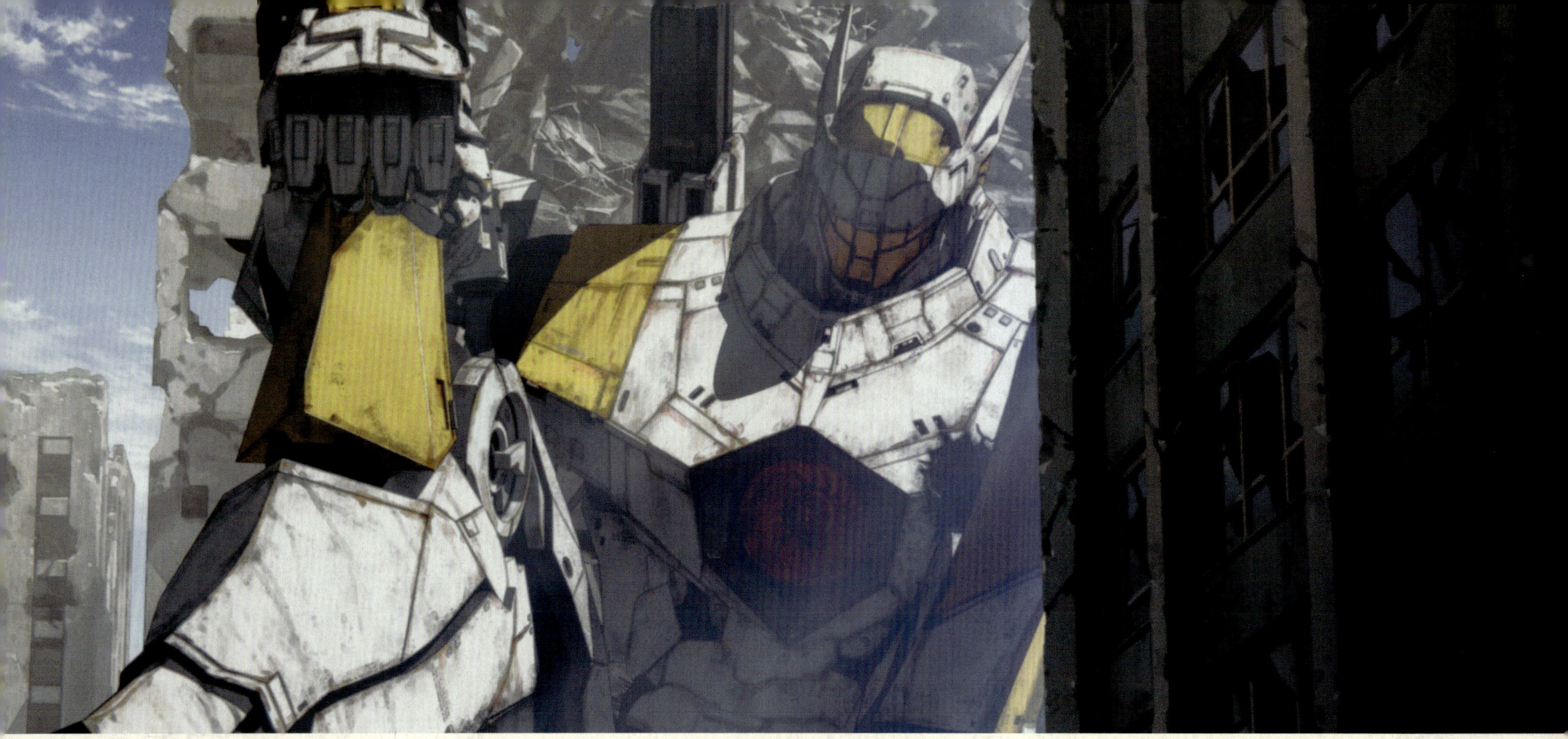

Sidonia. Tagged as a "Netflix Original Anime", it was the platform's first investment of that kind. It was made by the studio Polygon Pictures, which would make *Pacific Rim: The Black*. Shuzo John Shiota, Polygon's President and CEO, said in one interview that Netflix liked anime for its fan following and modest budgets. After all, anime could create big spectacles for relatively little money.

Polygon Pictures is far from an average anime studio. Founded in 1983, it's one of the oldest digital animation studios, from a time when few people knew what digital animation was. Indeed, Polygon often had to contend with a frosty attitude towards computer animation in Japan. Shiota approached American companies for work, and soon Polygon was making spinoffs from American properties.

In 2007, Polygon made the CG series *My Friends Tigger and Pooh* for Disney. In 2012, it adapted another Disney property in *TRON: Uprising*, spun off from the *Tron* cyberspace films. *TRON: Uprising* was important in developing Polygon's cel-shading techniques. Cel-shading is a kind of CG which makes computer animation look more like traditional drawn animation, using flat colors and shadows. It contrasts with the 3D CG approach of Pixar and DreamWorks, and it's more palatable to anime fans, who treasure 2D.

Above // Putting your giant robot next to a building is an easy way to remind the viewers of its scale.

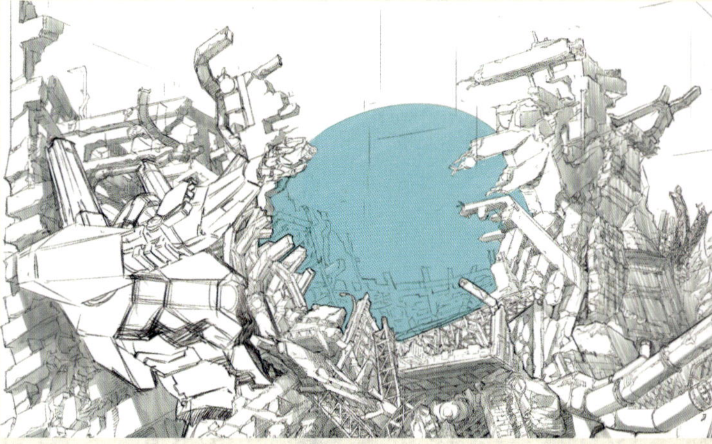

Polygon's other film and TV titles include the dark thriller *Ajin*, with monster mummies; *Ronja the Robber's Daughter*, produced by Studio Ghibli; and the fantasy series *Lost in Oz*. Polygon also worked on titles involving Kaiju—it made an animated *Godzilla* film trilogy, starting with 2017's *Godzilla: Planet of the Monsters*. Polygon also wrangled robots, working on multiple animated versions of the popular *Transformers* franchise.

The Polygon studio had long looked to territories outside Japan. The *Pacific Rim* franchise was a loving tribute to Japanese media from its conception. It might seem a no-brainer that Polygon would be chosen as the studio to animate *Pacific Rim: The Black*. At the time, though, it wasn't so certain.

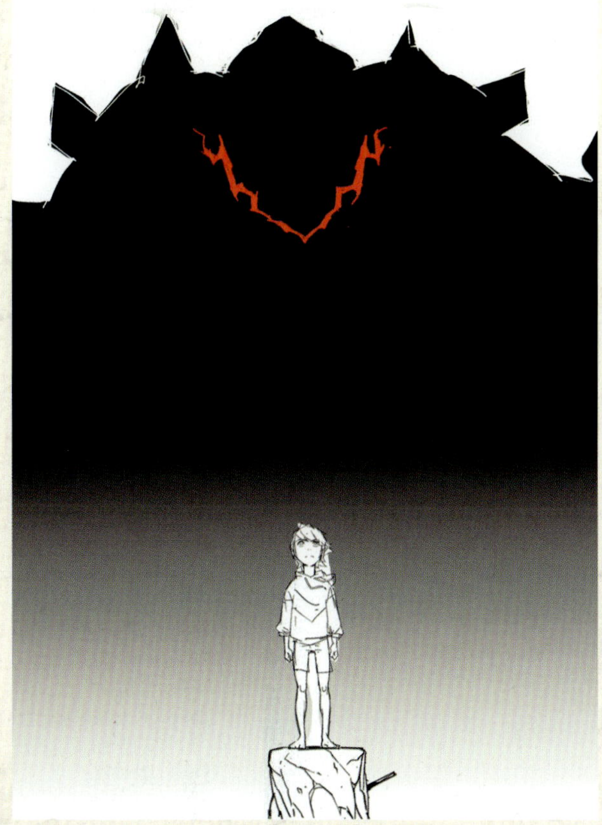

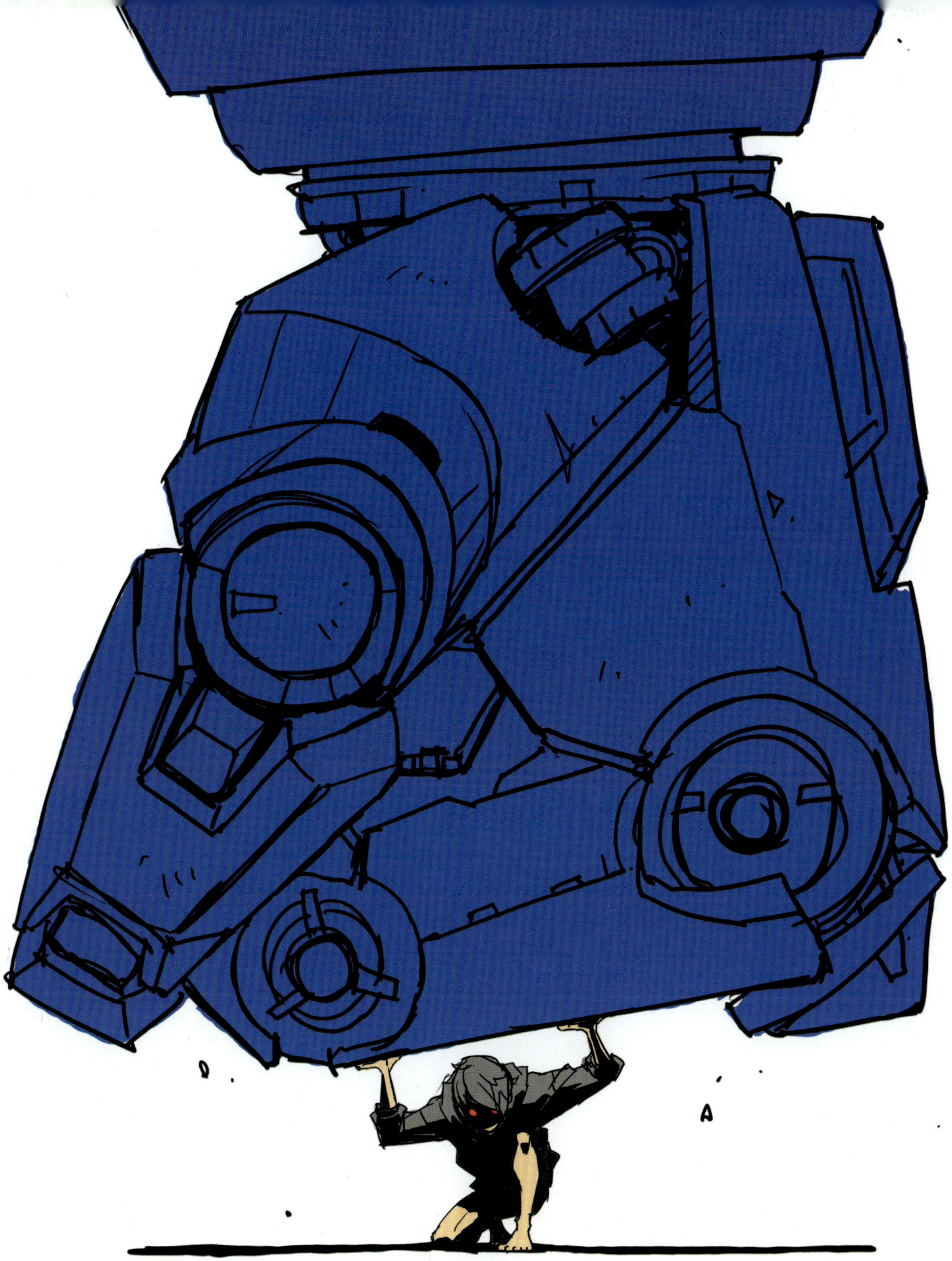

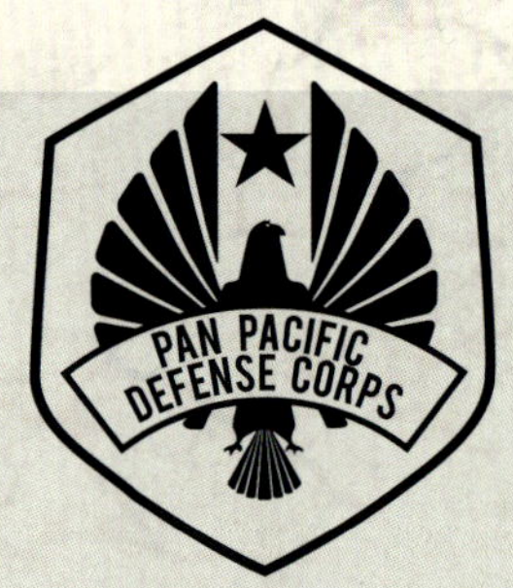

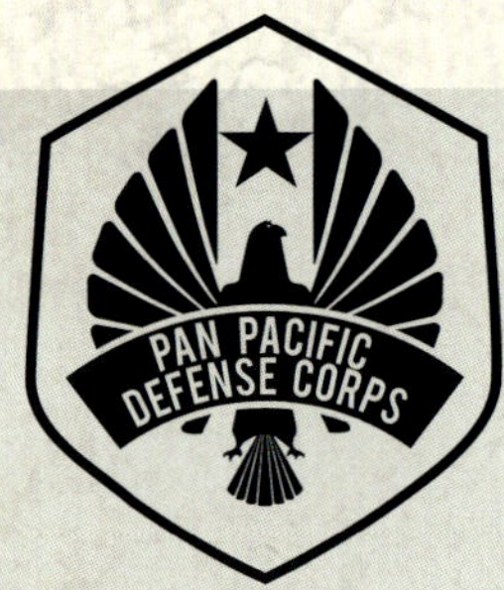

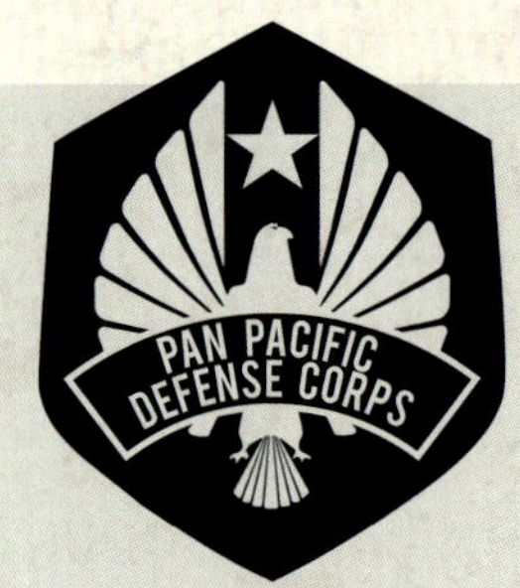

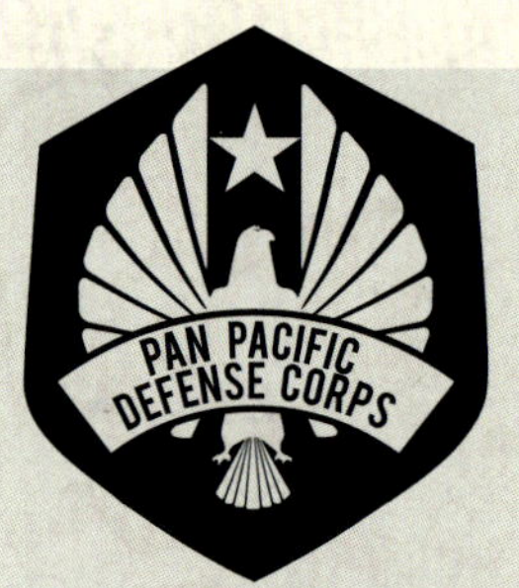

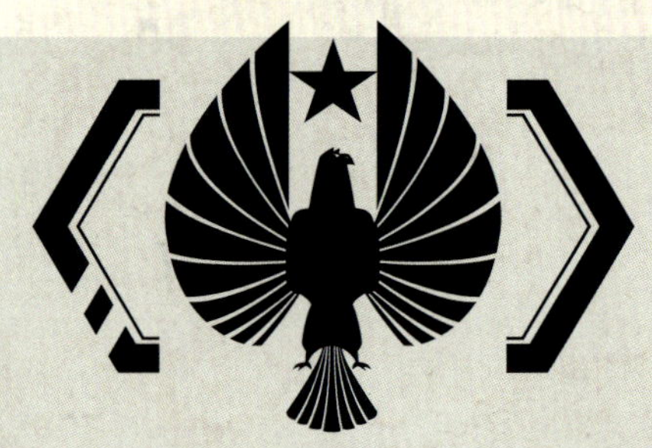

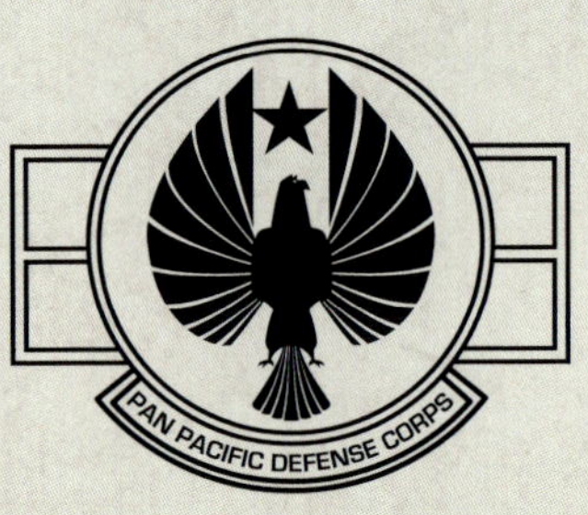

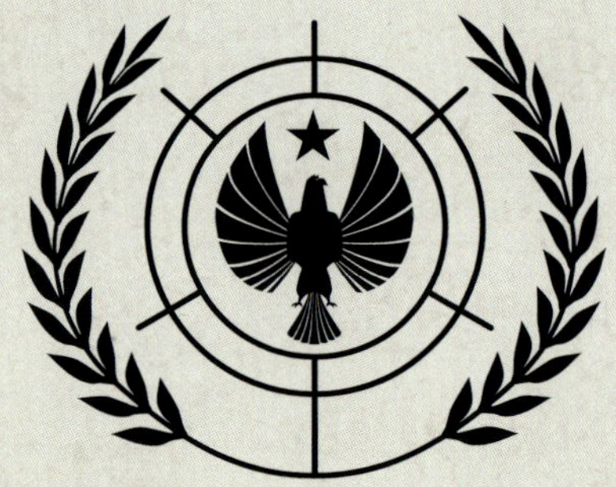

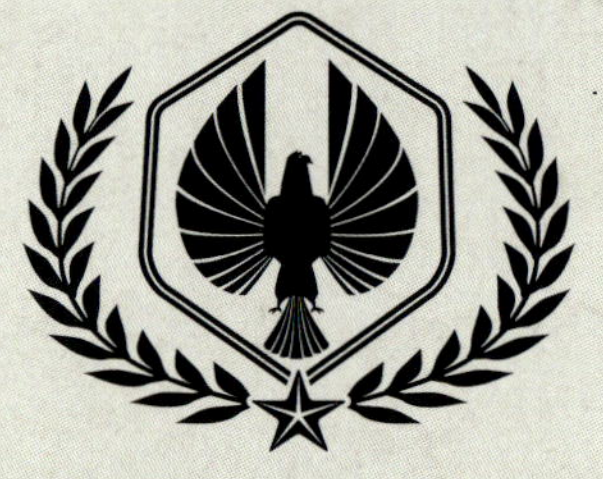

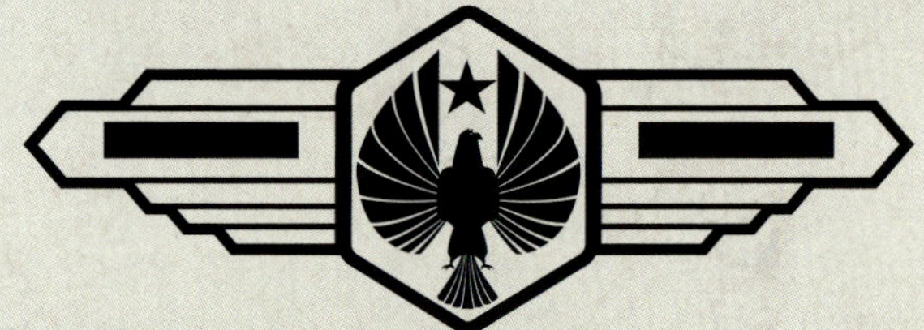

PPDC
PAN PACIFIC
DEFENSE CORPS

PAN PACIFIC
DEFENSE CORPS

PAN PACIFIC DEFENSE CORPS

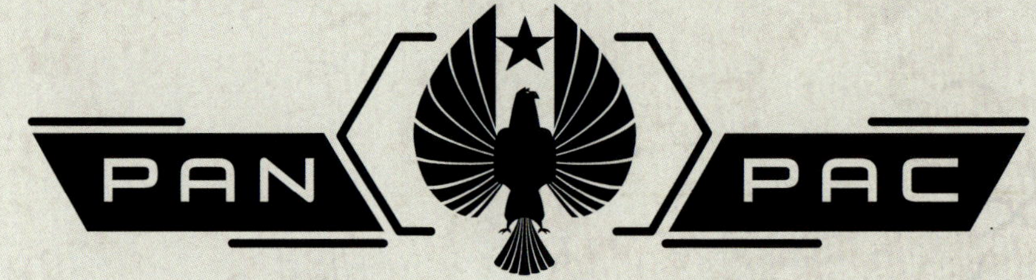

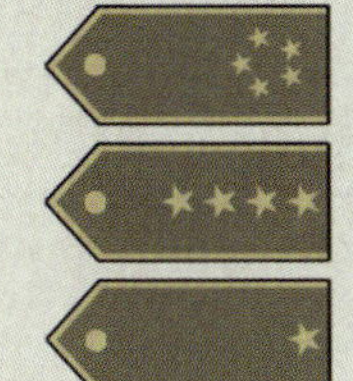

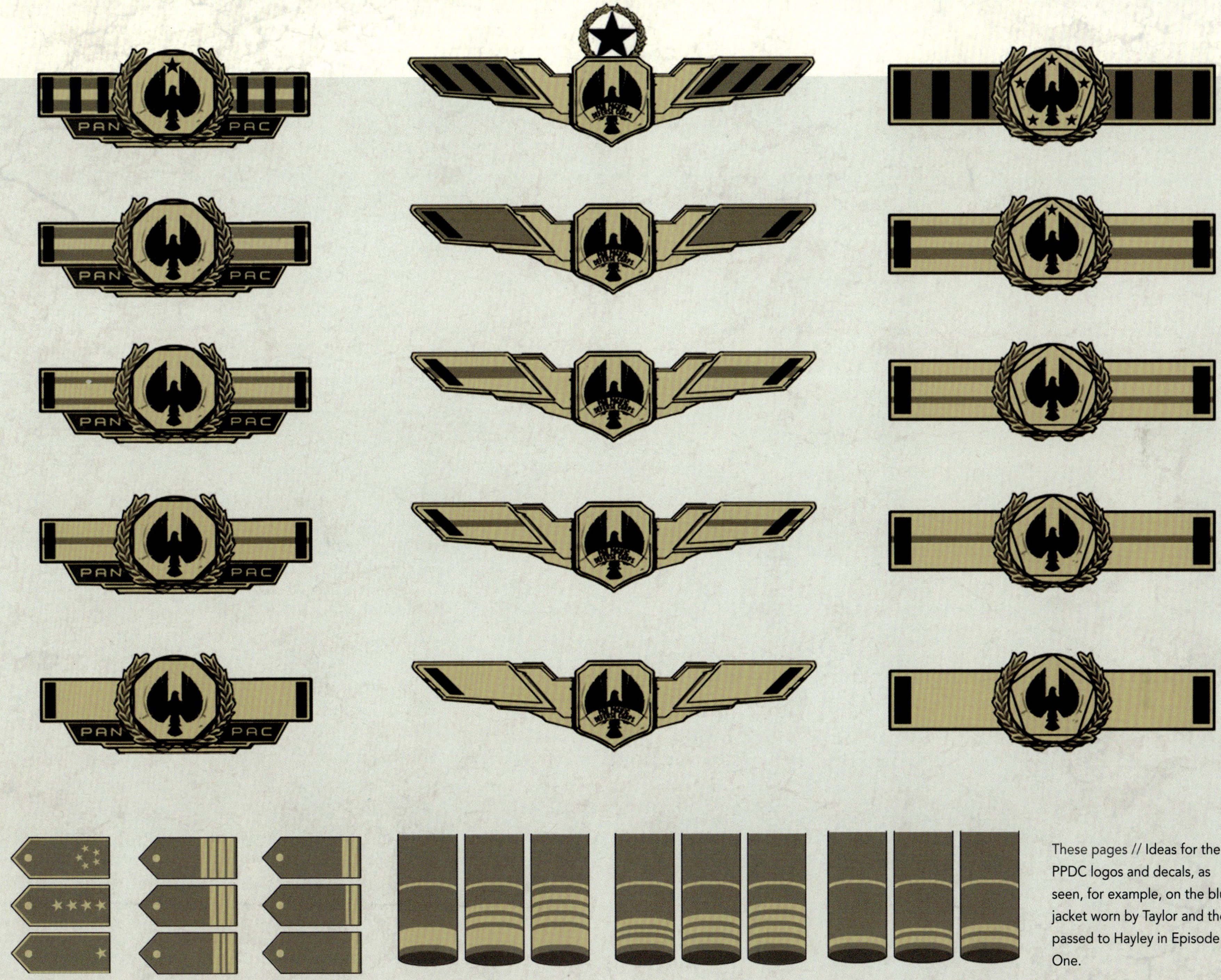

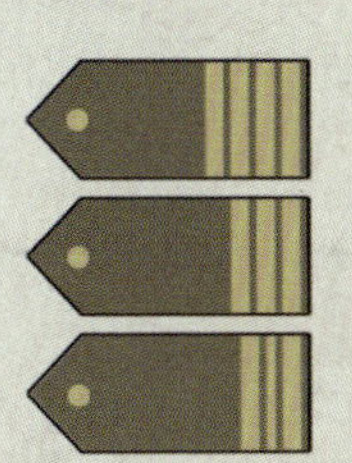

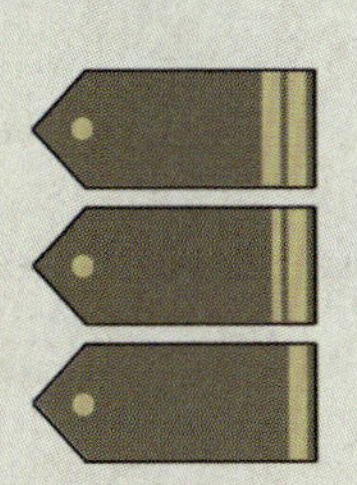

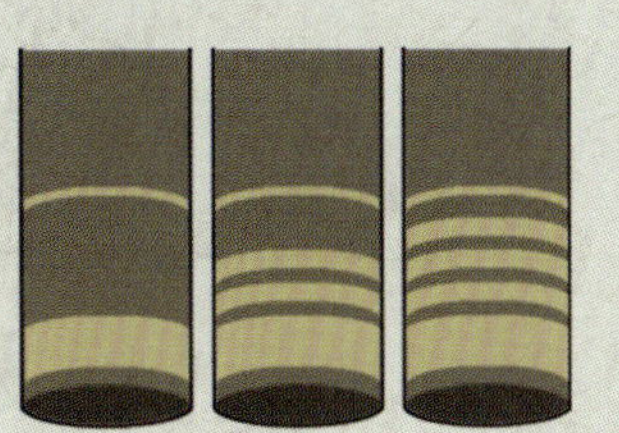

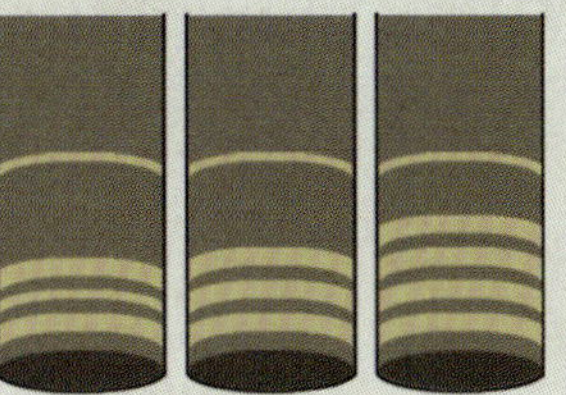

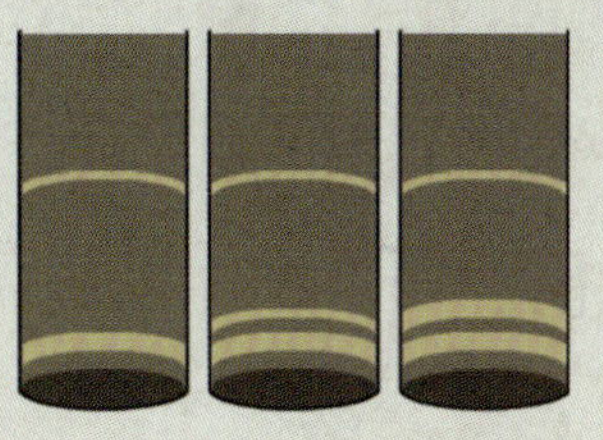

These pages // Ideas for the PPDC logos and decals, as seen, for example, on the blue jacket worn by Taylor and then passed to Hayley in Episode One.

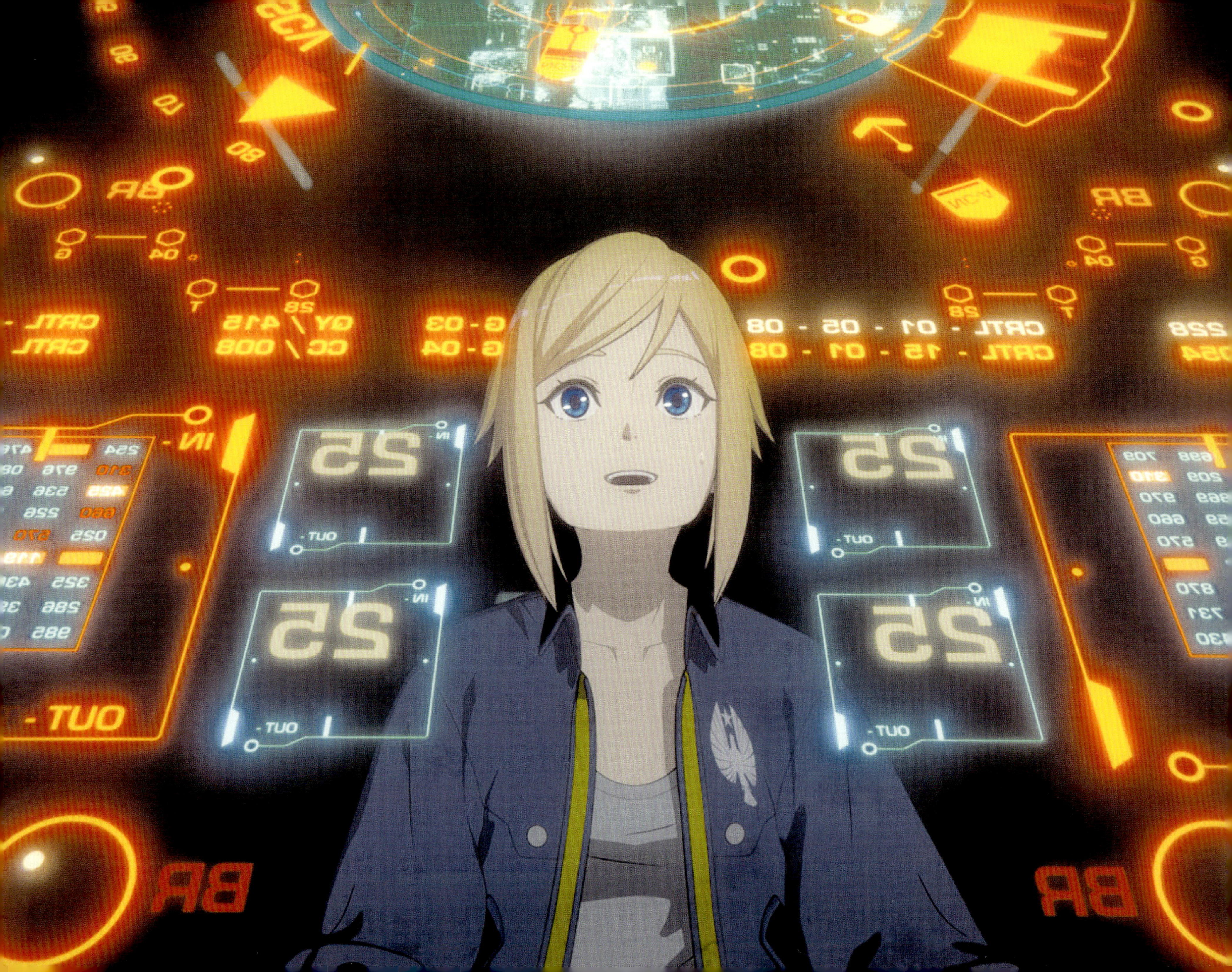

OPENING COMMUNICATIONS

When Ken Duer joined the *Pacific Rim* animated project as producer, the pitch by Greg Johnson and Craig Kyle had been chosen by Legendary for the series. "I knew Netflix wanted to try the Kaiju route," Duer comments. "The Kaiju genre has a big overlap with anime and animation fans."

However, Legendary hadn't chosen which studio would make the series. Duer recalls that when he joined, it also wasn't settled if *Pacific Rim: The Black* should look like 3D CG animation, or more like 2D. Duer acknowledges that, among anime fans, there's some resistance to titles that use CG.

"Anime fans are still very 2D-oriented," Duer says. "A lot of them don't consider CG to be anime. So we also had to think, 'What is anime?' I was born in Japan and grew up in Japan but that was long ago, and anime has moved on. It's a different philosophy now. So we had to really think, 'What is it that makes anime? Is it the storytelling; is it the design; and does it have to be 2D?' All of that had to be discussed."

Duer had worked with Polygon Pictures already. "We explored a couple of CG studios, but from my experience with Polygon, I knew they were one of the frontrunners of turning CG into something that looked like traditional 2D animation. I had worked with Polygon on *Lost in Oz* and had

"ANIME FANS ARE STILL VERY 2D-ORIENTED. A LOT OF THEM DON'T CONSIDER CG TO BE ANIME."
Ken Duer, co-producer

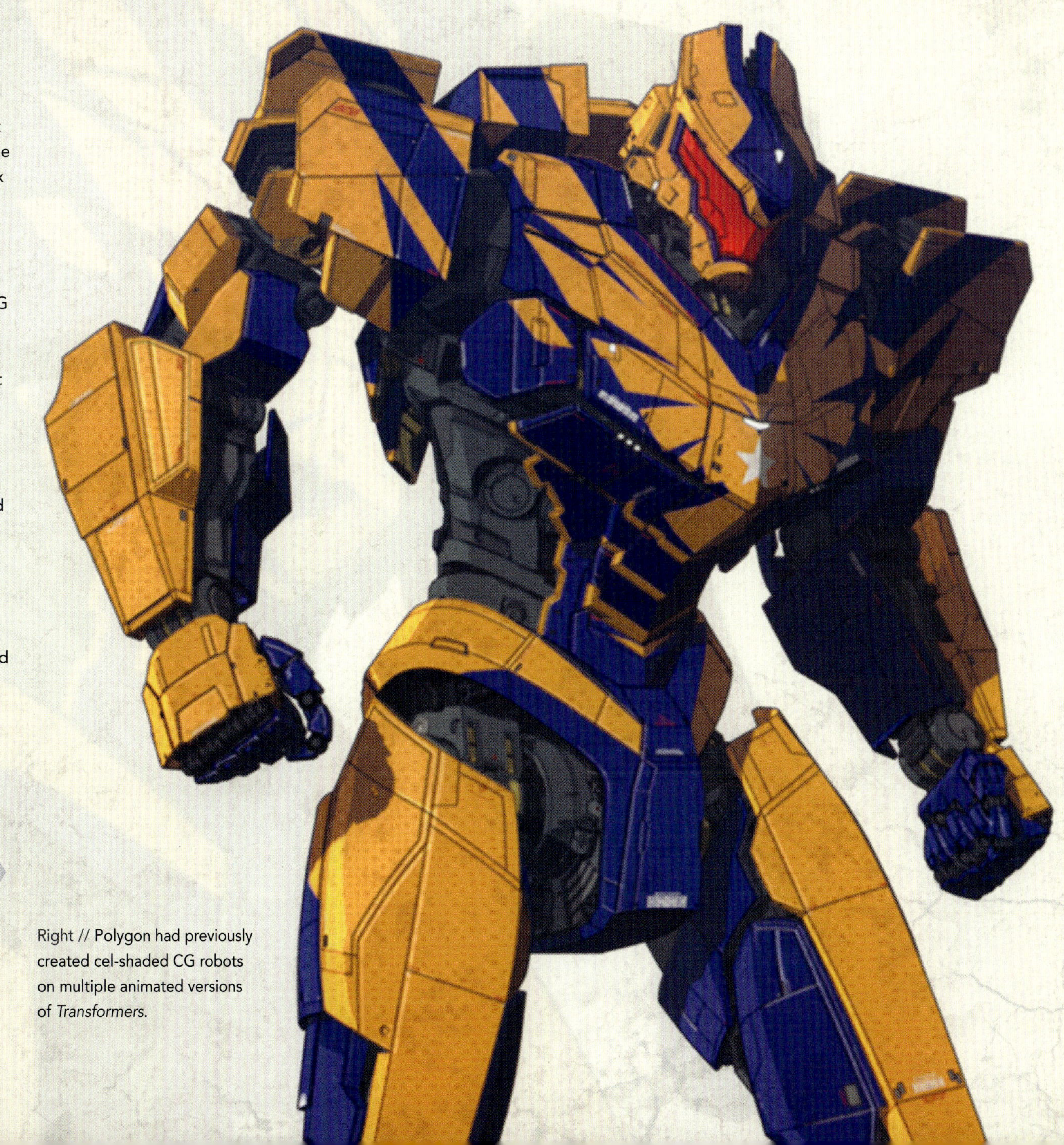

Right // Polygon had previously created cel-shaded CG robots on multiple animated versions of *Transformers*.

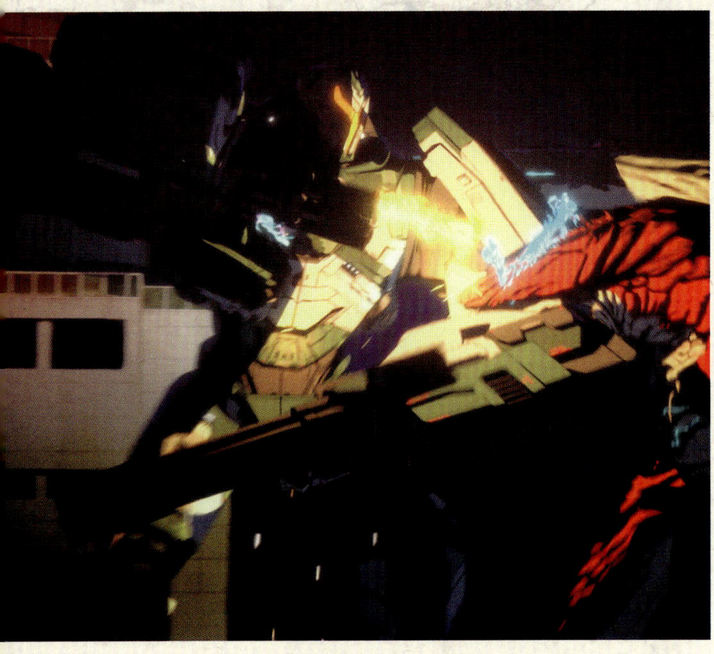

a very good experience with them. Looking at some of the studio's other titles, I thought Polygon could definitely pull it off, so we could keep the diehard 2D anime fans."

From Polygon's side, the studio was aware of *Pacific Rim.* "We'd been chasing the opportunity to animate the franchise for about seven or eight years," says the studio's CEO, Shuzo John Shiota. "The idea of *Pacific Rim* becoming an animated series came up and down, and we were aware of it from the first try, I think. *Pacific Rim* is a franchise that has a great respect towards the Kaiju culture that originated in Japan. It's not exactly the same—*Pacific Rim* has a Hollywood flair to it—but we felt a strong connection, especially with the first film.

"We were enamored with the franchise," Shiota continues, "and one of our friends got attached to the first attempt at animating it. We tried very hard to be attached, but the project did not go through. When it came around the second time, we heard about it through the grapevine. Jack Liang, the executive producer of Polygon Pictures, had an acquaintance at Legendary, and we started trying to get attached to the project through him. It was more an approach on our part initially."

Liang himself adds, "When the first *Pacific Rim* film came out, we felt that what Legendary and Guillermo del Toro and his team had created was very much a homage, done in a very good way. When we first saw it, a lot of our staff were very excited: 'If they ever do an anime, or an animation, Polygon has to be involved.' We wanted to be a part of it."

Some nostalgic Western viewers may link the spectacle of battling giants less with animation than with monster-suited actors on miniature sets. It's a tradition that encompasses films with names like *Godzilla vs. MechaGodzilla*, and also the robot fights in *Mighty Morphin' Power Rangers*, the Americanised version of Japan's *Super Sentai* franchise. The venerable *Ultraman*, which Guillermo del Toro named as an influence on *Pacific Rim*, is part of the genre too.

The genre's sometimes called *tokusatsu*, a Japanese expression meaning 'special filming'. "Yes, in Japan in the early 1970s there were *tokusatsu*, with the Kaiju and the

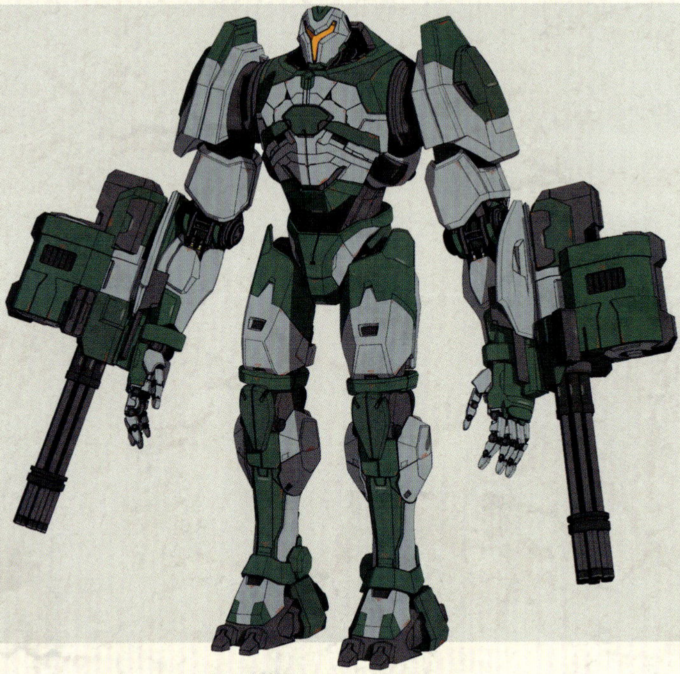

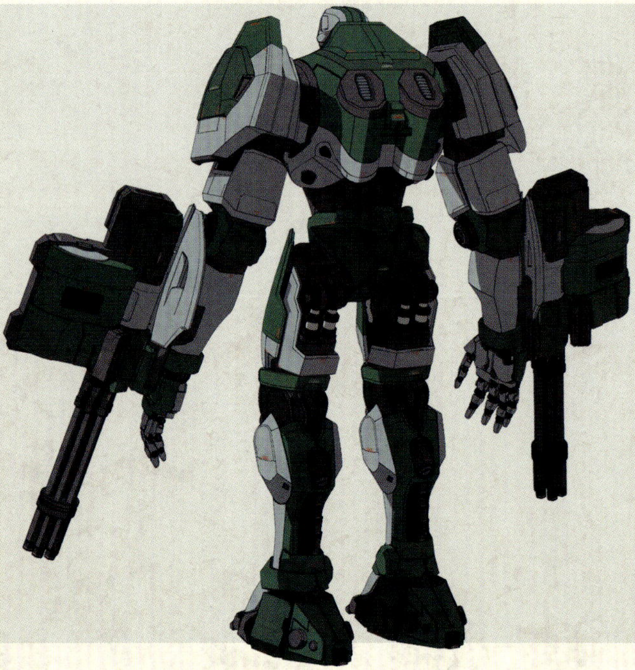

These pages // When you're making robot armies, much of their personality comes from the colors that you dress them in.

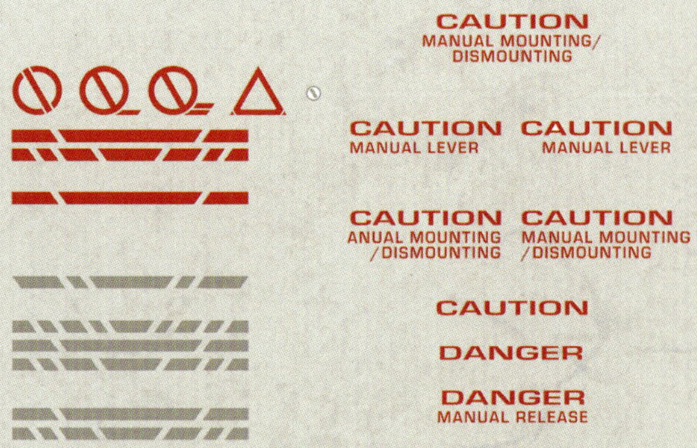

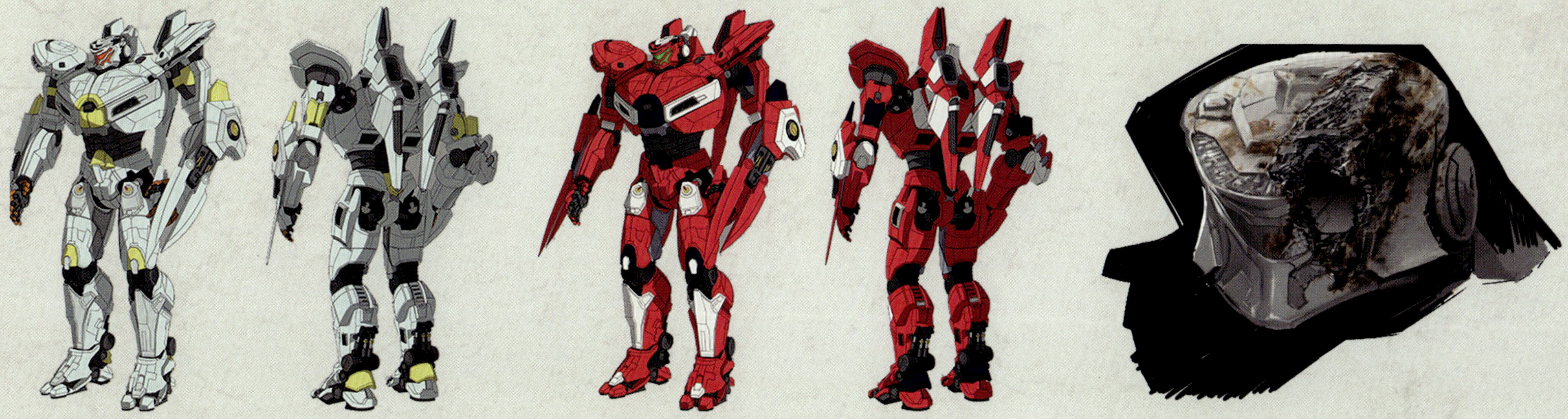

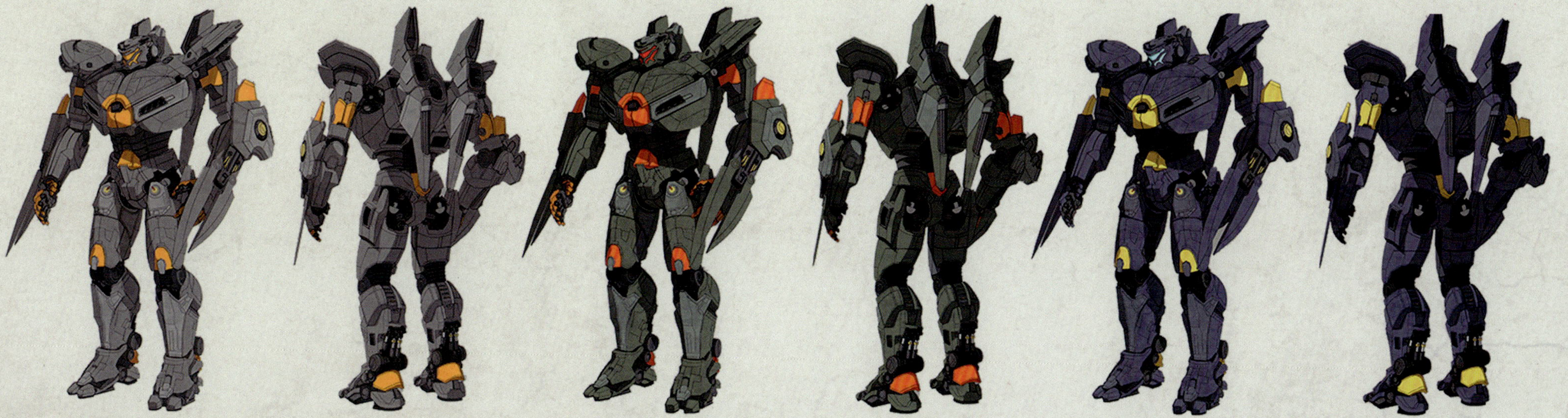

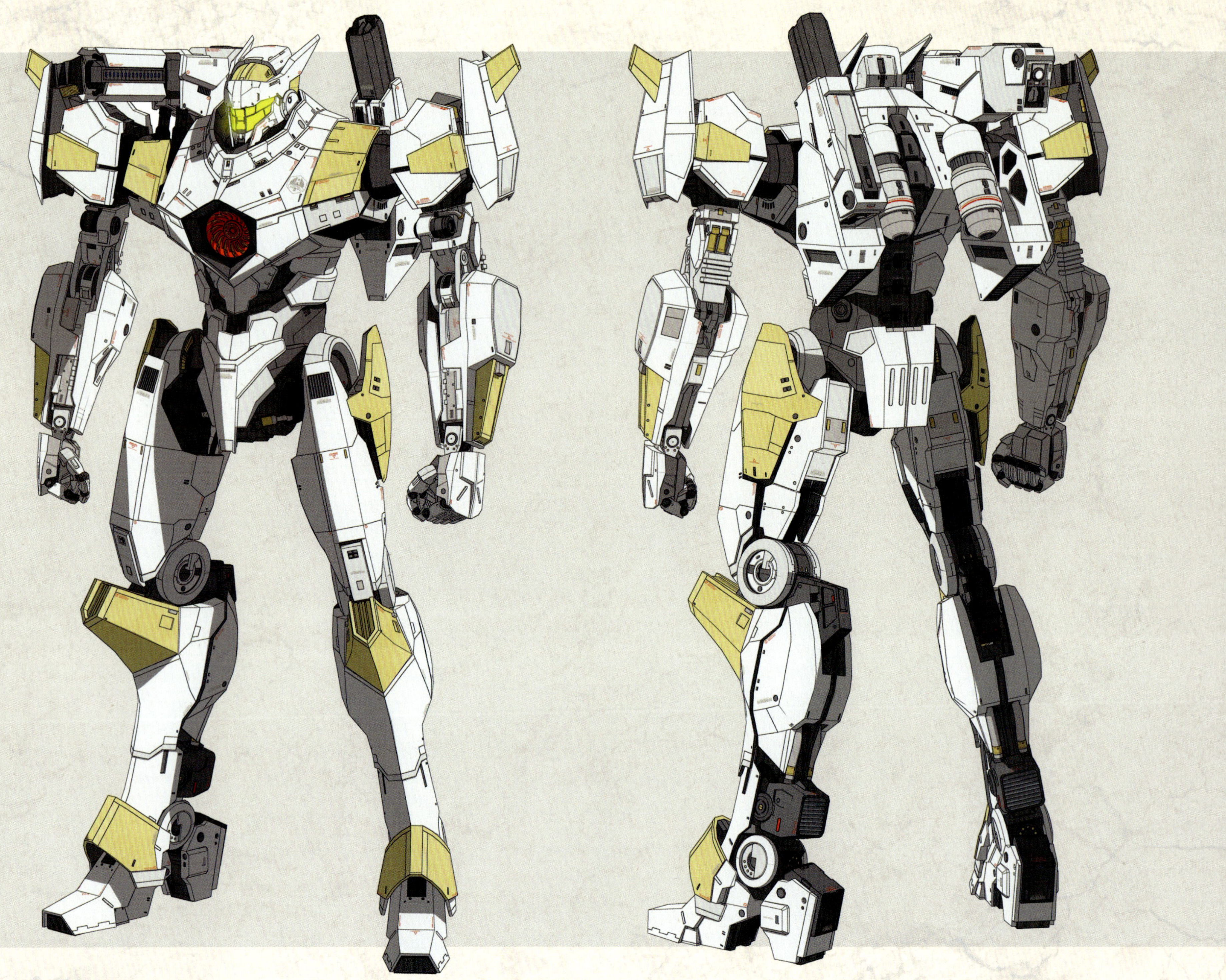

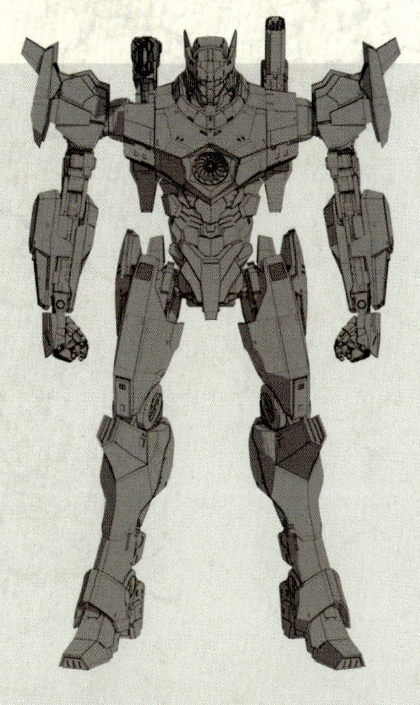

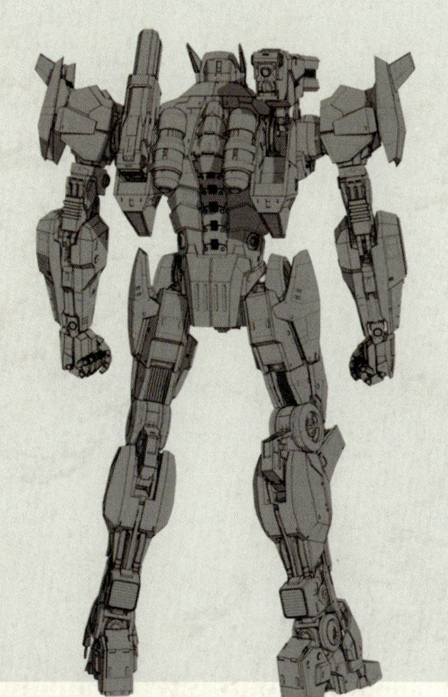

robots," says Shiota. "But there also was a rich history of animated robots, like *Grendizer* [shown on Japanese TV in 1975] and *Mazinger Z*. We grew up with these; for us, it doesn't seem like a jump to translate them to animation. It feels quite natural for us, especially for people my age. And obviously for later generations as well," Shiota adds, citing the hit anime *Neon Genesis Evangelion*.

"At Polygon, we do not do any visual effects, we do not do any live action," Shiota says. "Our thing is animation, and we felt that if *Pacific Rim* went into animation, we would be the best fit. Polygon has done tons of *Transformers*, tons of science fiction. Of course, the team had a challenge, in trying to portray the weight and the emotions of the characters, to execute those emotions comparably to a Hollywood film. It's one thing to translate a *tokusatsu* TV series into animation. It's another to translate a big Hollywood film. The challenge was huge in that sense, but portraying the genre in animation is nothing new to us."

Left and below // Hunter Vertigo, as piloted by the parents of Taylor and Hayley.

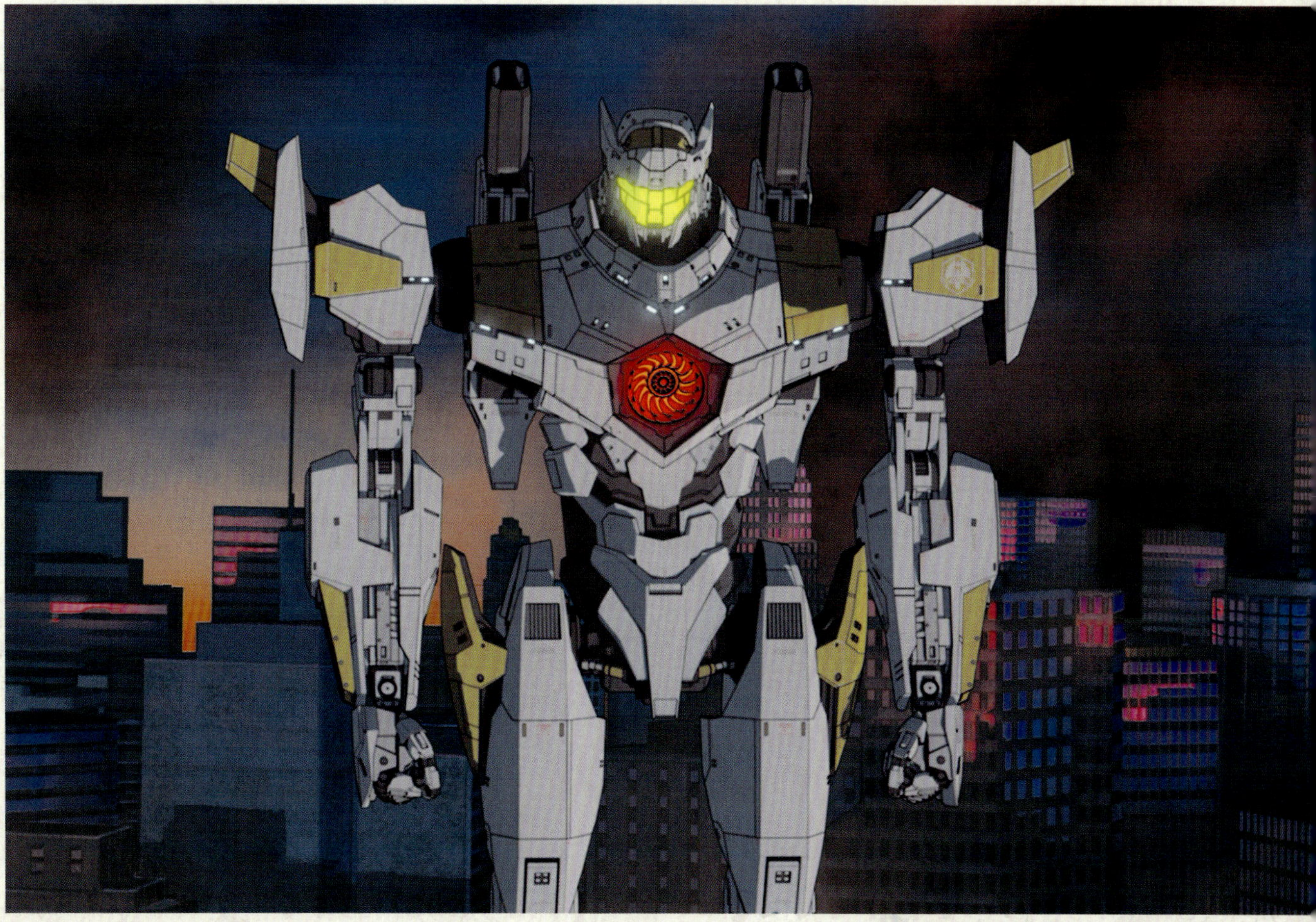

EAST MEETS WEST

Polygon Pictures was based in Tokyo, while the Legendary staff developing the series were in Los Angeles. Ken Duer wanted to bring the two sides together. "We got the Polygon studio a lot more involved in the creative process than we would normally do," says Duer. "We could have done all the designs and the scripts here in America and sent the package over to Japan and said, 'Please animate.' But if you really want to draw out the creativity and expertise of the Japanese staff, you should give them a lot more freedom and involvement in the creative process."

Johnson agrees. "We were excited by having Polygon artists in Tokyo spearhead the designs. They were our creative partner in the look of the show, and since this was to be an anime, it made sense to start the process there. For the most part, we would get a sampling of various designs to consider, and we'd start narrowing down our preferences until we had something that excited Craig and me, Legendary and Netflix. The process is always most labor-intensive at the beginning, as the look of the series is taking shape."

Compared to previous animated productions that Duer worked on, the process was different in several ways. "We normally don't send the script to the animation studio until we have the final draft," Duer says. "But with *Pacific Rim: The Black*, I would send Polygon outlines, synopses, first drafts, each version along the way. It was so the Japanese staff could see how the story was evolving, and that we weren't writing something that wasn't possible in the time and the budget."

Duer points out that writers on animated series aren't the same people as the animators or producers. "The writers just want to be creative and write something fantastic," says Duer. "A lot of the time we end up with a script and say, 'Holy cow, we don't have the time and the money to design and animate all this!' That was another reason we wanted to get so involved with the people who would actually do the

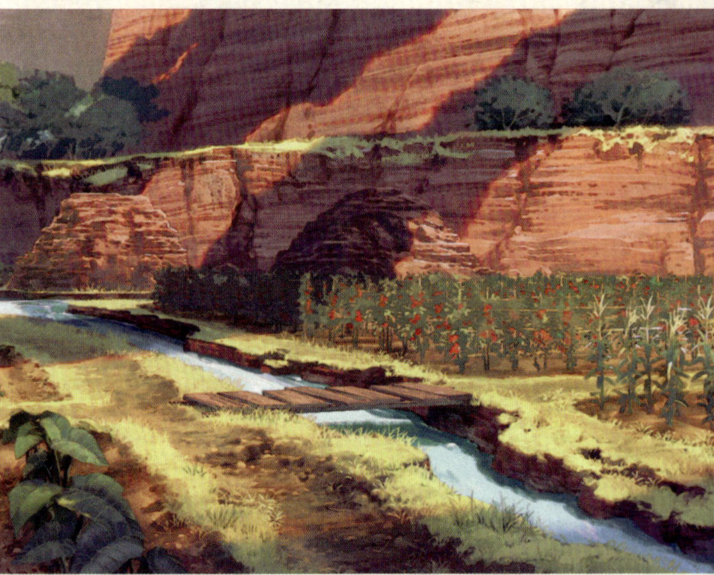

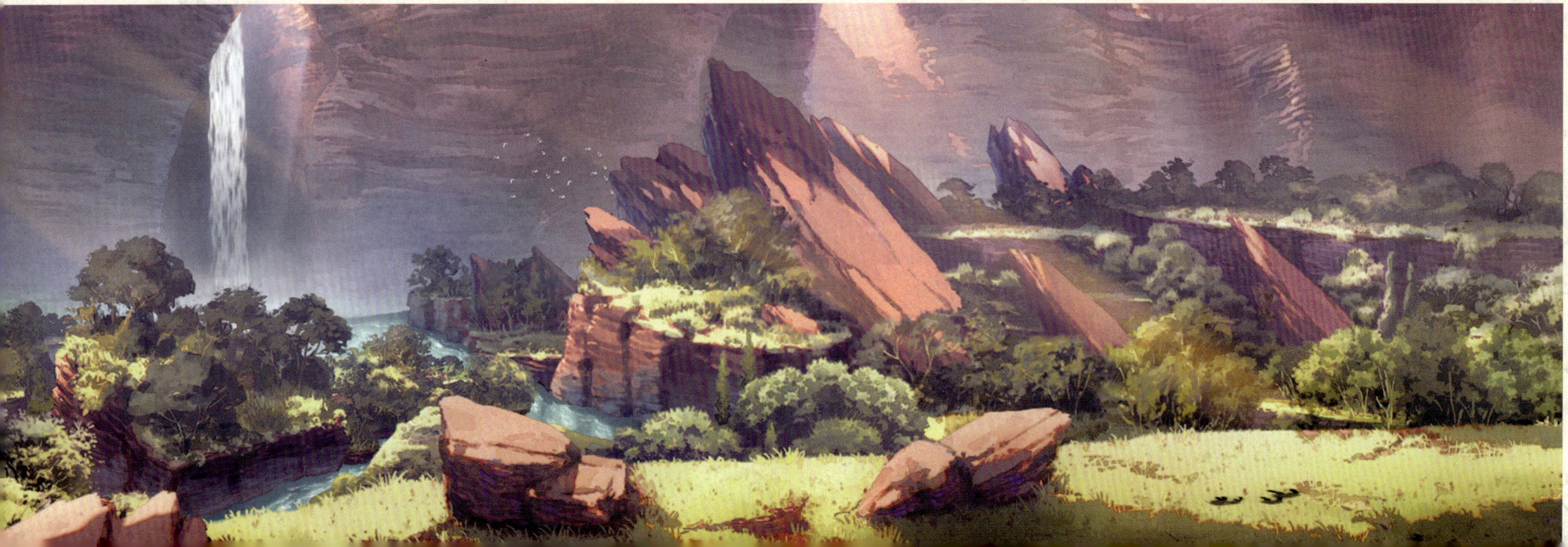

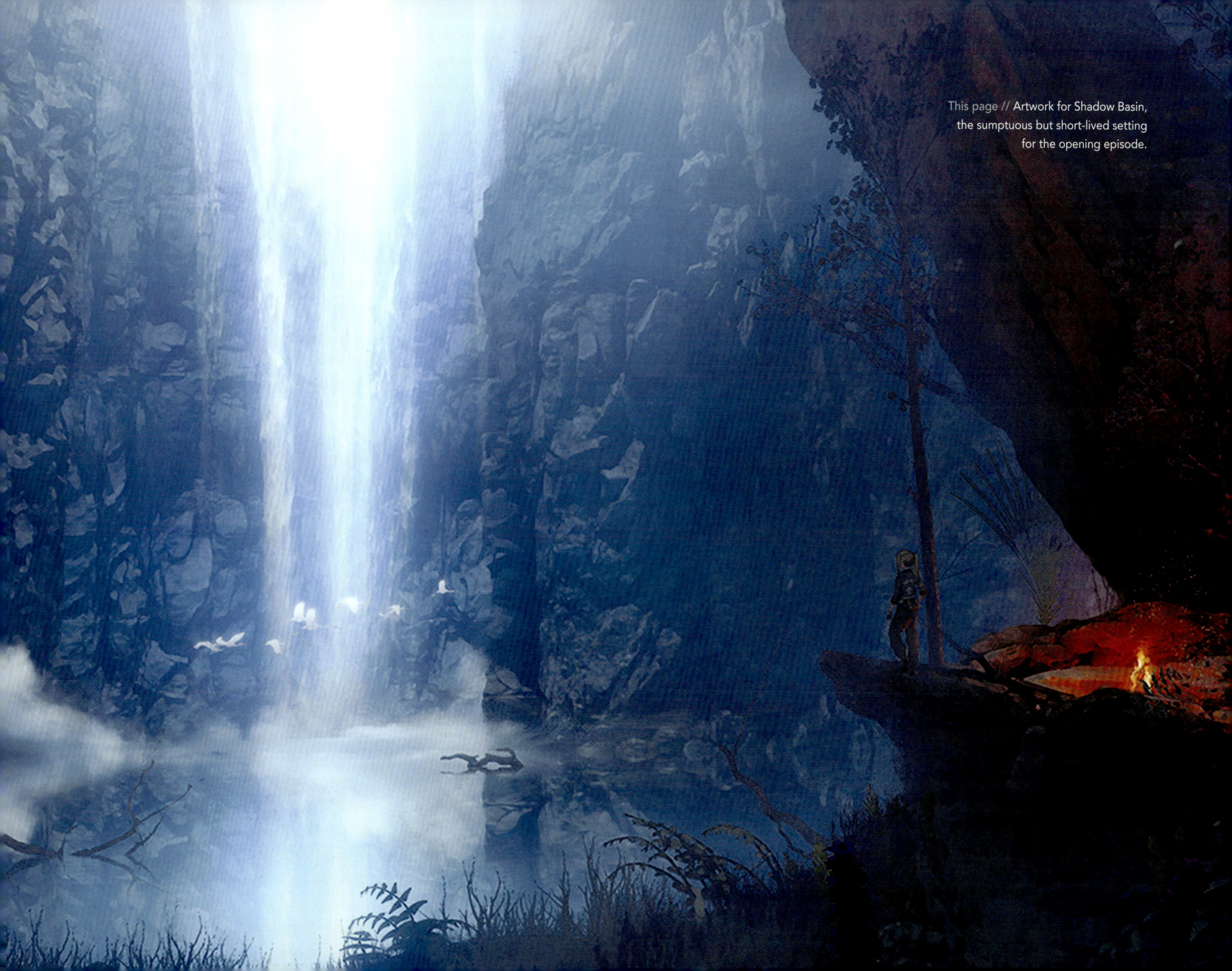

This page // Artwork for Shadow Basin, the sumptuous but short-lived setting for the opening episode.

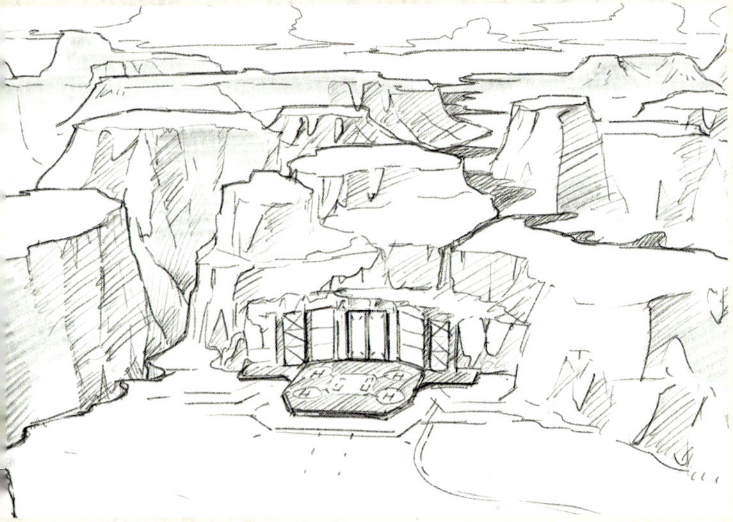

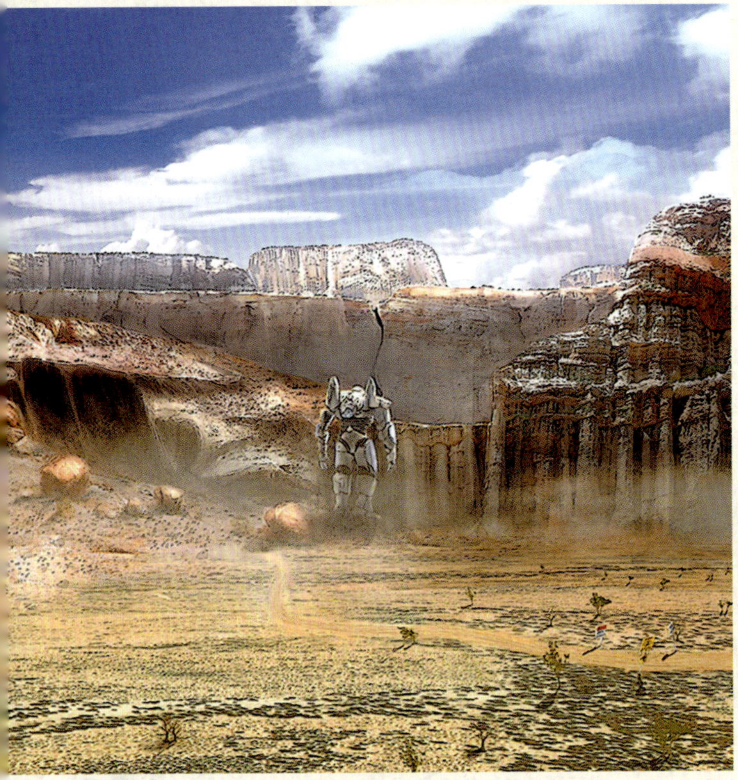

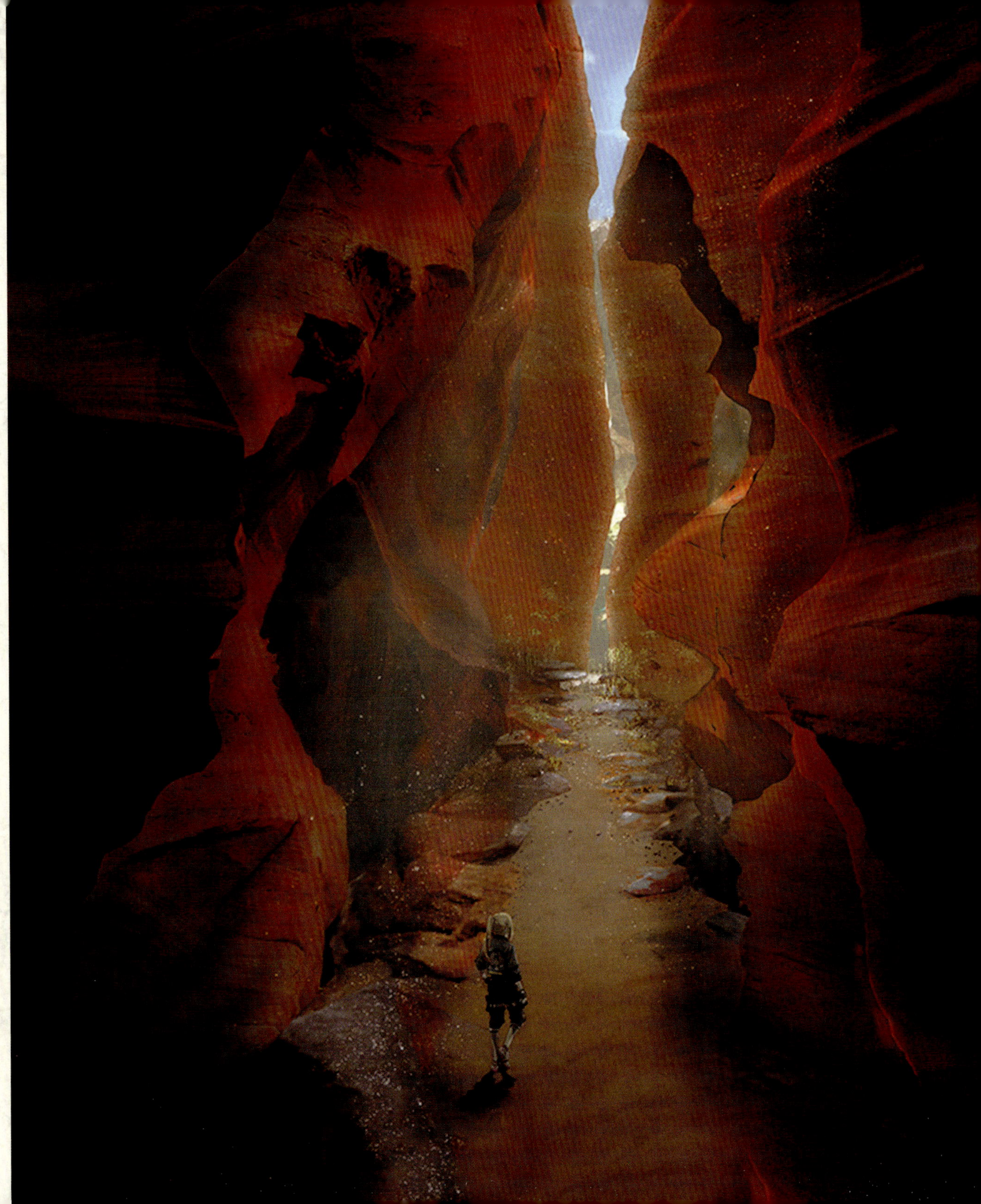

animation. Otherwise, we could spend twelve weeks writing the scripts and give it to the animators, only for them to say, 'Sorry, we can't do this.'"

For Duer, it doesn't matter where the animation is made; facetime is crucial. "Not just by email and phone calls and Zoom, but to actually go and meet the crew; to discuss every detail, not just technical ones, but creative details. It's convenient to use Zoom, but it doesn't beat being there, face to face, and having these subtle discussions which don't translate by email. We went over everything from designs to the final look, the lighting, the color, what kind of animation it should be."

Duer visited the Polygon studio in Tokyo before the Covid pandemic. He was accompanied by Johnson and the series' director on the American side, Jae-Hong Kim. "We were at Polygon for a week, and every day we would hash out the process with different teams," Duer says. "All the little things had to be thought out and discussed upfront, rather than being discussed later, because if we're doing this, we need to do this."

The director, Jae-Hong Kim, had also worked with Polygon on *Lost in Oz*. "I knew Polygon very well, they are the best! It was very important to have face-to-face meetings. I need to make sure we are on the same page, and they need to know what's the vision and direction for the show."

Like Duer, Kim didn't want to dictate. "As a supervising director, I like to give a lot of creative freedom on Polygon's side. If I just tell them, 'It's got to be this and that', then what's fun about doing the show?"

A lot of the discussions in Tokyo were conducted through pictures. "We traded drawings," Kim says. "Animation is an art medium, so instead of verbal explanations, we drew things—'How about this?', 'How about that?'—to see what worked the best."

Kim met with the top-level artists, episode directors, and art directors, as well as the supervising director on the Polygon side, Hiroyuki Hayashi. "They all had their own ideas," Kim says. "My job was: unite them all, but make a

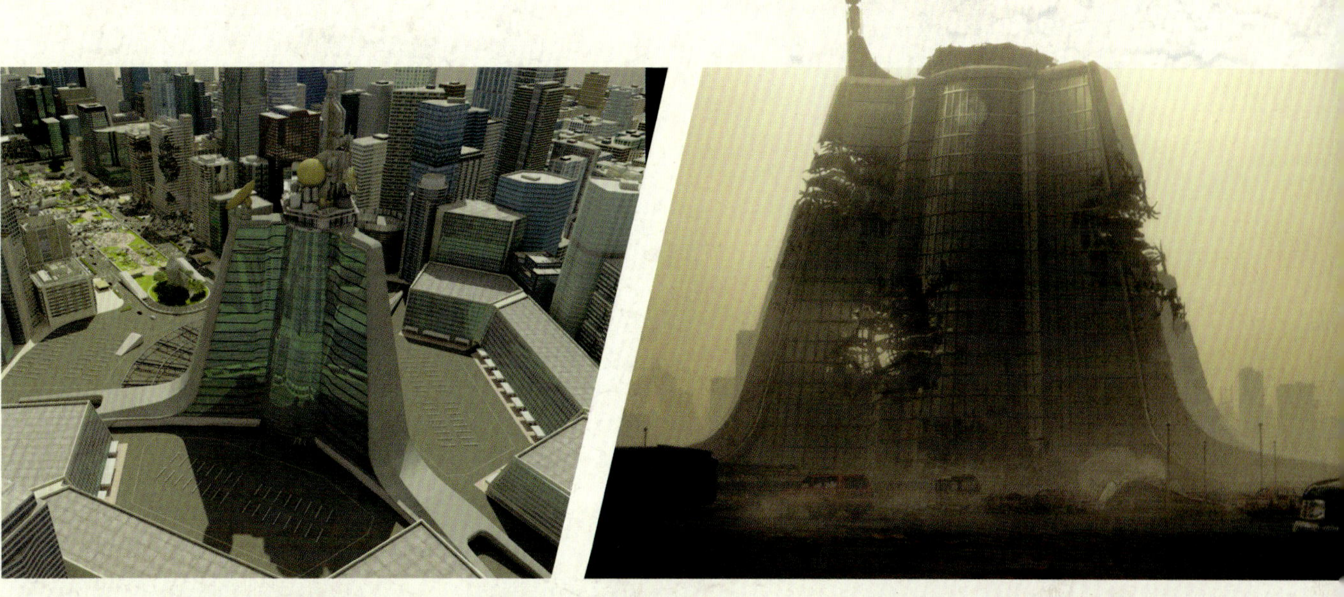

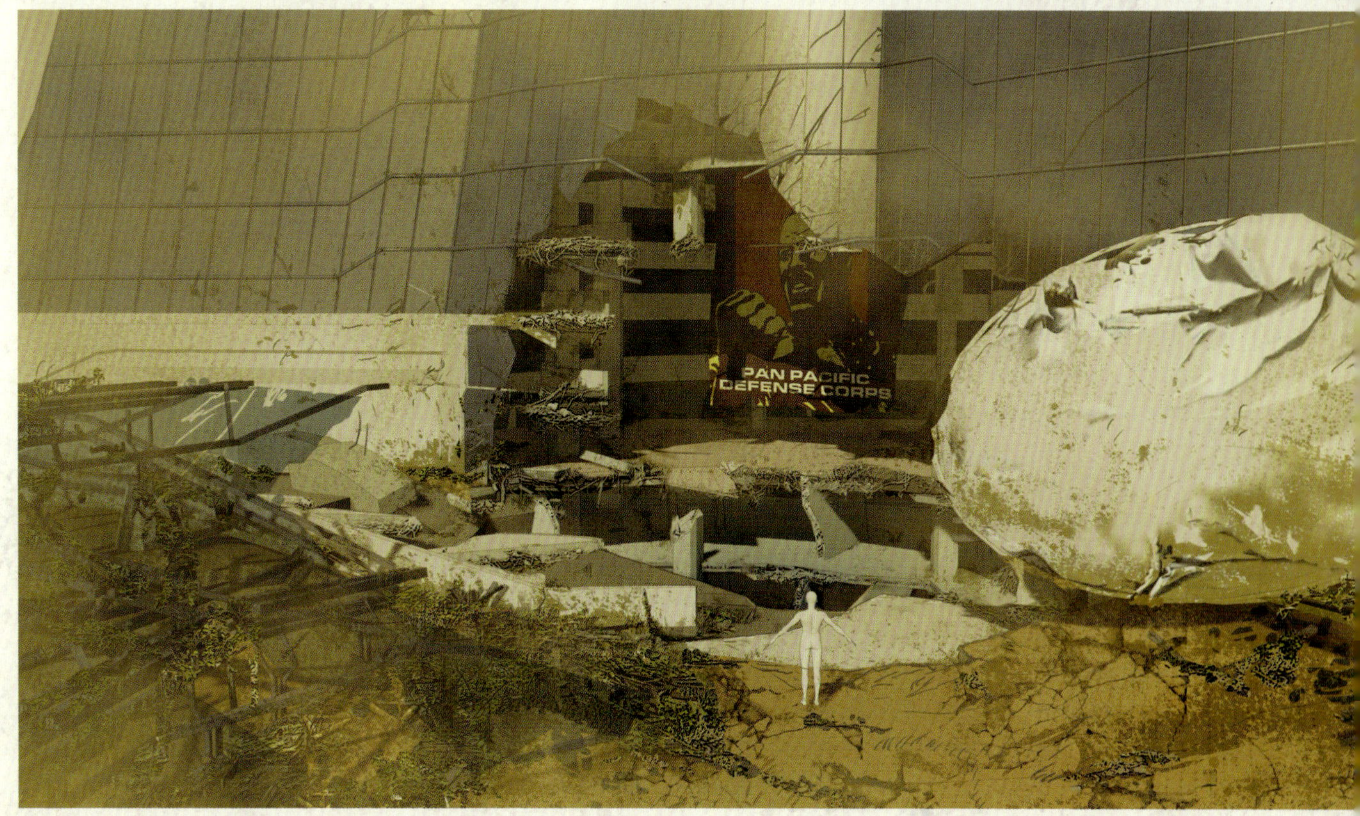

Left and right // Artwork for the rugged outback (left) and high-tech structures (right).

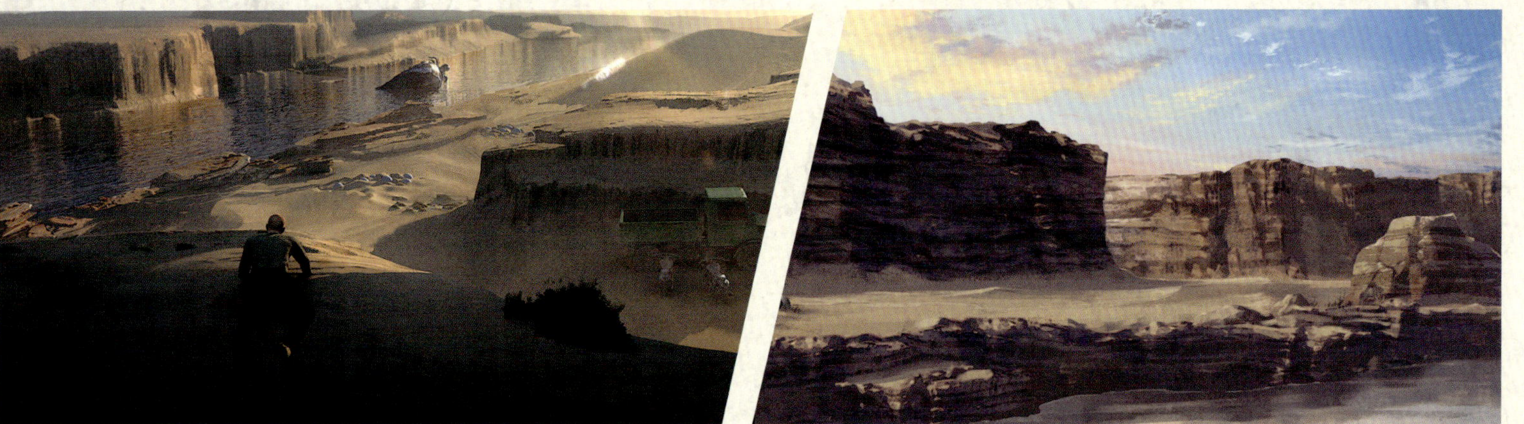

Left, below and right // The art on these pages would inspire the visuals in the third episode, set around a deadly river.

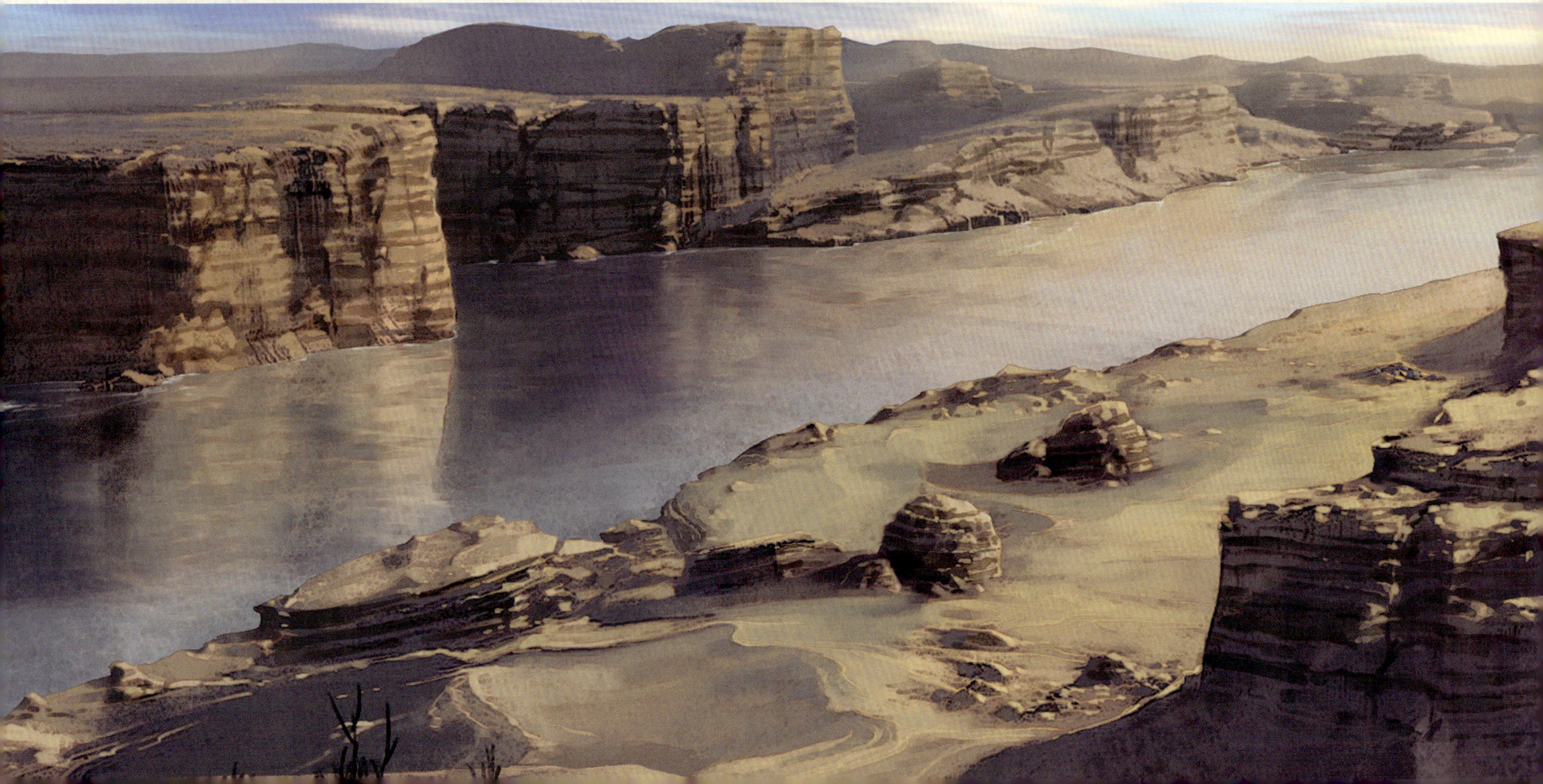

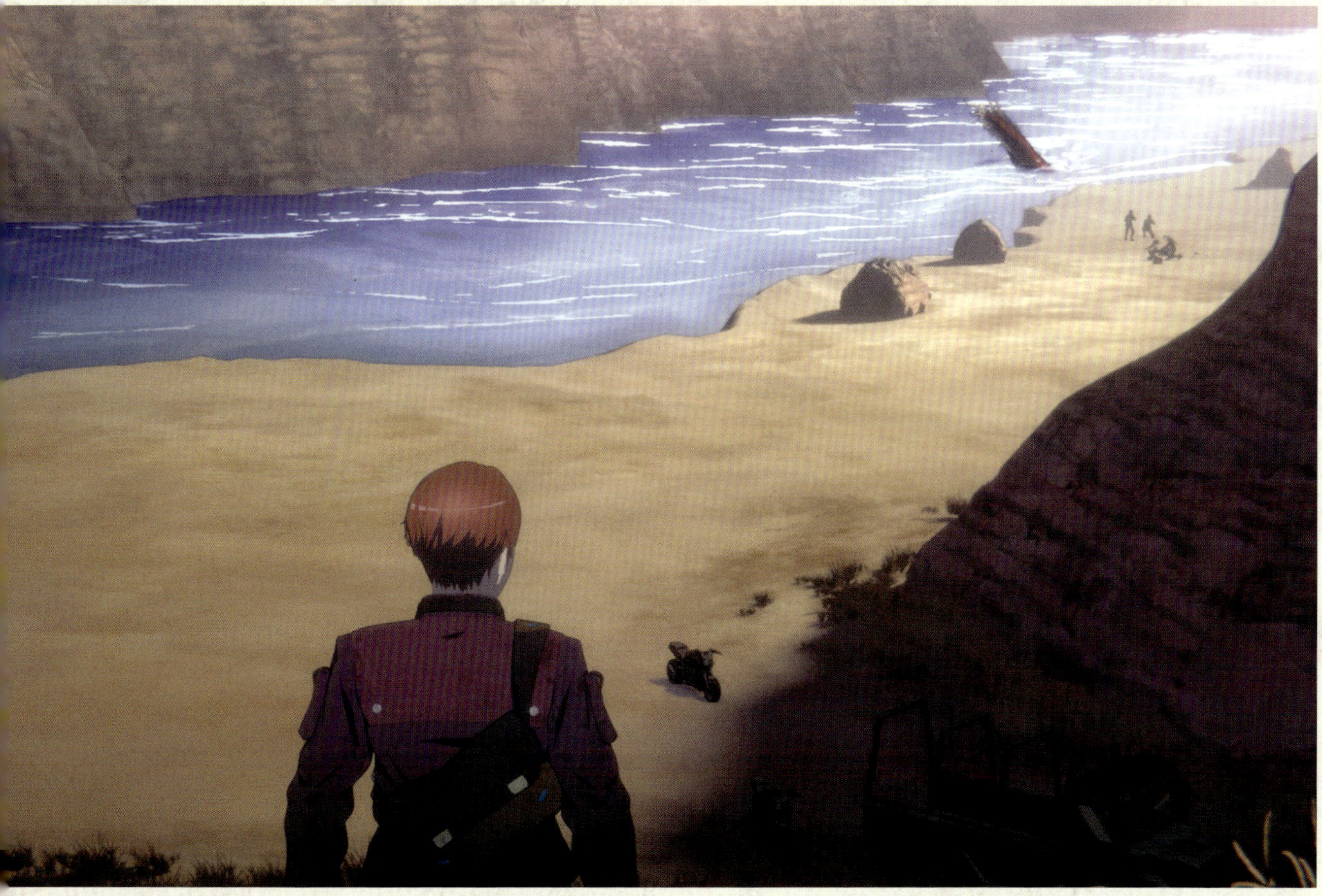

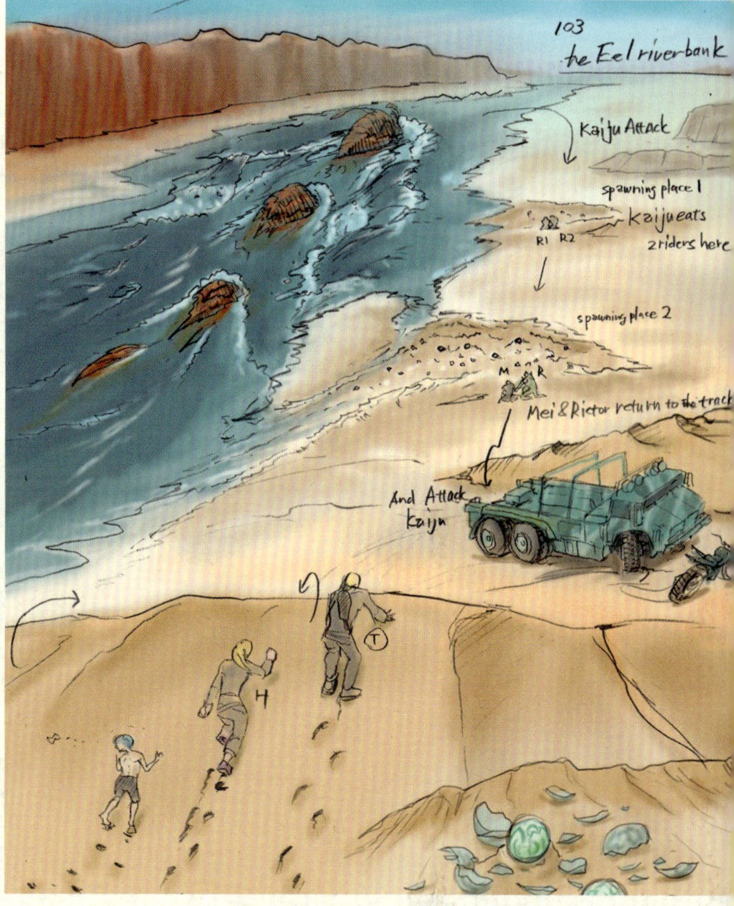

single decision. I had to give them a clear direction, a clear path. What needs to be done, what needs to be shown."

Following the Tokyo visit, the Los Angeles staff communicated with the Japanese side via video calls each Tuesday and Thursday. "We would look at designs and make comments," says Duer. "The Polygon staff would send us shots and we would discuss them, just like a live-action director would look at dailies. We would do that every week, twice a week, for two years, making sure the Polygon staff understood the sometimes subtle creative notes."

Kim set the direction for the show's style and look, and was involved in designs from the pre-production stage. "I worked on character designs, mecha (machinery), backgrounds, props… Usually the Polygon art director or artists sent me rough designs and I went over them for revisions or notes. If something went nowhere, then I had to provide a rough concept design and send it to Polygon."

Kim also went over the storyboards from Polygon, putting in more notes and revisions. "Also, the colors and directions for light and shadow, expressions and gestures in the animation, and the timing for acting and actions as well."

For Kim, there was one definite highlight. "Designing the Kaiju and Jaegers was the part that was the most fun!" he enthuses.

"INSTEAD OF VERBAL EXPLANATIONS, WE DREW THINGS TO SEE WHAT WORKED THE BEST."

Jae-Hong Kim, director

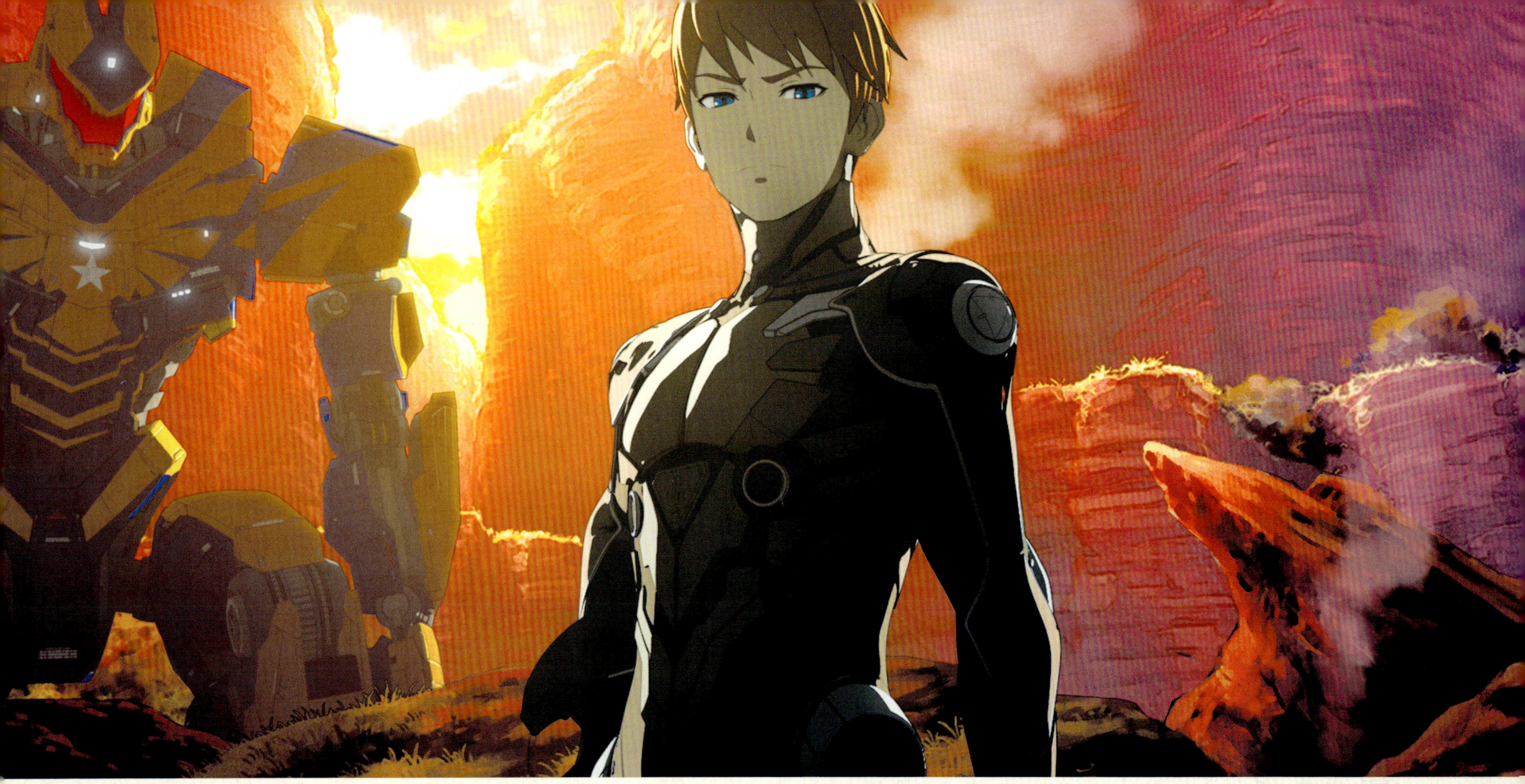

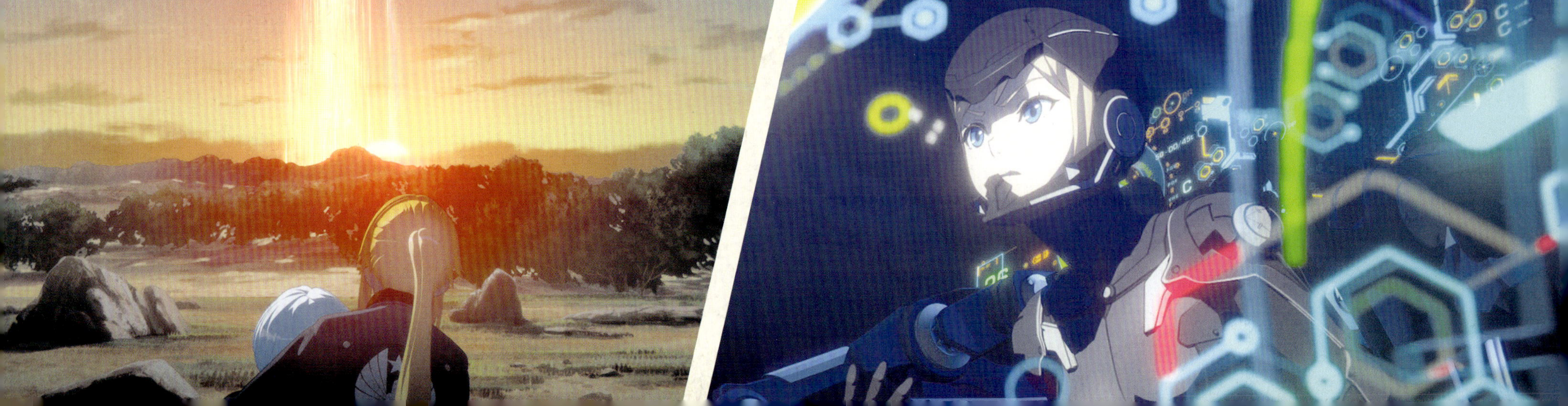

ASSETS AND STYLE

Anime often juggles its limited assets in particular ways, as Greg Johnson explains. "In many anime series and movies, a style has evolved from the careful use of assets. Huge set-piece sequences, where the hour-of-labor count is high, are typically saved for the big scenes in the story. The rest of the series typically relies on clever usage of restrained asset usage. There are slow panning shots, limited character movement, reduced lip synch, while the anime gives most attention to the expressiveness of the eyes to convey mood."

Johnson points out that anime, even action anime, lets its audience feel intimate with the characters, more than a blockbuster film. In Johnson's view, "The shaking of a hand, a slight turn of a head, a long shot of a lone figure—these are all artistic choices that help establish the mood and, by their very use, partly define what anime is."

All those considerations help determine where the money goes. "You have to look at the script and the storyboard as a collection of assets," says Johnson. "Backgrounds, props, characters, and effects; plus vehicles and, in our case, Jaegers and Kaiju. These assets take a certain number of hours or weeks to create. In budget terms, there is a price tag for each hour devoted to them. As a producer, I must work within those hours. At a certain point along the pipeline, I can't ask for a new scene in a new location without incurring overages."

Jae-Hong Kim concurs. "You can think of awesome drawings and what the color scheme is going to be, and

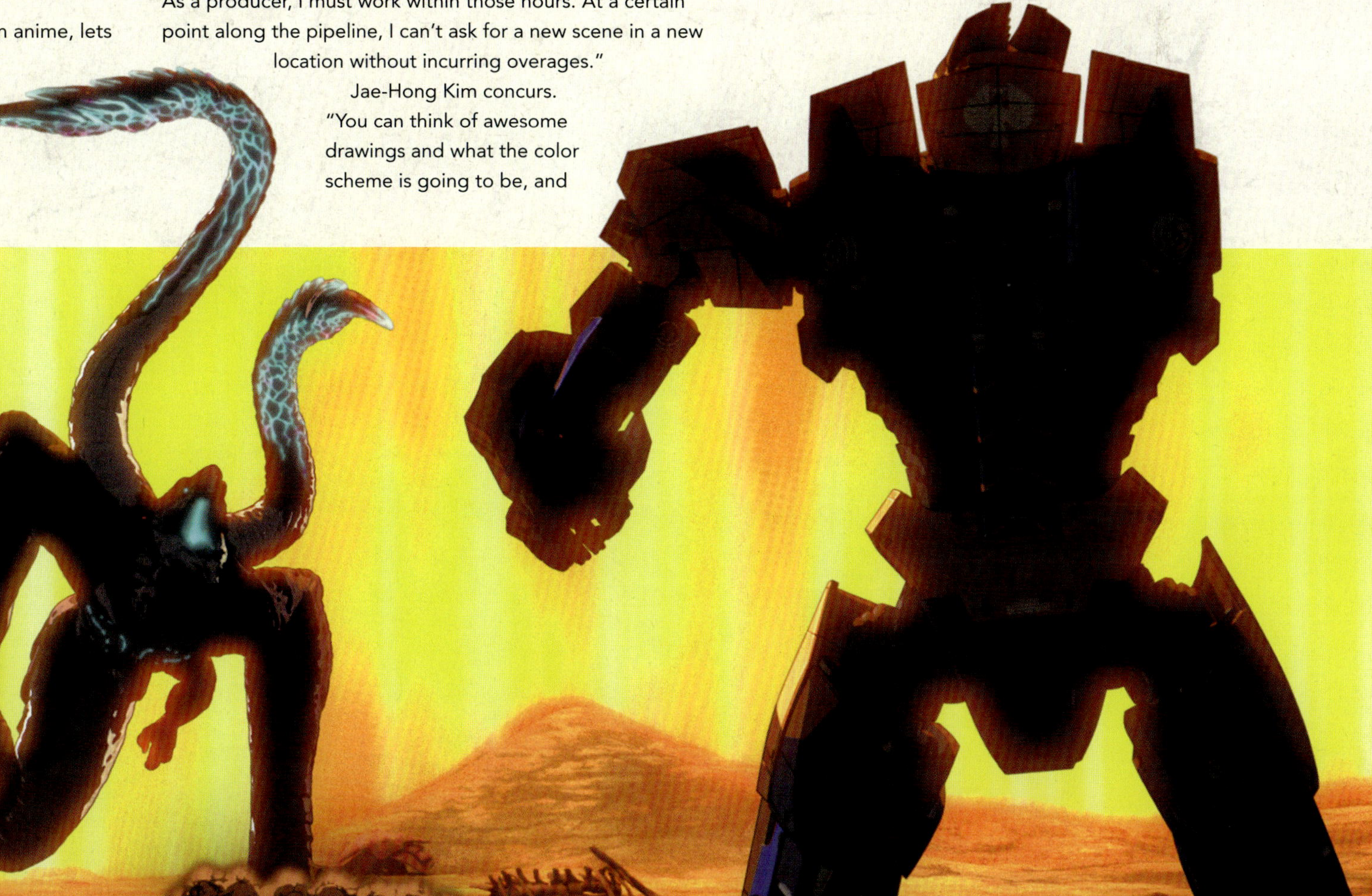

Below // Art for the fight between the Jaeger and the Acidquill from Episode Six of the series.

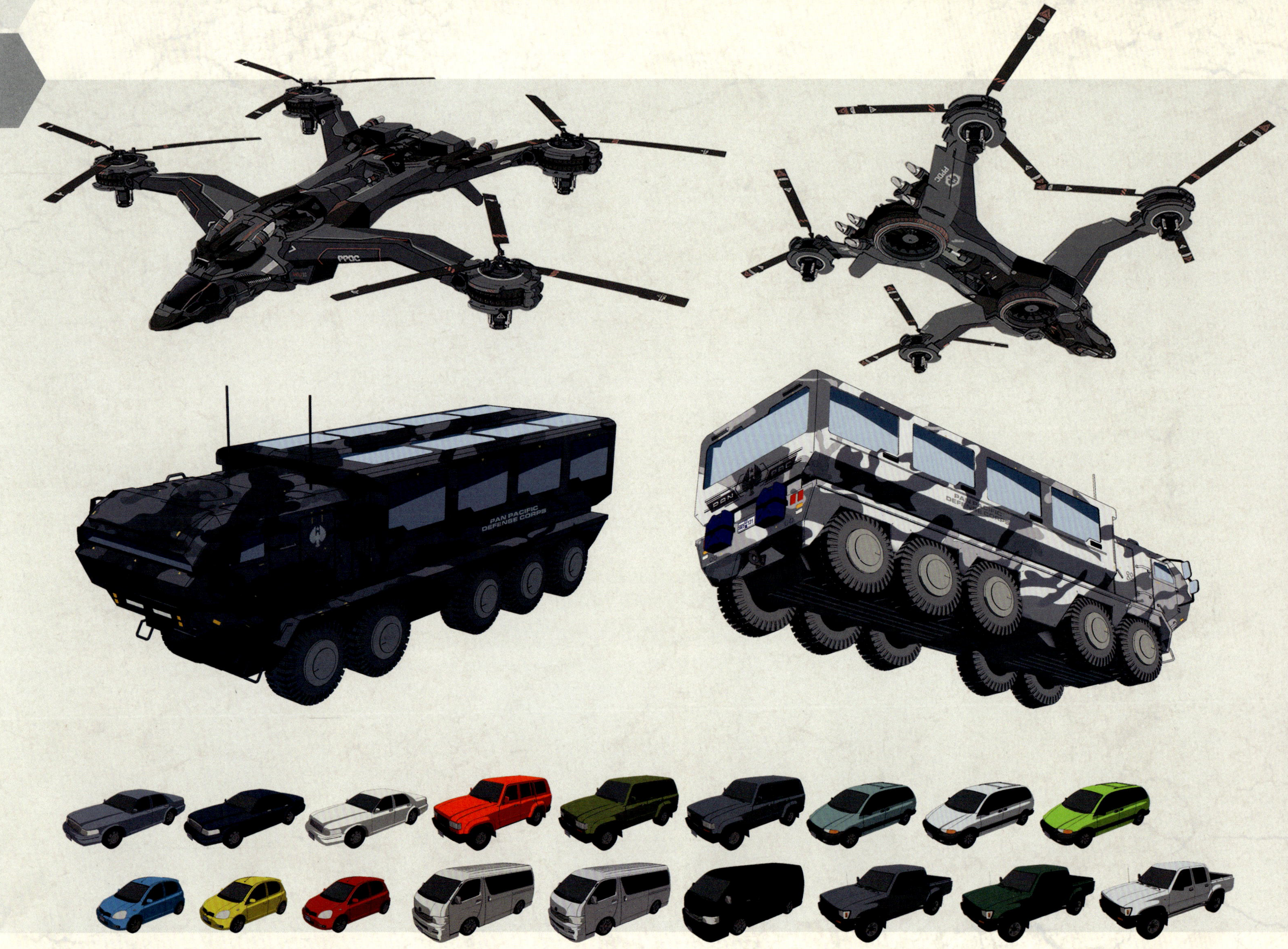
PPDC
PAN PACIFIC
DEFENSE CORPS

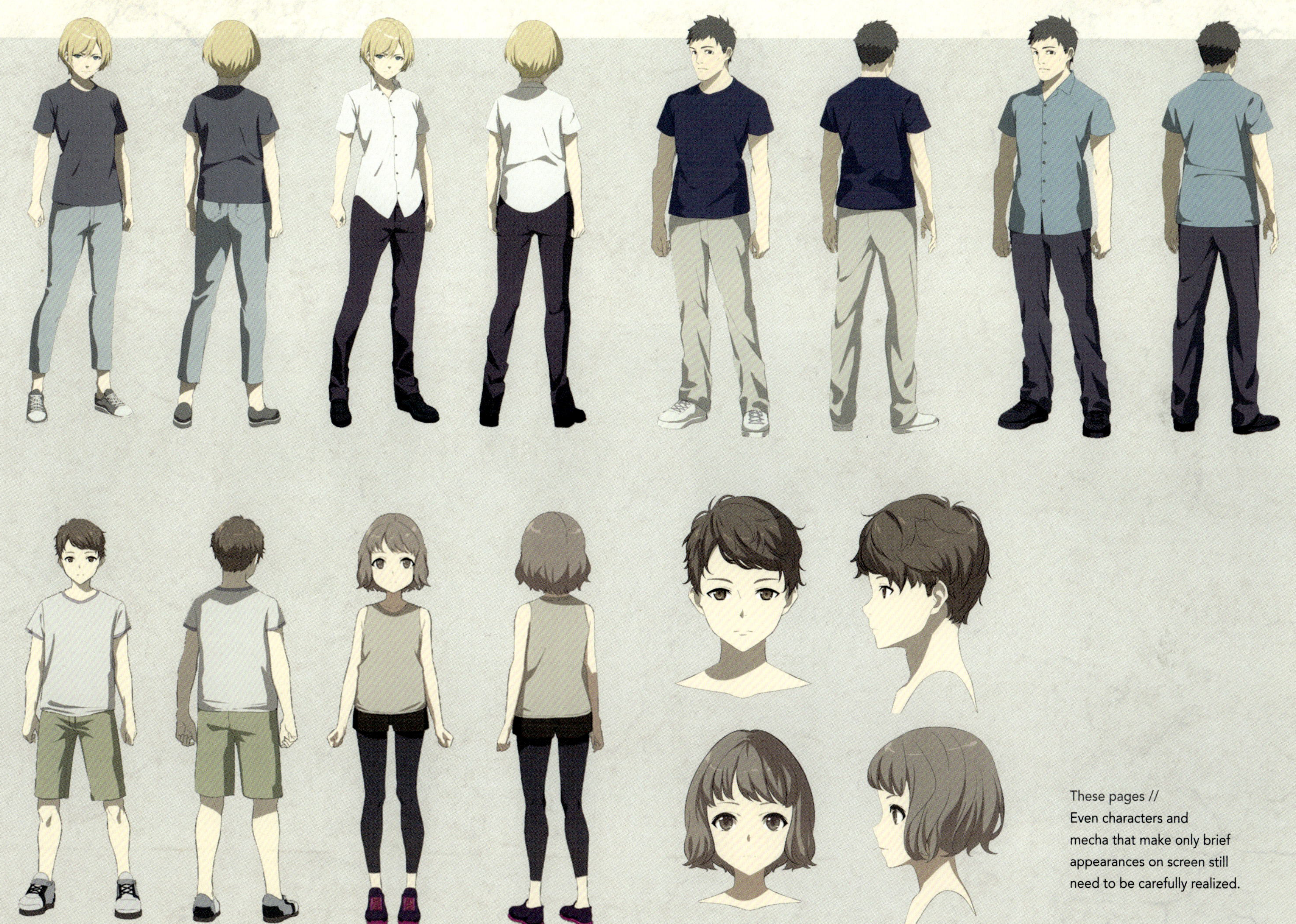

These pages //
Even characters and mecha that make only brief appearances on screen still need to be carefully realized.

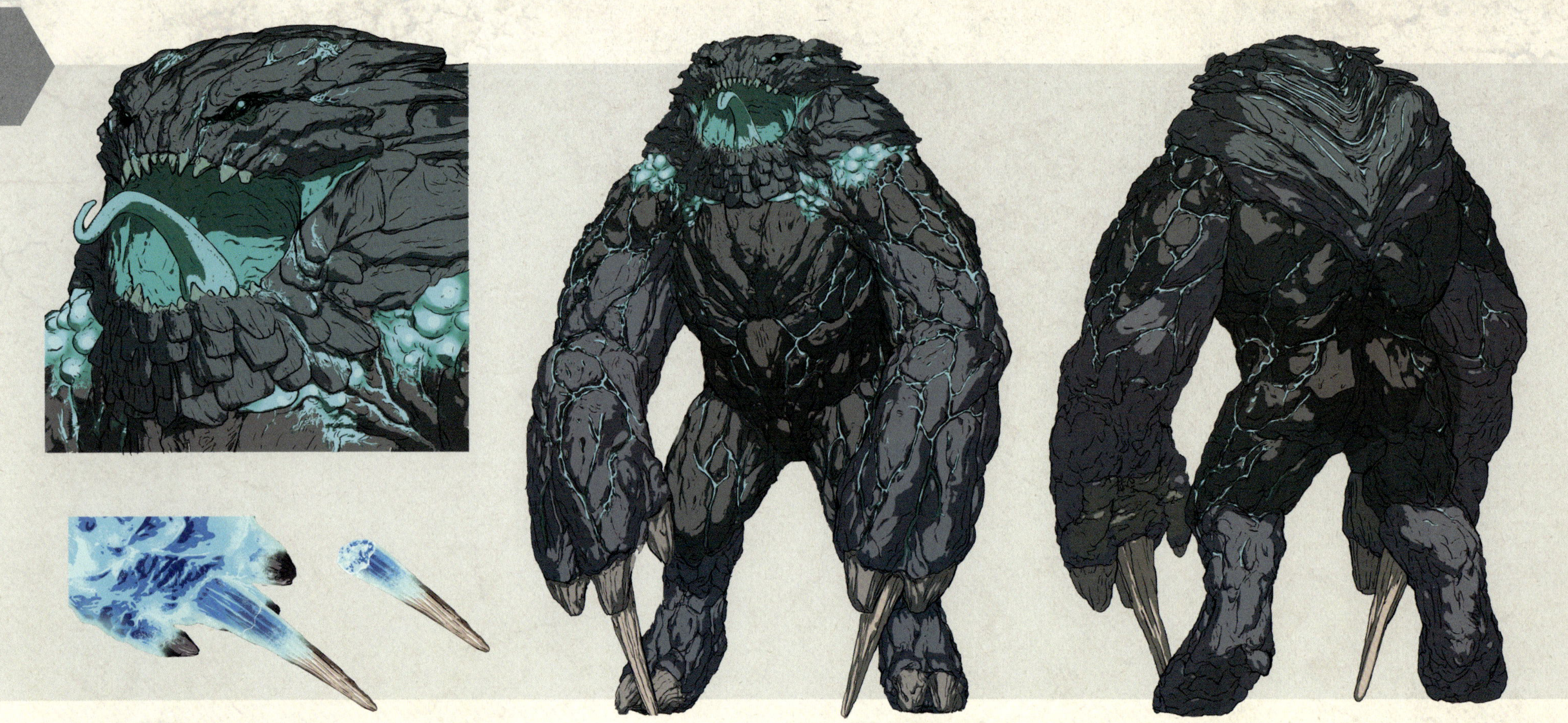

the look of the action. But at the same time, I have to know what kind of budget we have."

Duer stresses the importance of recycling. "Especially in CG animated series, it's all about repurposing, reusing the assets. If you design and build every asset for every episode, that starts to get very expensive. In CG, the more you reuse, the more you get to amortize your costs.

"When we go into production, we have to set rules—how many characters per episode, how many environments, how many locations. Let's say that in every episode, we can introduce and design five new characters. If the script calls for ten, the animators will go, 'Oh, you're going to have to cut someone…'

"In a show like this," Duer continues, "there are battles, destruction. To do all that in CG could be very expensive. If there's a huge battle between a Kaiju and a Jaeger, and the Kaiju smashes into every building and destroys it, that's cost-prohibitive. Those are the situations where we wanted feedback from Polygon, for the staff to call it out and say 'How can we do this so we don't have to smash everything, never to be reused?'"

Duer remembers the back and forth. "We would go back to the script and say, 'Let's cut this scene out,' or, 'Instead of going to this location, let's go back to this previous location.' That kind of thing was very helpful."

Jae-Hong Kim similarly remembers discussing script changes because of asset issues, or things proving prohibitive to animate. "We don't have a multi-million-dollar budget," Kim concedes. "Also, since this is not an animated feature film, there are a lot of limits in the production

Above // Kaiju are great, but there are limits to how many you can build.

"ESPECIALLY IN CG ANIMATED SERIES, IT'S ALL ABOUT REPURPOSING, REUSING THE ASSETS."
Ken Duer, co-producer

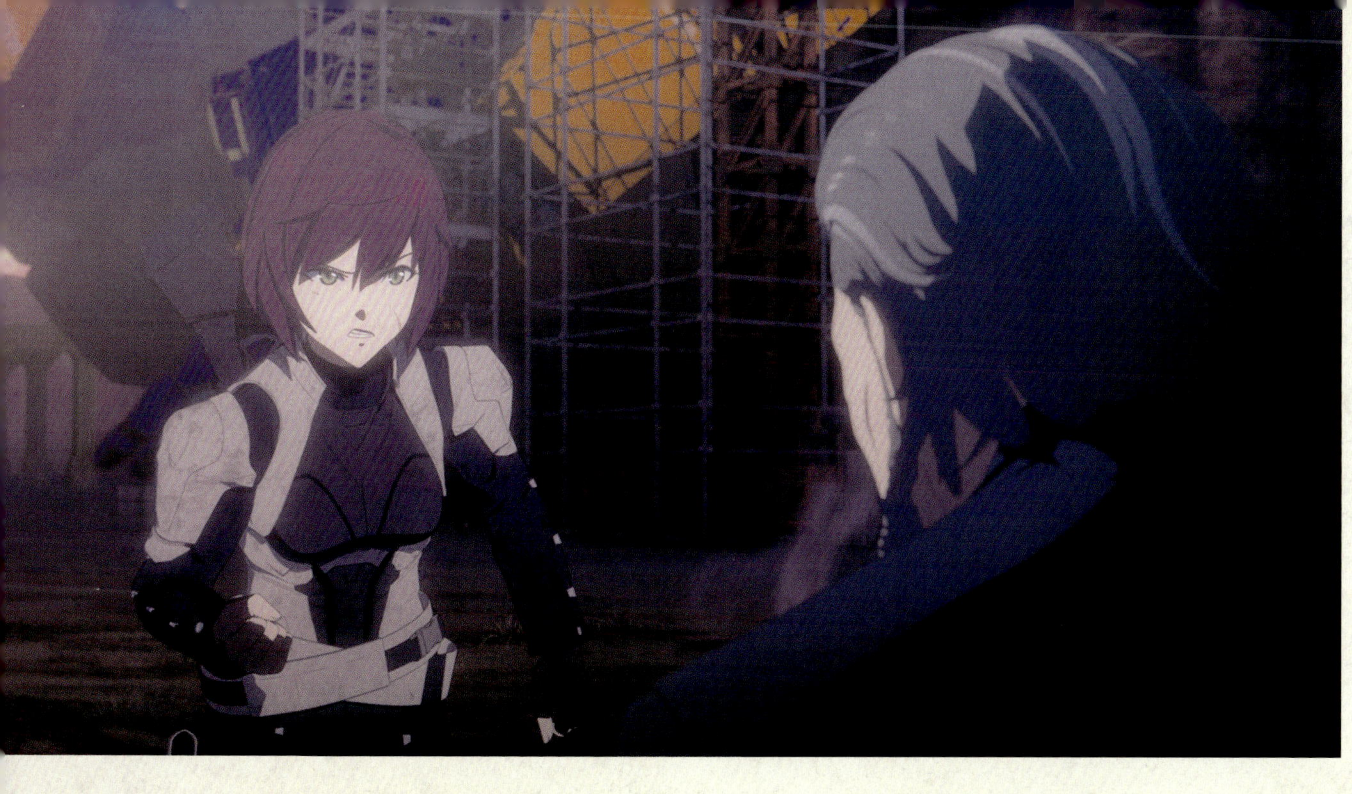

schedules. We had to balance that. I didn't want this show to look cheap, but at the same time, I had to calculate really well—what to lose, what to keep. I couldn't compromise on the designs of the Jaegers and Kaiju, but I could slightly lower the level of the visuals of the backgrounds…"

The live-action *Pacific Rim* films gave him some guidance about the show's look. But, Kim says, "My task was, how can I make the look of the series slightly different from the live-action look? Since we're using animation, I really wanted to steer the show slightly away from live action. I like to emphasise what anime can deliver to the audience. There are freedoms in what animation can do."

Of course, the look was filtered through Polygon's cel-shaded CG. Like Duer, Kim acknowledges the resistance of some anime fans to CG. "A lot of people have this barrier: 'I don't like CG, I love 2D animation.' But what if you could combine those two things so you have something animated in CG, but which definitely looks like 2D animation? I thought that was a good challenge."

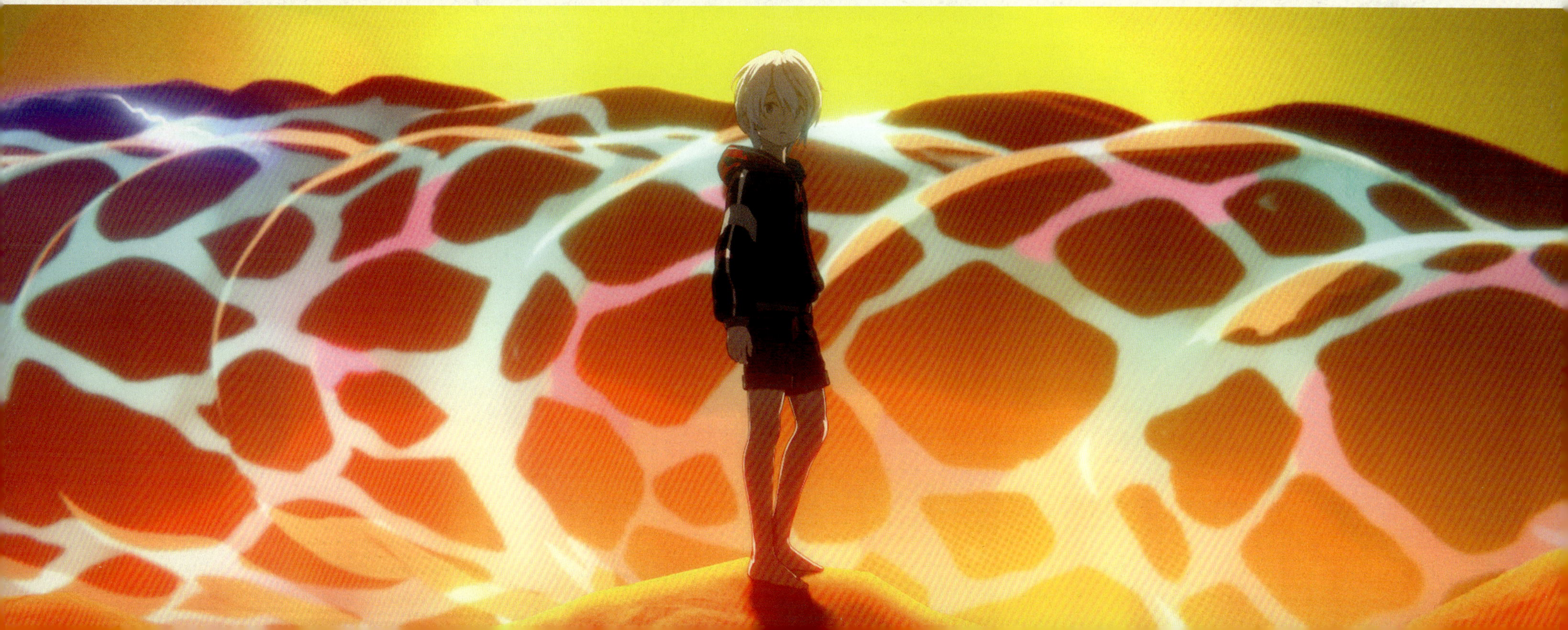

THE CONTINUING STORY

Pacific Rim: The Black tells an ongoing, serialized story, and that's a big part of its appeal. As Johnson puts it, "What really drives our characters forward, as well as our audience, are the unanswered questions that are established early on. Where are the protagonists' missing parents? How do the Kaiju exist in a land where they can't do what they were made to do; fight? And can our characters make it out of Australia with so much against them: their inexperience, naivete, and emotional baggage, and a training Jaeger with no weapons?"

Johnson sums up the show as, "Big mysteries, little mysteries, keeping viewers on their toes with surprise left turns, and not wrapping up the conflict at the end of every episode."

Serial storytelling used to be rare in animation for the American market. Ken Duer remembers, "I've been in animation for quite some time, over 30 years. Traditionally, animated series in the United States, and maybe in Britain and Europe, have one-off episodes. Each episode ends and it doesn't really continue on."

It's done differently in Japan. "The Japanese have always been animating series in a serial form," says Duer. "The story continues on, and it's a long journey for the characters. We were never really able to do that here."

In Duer's view, that changed with the dramatic rise of streaming platforms. "They allowed a different storytelling process," Duer says. "For me specifically, *Lost in Oz* [the Polygon-animated series] was a rare moment when we could make a serial running 26 episodes. The writers, the showrunners, everybody had great fun. We could tell a deeper story with the characters' relationships, of not just a physical journey but an emotional journey. You can't really do that in 22 minutes."

As the supervising director, one of Jae-Hong Kim's jobs was ensuring the episodes were paced properly. "I need to double-check the pacing," Kim says. "I had to orchestrate the emotion lines for each character and adjust their chemistry, not for two hours but over multiple episodes."

"I HAD TO ORCHESTRATE THE EMOTION LINES FOR EACH CHARACTER AND ADJUST THEIR CHEMISTRY."
Jae-Hong Kim, director

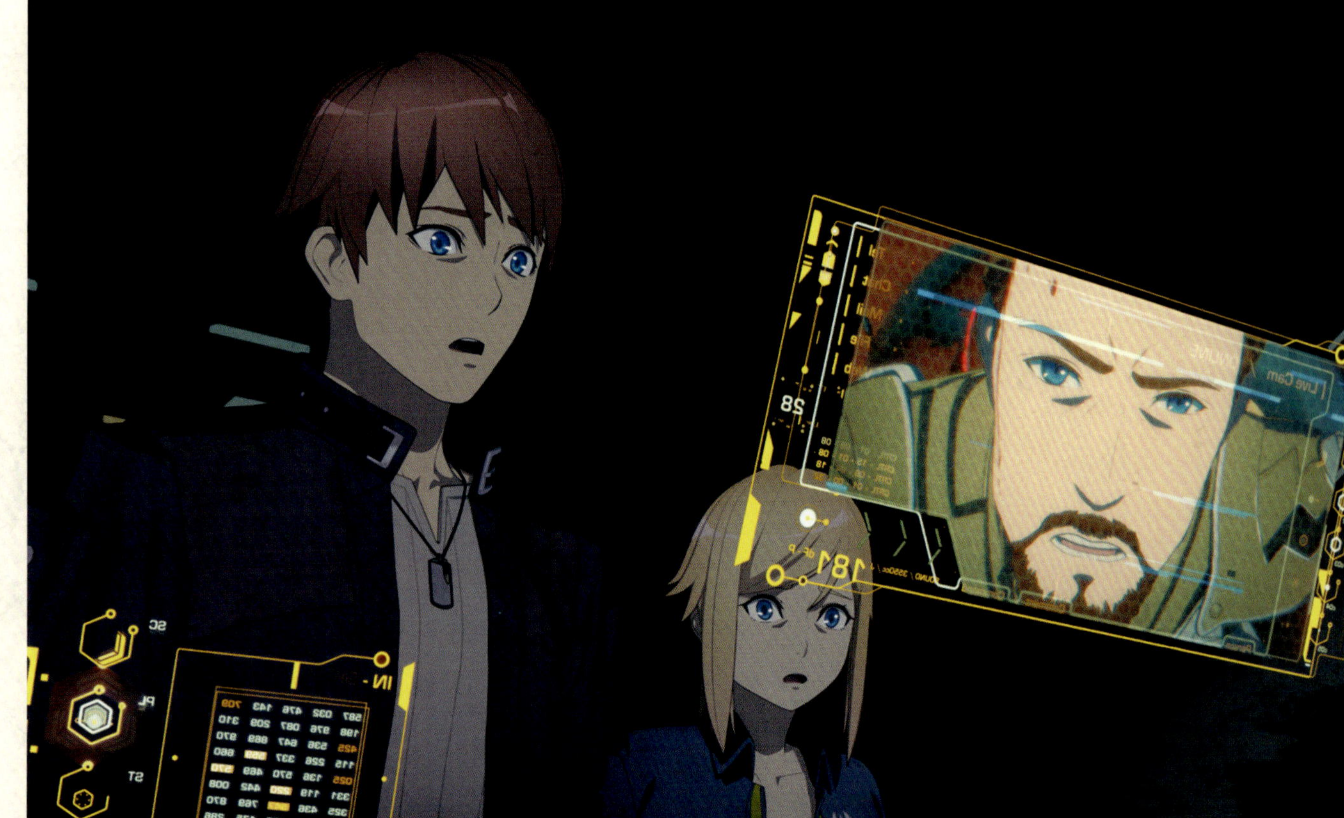

Right // In Episode Seven, Taylor and Hayley catch an agonizing glimpse of their missing father.

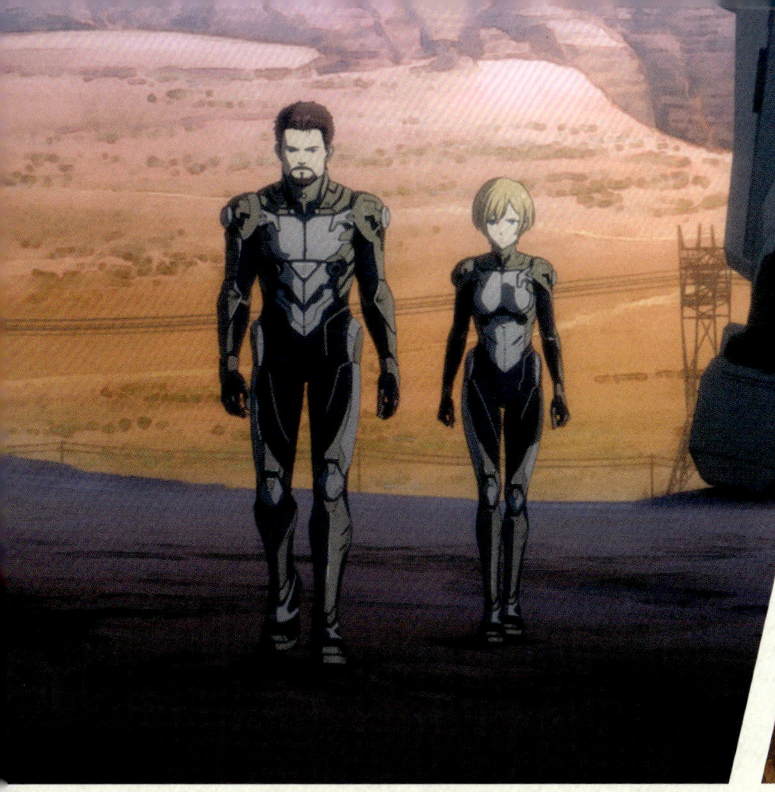

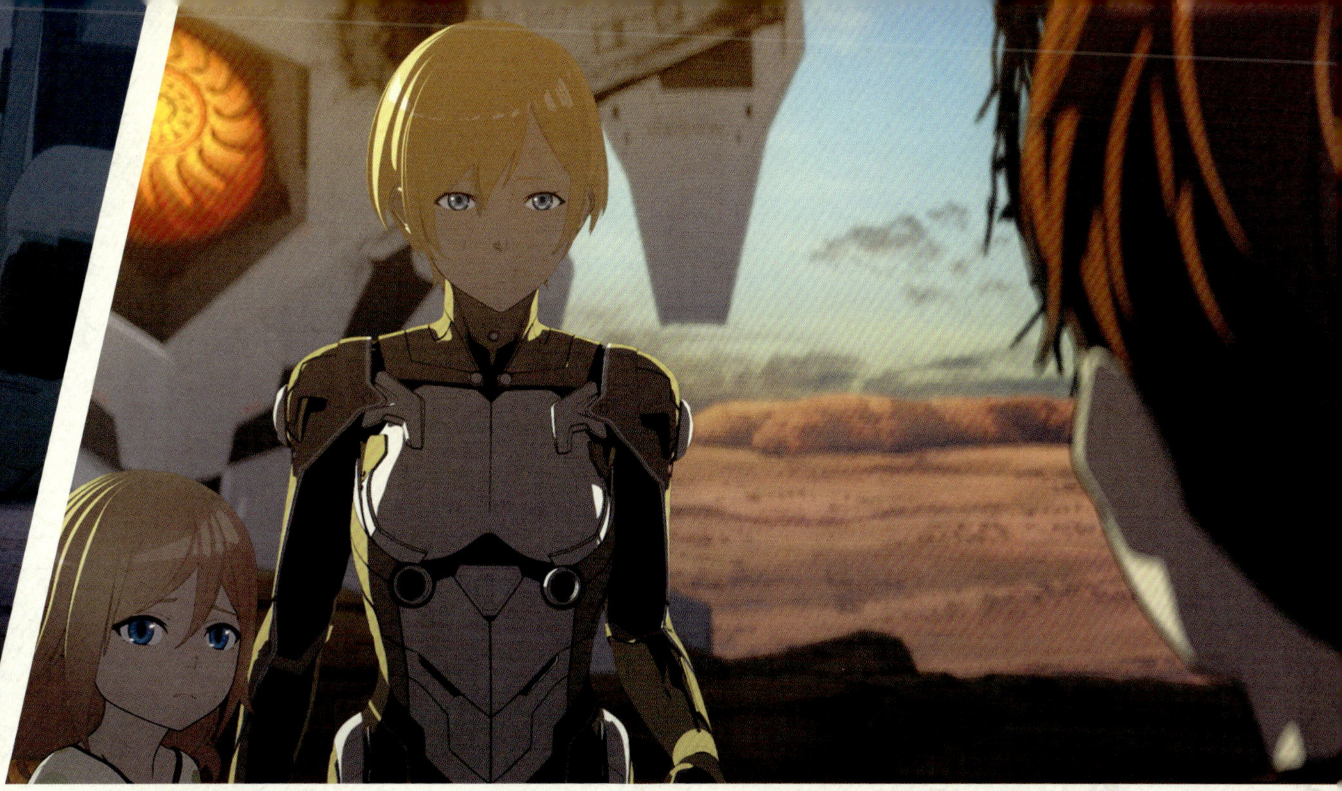

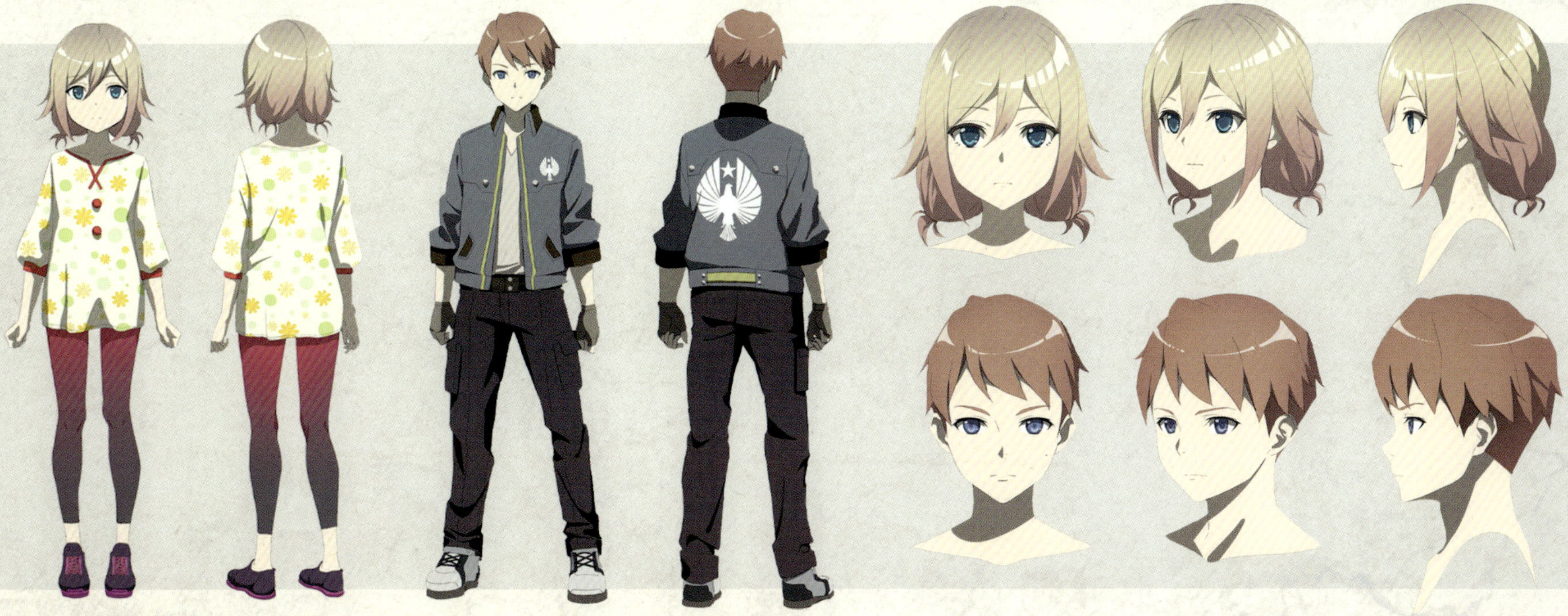

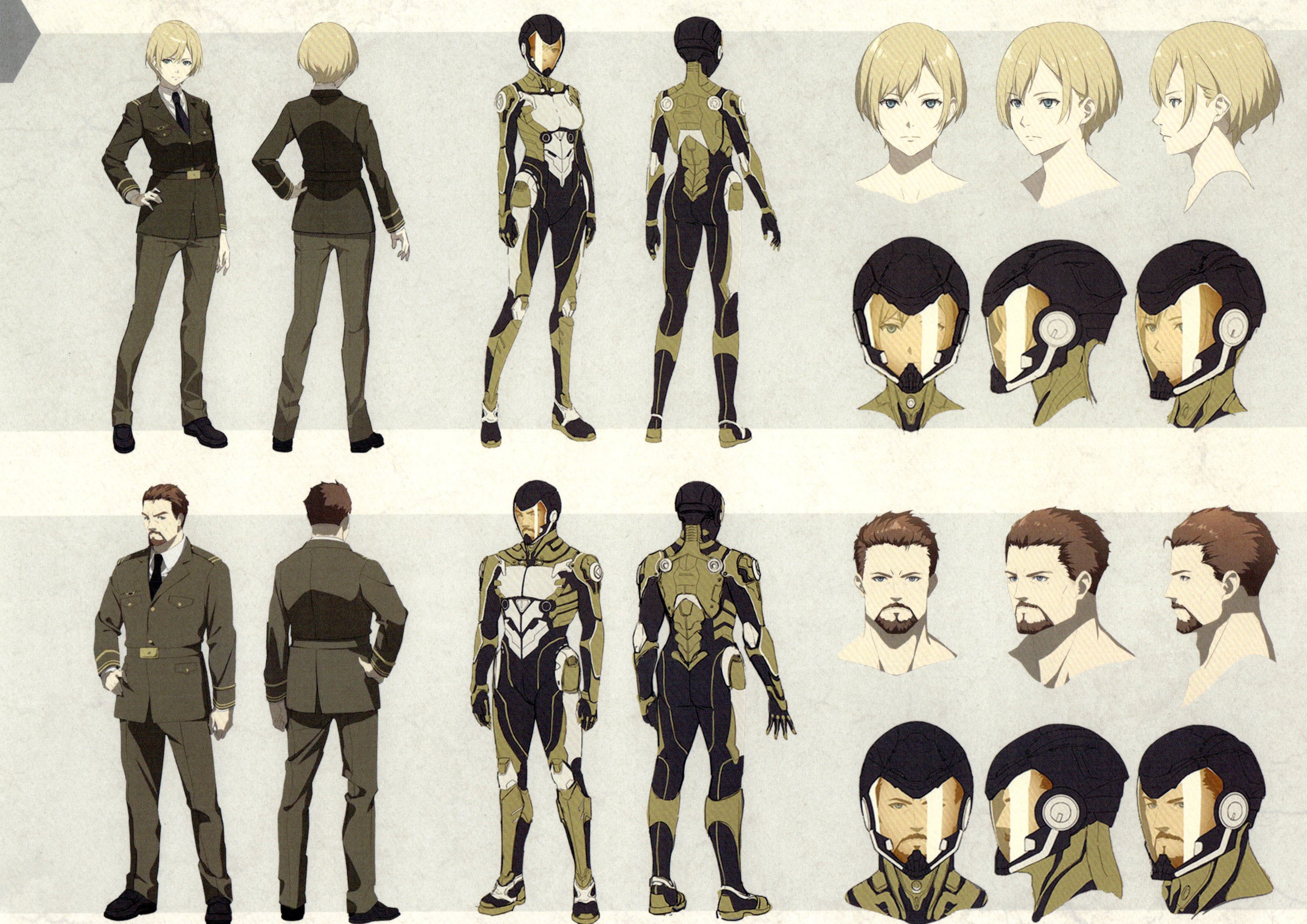

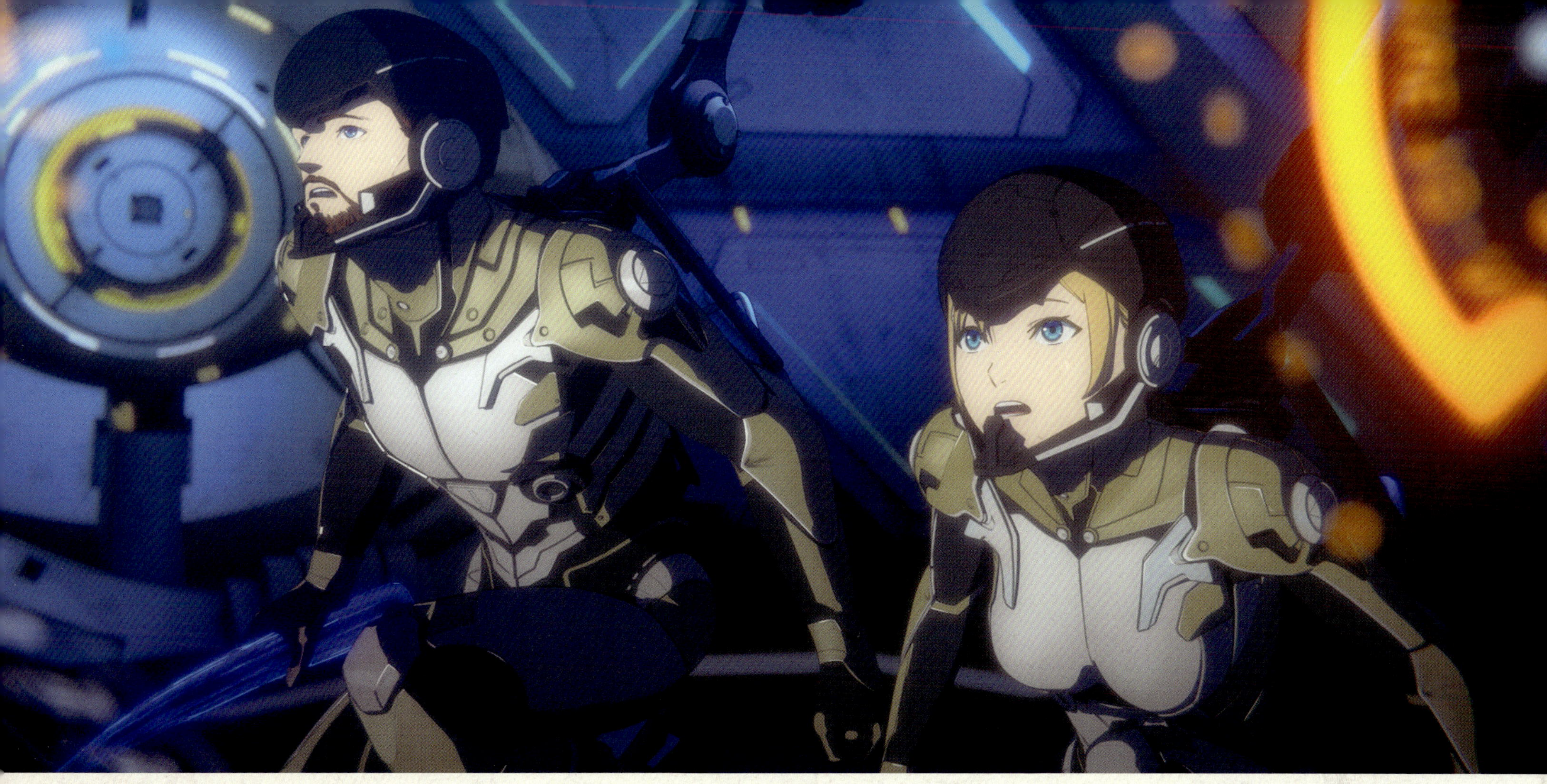

“WE COULD TELL A DEEP STORY OF THE CHARACTERS’ RELATIONSHIPS, OF NOT JUST A PHYSICAL JOURNEY BUT AN EMOTIONAL JOURNEY.”
Ken Duer, co-producer

At the start of *Pacific Rim: The Black*, a plethora of ‘breaches’ open in the ground of Australia. Anyone who’s seen the *Pacific Rim* films knows what that means. The breaches are passages to an alien world; this world’s inhabitants are called ‘Precursors’, and they mean to claim Earth as their own. Rather than come through the breaches themselves, the Precursors send the Kaiju they’ve created to cleanse the Earth of humanity.

Episode One of *Pacific Rim: The Black*, “From the Shadows”, begins with the kind of scene that wouldn’t look out of place in a *Pacific Rim* film, and it’s very unlike most of the animated series. The Kaiju are shown tearing their way through Australian cities, while the Jaegers fight back desperately. But this time—and this was the basis of the initial pitch—the Kaiju are winning. A continent-wide evacuation of Australia has been ordered.

The first moments take a similar viewpoint to the films, putting us with the Jaeger pilots in their huge robots. Specifically, we’re with a husband-and-wife team: Ford and

Above // Jaeger pilots Ford and Brina Travis, frantically defending a city—and their two children.

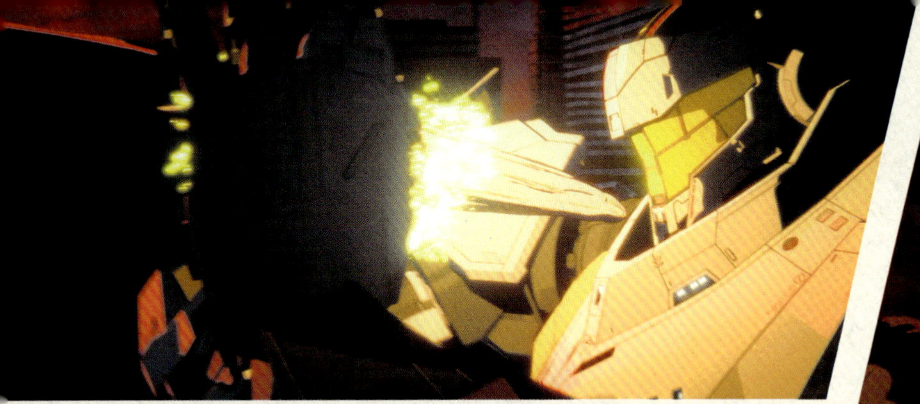

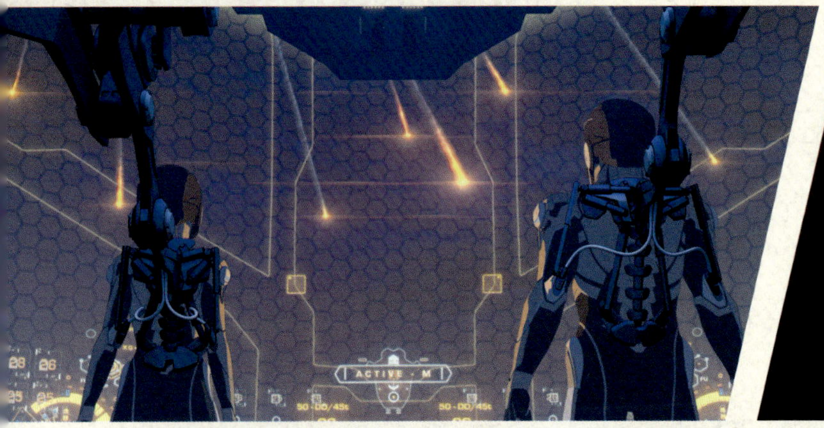

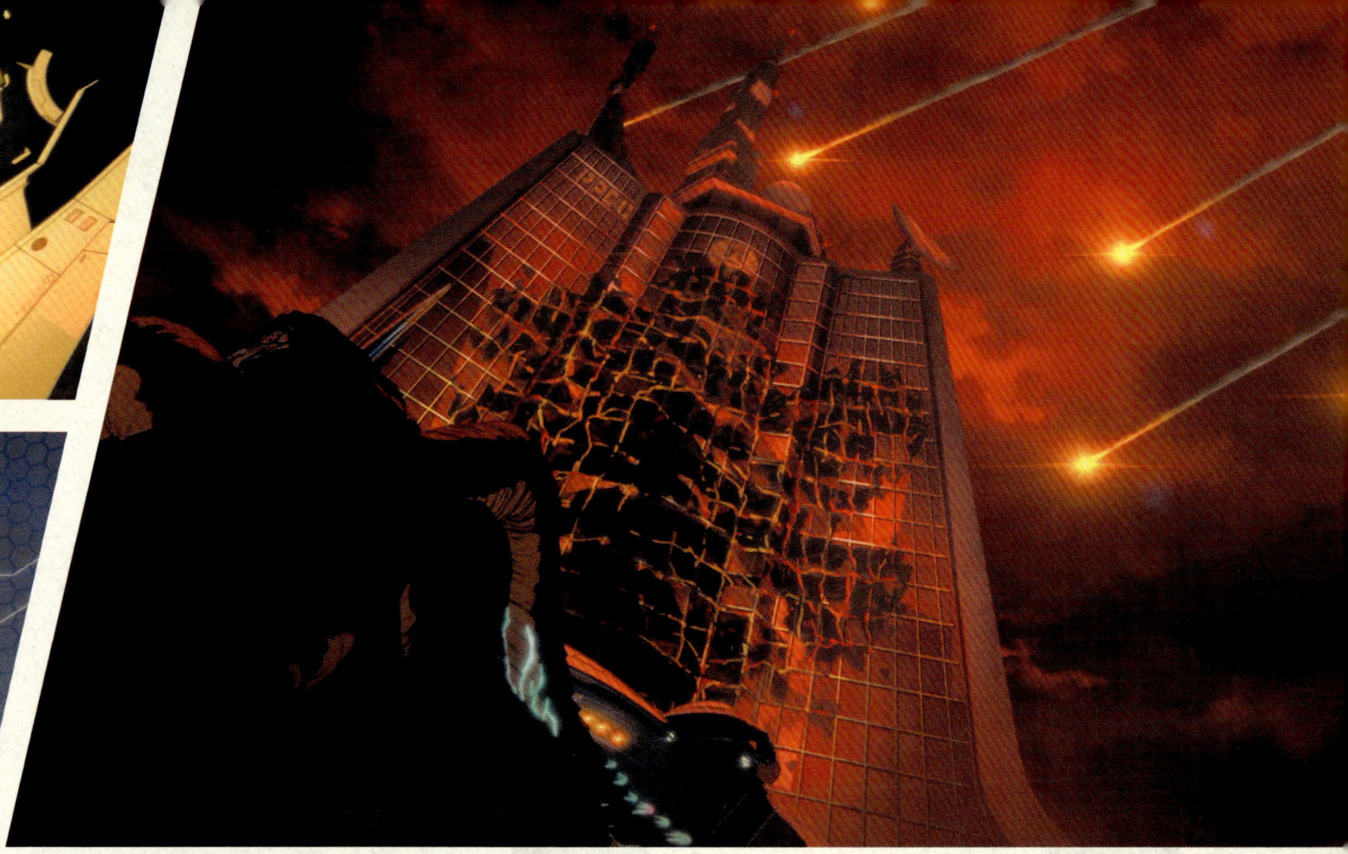

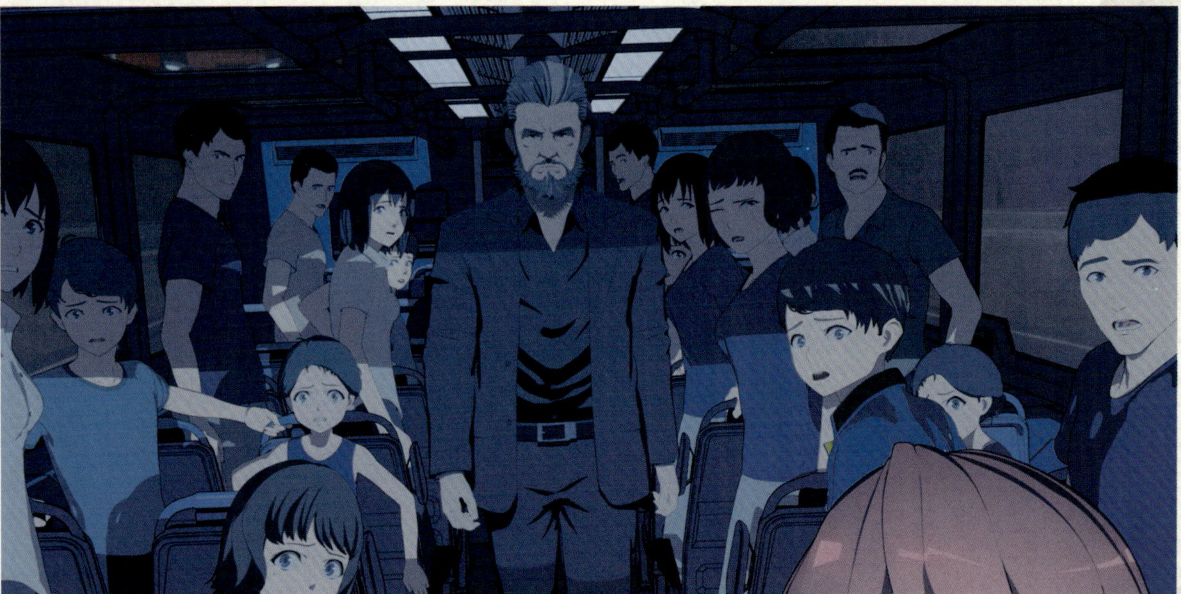

Brina Travis, who are piloting their Jaeger, Hunter Vertigo, in defence of the fictional city of Meridian. The couple has an especially personal stake in the battle.

The perspective changes to a busload of scared kids at street level. It's a new focus for *Pacific Rim*, though viewers may be reminded of the flashback in the first film where a little girl flees from a Kaiju in Tokyo. Here, the focus is on two kids in the bus: Taylor and Hayley, the young son and daughter of Ford and Brina.

Their parents save the kids, the Jaeger carrying the bus to safety even as Ford and Brina's comrades die around them. One new type of Kaiju glimpsed in these scenes is the Acidquill, with two luminous blue tendrils growing from its back, which it wields as whips or daggers. We'll see many more of its kind later.

As the characters escape, they see a satellite array crash down in flames to Earth. The authorities have initiated 'The Black', a blackout of the whole of Australia, now designated a lost continent.

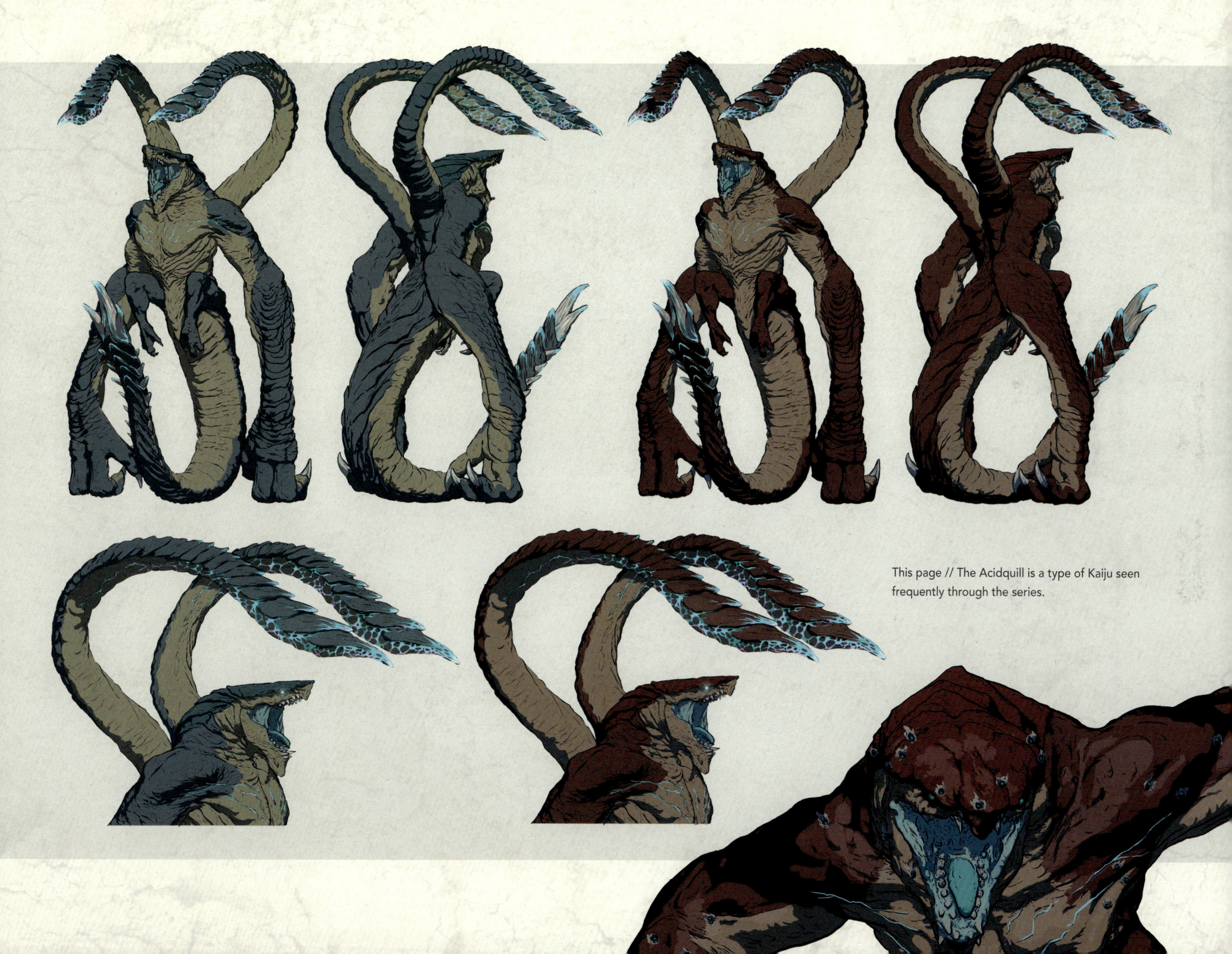

This page // The Acidquill is a type of Kaiju seen frequently through the series.

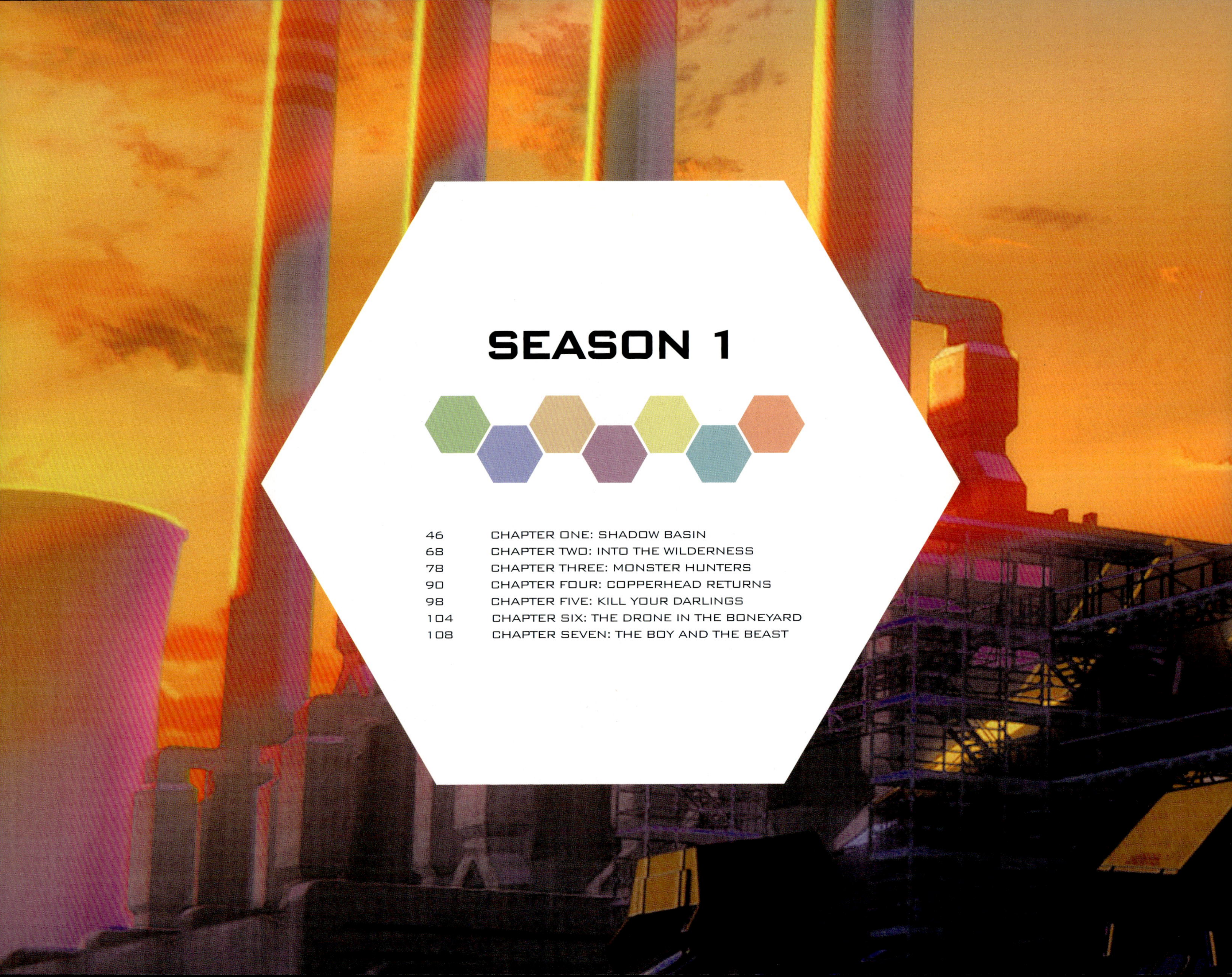

SEASON 1

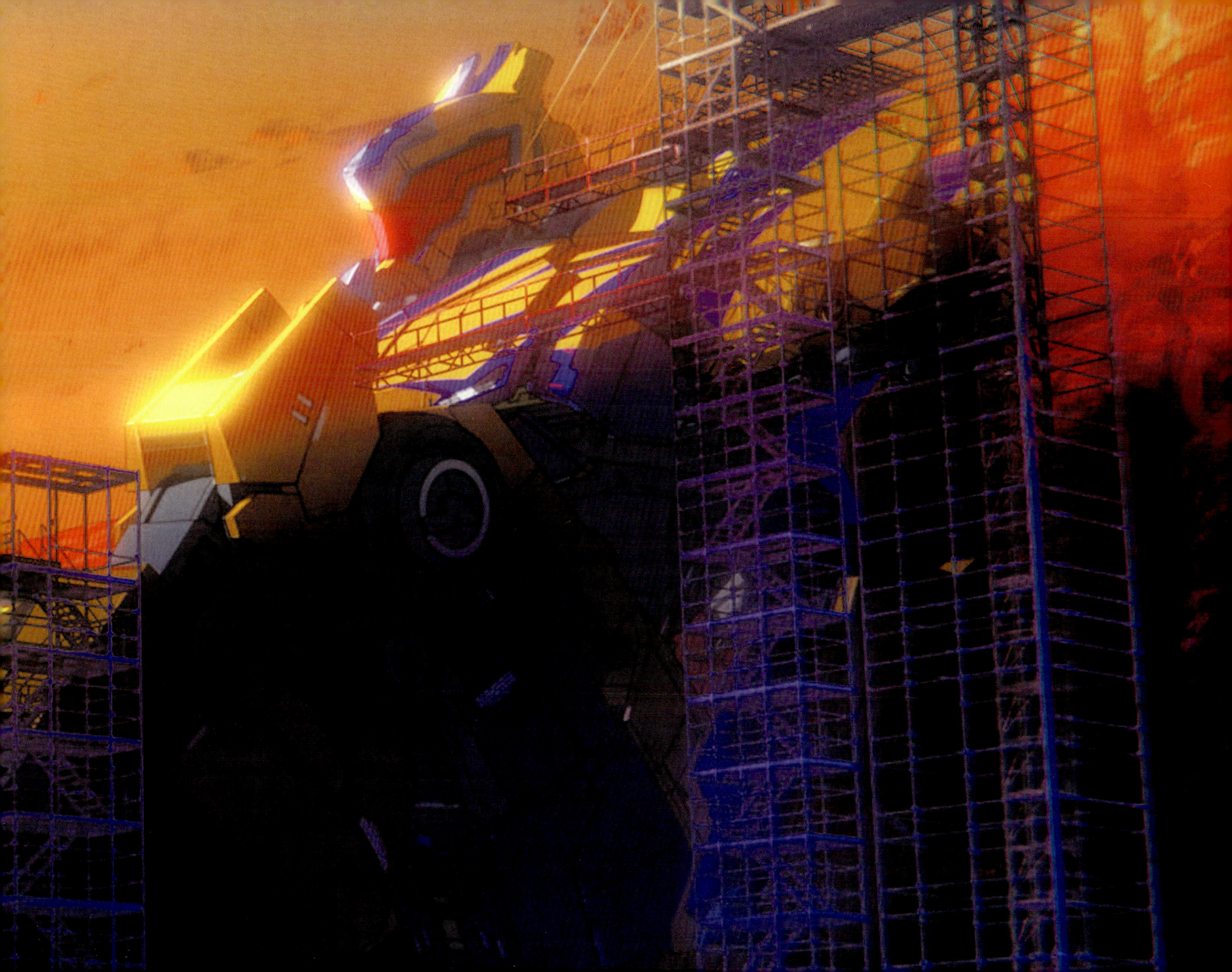

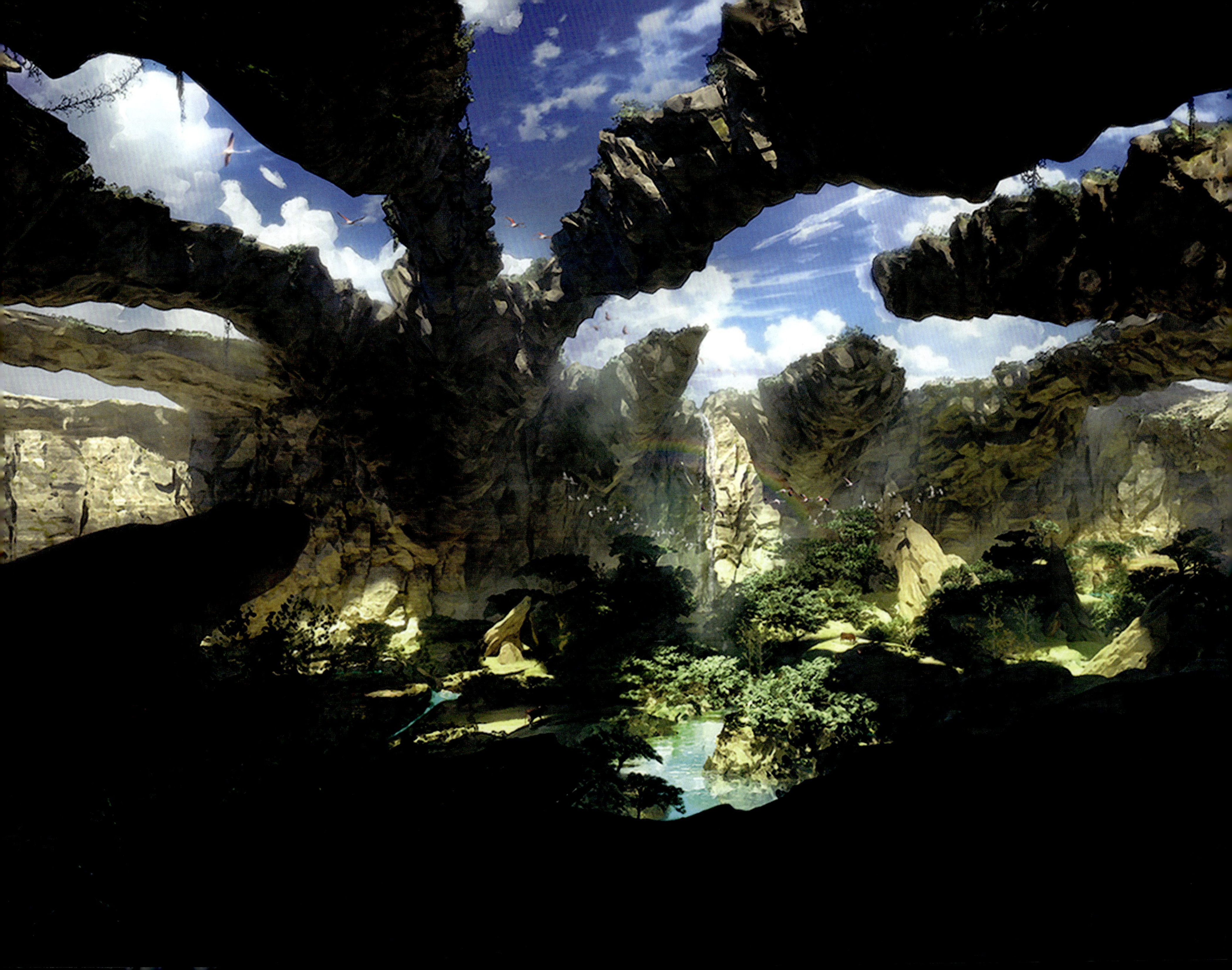

CHAPTER ONE
SHADOW BASIN

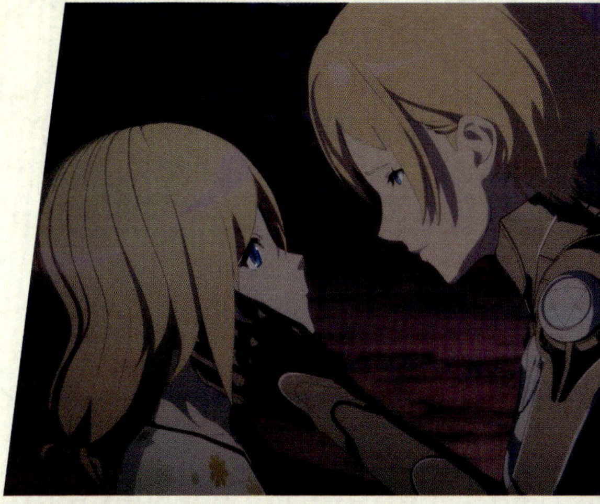

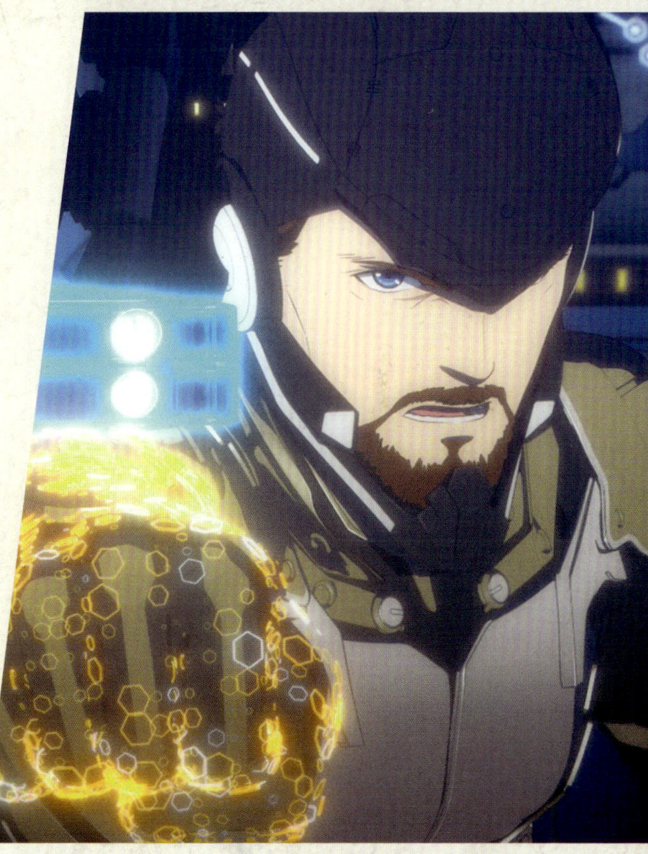

Hunter Vertigo bears the busload of kids into the desert, heading for the Jaeger's home base. However, Ford and Brina find the base has been sealed underground and abandoned by the retreating army. After fighting off another Acidquill, the grown-ups leave the children, including Taylor and Hayley, at Shadow Basin, a secluded arena protected by rock and fed by waterfalls.

The parents will take Hunter Vertigo to Sydney, where the Jaeger forces are retreating, and get help to evacuate the children. Ford and Brina promise they'll return in two weeks, and march off in the Jaeger, Taylor and Hayley staring after them.

Cut to five years later. Ford and Brina never came back to Shadow Basin, which is now home to Taylor, Hayley and the other children. Shadow Basin is rendered in warm and comfortable colors, suffused by a peaceful atmosphere. It wasn't based on a real location, being entirely created by the series' artists.

"The concept of Shadow Basin is like Paradise, it's like an oasis," says Jae-Hong Kim. "Out there in the continent, it's crazy, Kaiju ruling… and then there are a few human survivors hiding in here. The Basin looks big compared with the human characters, but compared with the continent, it's really small."

Kim continues, "We came up with the idea that the Basin has to look beautiful, with waterfalls, and the humans farming in there. We wanted to show more of that—how the humans are living there, how they've settled down there. That's why we have a little shot in Episode One of the characters sitting around their campfire and chatting—originally we had more of that."

Hiroyuki Hayashi was the supervising director on the Polygon side. "Shadow Basin only appears one time in the whole series," he says. "We wanted to make it look unique, in a way. It's like a colony that has separated from the other parts of the world."

Yuki Moriyama was art director on the series, having been character designer on earlier Polygon anime, including *Knights of Sidonia*, *Ajin*, and the studio's *Godzilla* films. "Legendary gave us a series bible, with all the designs and concepts they were thinking about," Moriyama explains. "The concept image for this location stood out to me because it was an area that was surrounded, enclosed. It was all about translating that concept image into a 3D set."

Light and shadow were crucial. "Because of the rock surfaces hanging down from the sides and from above, we felt it would be a good idea to use light and shadow to create a beautiful look for the location. There are some places where the light might not be hitting, but then it might be hitting the gaps between different rock surfaces… That's something we paid attention to, to create a beautiful look."

We see an angry exchange between Taylor and Hayley. A lot of antipathy has built up between the siblings in five years. Taylor, the big brother, is determined to keep the Shadow Basin community safe and wait patiently for help. Hayley, on the other hand, has lost faith that their parents will ever come back. She insists that they must make their way across Australia themselves.

Both the brother and sister have characteristic anime faces: for example, Hayley has a sharp chin and much bigger eyes than her brother. According to Hiroyuki Hayashi, the 'typical' anime style was a conscious decision. "Legendary wanted to go for an anime type of look," he says. "Normally, that's how characters look, I guess, in anime projects. But one thing that we discussed with the showrunners is that there are a lot of different types of anime. Some anime have a more realistic look, some a more 'deformed' look. We had some back and forth with the showrunners to strike a balance between those sides, and the result is what you see."

"[SHADOW BASIN] IS LIKE A COLONY THAT HAS SEPARATED FROM OTHER PARTS OF THE WORLD."
Hiroyuki Hayashi, director

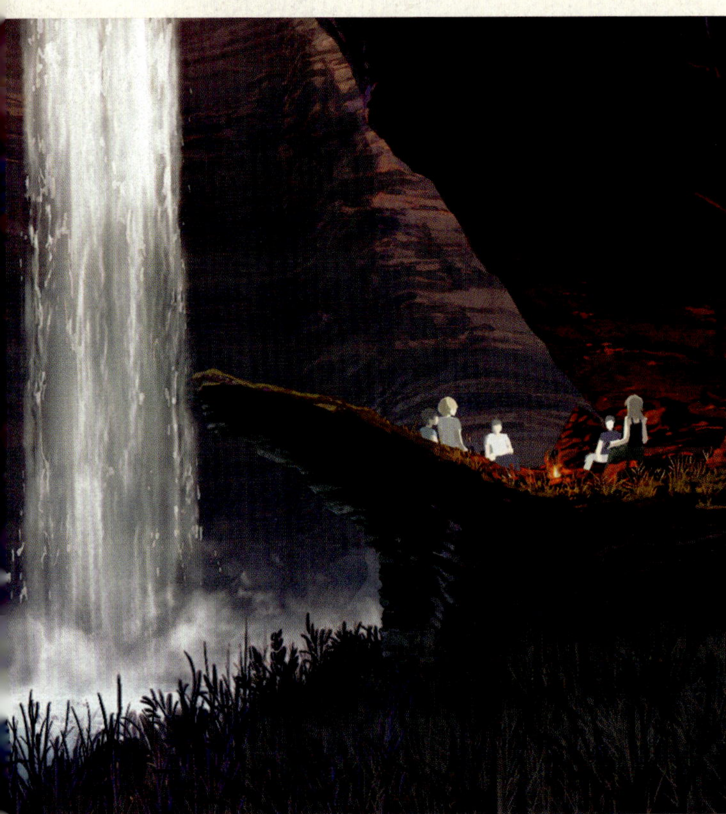

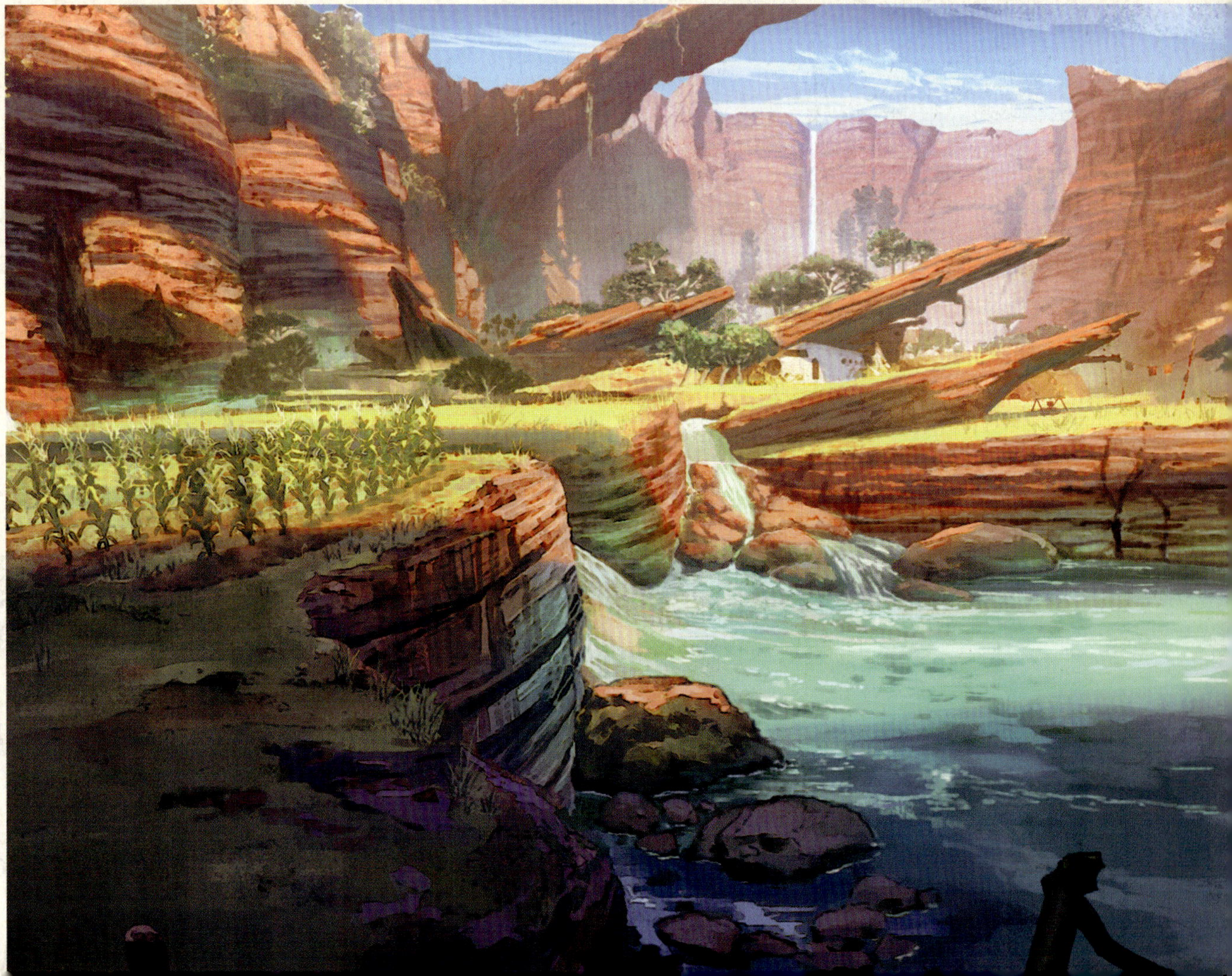

Above and right // The Edenic surroundings of Shadow Basin.

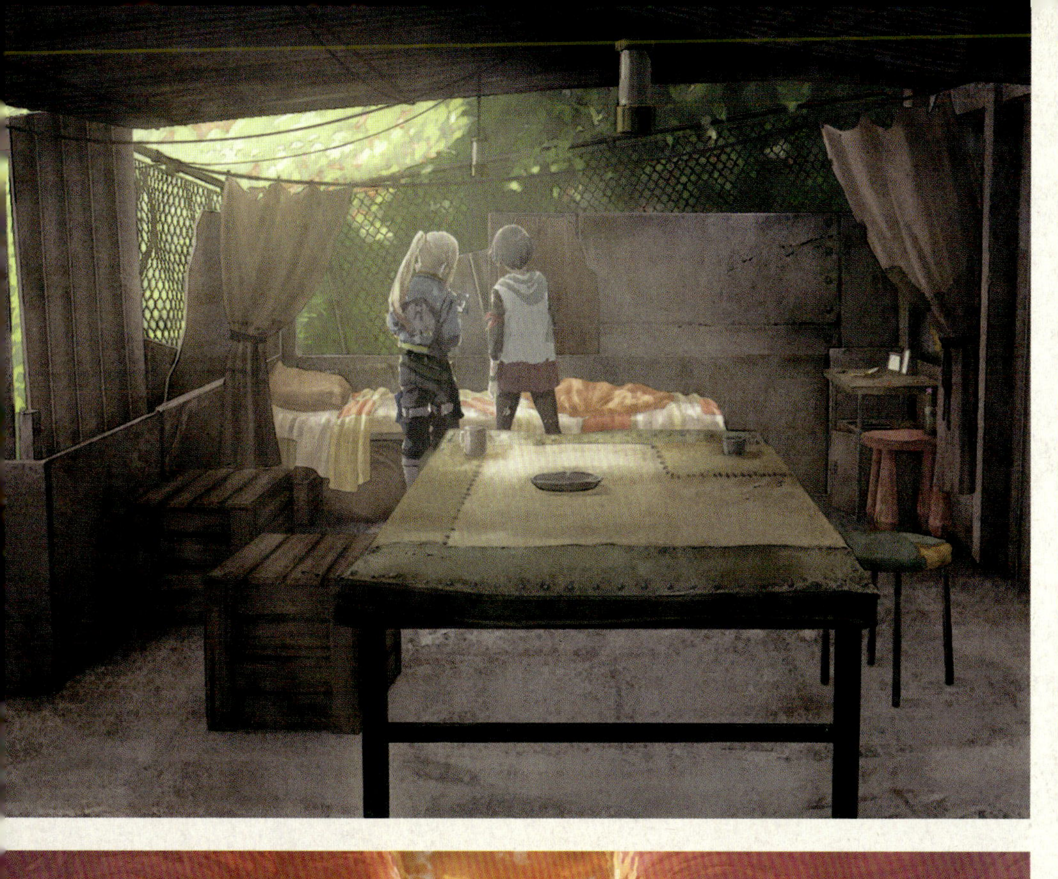
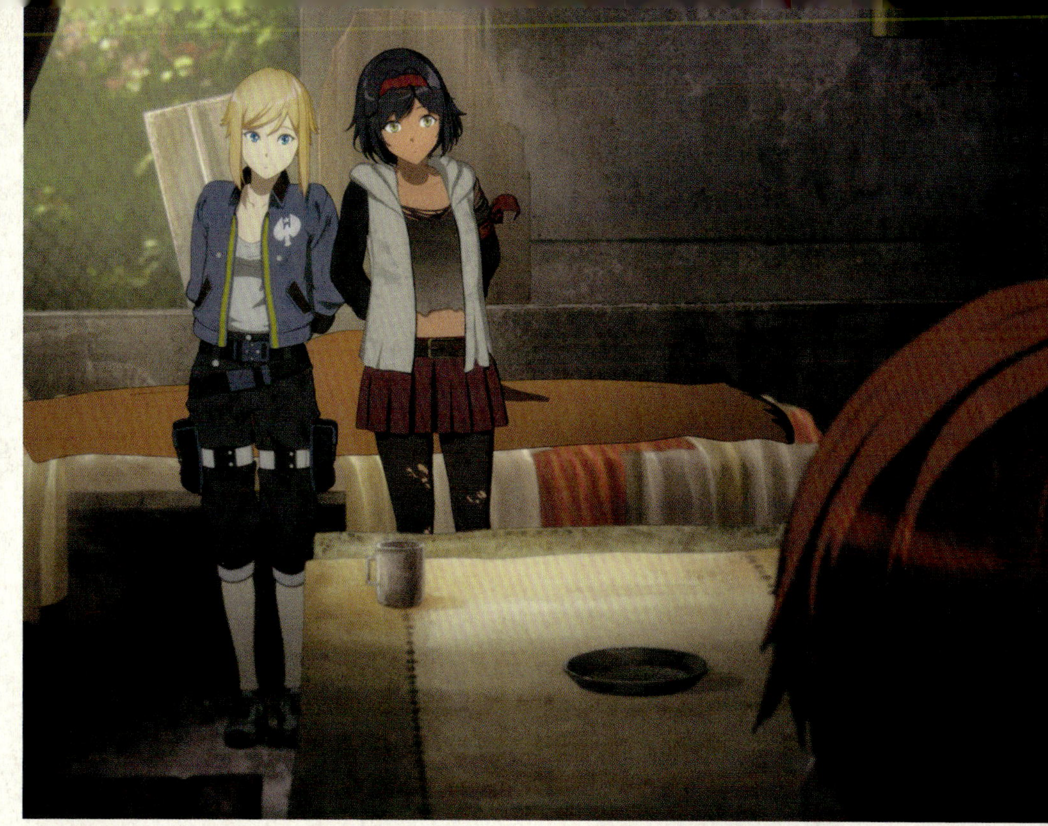
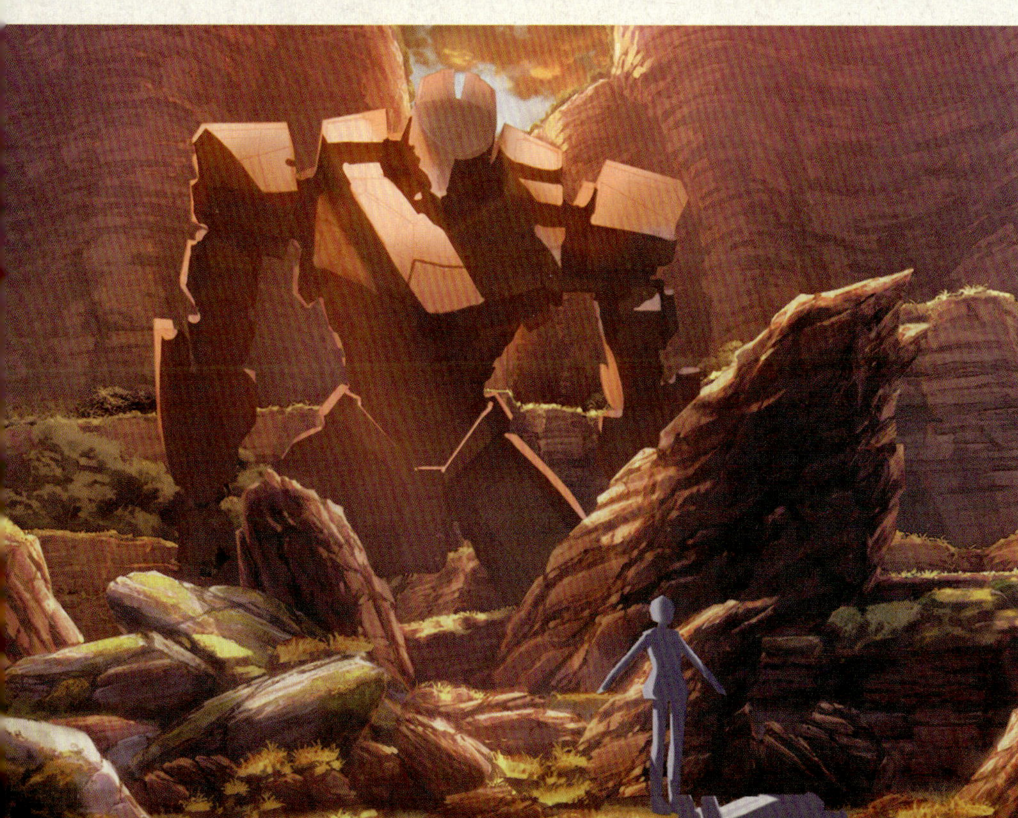
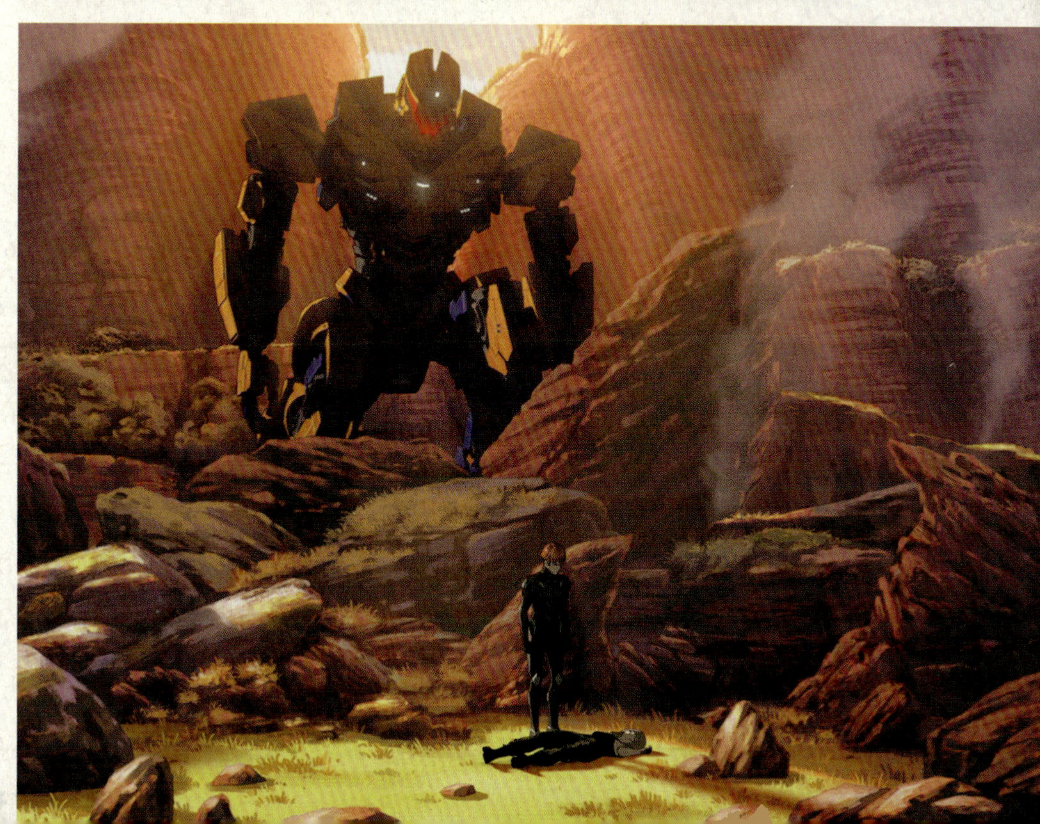

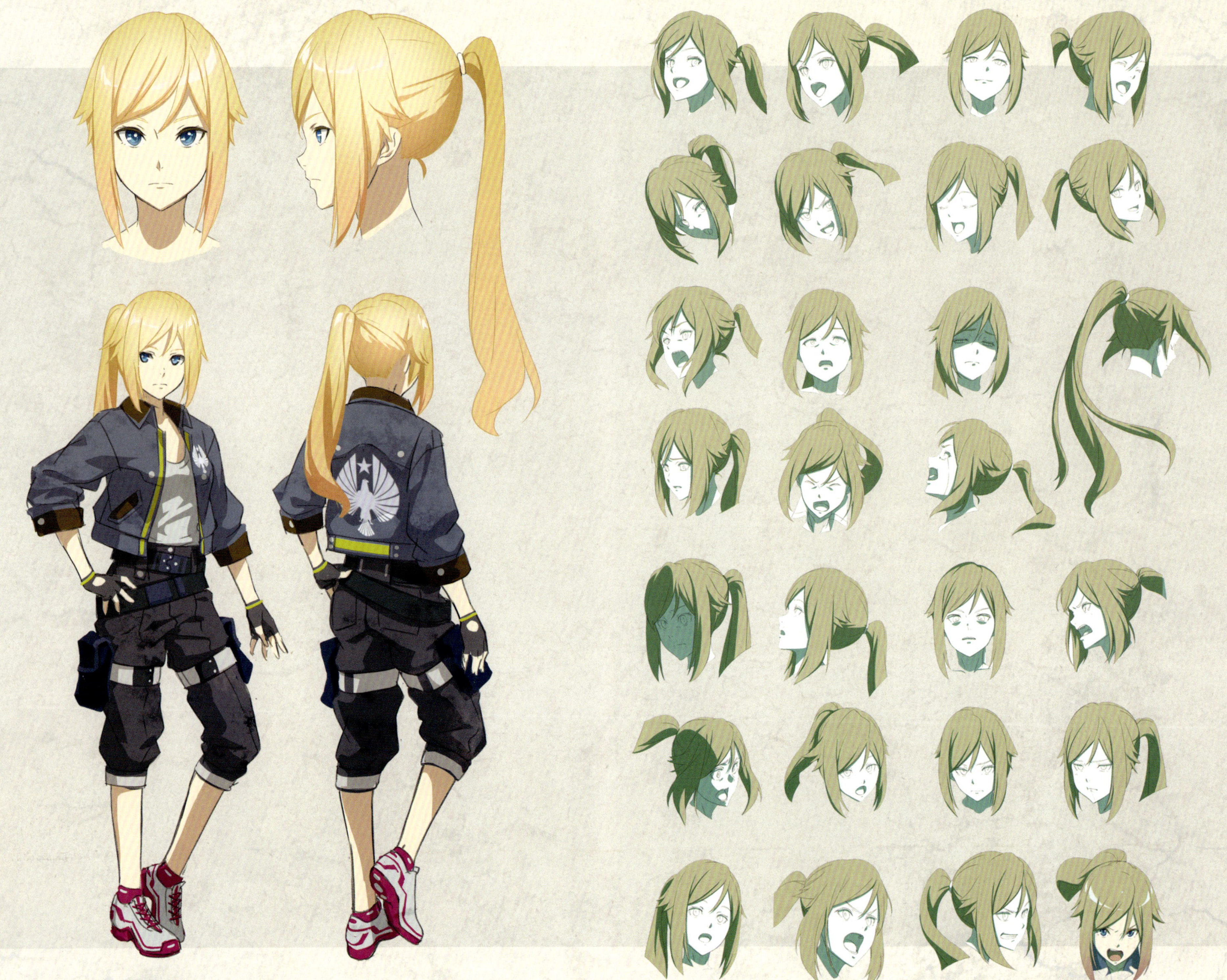

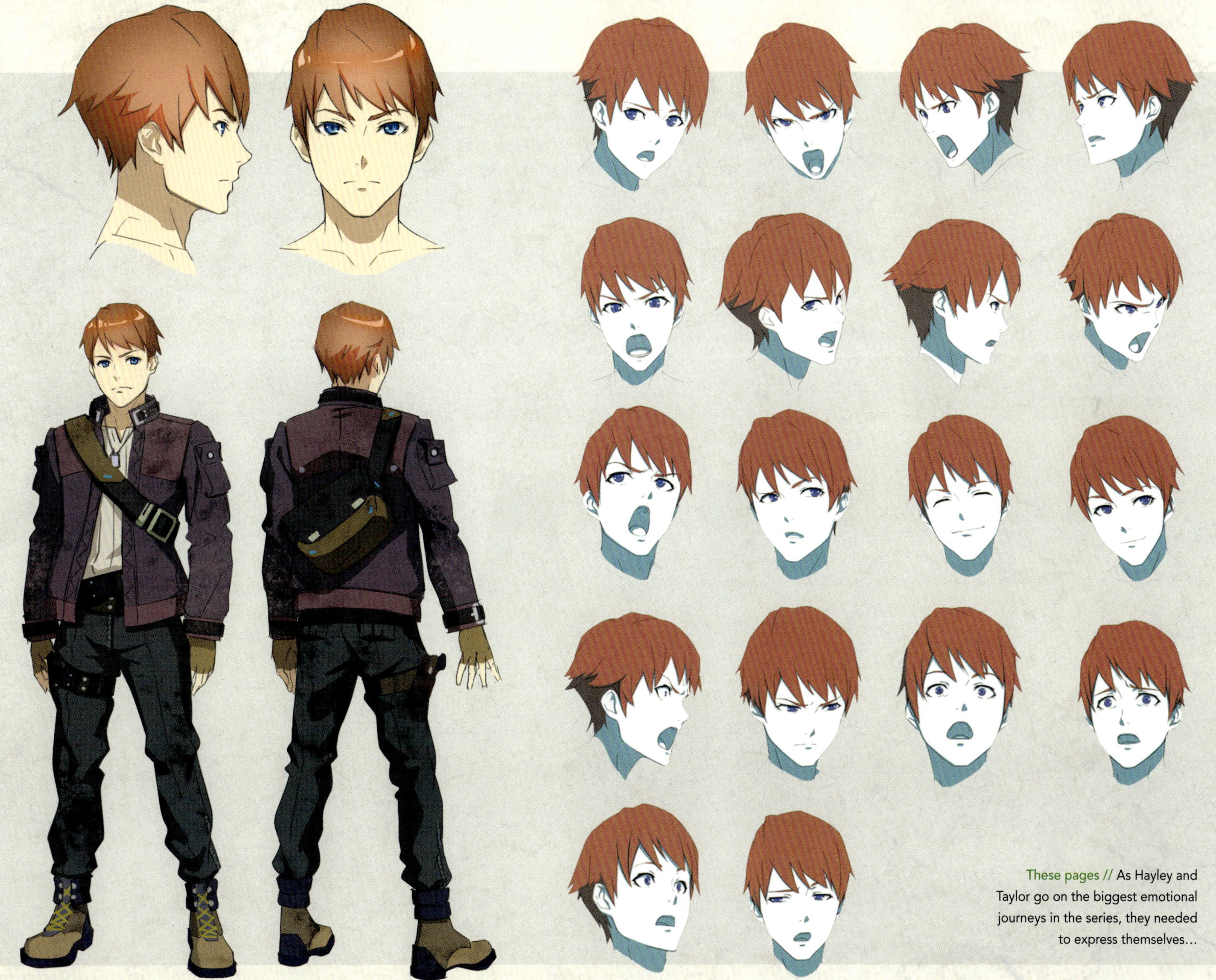

These pages // As Hayley and Taylor go on the biggest emotional journeys in the series, they needed to express themselves...

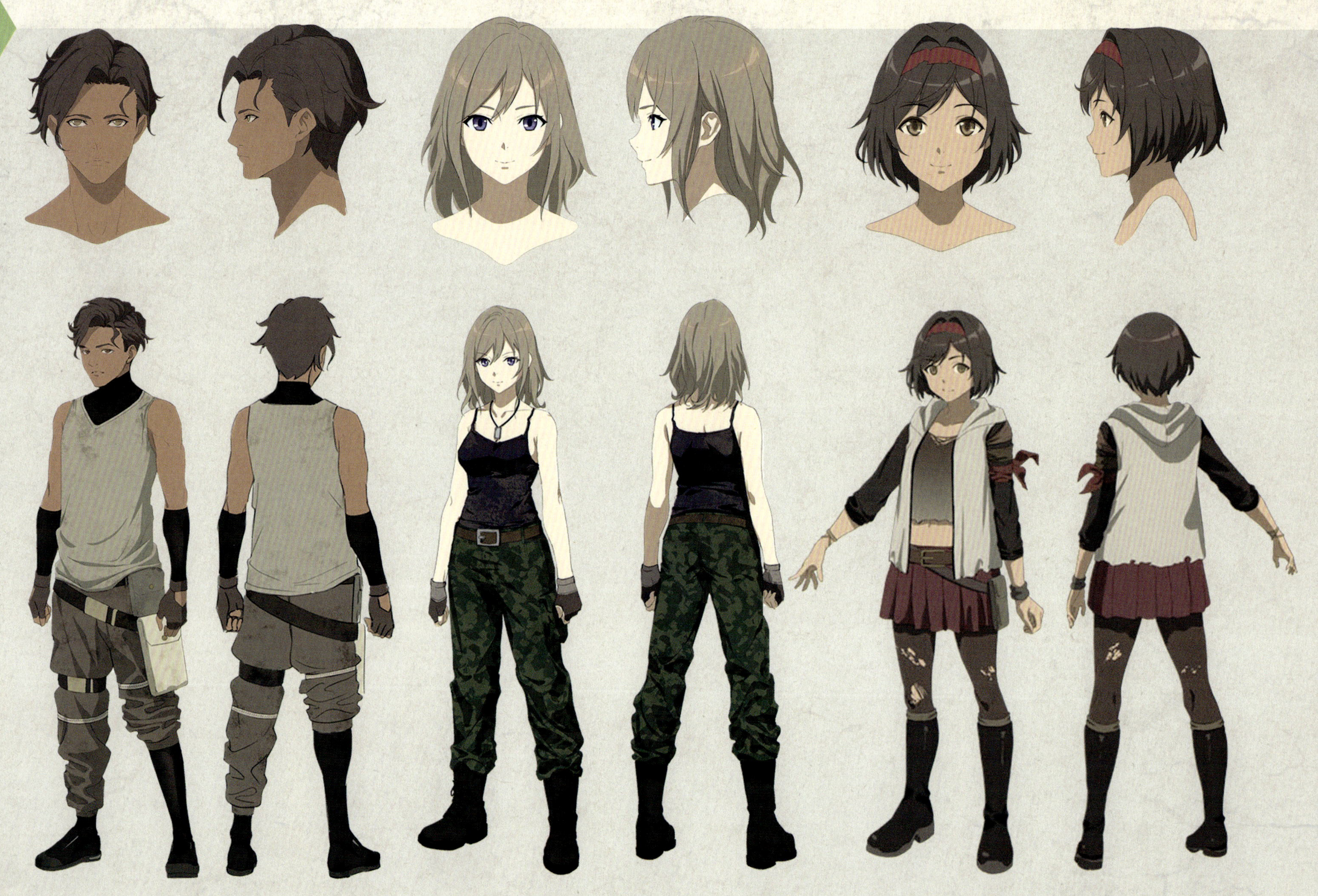

Jae-Hong Kim says, "It was Polygon's distinctive design style… The look of the 2D anime style in CG."

Jack Liang, Polygon's executive producer, explains the animation of the humans in the series did not involve motion capture—that is, animation which uses recorded movements of real people, as often seen in videogame cutscenes. "We didn't use any motion capture at all in *Pacific Rim: The Black*," says Liang. "Polygon has usually used it for specific little things, [but] we haven't used it through an entire production. For *Pacific Rim: The Black*, we went into the series with no intent to use motion capture; everything's just keyframe animation." Keyframe animation is a form of digital animation which doesn't use motion capture.

Liang points out if the human animation had been motion-captured, it wouldn't have looked like the typical anime style. "When it goes in that kind of stylistic way, motion capture is not the most ideal. The characters' expressions are so different compared to a photo-real type of project."

Hiroyuki Hayashi adds, "When we use manual keyframe animation, there are certain things we can do which we can't do with motion capture. We had a collection of highly skilled animators on this project, so we wanted to use them to the best of their abilities, which meant we did not use mo-cap, and had the animators do it themselves."

Producer Ken Duer points up a different issue with the human movement. "Did we need to sync the lip movements?" Duer says. "In America, we do. In Japan, it's really not lip-sync, just random movement."

Duer explains, "In the USA, we tend to have eight to twelve mouth shapes or more, depending on the complexity of the character designs. In Japan, for normal TV animation, they have maybe four mouth shapes. Because we wanted to make this anime and not American animation, we went for halfway. So we had a lot more lip sync than a normal anime, but less than what we would have in an American animation—about eight mouth shapes."

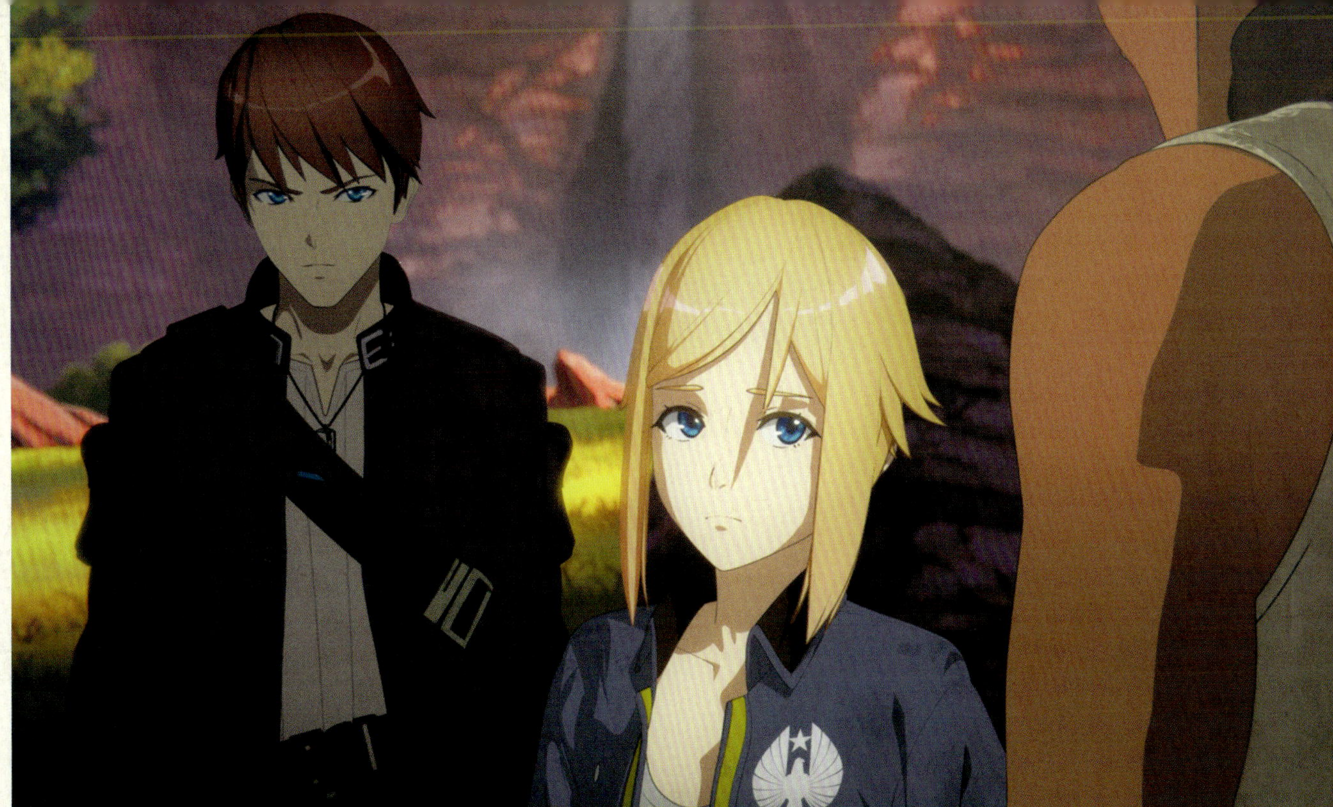

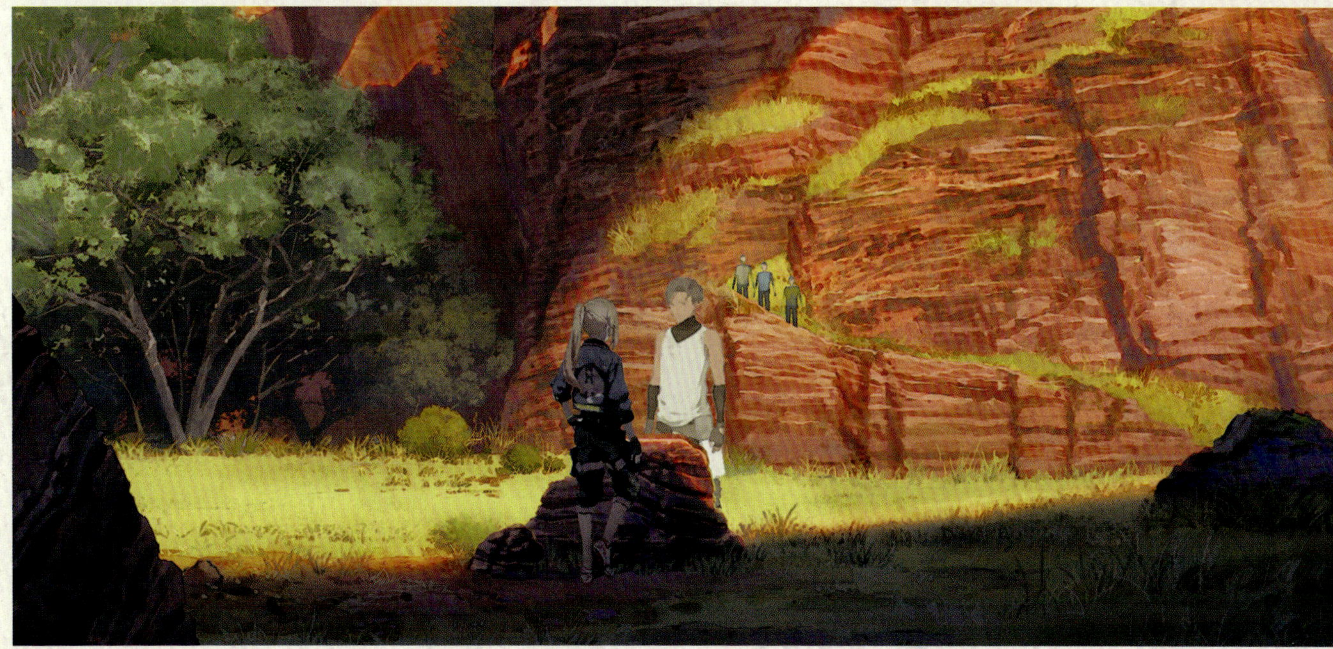

Right // Even surrounded by beauty, the teen Taylor and Hayley aren't at ease.

THE BURIED GIANT

After rowing with Taylor, Hayley stomps to the edge of Shadow Basin. But she stomps too hard—the ground gives way, and she falls into a hidden tunnel, with metal, glowing walls. She's just found the abandoned Jaeger base that her parents were seeking when they came to Shadow Basin, sealed for five years.

Following the tunnel, Hayley finds… a Jaeger, intact and operational! It's Atlas Destroyer, the 'hero' robot of the series. It's painted in bright blue and yellow, colored more gaily than Hunter Vertigo. That's because it's not a combat Jaeger. When Hayley eagerly enters its pilot cockpit (called the Conn-pod), located in the Jaeger's head, she's greeted by Loa. She's Atlas Destroyer's inbuilt Artificial Intelligence, manifesting as a pulsating globe of blue and red.

Loa hovers in the space of the Conn-pod, which is a sea of glowing, blue-toned status displays. We sometimes see the Conn-pod through Loa's artificial vision, overlaid with hexagons. Loa greets Hayley as a new cadet—a humorous subversion of the 'Jaeger cadet' idea which Greg Johnson and Craig Kyle rejected when they sketched their proposal for the series.

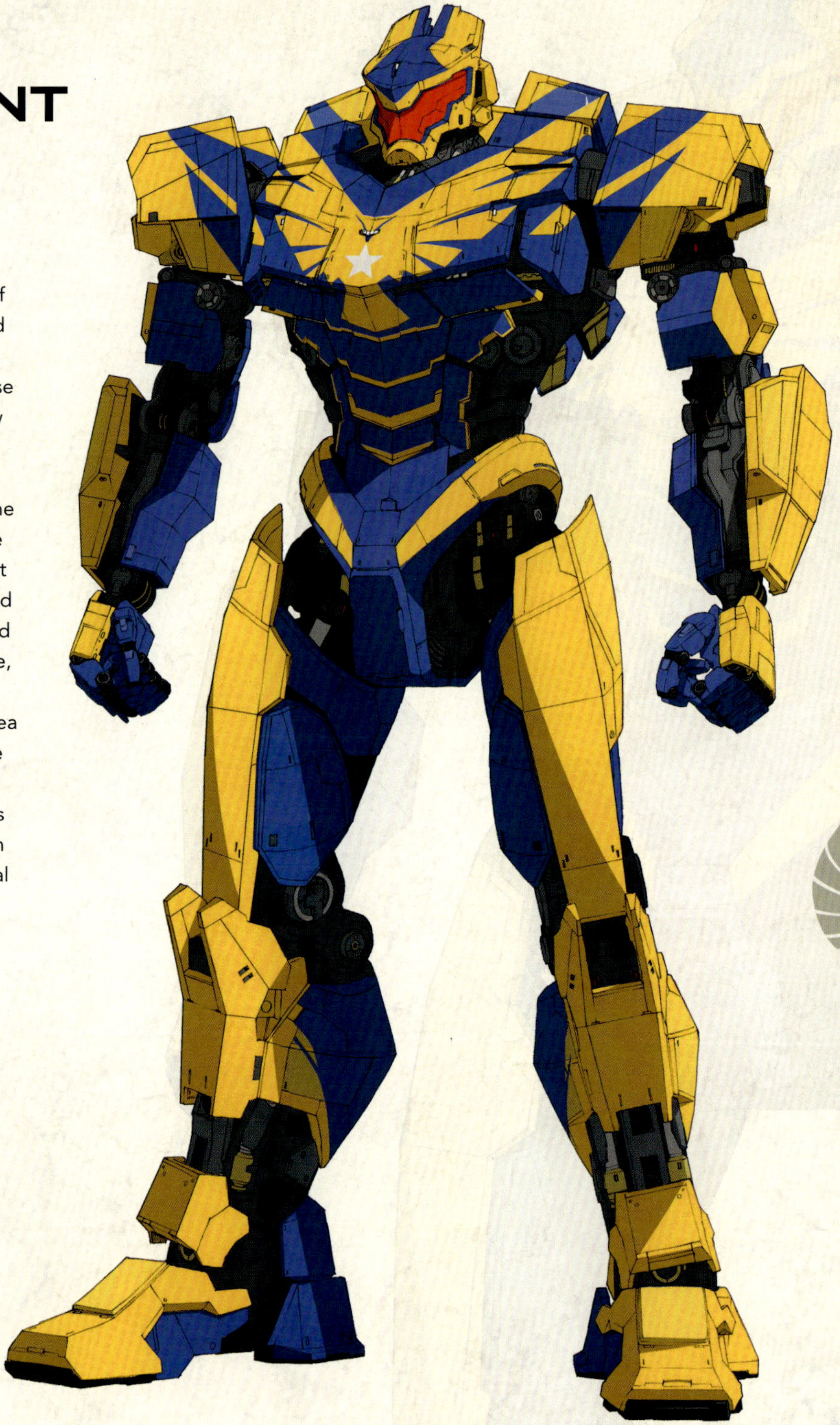

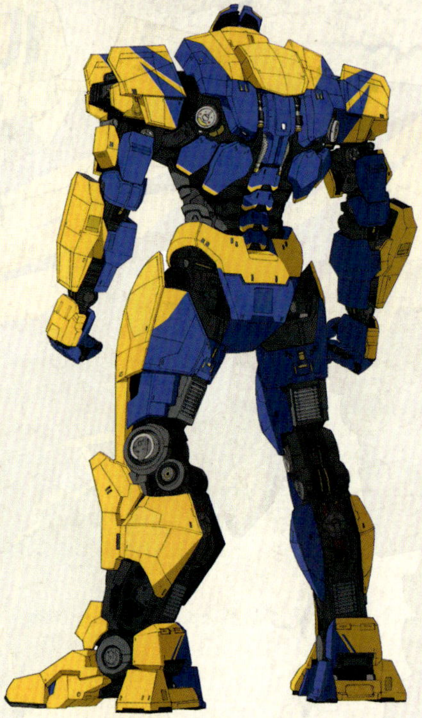

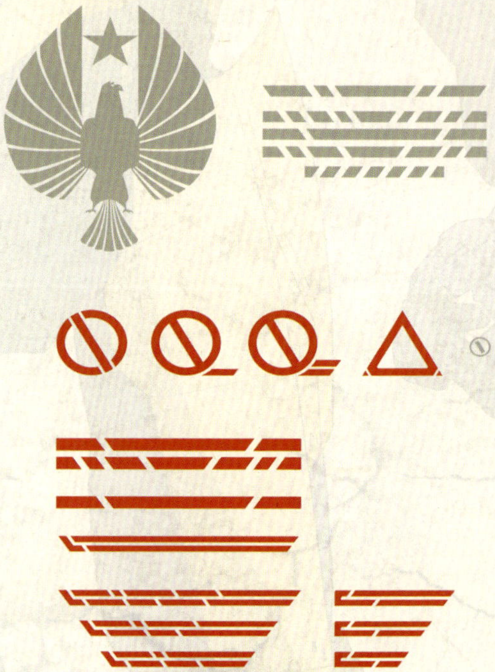

Right // Introduced in Episode One, Atlas Destroyer will be another of the series' lead characters.

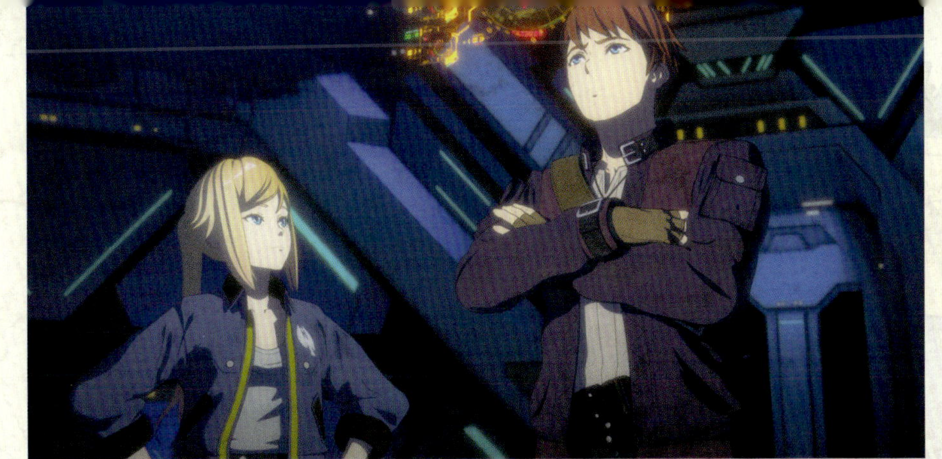

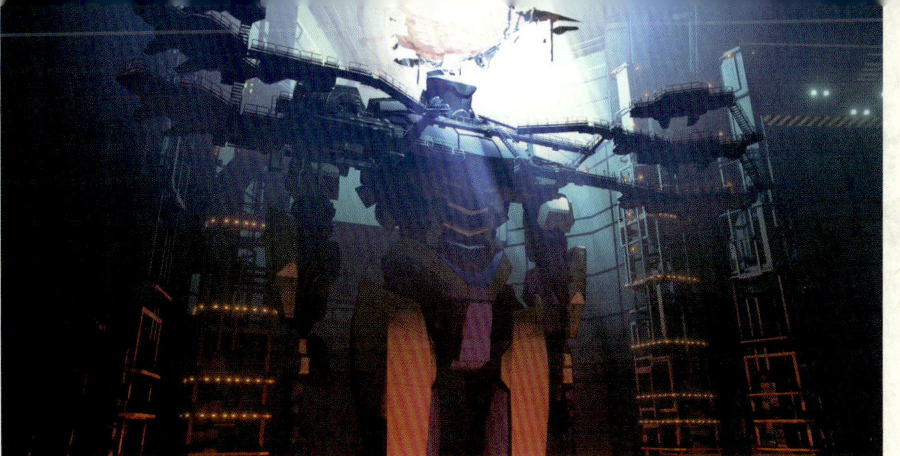

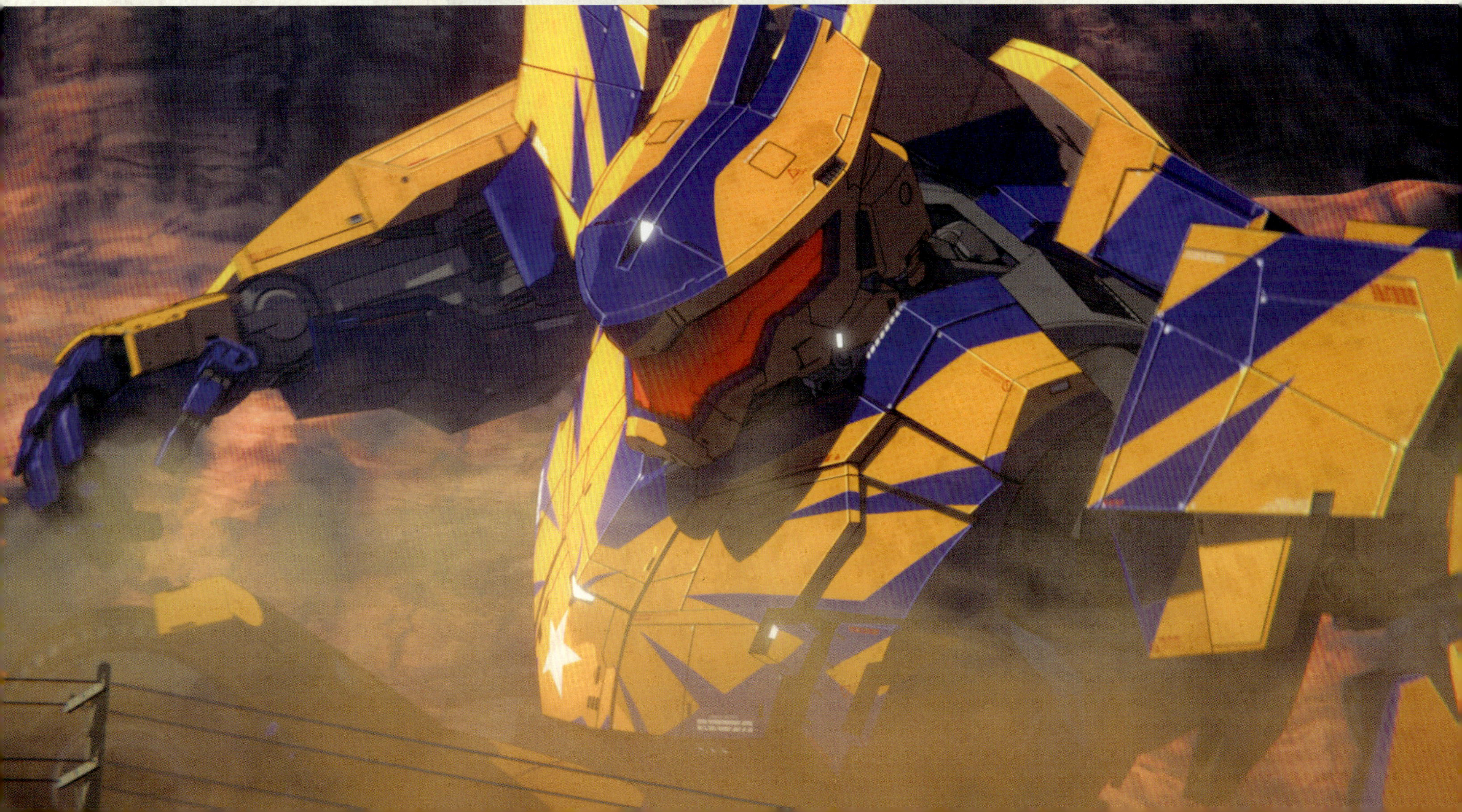

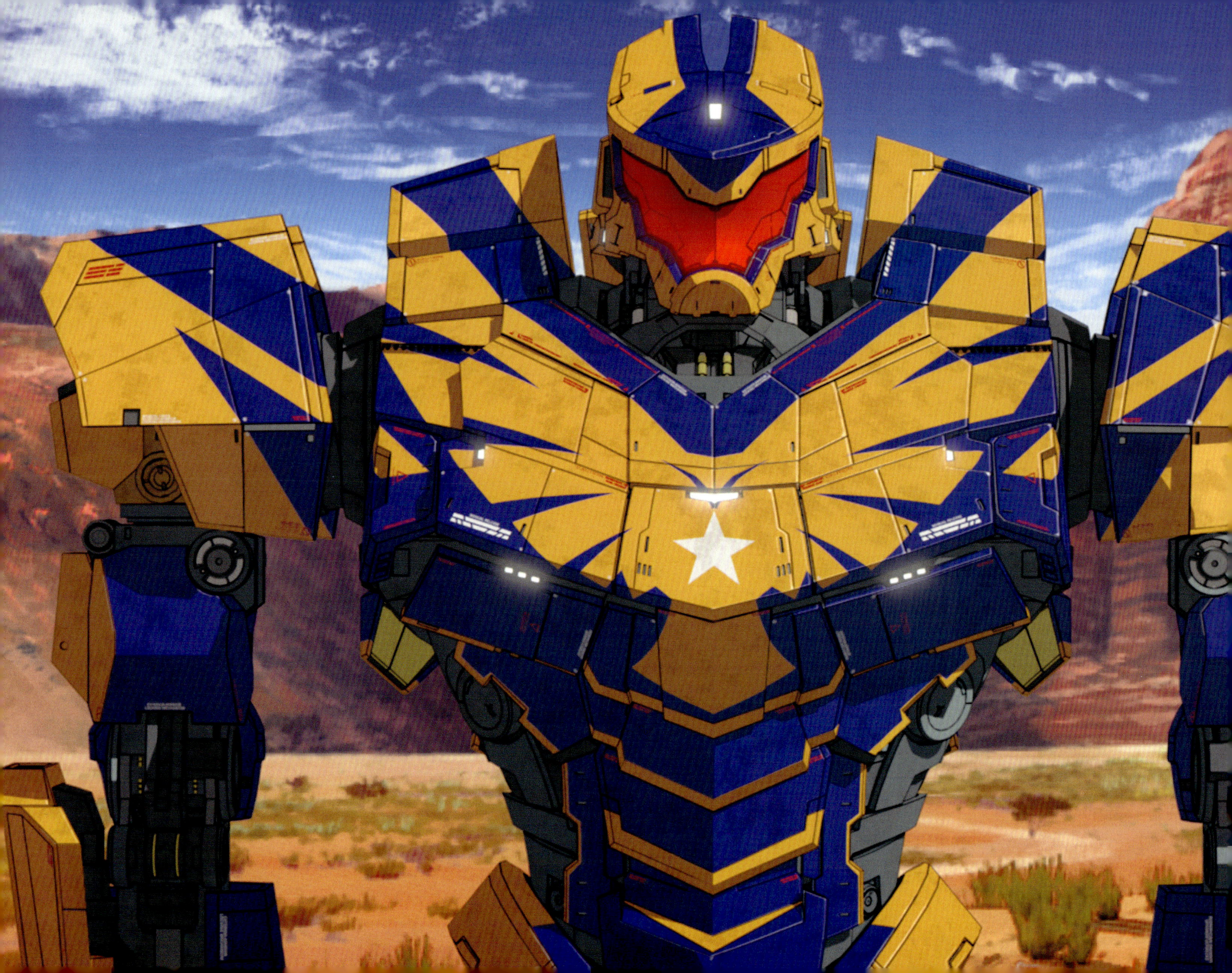

Atlas Destroyer is a teaching robot; its function is to train up Jaeger pilots, which is why it was left behind. Now, Loa asks Hayley if she wants to start her own Jaeger training. Does she ever...

"Since Atlas Destroyer is a training Jaeger," says Jae-Hong Kim, "it has a paint palette with a noticeably bright color scheme, just like an air force jet plane. I wanted to add numbers on its shoulder or on the corner of its chest, but it didn't work out." Later on, Atlas Destroyer will often be seen striding through the desert. "One of my main concerns was making sure it did not blend too much with the desert background!" Kim recalls. "So I had to change the yellow into a more orange color."

One detail that mecha fans may spot is that Atlas Destroyer lacks the characteristic circular power 'turbines' that the combat Jaegers have on their chests, including Hunter Vertigo earlier. As Kim points out, it was another way to differentiate the animated series from its own 'parents', the live-action films. "We're just dealing with a training Jaeger, so Johnson and Kyle had an idea; how about we remove the turbine?" Kim says. "I thought that was a good idea."

As the 'mind' of Atlas Destroyer, the A.I. Loa will come to serve as a parental presence for Taylor and Hayley. Her beautiful, organic-seeming appearance makes the Jaeger feel more alive. "Our original name for the A.I. was Aura," Johnson says, "as in the distinctive qualities of a person emanating from, in this instance, a robot. But all names need to clear legally, and 'Aura' didn't. So we researched other names that might have a different spiritual significance."

"WE'RE JUST DEALING WITH A TRAINING JAEGER; HOW ABOUT WE REMOVE THE TURBINE? I THOUGHT THAT WAS A GOOD IDEA."

Jae-Hong Kim, director

Far left // Atlas Destroyer was given a more orange shade to help it stand out from the desert.

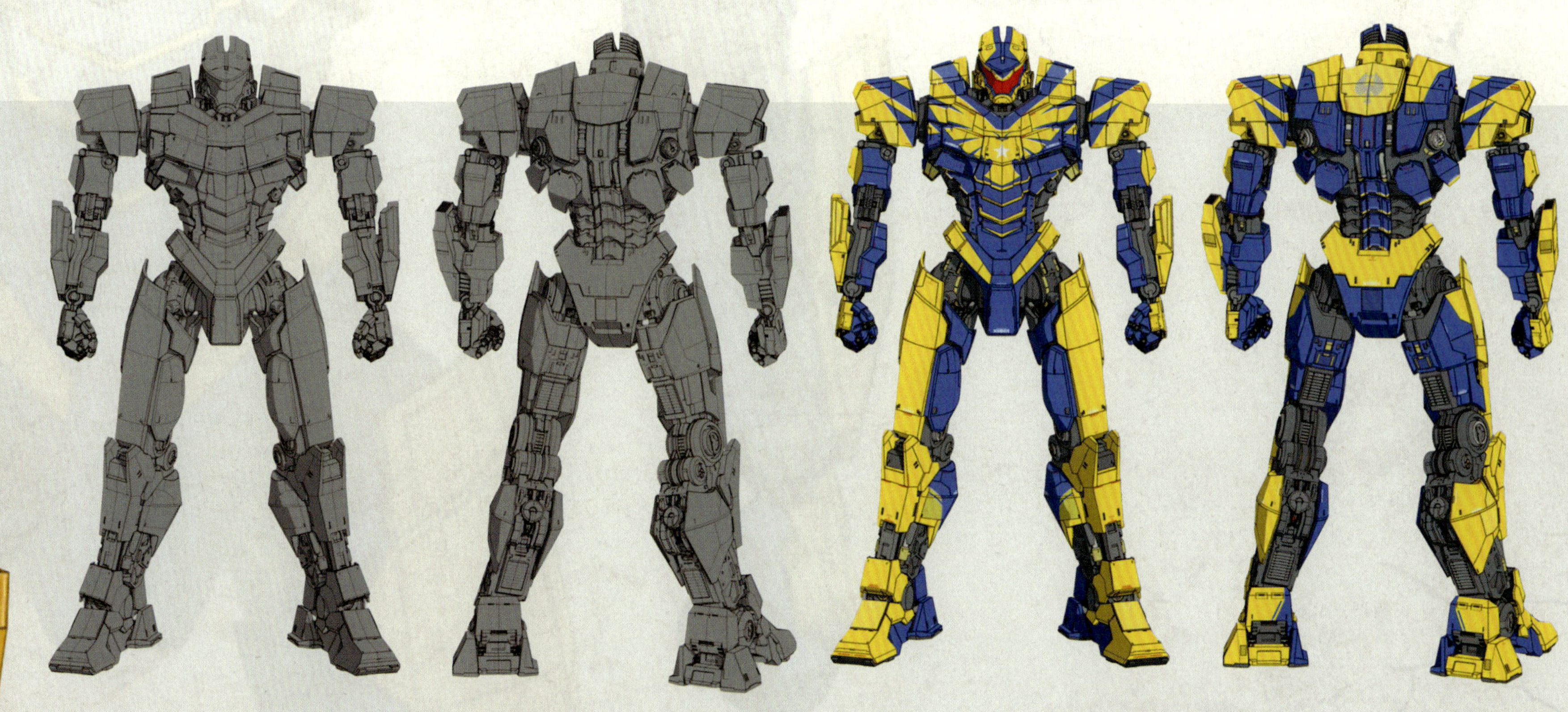

This led the writers to Voodoo beliefs. "The spirit 'Loa' in Voodoo is an intermediary between humans and higher beings," Johnson says. "It felt like that fit, as Loa was the conduit for our characters to interact with the Jaeger. It was also an easy name to say, and yet it wasn't common enough to be overused elsewhere."

Loa starts to 'train' Hayley, presenting her with six months' worth of lessons that the impatient girl skips through in minutes. Meanwhile, Taylor has gone looking for her, and finds the buried Jaeger as well. When he enters the control room, Hayley impulsively introduces him to Loa as her co-pilot. As Hayley has 'finished' her training, and Taylor passed the written Jaeger test when he was younger, Loa assumes the pilots are ready for the next stage, and starts the Jaeger's walk cycle. It's an act that will bring the youngsters' safe world of five years to a terrible end.

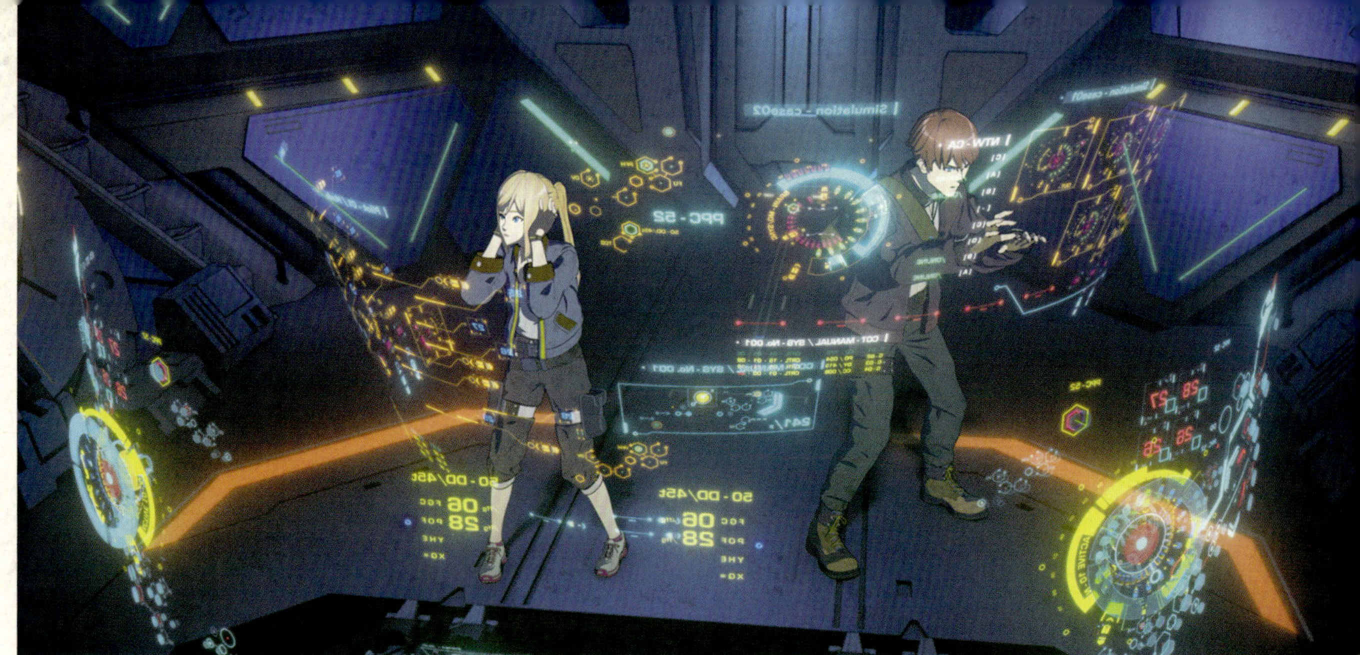

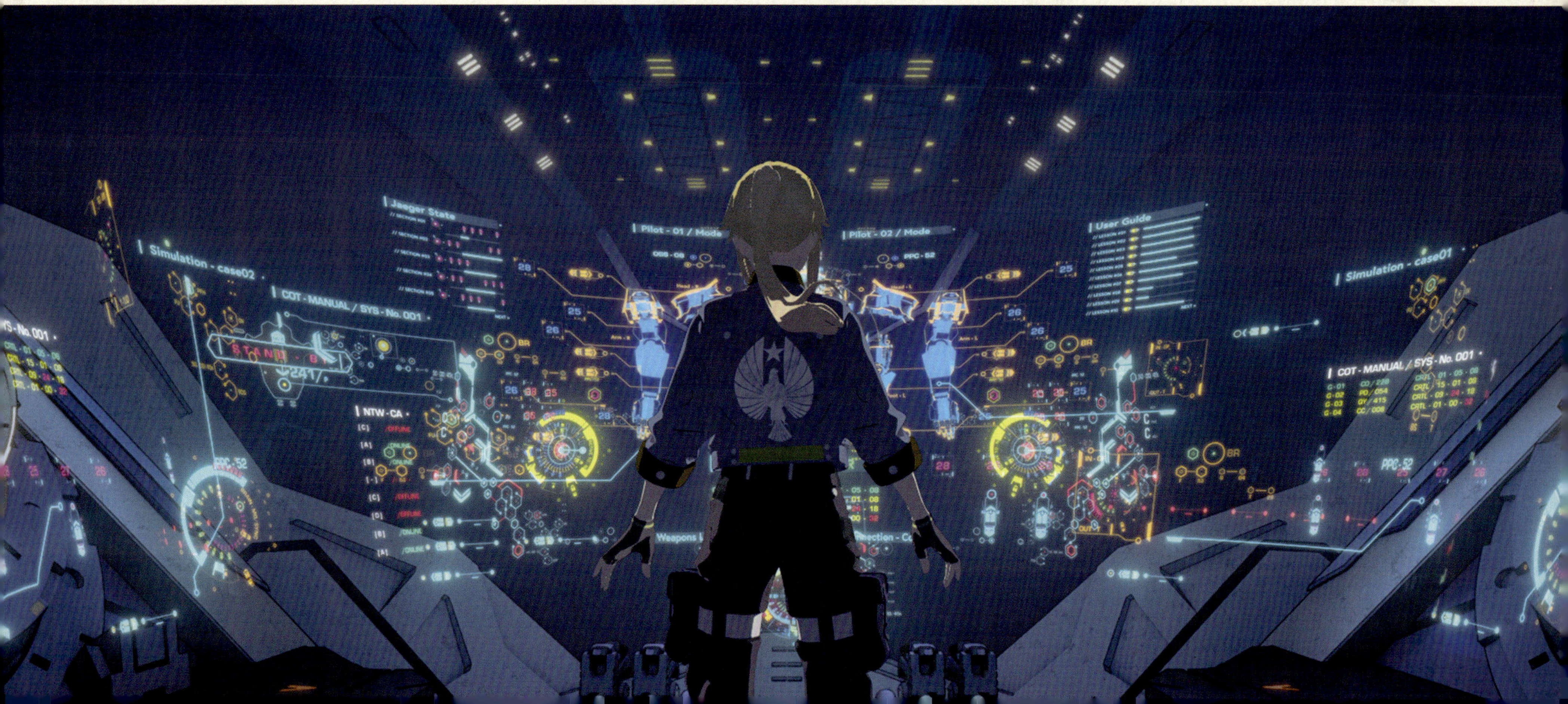

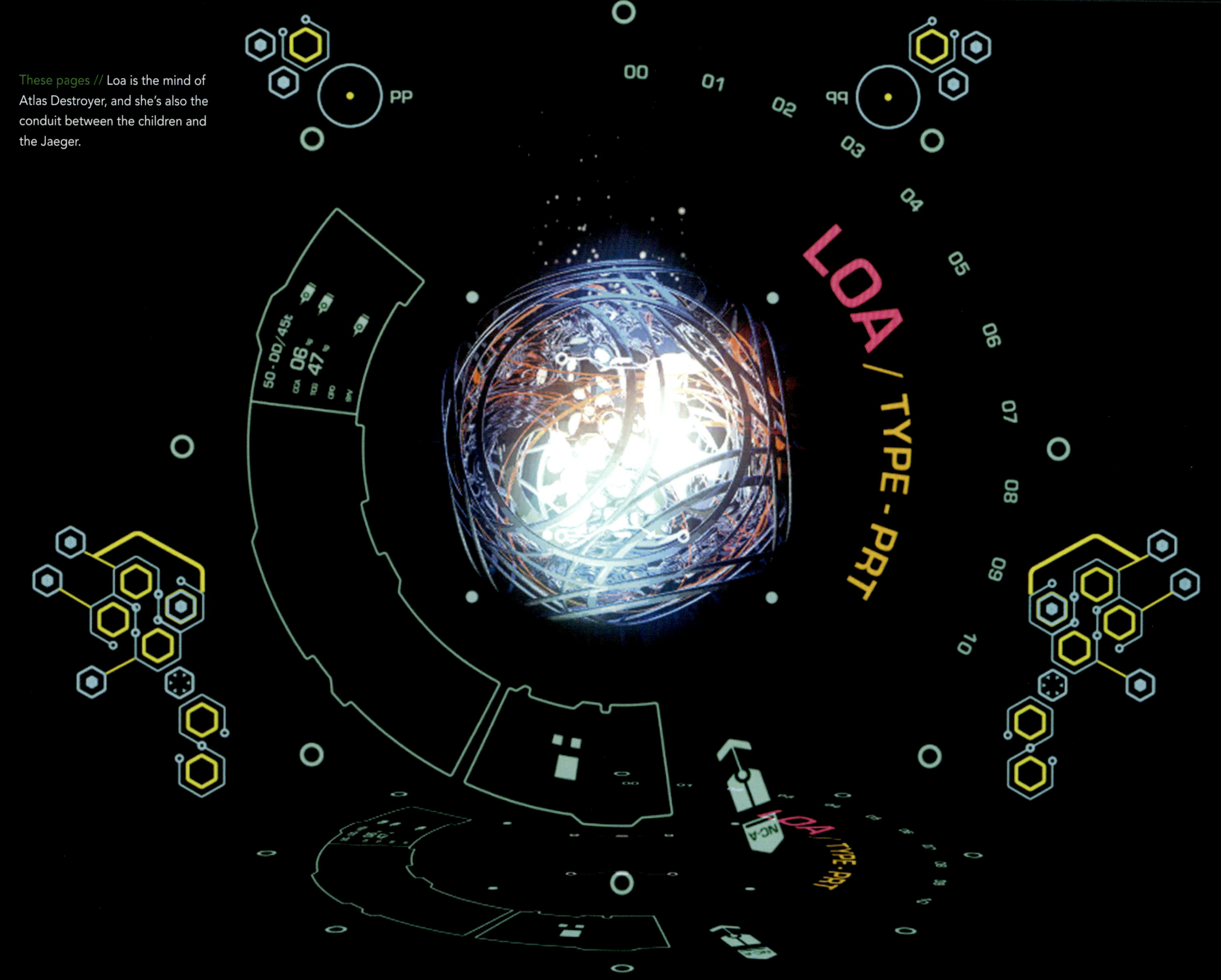

These pages // Loa is the mind of Atlas Destroyer, and she's also the conduit between the children and the Jaeger.

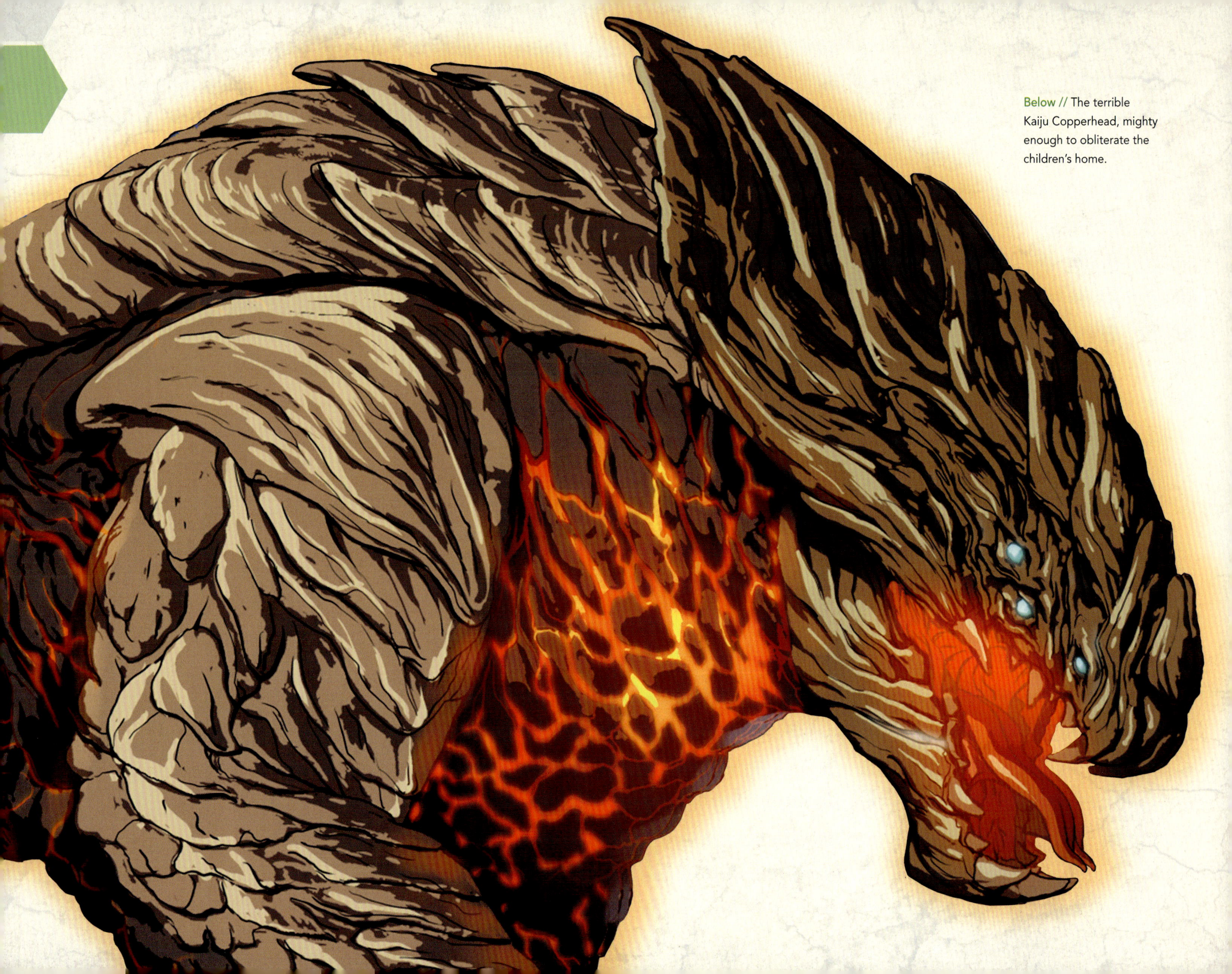

Below // The terrible Kaiju Copperhead, mighty enough to obliterate the children's home.

REIGN OF COPPERHEAD

As the Jaeger's walk cycle prompts a buried hangar door to start opening, sirens automatically sound, the din blaring outside the base. It would be a minor detail in the live-action *Pacific Rim* films, but it's catastrophic in *Pacific Rim: The Black*. The youngsters have only survived in Shadow Basin so long because they were beneath the Kaiju's notice. The activation of Atlas Destroyer has just changed that…

A shadow falls on Shadow Basin—that of a Kaiju, Copperhead, attracted by the sound. Striding nimbly on its four great legs, the monster looks like a gigantic boulder come to life. Its belly is a latticework of glowing lava-lines; its wrinkled skin is textured like layers of strata. It will be the 'main' Kaiju in the series' first season, and one of Taylor and Hayley's recurring enemies.

"Copperhead had to be unique, different from the Kaiju in the movies," explains Jae-Hong Kim. "In the live-action films, the Kaiju are generated by an alien species, and come through the portal of the Pacific Ocean. But *Pacific Rim: The Black* is set long after that. By now, some of the Kaiju have adapted to Earth."

The staff worked out backstories for all the new Kaiju, though many of these backstories never made it to the screen. "Copperhead was born in lava," explains Kim. "We had some ideas like showing him drinking lava and sleeping right next to lava. But we had to put all these cool ideas in the locker because we didn't have the time and budget. It was a shame."

It was crucial that the Kaiju looked like organic creatures, not machines like the Jaegers. Art director Yuki Moriyama highlights how Copperhead's belly tends to stretch, expanding and contracting greatly as the monster moves. "Of course, trying to make Kaiju look like living things is something we were considering

"COPPERHEAD HAD TO BE UNIQUE, DIFFERENT FROM THE KAIJU IN THE MOVIES."
Jae-Hong Kim, director

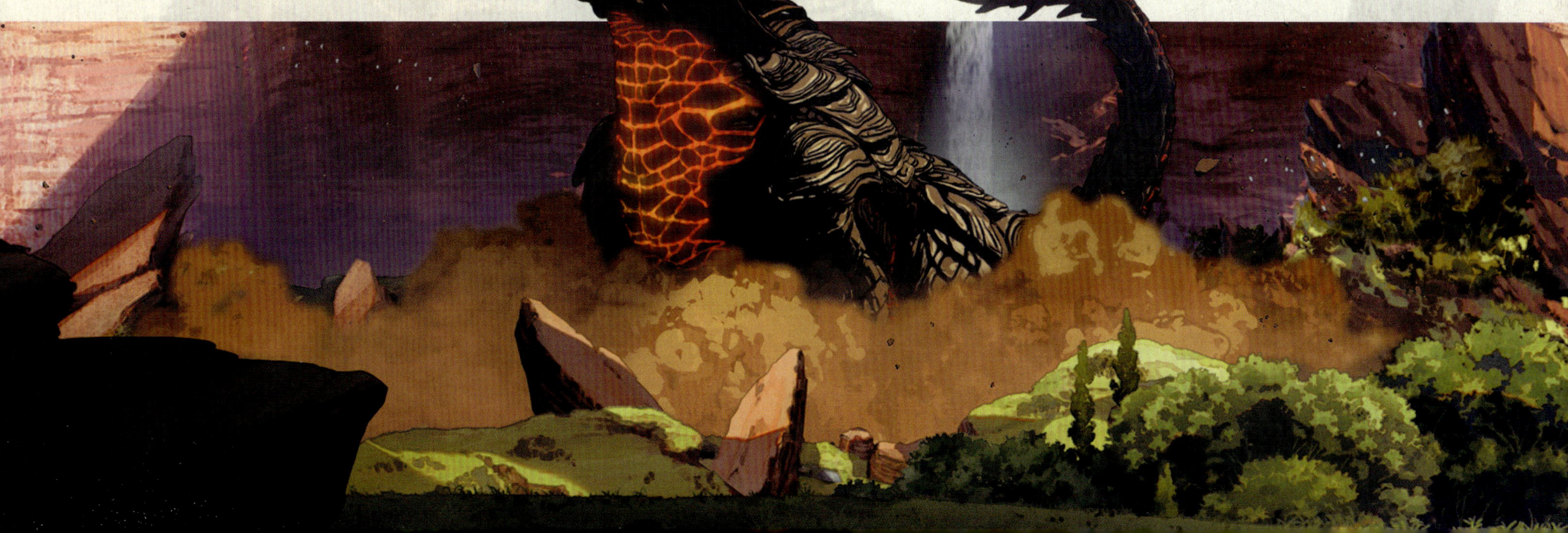

Below // Copperhead rampages through the defenseless Shadow Basin.

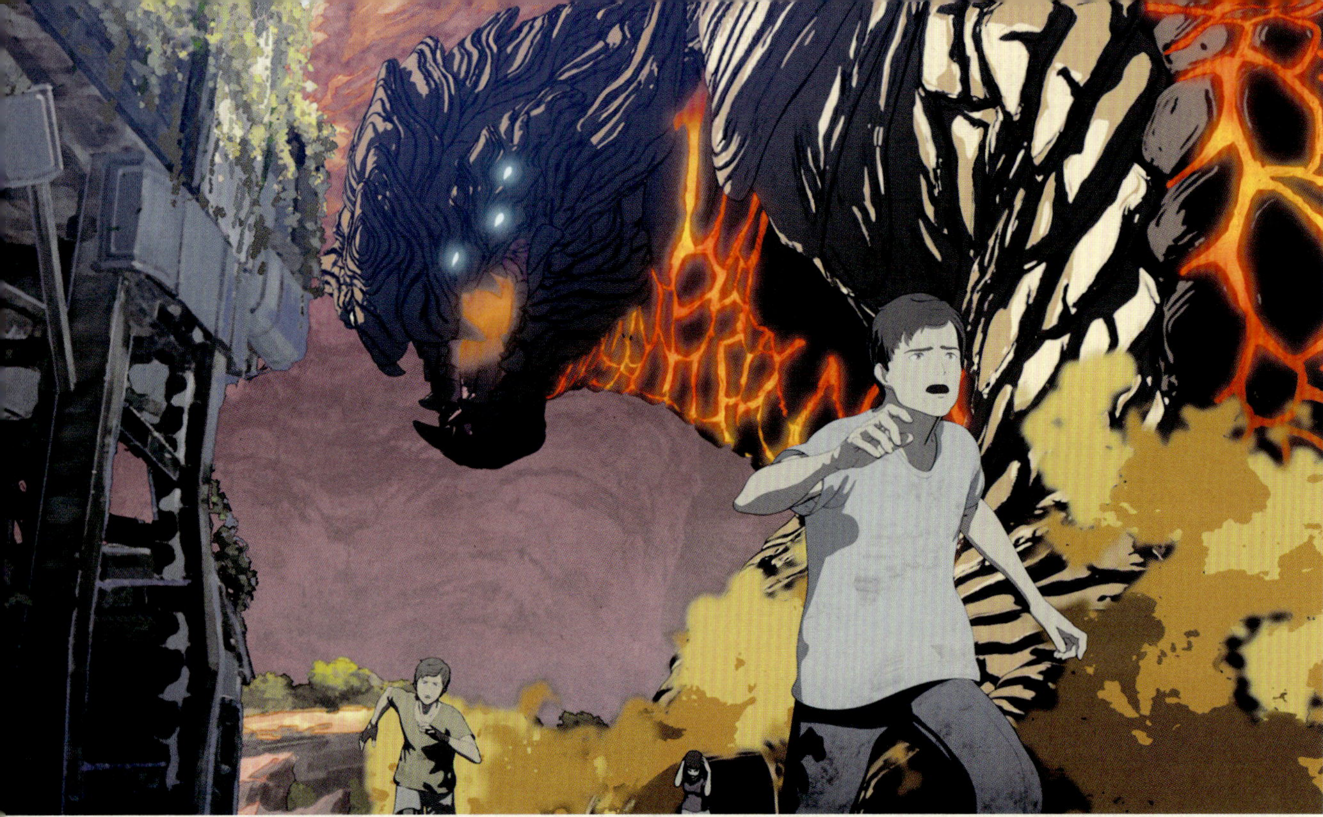

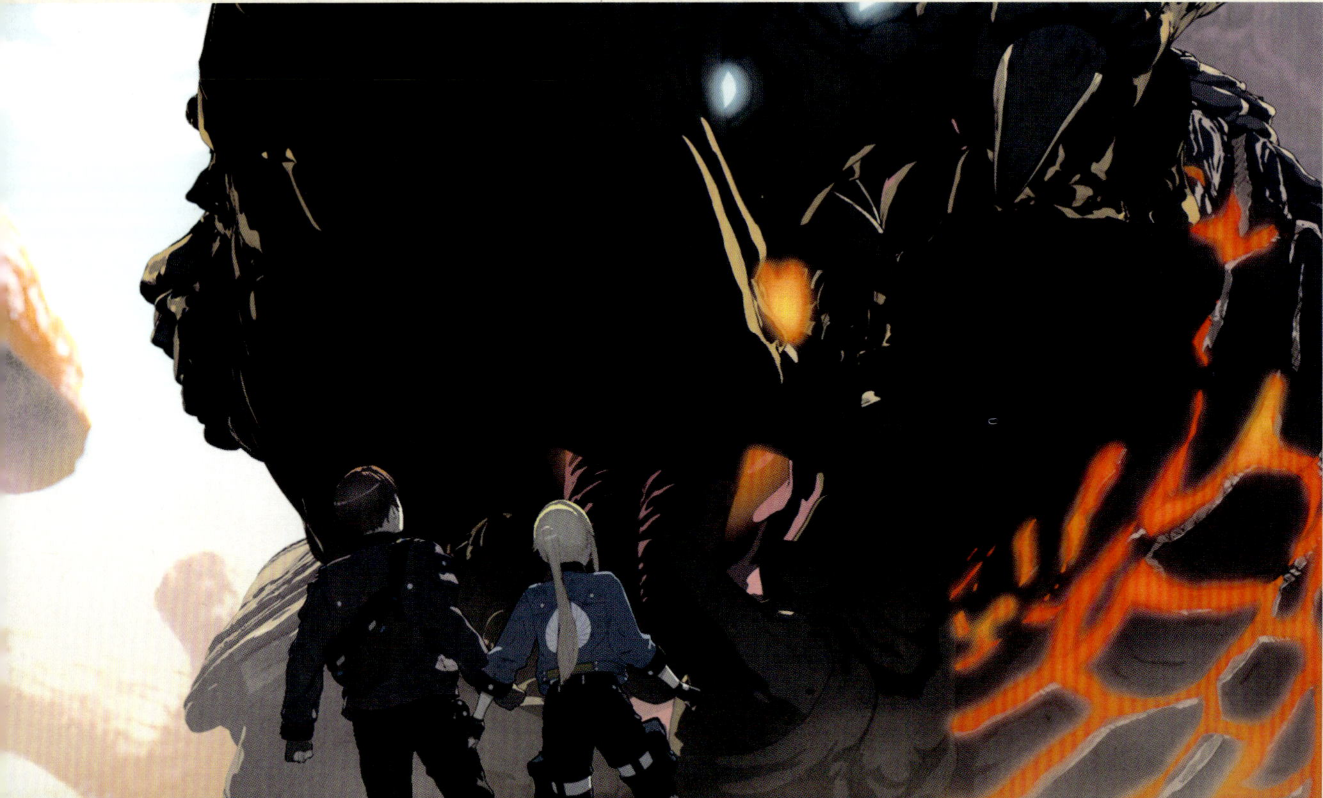

from the design stage," says Moriyama. "We paid particular attention to the flesh; trying to make clear the Kaiju were flesh-and-bone creatures.

"In order to do so," continues Moriyama, "because the Kaiju are so gigantic, we tried to add wrinkles, creases in the flesh that could expand and contract as the animators moved them, to make them look more organic, to look like they had meat on them."

"Ultimately, it is up to the artistic eye and the sense and creativity of the individual animator," says supervising director Hiroyuki Hayashi. "Of course, you can get a certain idea by looking at references and videos of actual huge animals, but Kaiju are considerably larger than any animals that exist. They can destroy mountains and entire buildings, so part of the struggle of designing them is imagining how something that massive would move. Internally we did discuss how to create references for that kind of thing, and we imagined how to make them convincing."

Rushing out of the base, Taylor and Hayley are horrified to see Copperhead wreaking havoc in Shadow Basin and crushing all their friends. As the monster suddenly notices the pair, they realise their only hope is to pilot the Jaeger, and they race back to the machine. But first, the siblings must synchronise with each other, and in *Pacific Rim*'s world that means 'Drifting'.

Drifting was central in the first live-action film. It showed how the pilots had to open their minds to each other while their neural pathways are intertwined via the pilots'

"PART OF THE STRUGGLE OF DESIGNING KAIJU IS IMAGINING HOW SOMETHING THAT MASSIVE WOULD MOVE."

Hiroyuki Hayashi, director

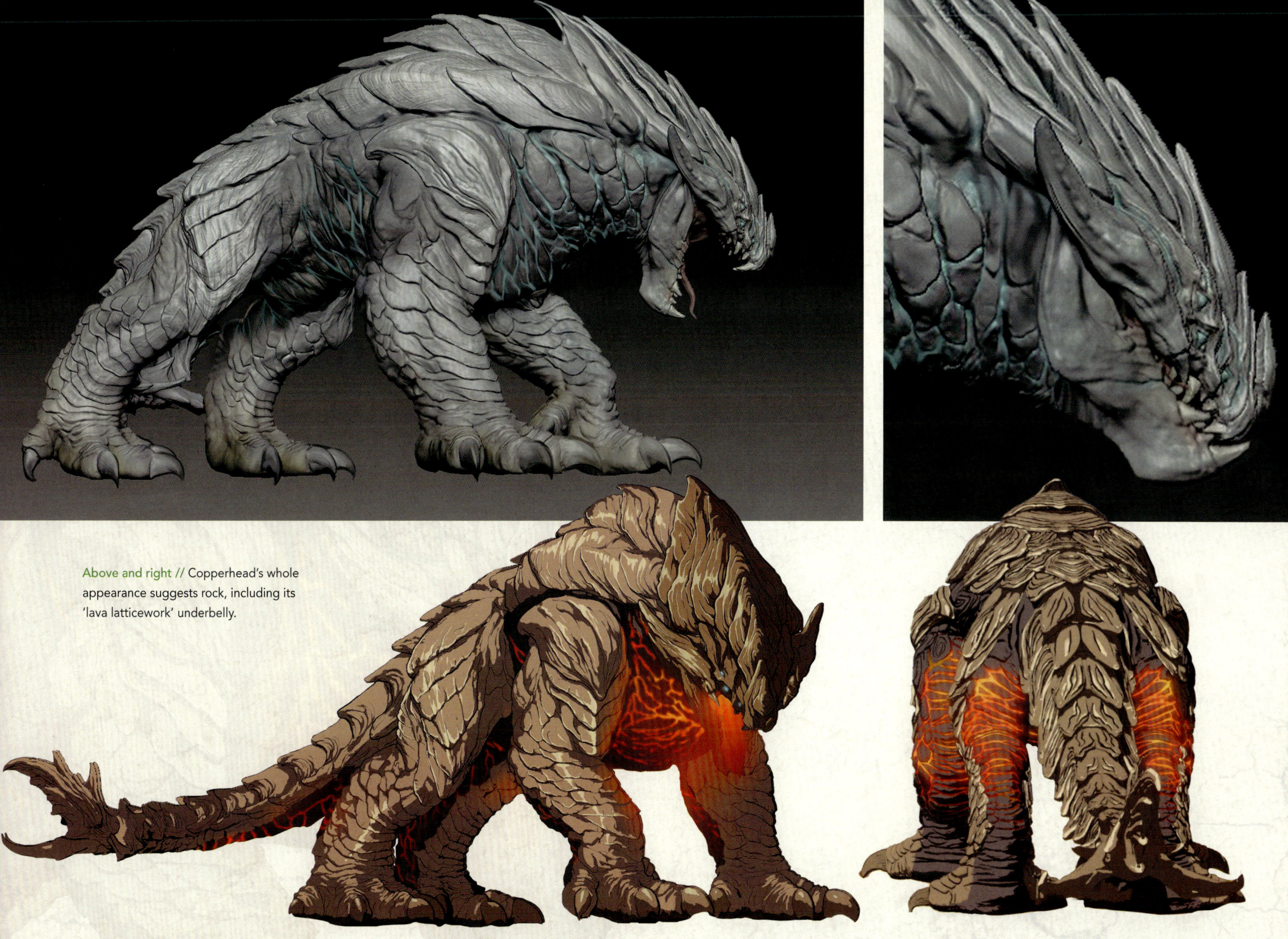

Above and right // Copperhead's whole appearance suggests rock, including its 'lava latticework' underbelly.

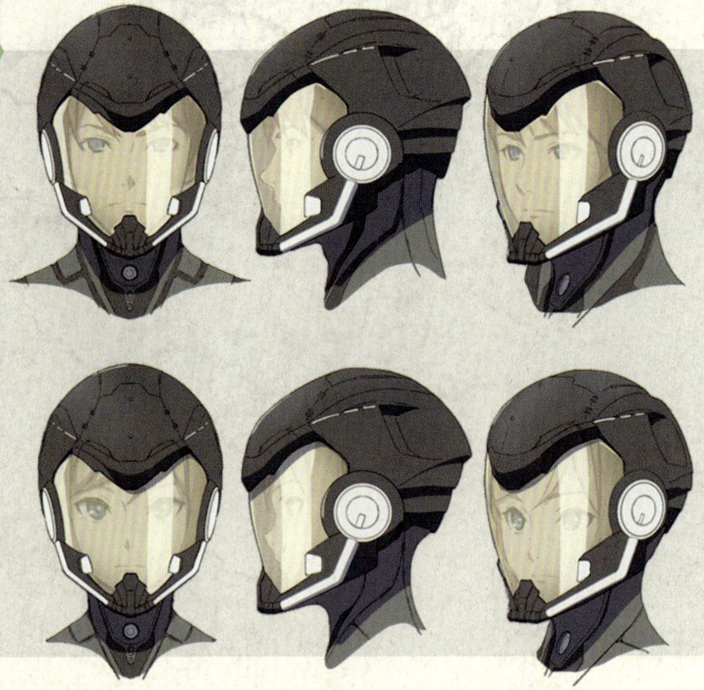

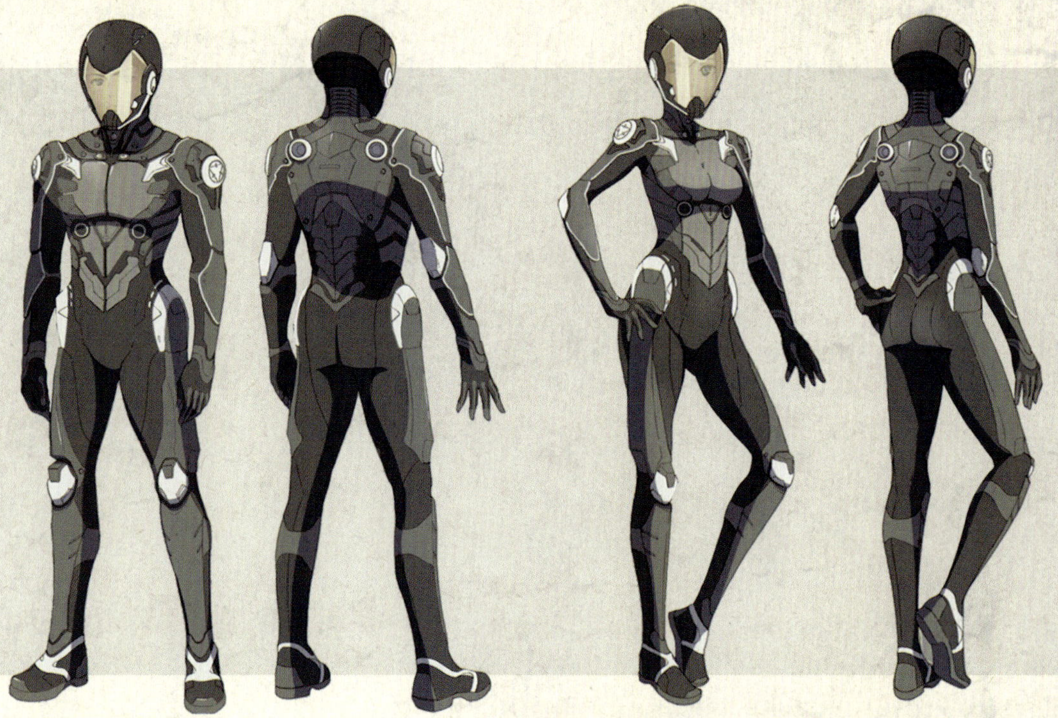

helmets—what the script calls a 'neural handshake'. When Taylor and Hayley first drift together, the inexperienced Hayley finds herself lost in her own memories, hampering her link with Taylor. The delay is long enough for Copperhead to find Atlas Destroyer and yank it from the ground like a child's toy.

Drifting will be a huge part of the animated series. "The Drift really intrigued us as a storytelling device," says Greg Johnson. "We had to establish more of its infrastructure so we could build off it. A 'Drift Space' where the pilots would appear as a neural link was established; a void where the pilots could communicate mentally, where memories would float like bubbles."

Indeed, the animated series finds a whole new way of visualizing Drift Space based around liquid, water and bubbles. Jae-Hong Kim explains, "We realised that we need a visual image for the Drift, which was never done in the live-action films. So what would the visual be? It should be different from a portal… It had to be unique and sort of surreal."

Kim remembers Johnson bringing up a 'watery' image, evoking the zero gravity of outer space and the abysses of the ocean. "That struck me," says Kim, "and it was clear to me how the image should look. The 'liquid' idea came from the US side, and Polygon nailed it."

Hiroyuki Hayashi says, "With the Drift scenes in the live-action movies, you had the advantage of being able to actually film scenes showing the characters' pasts, to show those scenes in quick flashes. So we tried to come up with a different way to show the connection between the Drifting partners in the Jaegers.

"Water, the surface of water, could be used as a symbol of the connection," Hayashi continues. "Water can move and form, so by having this wall of water, you could express the pilots' connection. If the connection is strong, that wall could be broken through, and if the connection is weak, then it won't. Water itself is very fluid and beautiful, so we were able to create some artistic looks but also have that emotion, that connection, expressed in the liquid."

The globe-like appearance of the AI character Loa fits with the liquid theme, and Polygon's art director Yuki Moriyama explains that was happy chance. "The art

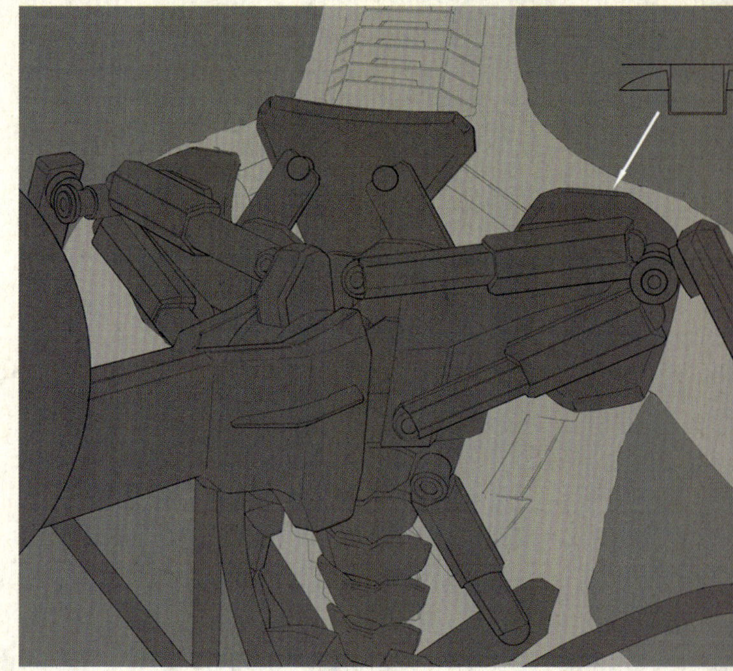

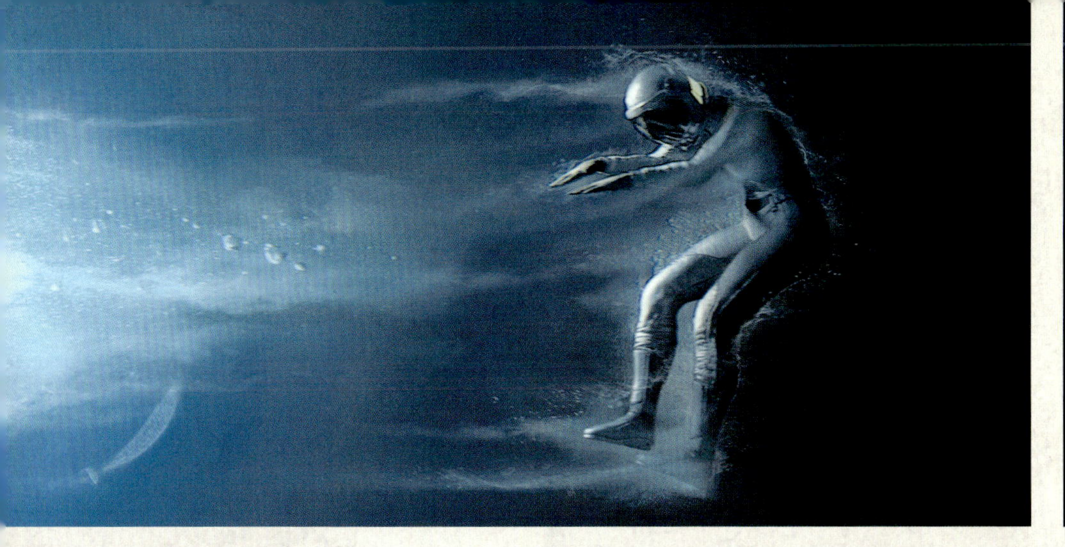

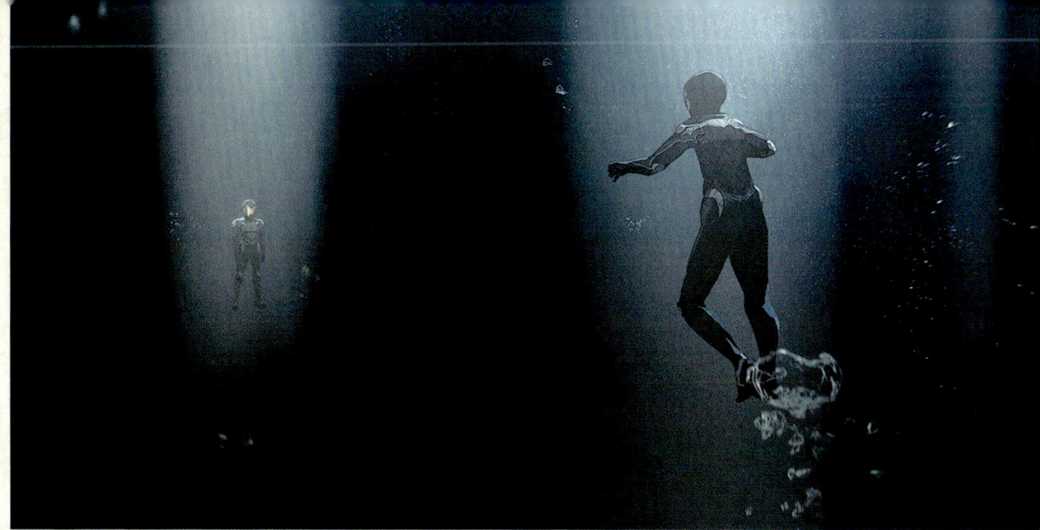

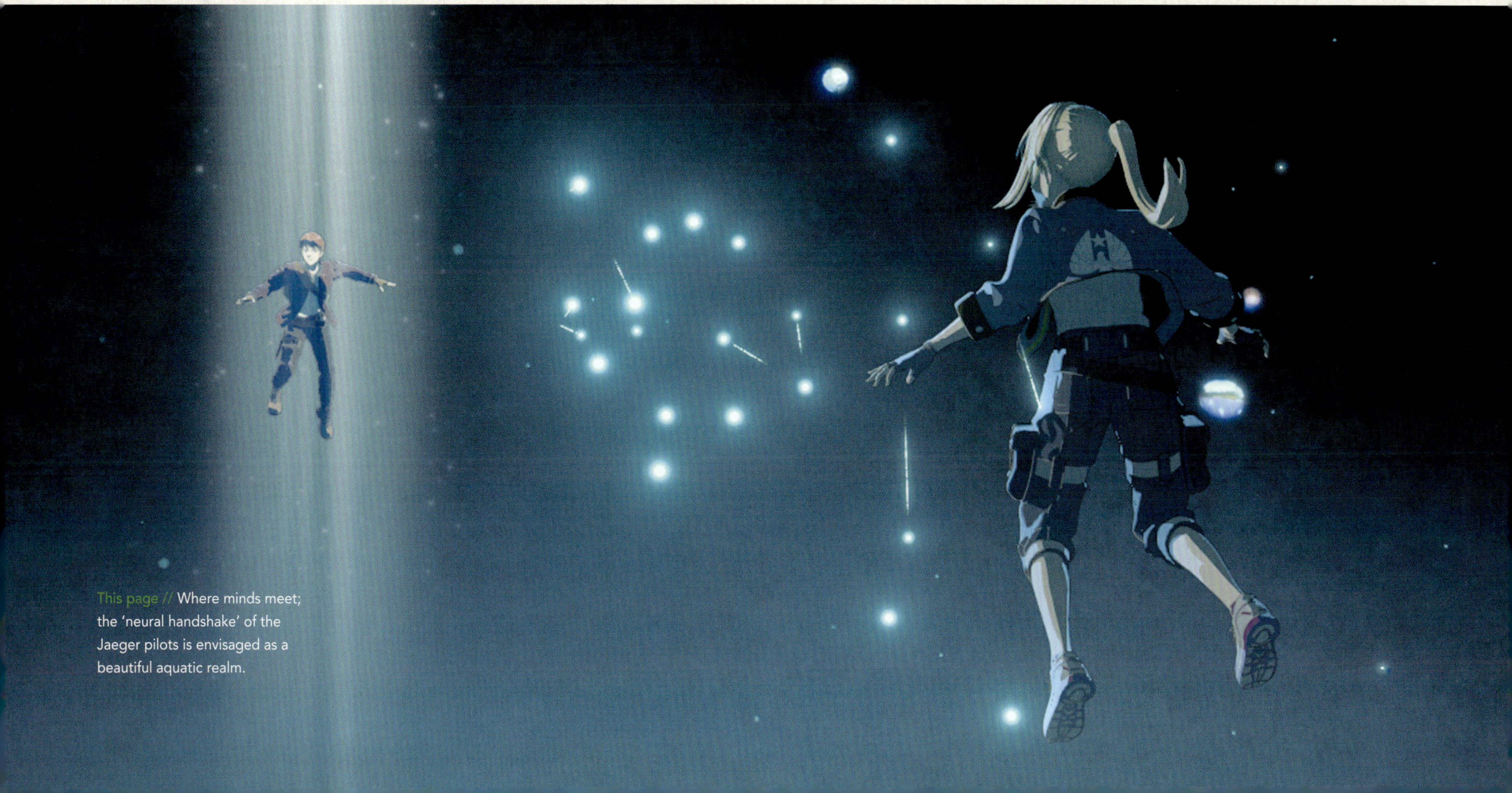

This page // Where minds meet; the 'neural handshake' of the Jaeger pilots is envisaged as a beautiful aquatic realm.

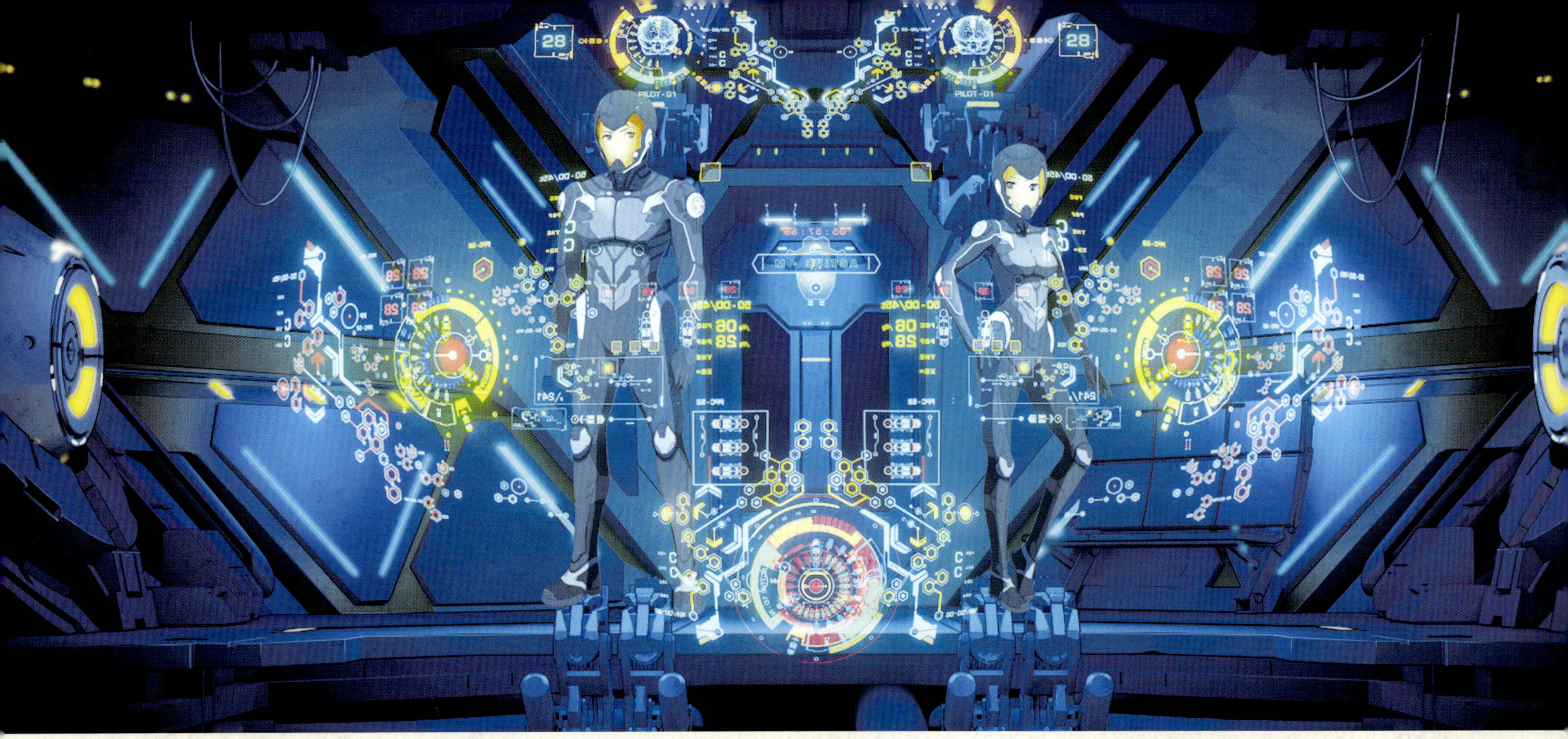

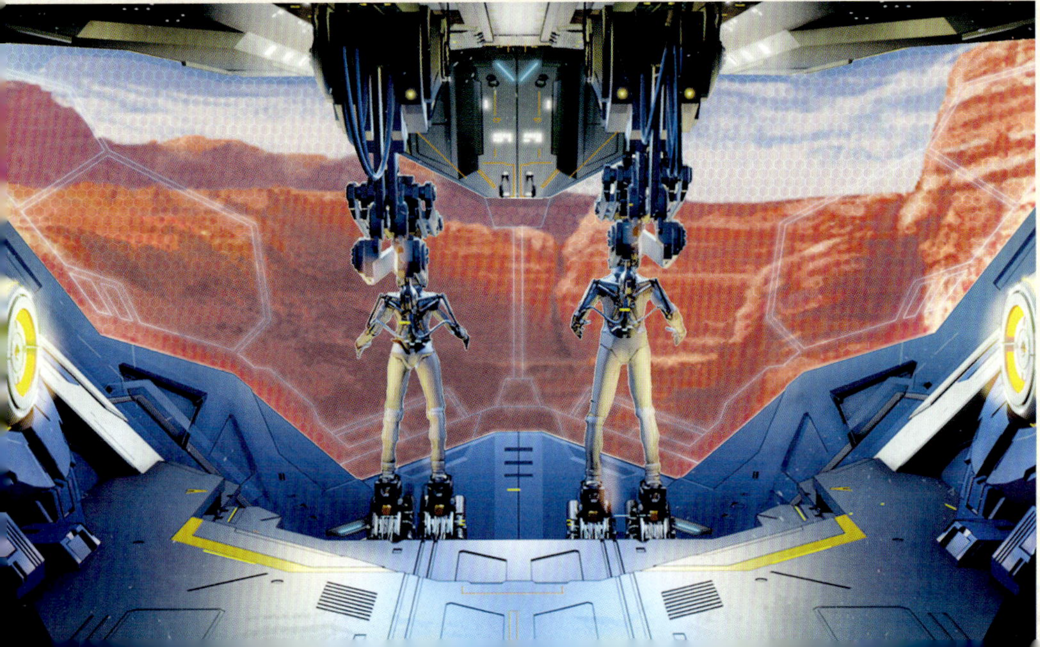

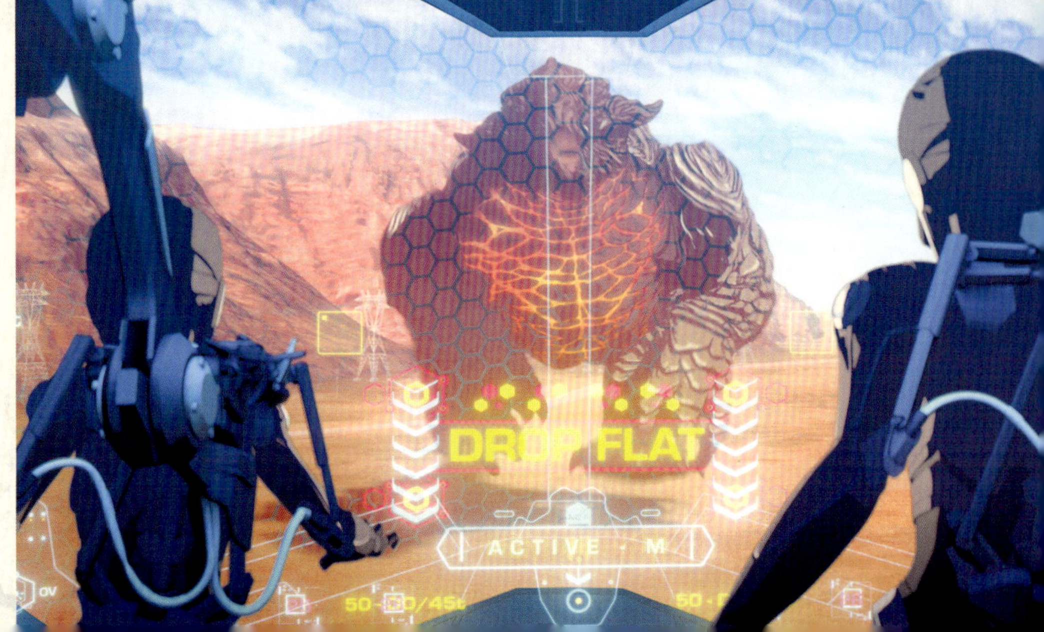
DROP FLAT
ACTIVE · M

development for Loa was done at a different time from the Drift sequences. When we designed Loa, we wanted to come up with a way to show the emotion of the A.I. Again, we came to the image of water because it is very fluid, and you can almost make it show different feelings by animating it in certain ways. That's how we came to the conclusion of using liquid again for Loa."

Ripped from the ground by Copperhead, Taylor and Hayley desperately try using Atlas Destroyer to fight. They discover, however, that the training Jaeger is not kitted out with any missiles. The siblings must fight Copperhead effectively hand to hand. Atlas Destroyer, unsurprisingly, gets the worst of it.

Jae-Hong Kim wanted the audience to feel the impact in the animation when the giants fight. In the first brief bout, there are showers of yellow metal when Copperhead strikes the Jaeger, rubble-clouds of rock when the monster brings down its huge spiked tail onto the ground, and a far bigger explosion of rock and earth when the Jaeger is sent flying once again, crashing hard down to earth.

"I gave the Polygon staff a lot of notes about the special effects," Kim says. "Quite often, people forget about them. For example, when a Jaeger punches a Kaiju it's an action, but what happens next is the reaction. What could be the reaction? The saliva coming out of the Kaiju's mouth, or some particles coming off from its skin. When a Kaiju smashes into a building, that creates huge destruction… That's what I call the reaction. All these special effects, the saliva, the skin particles, the collapse of a building creating smoke and debris, chunks of rock. I requested all these things."

"WE WANTED TO SHOW WHAT EFFORT IT TAKES FOR TAYLOR AND HAYLEY TO ULTIMATELY RISE UP AS HEROES."
Greg Johnson, showrunner

The kids are saved by Loa, who gets Atlas Destroyer to duck while Copperhead hurtles over it and into a chasm. The children return to Shadow Basin, but it's too late. All their friends at the Basin perished in Copperhead's attack; there are no survivors. The farmland they cultivated for five years is buried under shards of rock.

For Hayley, there's no hiding from the truth; this disaster is her doing. Few other series hit a young lead character so hard so early. When she found Atlas Destroyer, Hayley reacted like the 'chosen' hero of a thousand adventures. Now she faces the cruellest of reality checks.

For Greg Johnson, the destruction of Shadow Basin was a story necessity. "We wanted to take away the option of Taylor and Hayley simply giving up and going back to Shadow Basin. And it made sense that Copperhead, the Kaiju responsible for destroying that safe oasis, would physically represent the memory of that massacre as it continued to hound our siblings across the land. Copperhead became a constant reminder that Taylor and Hayley's actions, however unintentional, could not be put too far behind them.

"We wanted to show what effort it takes for Taylor and Hayley to ultimately rise up as heroes," Johnson adds. "That's only effective if they start low, like Hayley had to."

Jae-Hong Kim comments, "I guess nobody expected that a beautifully crafted location would be destroyed in the first episode. The Polygon people said, 'Oh, it's a real shame,' but we had to destroy it. We'll never come back to here! We felt the same way… but at the same time, that's what I like about the script. Sometimes it goes beyond your expectations, which I love."

With their home wiped out, the journey of Taylor and Hayley begins.

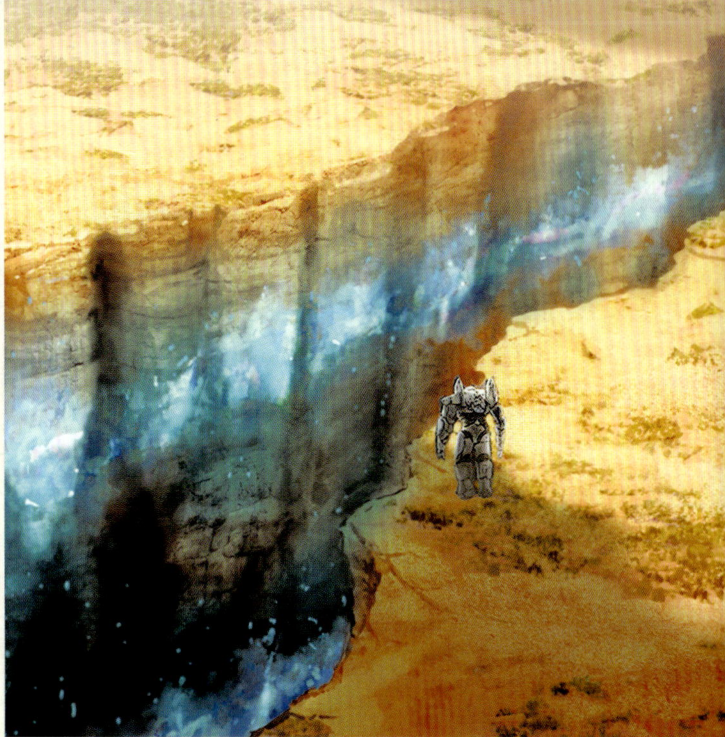

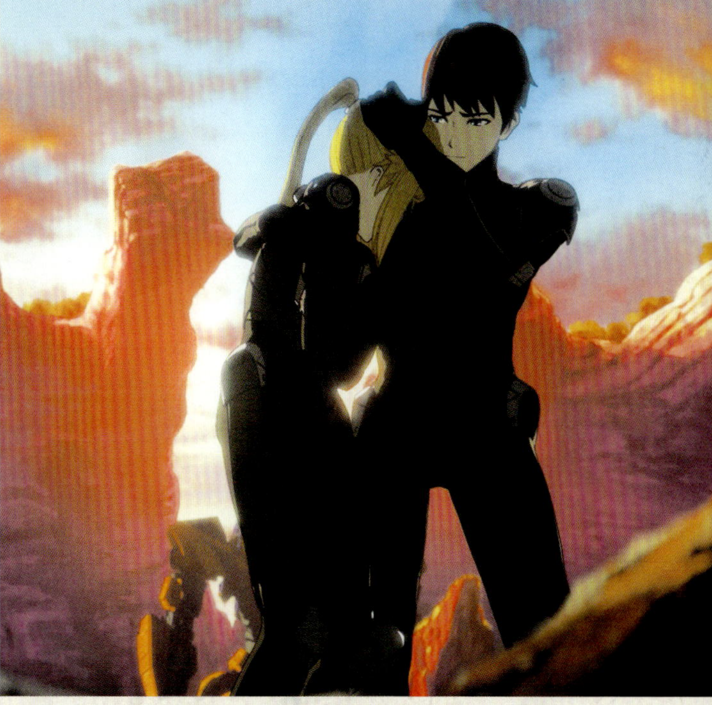

Right // Hayley and Taylor are shattered by the destruction of their home and the deaths of their friends.

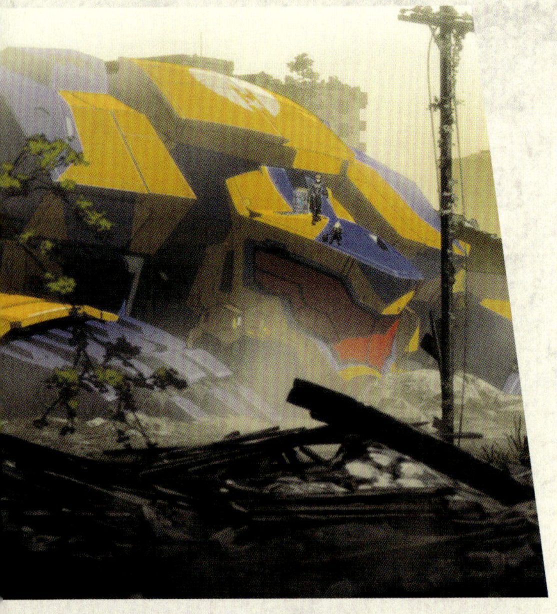

CHAPTER TWO
INTO THE WILDERNESS

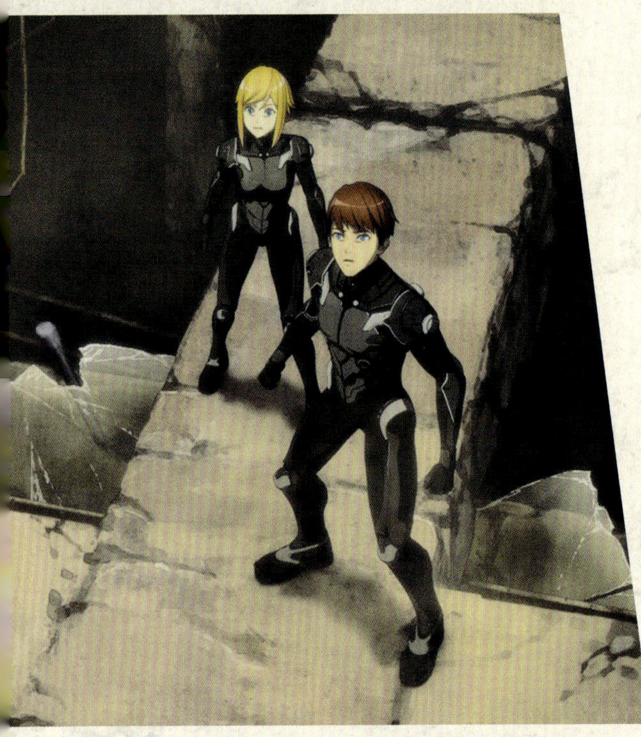

Episode Two, "Into the Black", starts with Hayley remembering the friends whose deaths she caused, and fearing her parents are gone too. Actually, it's not just a nightmare. Hayley's in the Drift with Taylor, who can't hide how, deep down, he blames his sister for what happened.

Loa 'wakes' the youngsters from their Drifting. Atlas Destroyer's energy is drained, and the Jaeger needs a new power cell. Loa has brought them to the outskirts of Meridian, five years after the kids fled the city. Taylor and Hayley must leave the Jaeger and head for the PPDC Recruitment Centre to find another power cell. PPDC, often namechecked in the script, stands for the Pan Pacific Defence Corps, the global anti-Kaiju force in the live-action films.

There's a stark contrast in settings, from the soothing tranquillity of Shadow Basin to the grey, sinister city. Hayashi says, "We wanted to show Shadow Basin to be almost heavenly, like Paradise, because everything after that is pure destruction and devastation. We tried to make Shadow Basin look as beautiful as possible… and then move to all these destroyed locations."

To create the look of the smashed cities, the staff went through images of ruined cities in the real world. Hayashi mentions one location they looked at was a famous Japanese island, commonly called 'Gunkanjima' or Battleship Island. Located near Nagasaki, the tiny island used to be a thriving mining community, but it was abandoned in the 1970s and left to be battered by wind and waves.

"But more than that," Hayashi explains, "we tried to imagine the big cities in the world today, and what they would look like destroyed in the future. So we looked at concept images for that [situation], created some concepts of our own, and saw how that would look."

Art director Yuki Moriyama looked at videogame concept art. "In the series, the Australian landscape has been destroyed, but also time has passed. That means that it's difficult to find real images of such locations, where

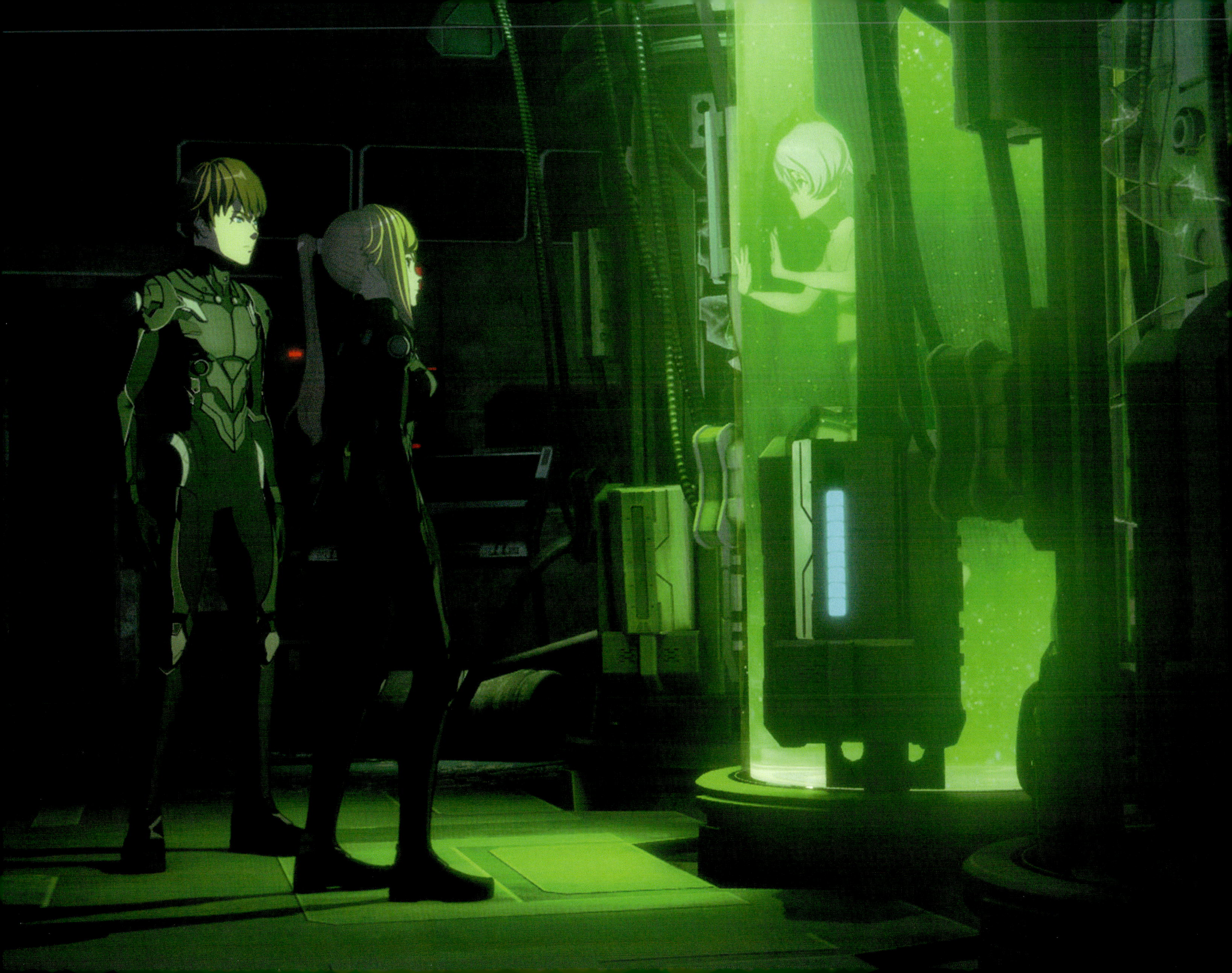

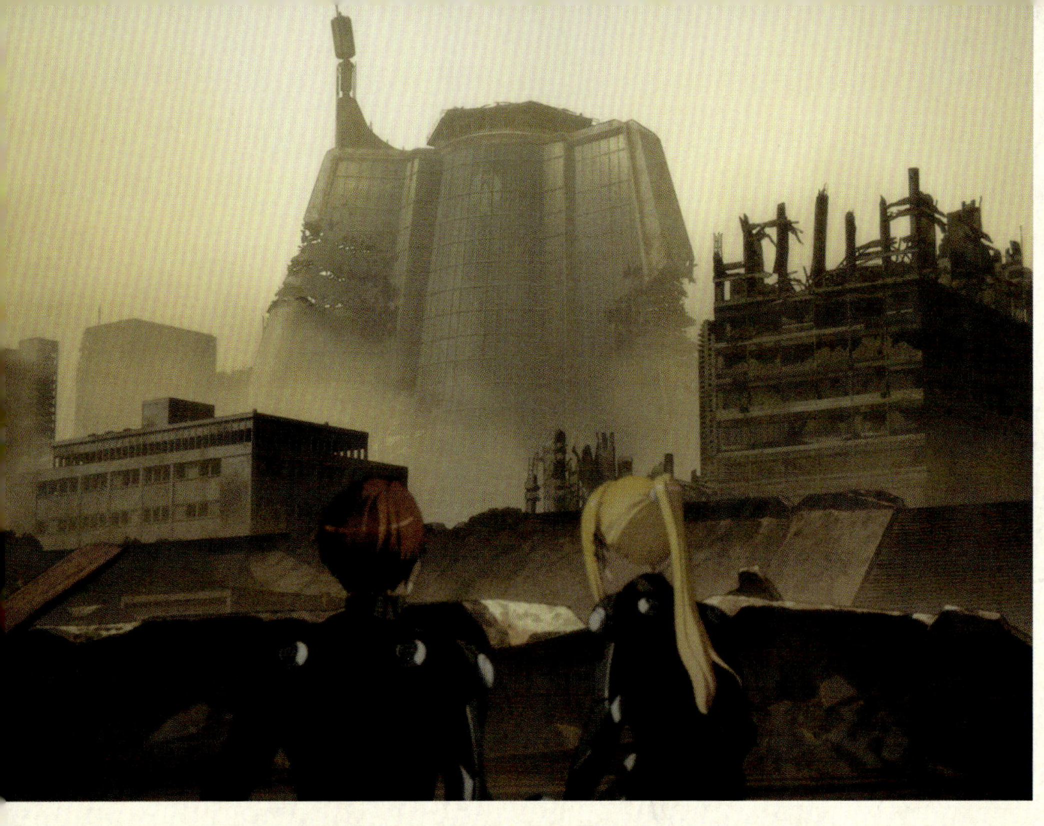

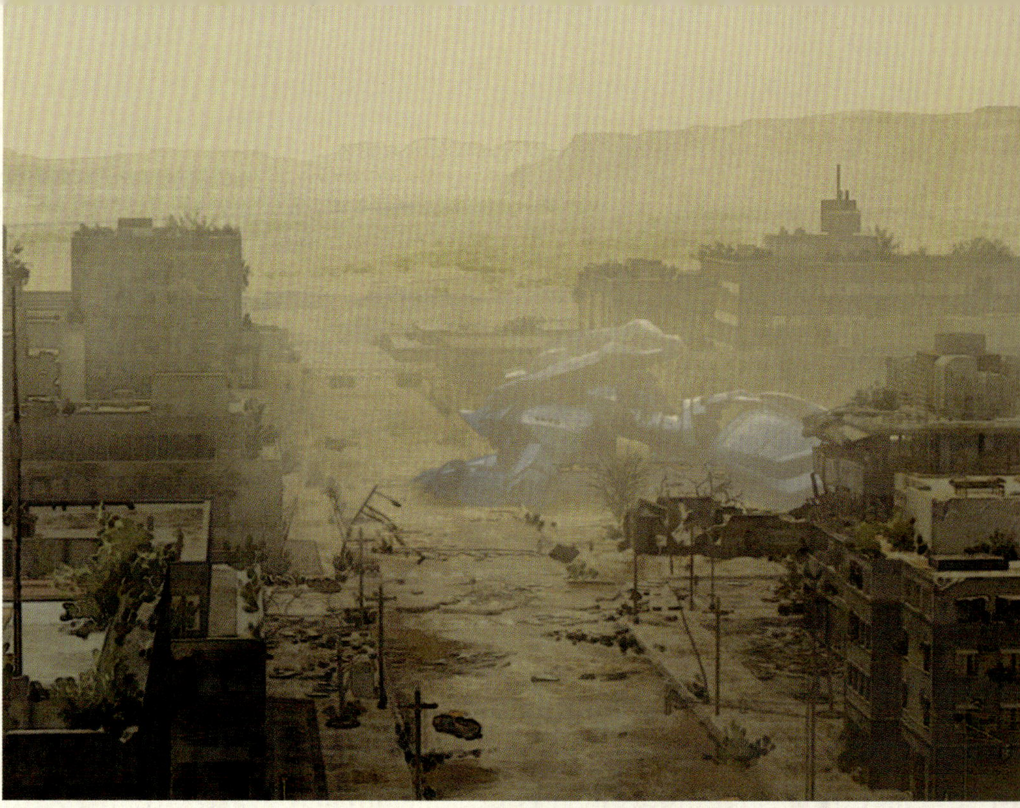

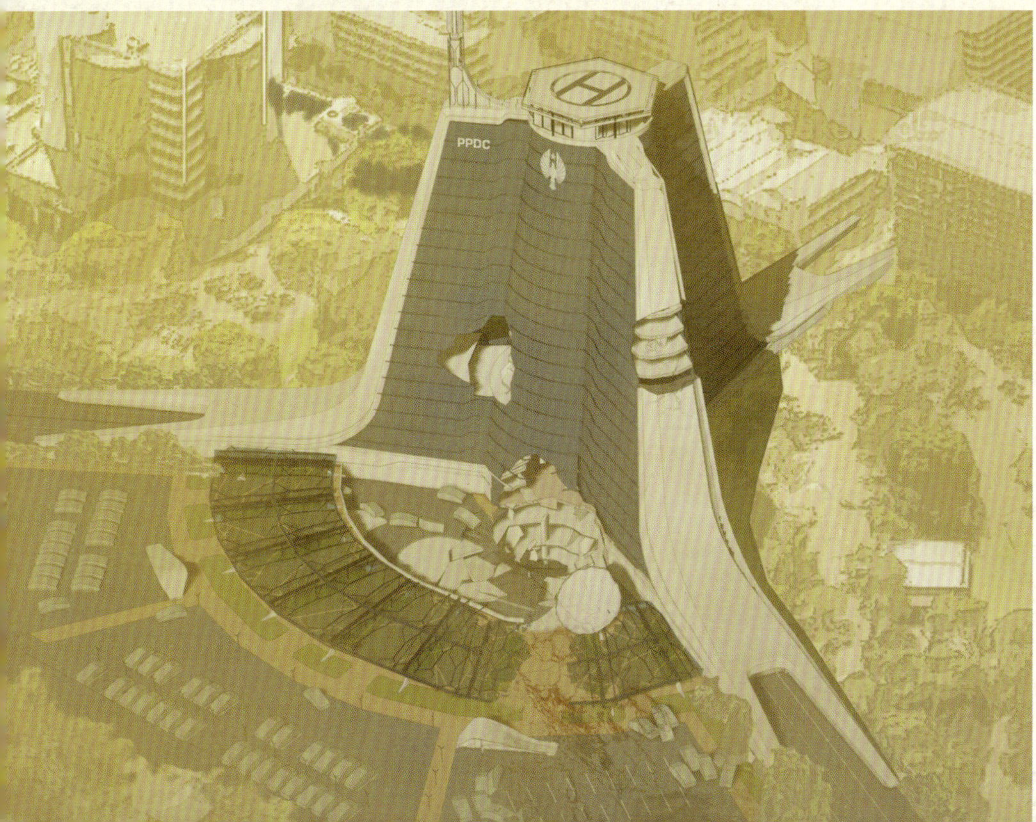
PPDC

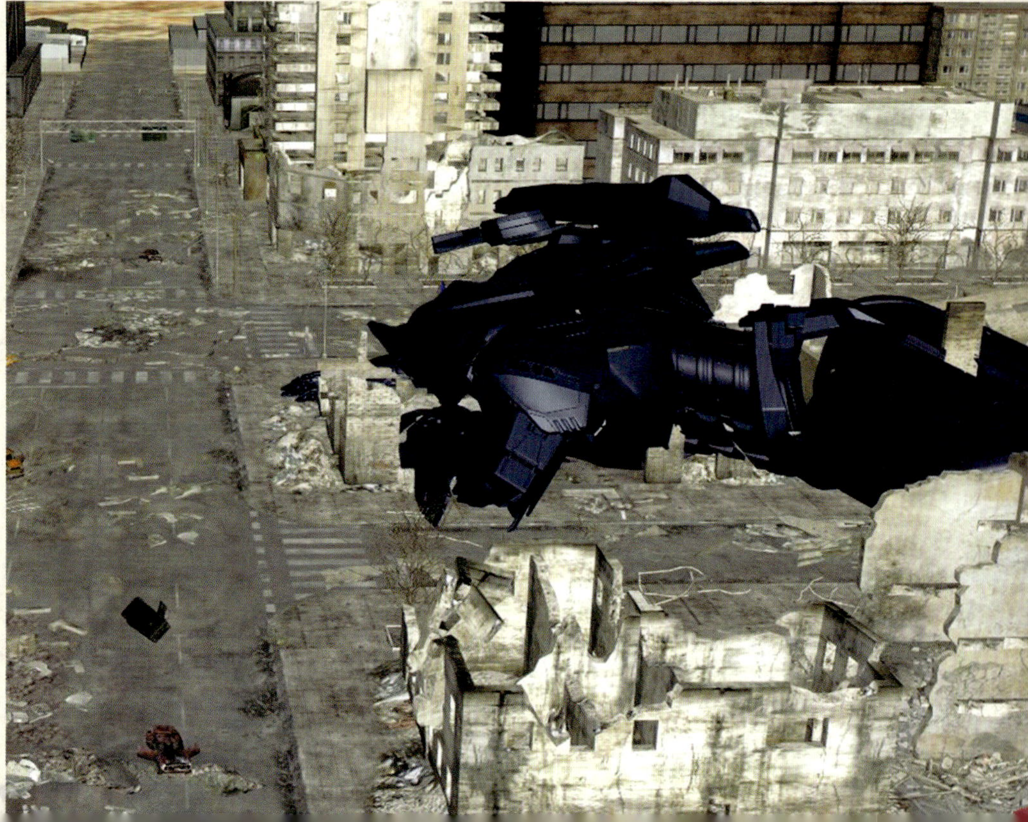

nature has been growing; it's destroyed but there's life. But in the videogame world, there are a lot of games with that kind of location. It was very useful to look at videogame concept art to see their interpretation, and then try to distill it into our own design."

Jae-Hong Kim remembers, "There's one shot where Taylor and Hayley are walking into the abandoned city, and a building has collapsed diagonally." (The shot is in Episode Two, as the youngsters begin their journey into Meridian.) "I did a sketch for that, and then the Polygon people thought that was cool, so they just nailed that right away."

As Taylor and Hayley move into the city, they're waylaid by another kind of Kaiju. This kind is smaller than Copperhead and the Acidquills, but still deadly. Full of malign personality, the new creatures suggest giant wolves, but viewers may think of something more reptilian.

Jae-Hong Kim confirms, "Normally Kaiju are gigantic, but we needed these Kaiju small enough to chase after the

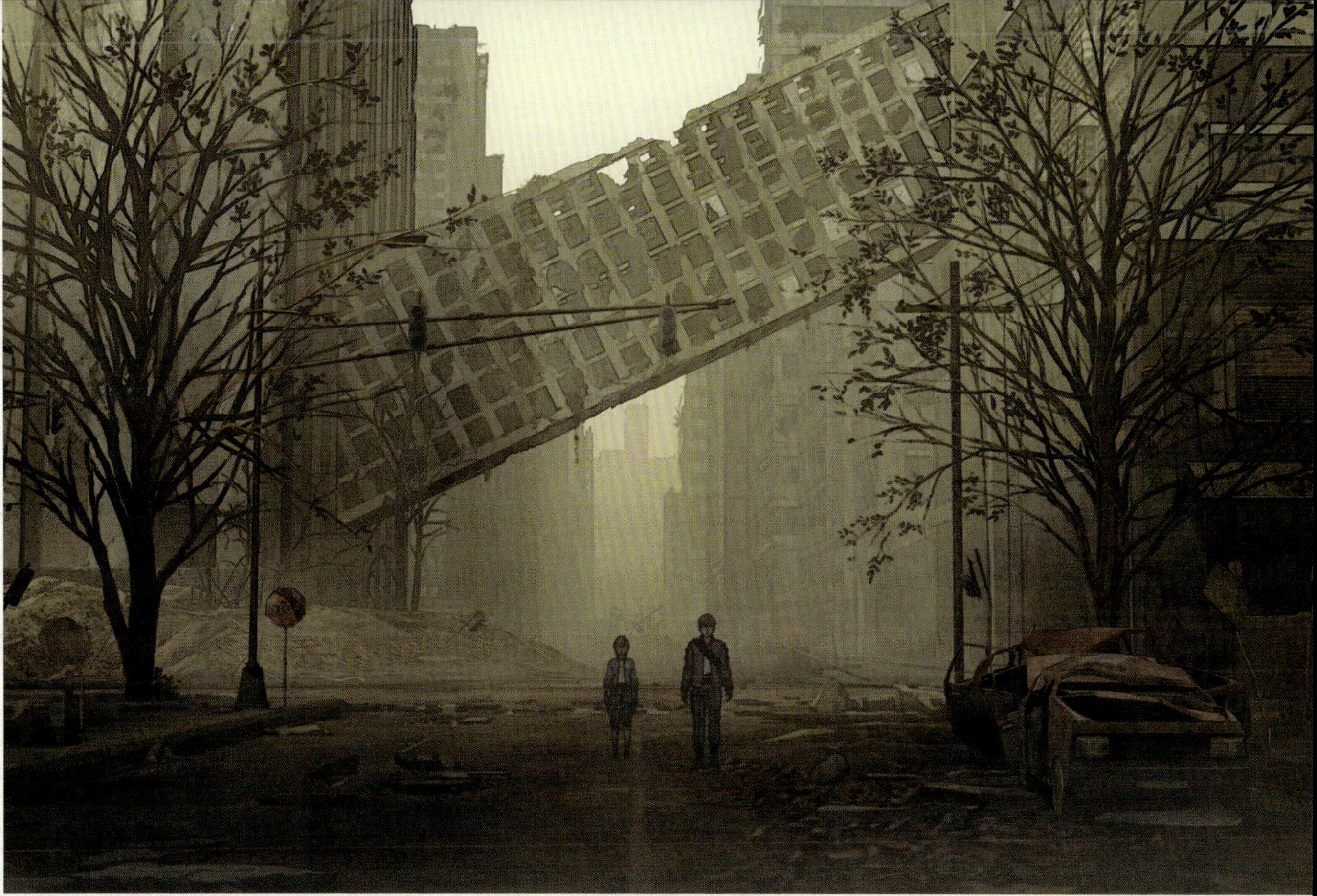

These pages // Five years after the fall of civilization, the children brave the sinister, monster-infested city of Meridian.

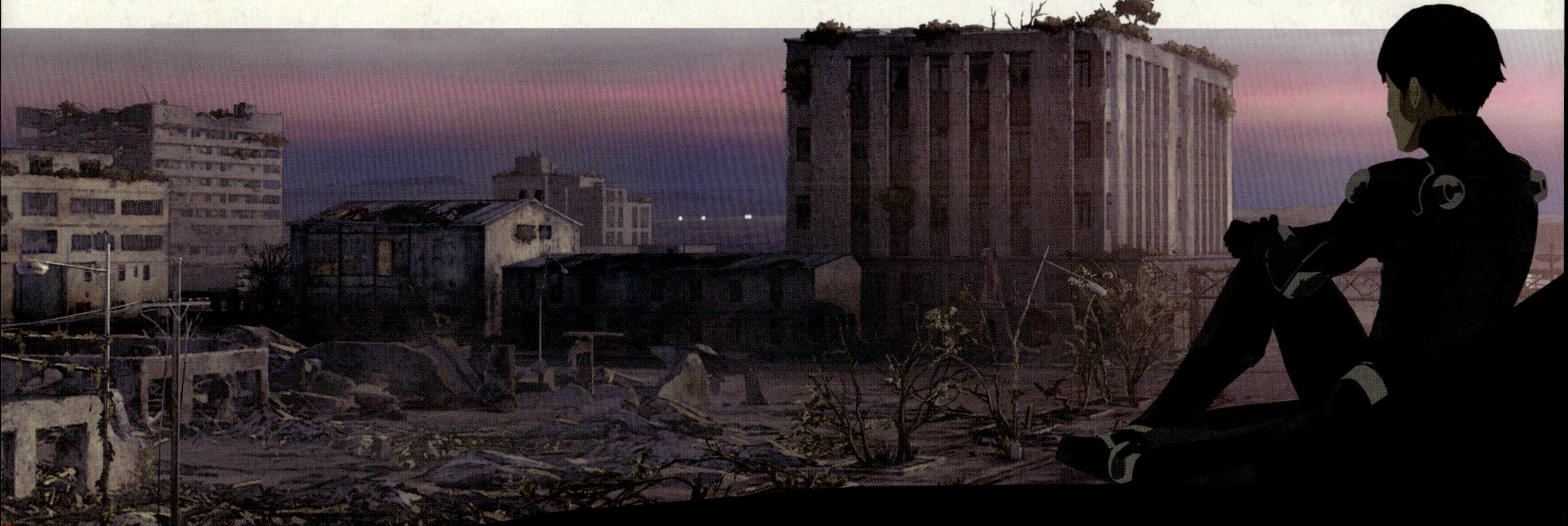

kids and enter the buildings. What animals are fast and scary enough to be a threat to kids? Surely these are Kaiju raptors! The Polygon team created a number of designs, and we picked one—slick, with an aerodynamic body shape. It looks like a dog, but what if a dog was mixed up with Kaiju blood? With no eyes, and two tentacles waving in the air (where the ears would be on a dog or wolf). We all thought it was a cool idea!"

As with Copperhead, the idea behind these Kaiju—dubbed Rippers in the series—is that a new generation has adapted to the Earth. Hiroyuki Hayashi remembers, "There was a series bible giving all the information about the world. The Precursors send these gigantic Kaiju, and part of their grand plan is not just destruction but assimilation. The difference in this series is there aren't just these huge Kaiju. There are Kaiju which have acclimated and adapted to Earth's environment, and mixed and hybridised and mimicked Earth life-forms.

"That's why the Rippers are similar to wolves, creatures that exist on Earth," Hayashi continues. "They aren't as gigantic, they don't have the terrifying, city-destroying power, but the hybrid Kaiju are still a terrifying threat. They fulfill a different role because they're more hunters and trackers."

The creatures nearly prove the death of Taylor and Hayley, chasing them through the city—though one Ripper is suddenly snatched out of the chase and devoured by a shadowy red-eyed giant. After Hayley saves Taylor from

"WHAT IF A DOG WAS MIXED WITH KAIJU BLOOD? WITH NO EYES AND TWO TENTACLES... WE THOUGHT IT WAS A COOL IDEA."
Jae-Hong Kim, director

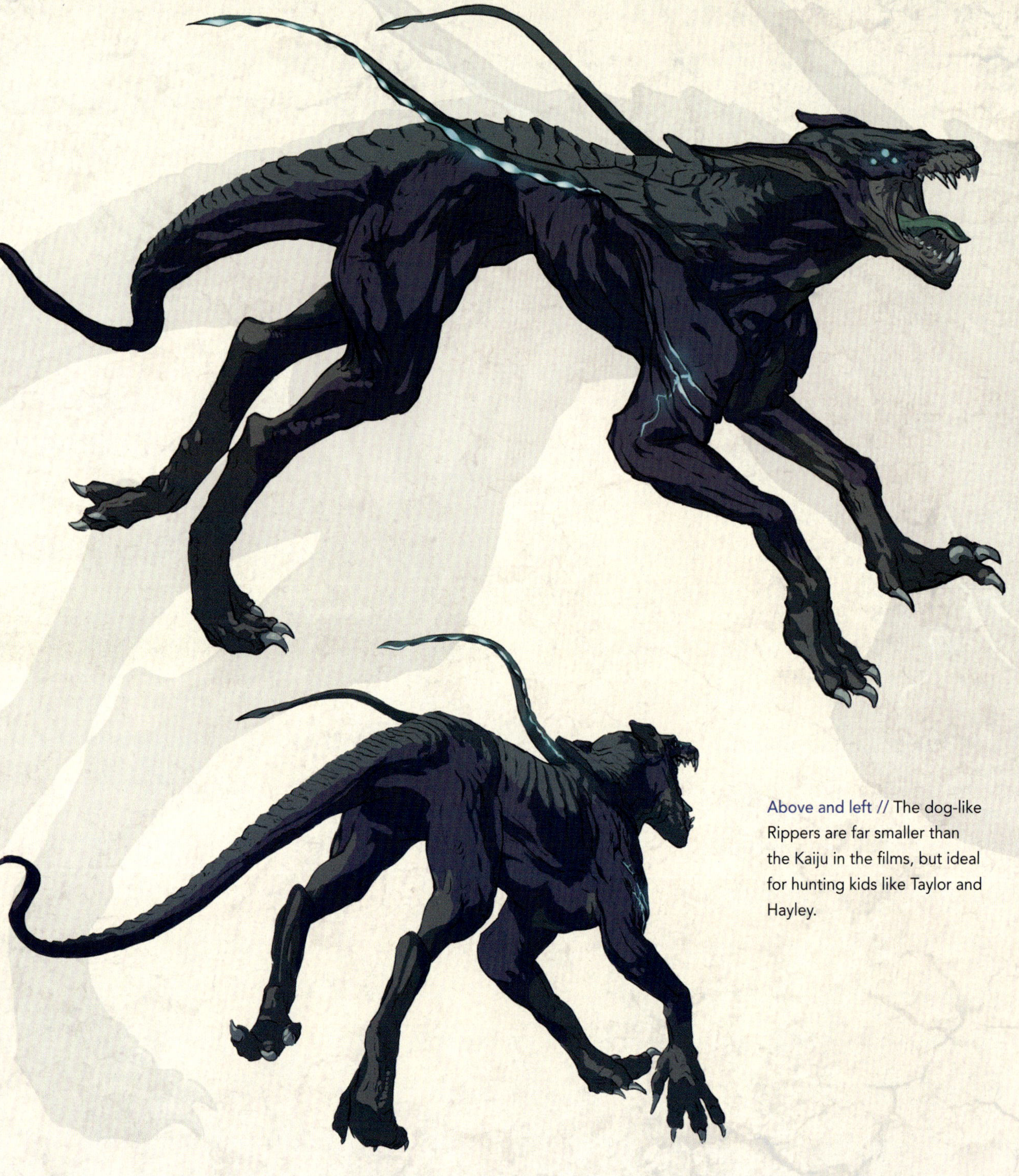

Above and left // The dog-like Rippers are far smaller than the Kaiju in the films, but ideal for hunting kids like Taylor and Hayley.

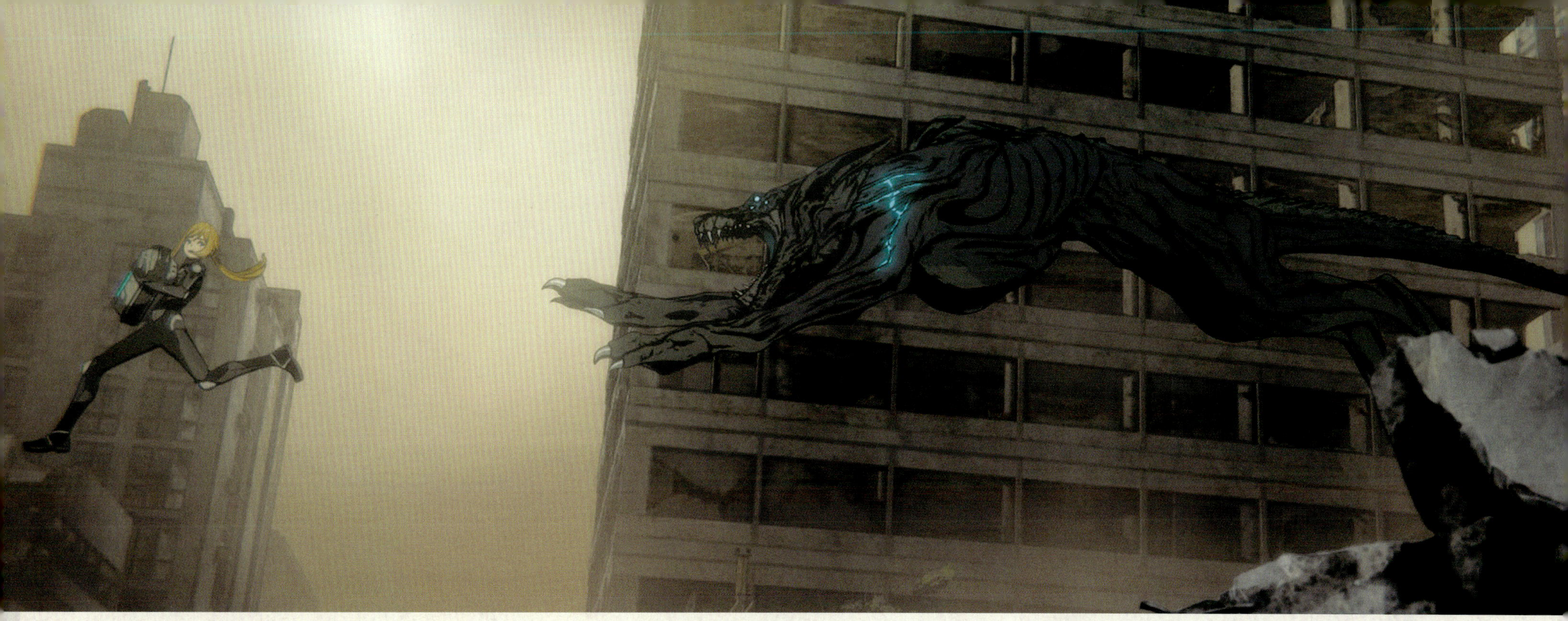

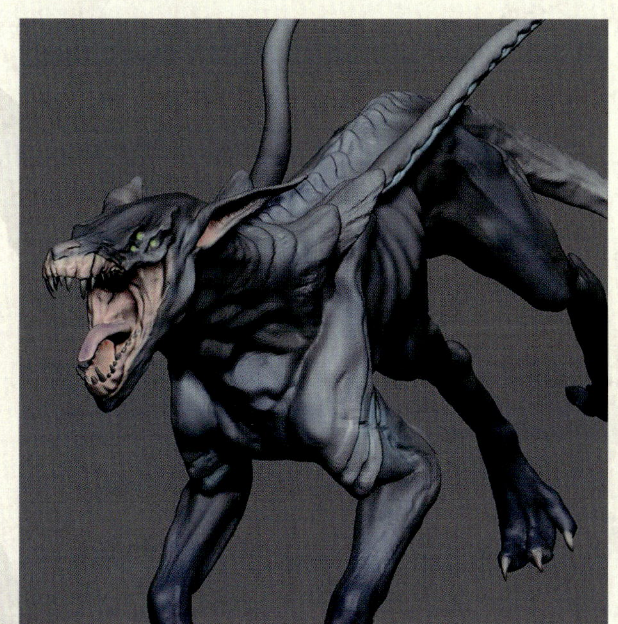

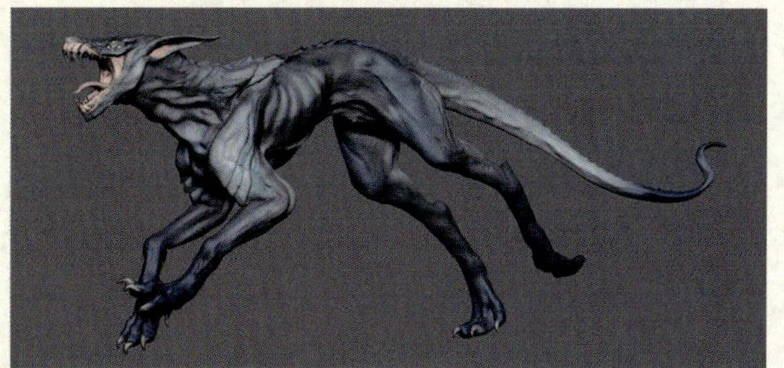

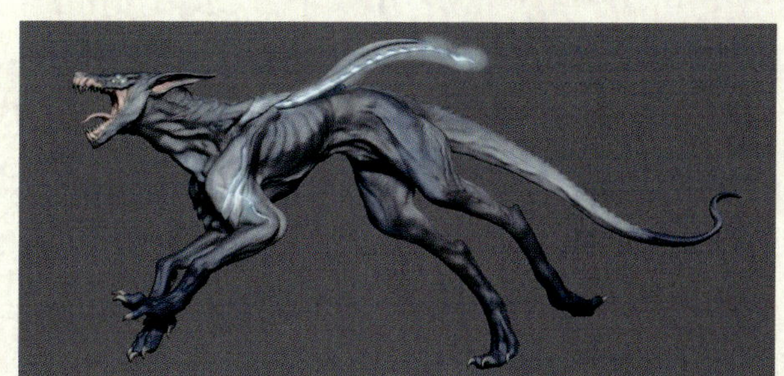

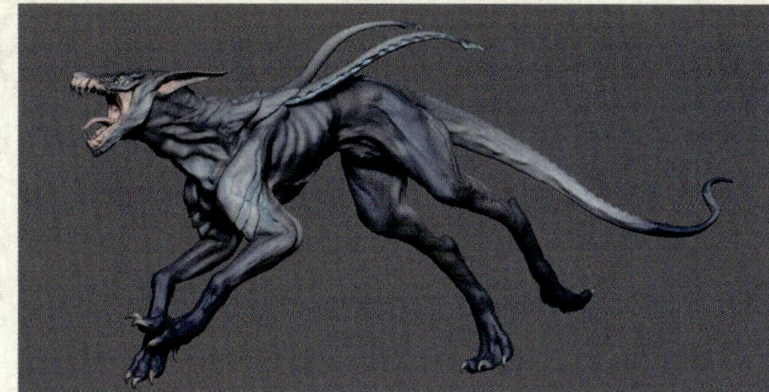

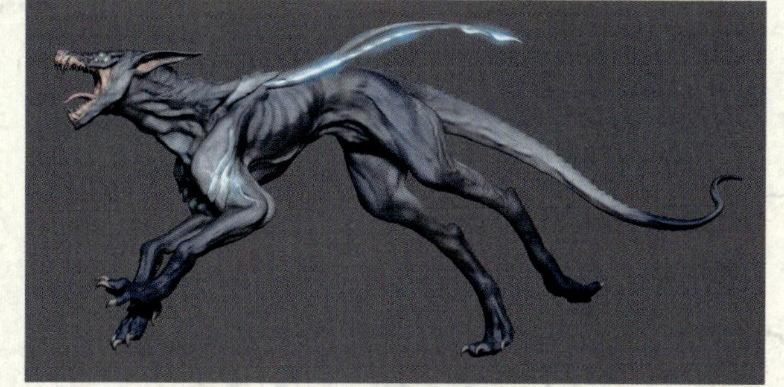

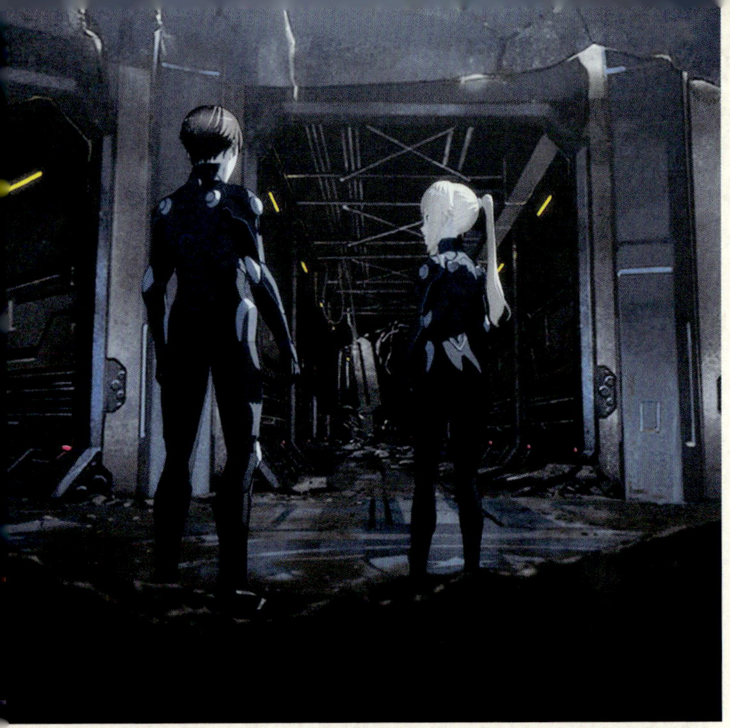

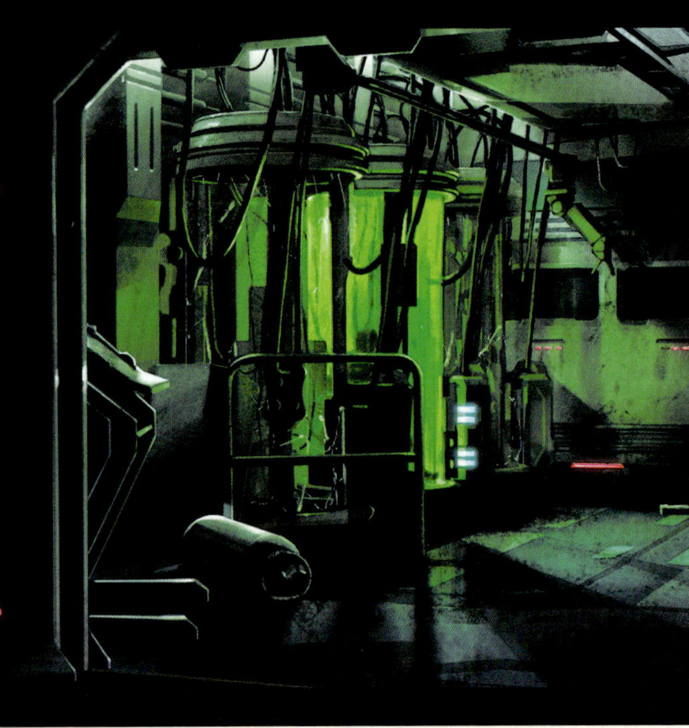

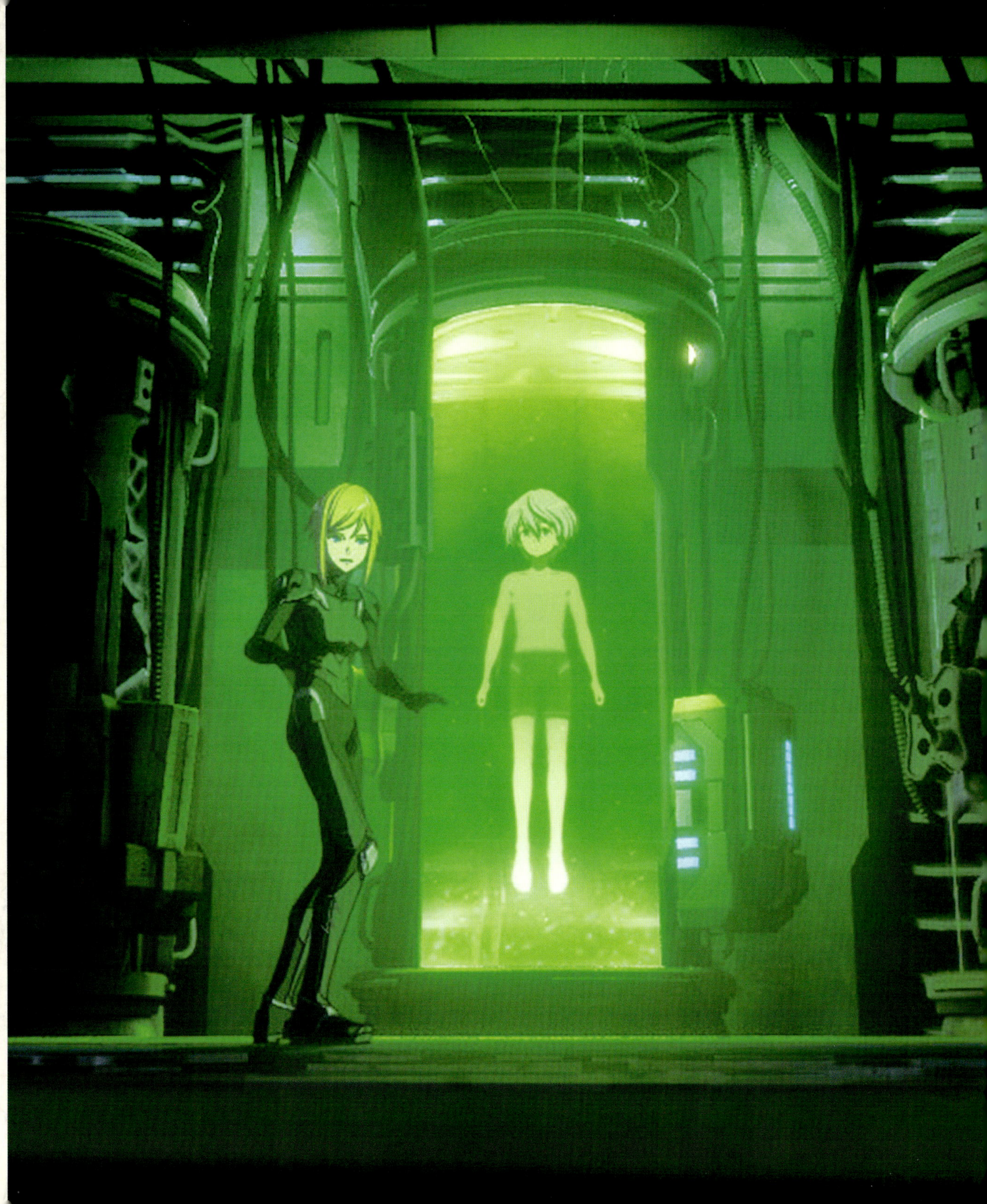

drowning, the siblings finally reach the PPDC Recruitment Centre. Descending into the lower levels to look for power cells, the teens split up, and Hayley comes across a huge transparent tank, glowing a lurid green. Inside the tank is… a little boy.

bOy, as he's officially named in the series, is plainly unearthly from his first appearance. He looks very young and cute, nearer Hayley than Taylor. (Appropriately, Hayley will become extremely protective of bOy.) Anime often has characters with multi-colored hairstyles, but bOy is the only character in *Pacific Rim: The Black* to have 'strange' hair, colored light blue.

"From the beginning, bOy was set as a mysterious one," says Jae-Hong Kim. "Our task was to create that mystery look for him. The color of his hair and eyes would be the only elements we could play with. Also, I wanted to create a very opposite image when he transforms. So it was important that we made him look vulnerable and pure."

Hiroyuki Hayashi says, "For the design of bOy; as you know after you've watched the show, he's like a human but he's not. All the other characters in the show are basically humans. We had normal hair colors, normal eye colors for them. But for bOy, we wanted to drop a hint that maybe he's not just a boy; maybe he's something more.

"So that's why we adjusted the hair color to something that a human normally wouldn't have," Hayashi continues. "And also with the details on the eyes, we tried to adjust them a little bit, to drop some hints to the audience that something might happen with this character." bOy's eyes look even wider than Hayley's, with strange moon crescents in their pupils. As with Loa, we sometimes glimpse the world through his eyes; he sees Hayley with an inner gold glow.

"FOR BOY, WE WANTED TO DROP A HINT THAT MAYBE HE'S NOT JUST A BOY, MAYBE HE'S SOMETHING MORE."
Hiroyuki Hayashi, director

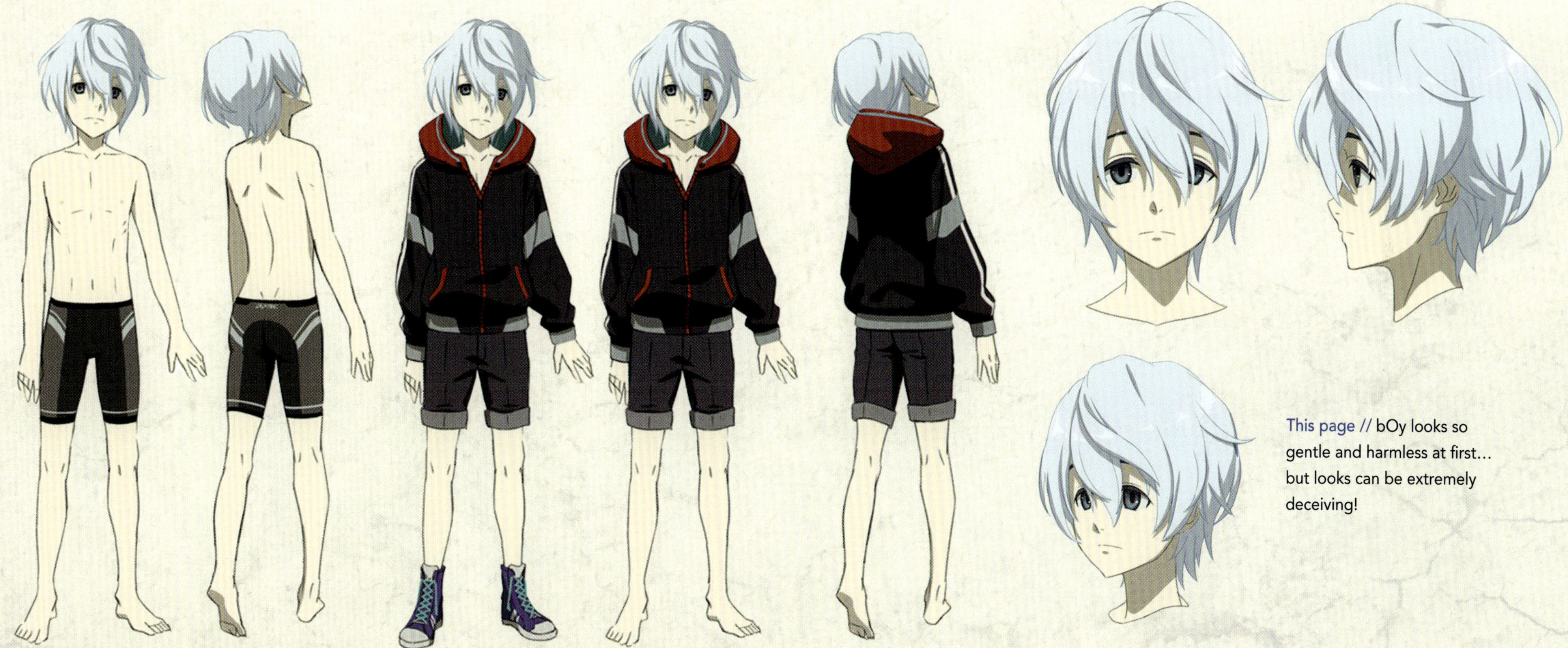

This page // bOy looks so gentle and harmless at first… but looks can be extremely deceiving!

Hayley insists she and Taylor can't leave the child to die, and she breaks him out of the tank. That alerts the remaining Rippers, who pursue the trio mercilessly. However, the giant figure from earlier returns and kills the Rippers before fading into the mist.

The exhausted kids reach the safety of Atlas Destroyer. They'd picked up a power cell in the PPDC building, but find that it's damaged and useless. Still, the siblings have bonded through their terrifying adventure. Hayley leans instinctively on her big brother's shoulder. bOy just sits, separate and silent...

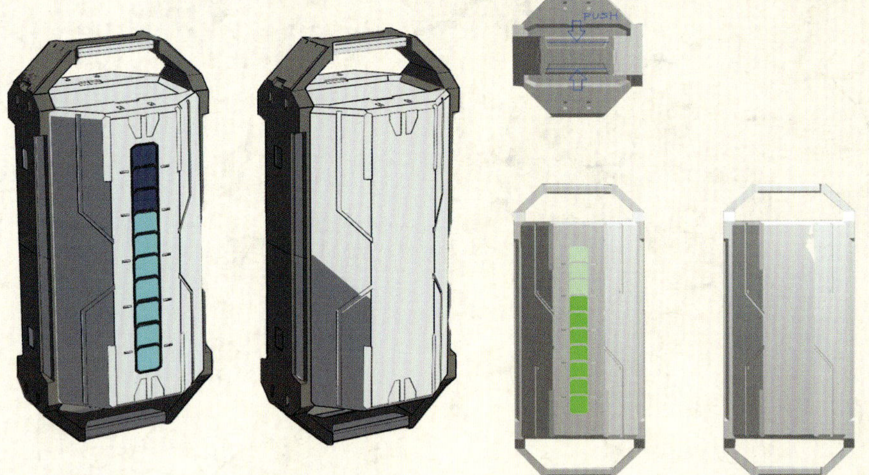

Right and below // The Jaeger's power cells will cause the characters a great deal of trouble.

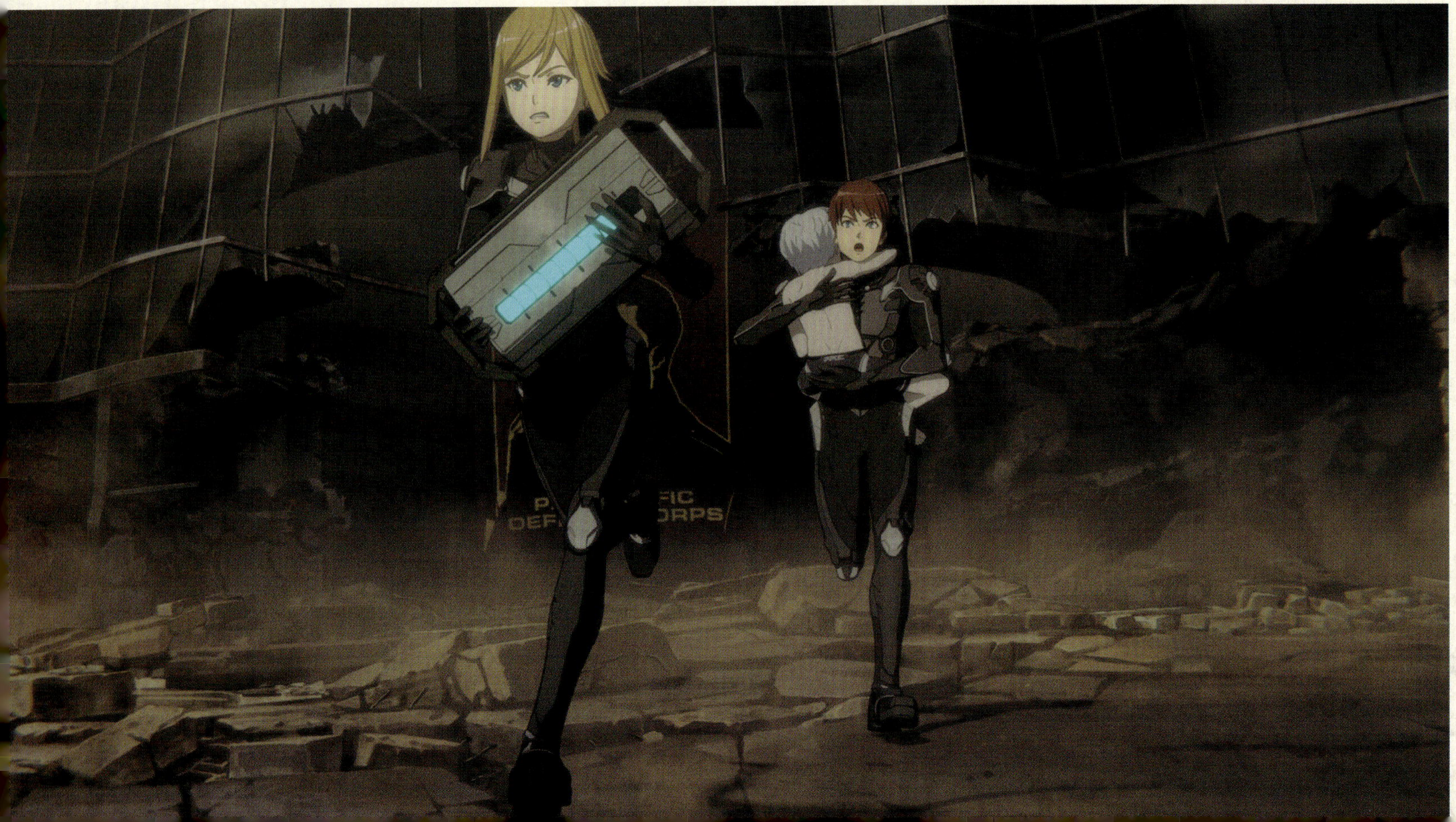

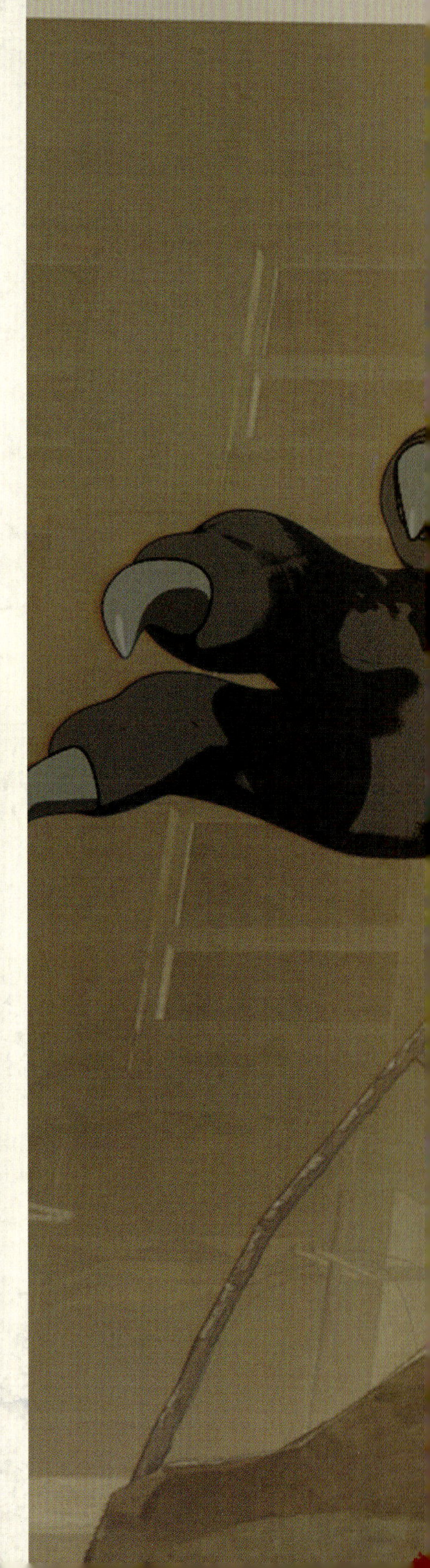

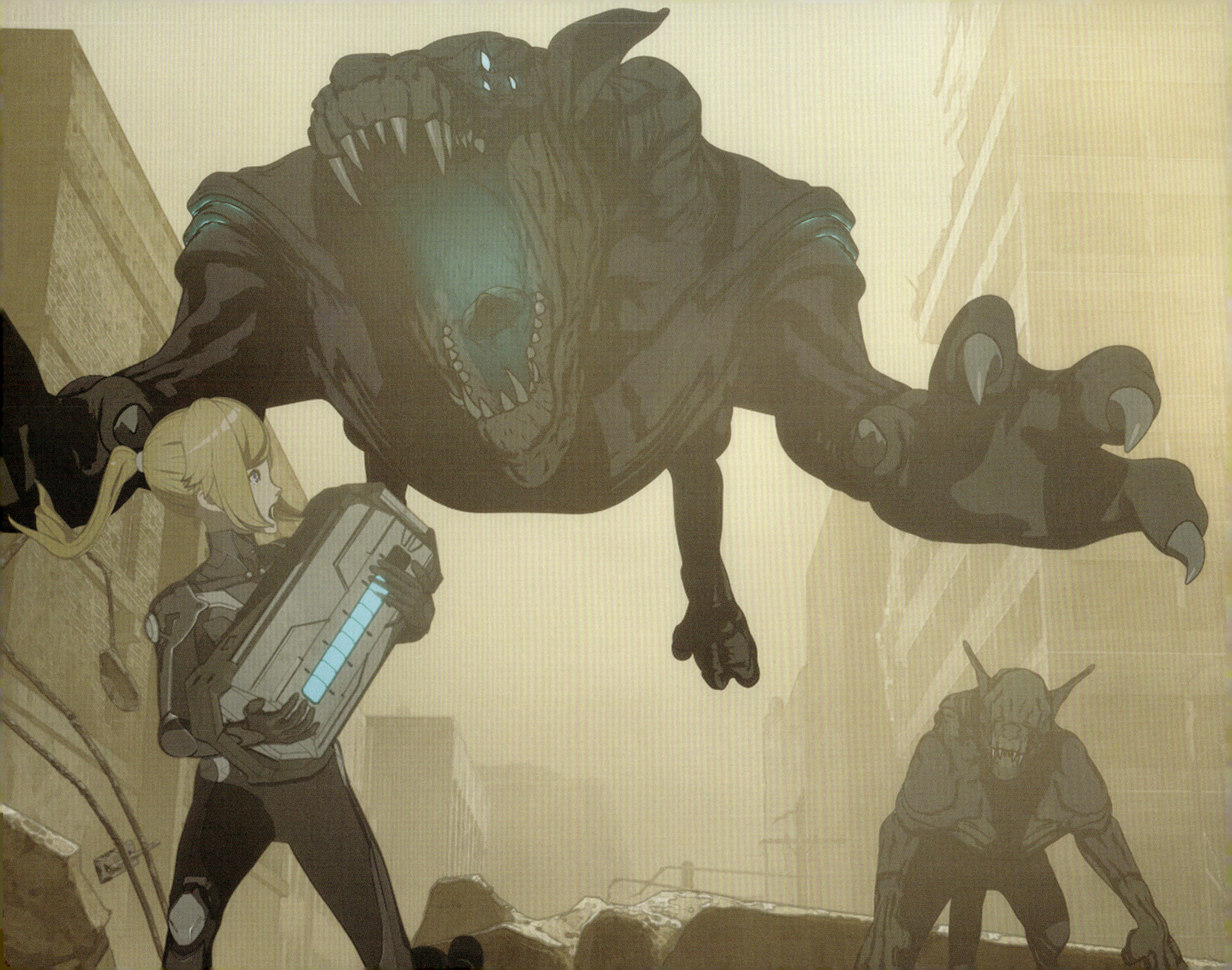

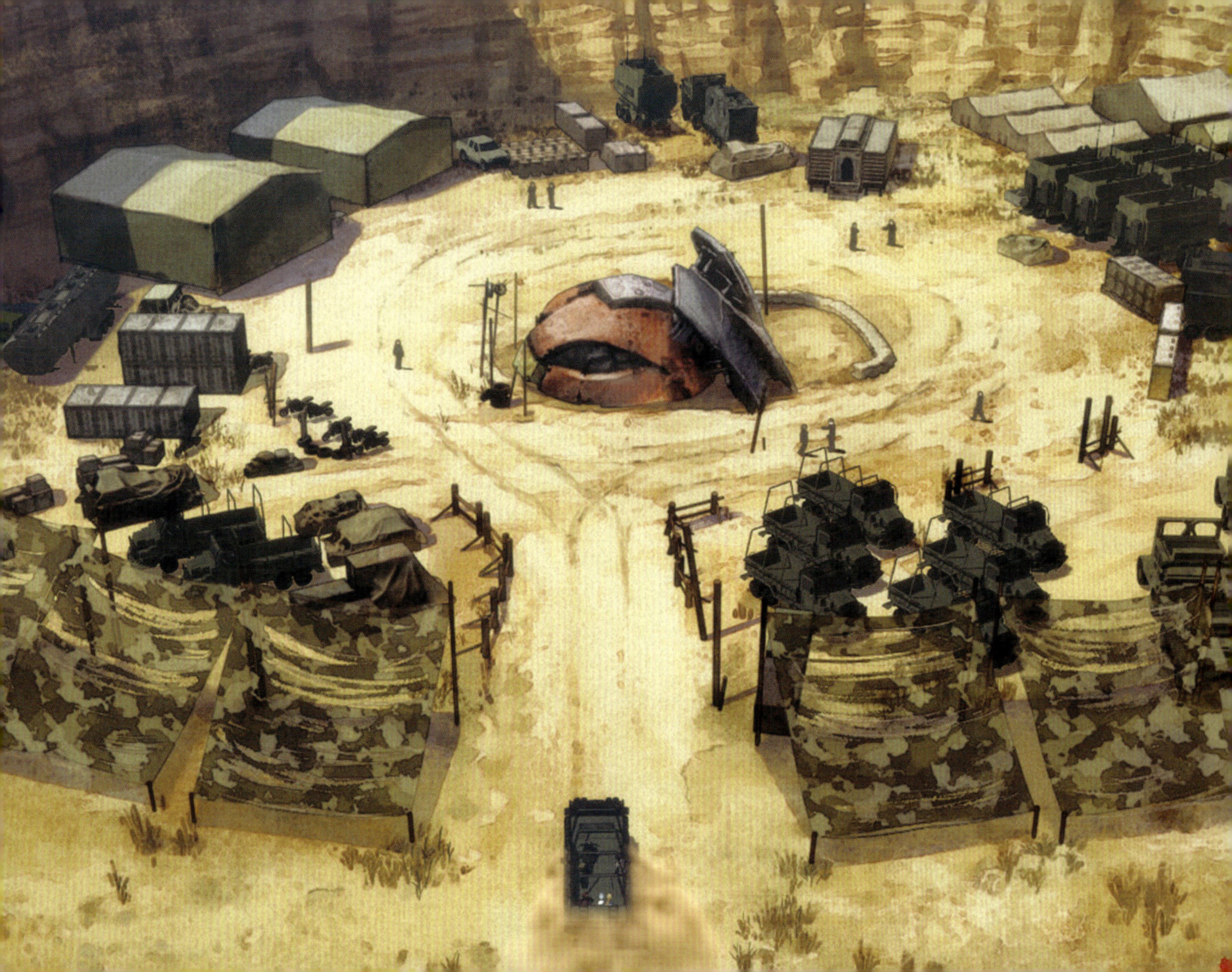

III

CHAPTER THREE
MONSTER HUNTERS

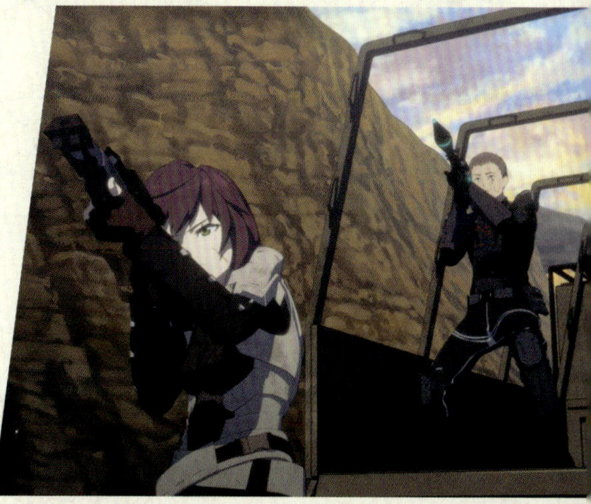

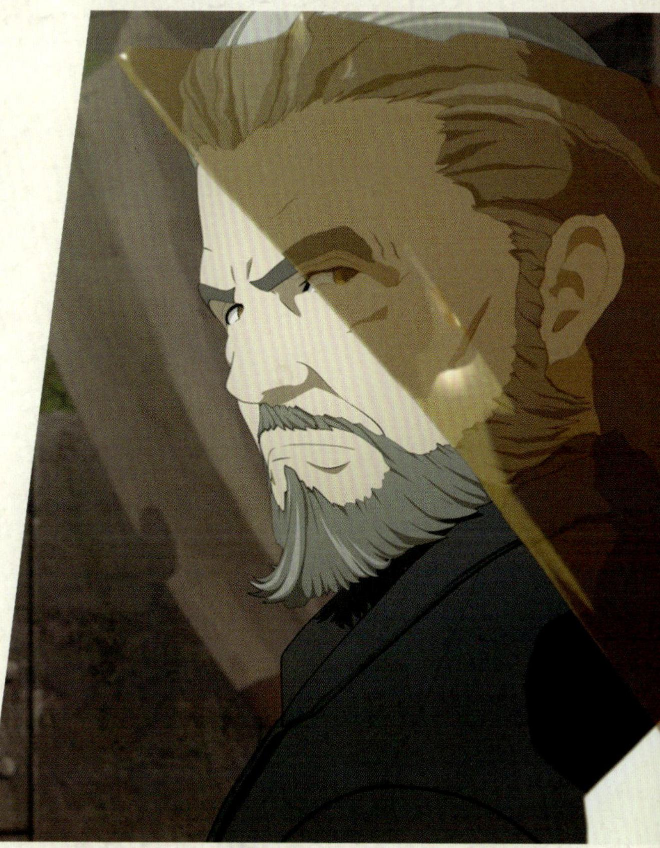

The third episode, "Bogan", starts with Taylor sitting on the immobilised Jaeger at sunrise when he sees an incredible sight—vehicles heading into the wilderness outside Meridian. Excitedly, Taylor calls Hayley and goes after them. As Loa's not programmed for babysitting, they must take bOy along too.

Cue the appearance of another new Kaiju. It's an aquatic monster that looks like a finned eel, swimming in a river. The people Taylor saw aren't out to fight it but to steal its eggs, which it lays on land. Once again, the children's actions will have unforeseen—and fatal—consequences.

Hayley and Taylor are watching from a distance when bOy sees the Kaiju Eel and runs towards it, oblivious to danger. The Eel scents him and turns towards land, where it spots the other intruders on its territory...

The Eel's horrible grinning head may remind film fans of the stop-motion dinosaurs in the original *King Kong*. "Greg Johnson and Craig Kyle wanted a Kaiju based on a water animal," says Jae-Hong Kim, "and they specifically pointed out an eel with short legs. It's not just about the swimming in the water. It looks like an eel, but it can crawl on the ground, and it lays eggs on the land. We thought 'Huh?' at the beginning, but I guess it turned out good at the end. Especially when the Eel slithers along the ground, that was a good scene!"

The Eel does indeed storm up on land, crunching up two egg thieves in its jaws. The other characters seem doomed as well, but the group's leader, an inhumanly fearless woman called Mei, fires a bazooka into the Eel's jaws, blowing its head off. Mei's underling, a scowling youth called Rickter, is all for killing the children too, but Mei overrules him. Curious about how on Earth these kids are here, Mei tempts them to come along and get some food at a "settlement".

After Shadow Basin and the ruined city, Episode Three takes the story into the desert. None of the series' staff had the chance to do location research on the ground. "The best way to do research would be to go to Australia, but we couldn't," acknowledges Jae-Hong Kim. "We used many photos from internet image searches; we searched a lot of visual references from movies for the desert scenery and the look of the show."

Kim continues, "I shouldn't forget about the medium I was using, which is anime, but at the same time I really wanted to capture the feel of the environment, the look, the color, the atmosphere of Australia. It's desert, but it's not just desert; there are a lot of different environments. The

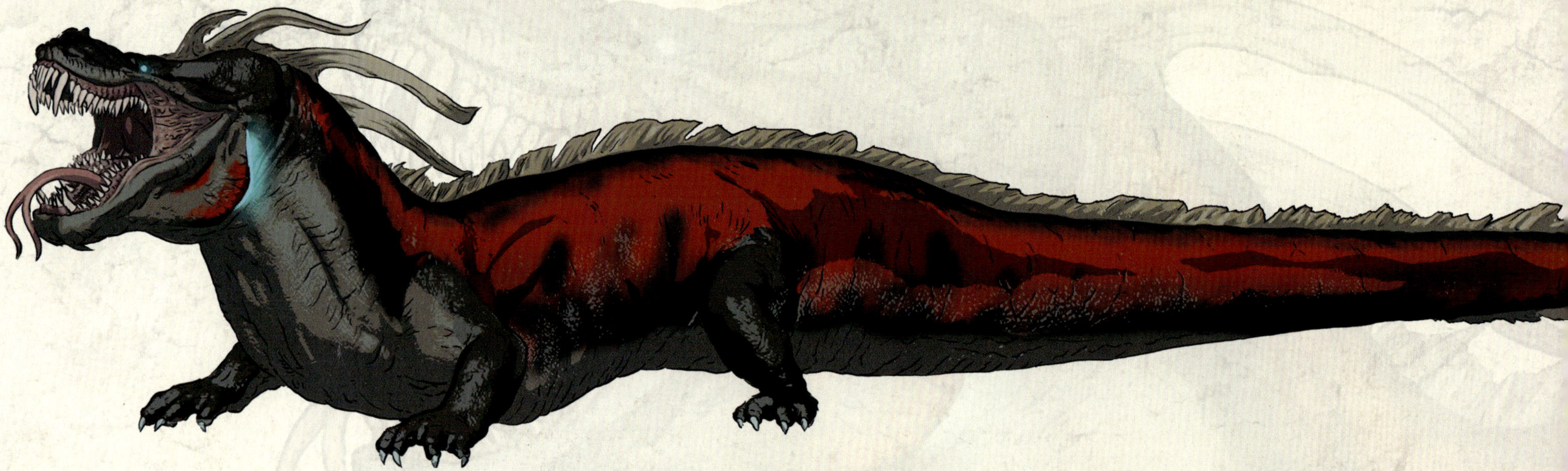

Above and below // The man-eating, egg-laying Eel Kaiju is a source of danger, but also of potential profit, to the people of Bogan.

Polygon staff and I did a lot of research and came up with many different versions of the look of the desert. It was a hard but fun process."

Art director Yuki Moriyama notes, "Because this series is set in the future, and it's centred on a destroyed landscape with big cities, we actually used Las Vegas as one of our big reference points, the desert areas round Las Vegas."

Jae-Hong Kim confirms that the inclusion of images of overbuilt vehicles rushing through the desert was deliberate. "We wanted to create the world after the apocalypse, on a continent of roaring monsters! The technology should not be too high-tech, but slightly more advanced than it is now."

Later in the episode, a character arrives in an outrageously overbuilt white limousine, with huge hydraulic wheels. "Polygon came up with the limousine idea, and we thought it was funny and silly!" says Kim. "But it fit very well."

The limousine is part of the story's worldbuilding. The ungainly-looking vehicle is shown towing cannibalised Jaeger parts, and it uses cannibalised parts itself, plainly

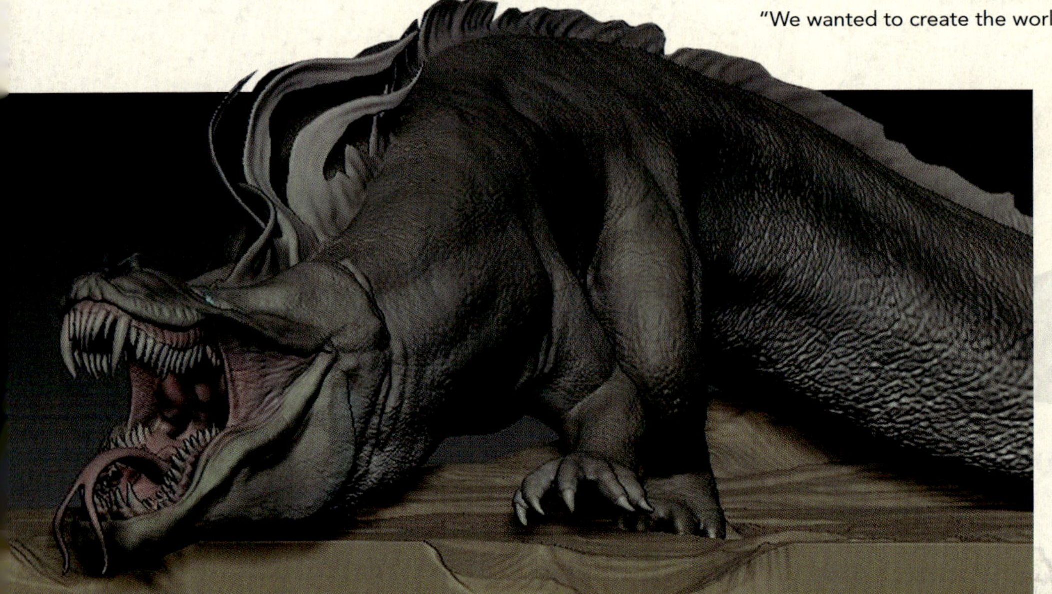

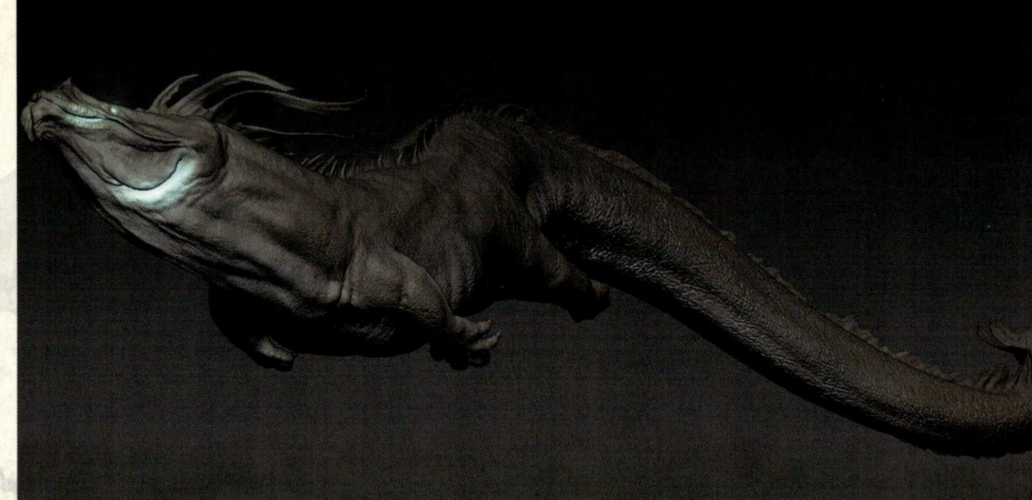

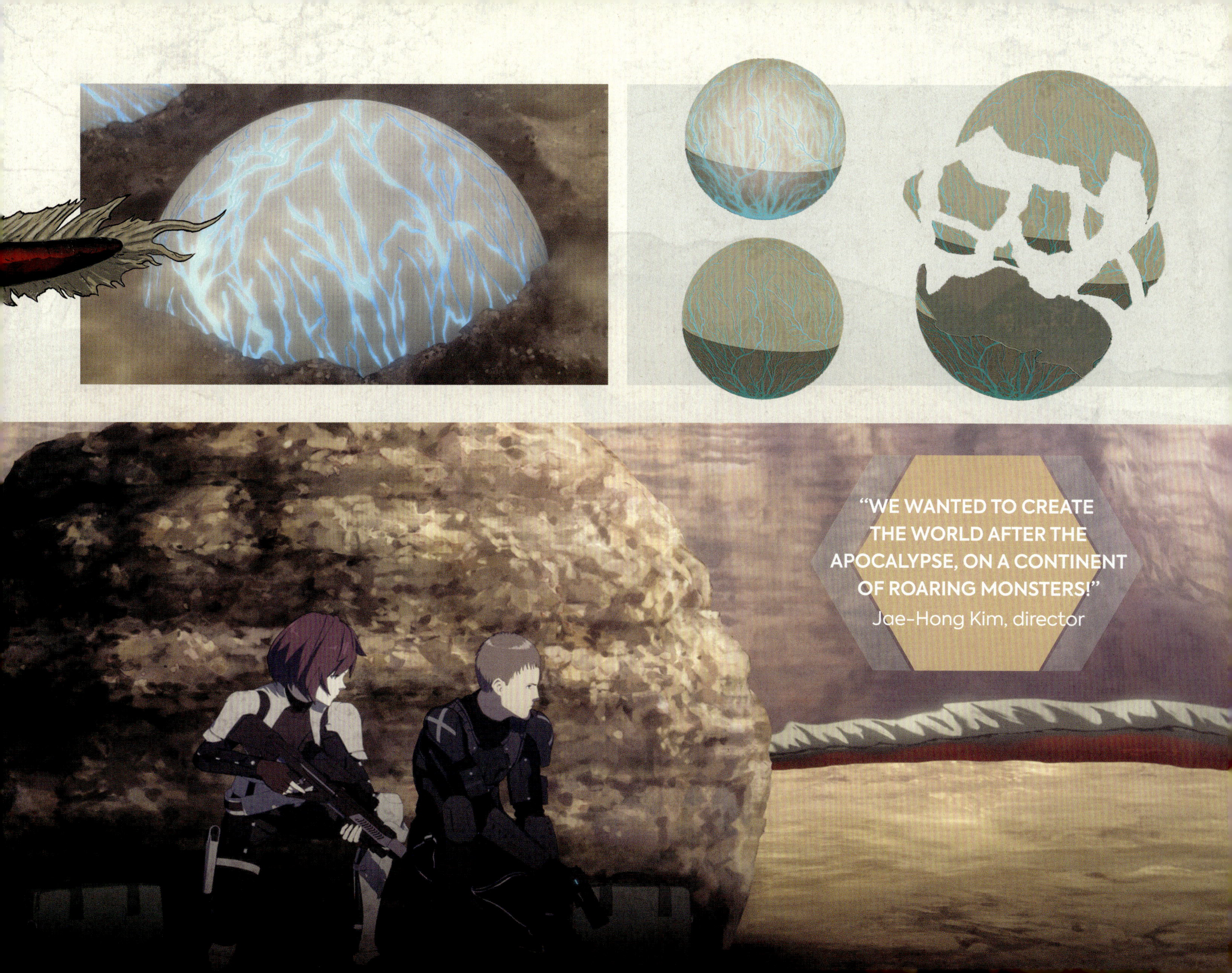
"WE WANTED TO CREATE
THE WORLD AFTER THE
APOCALYPSE, ON A CONTINENT
OF ROARING MONSTERS!"
Jae-Hong Kim, director

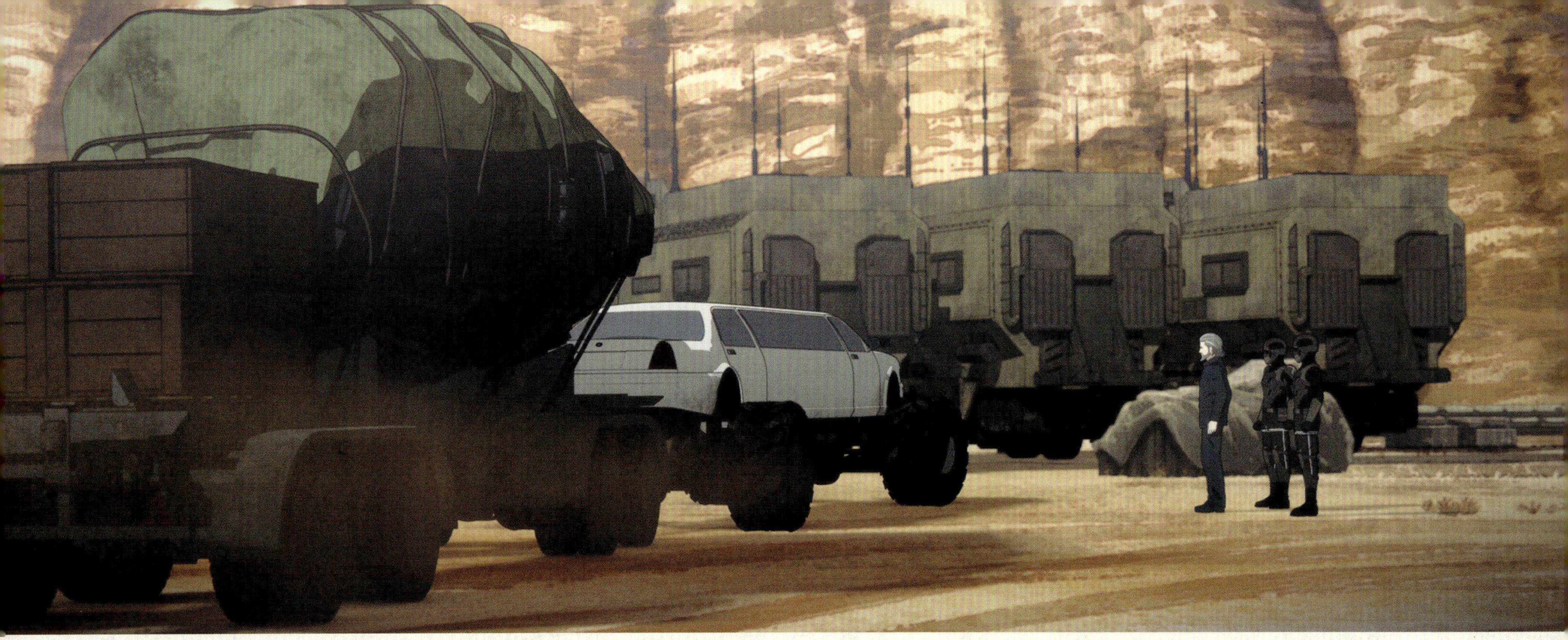

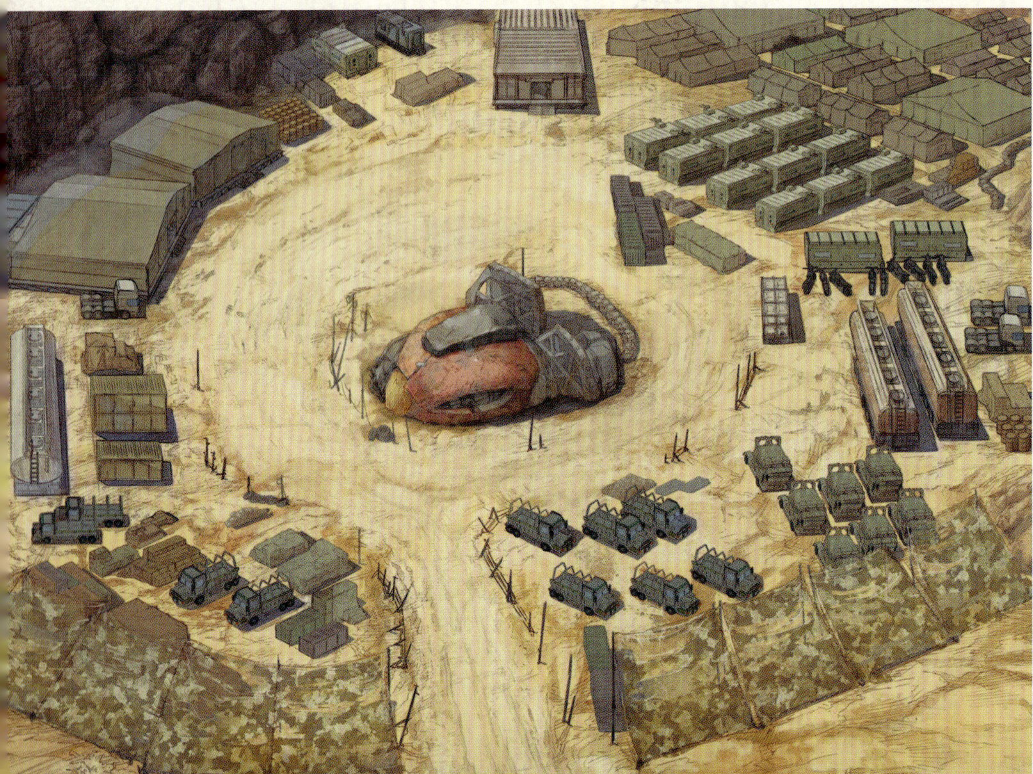

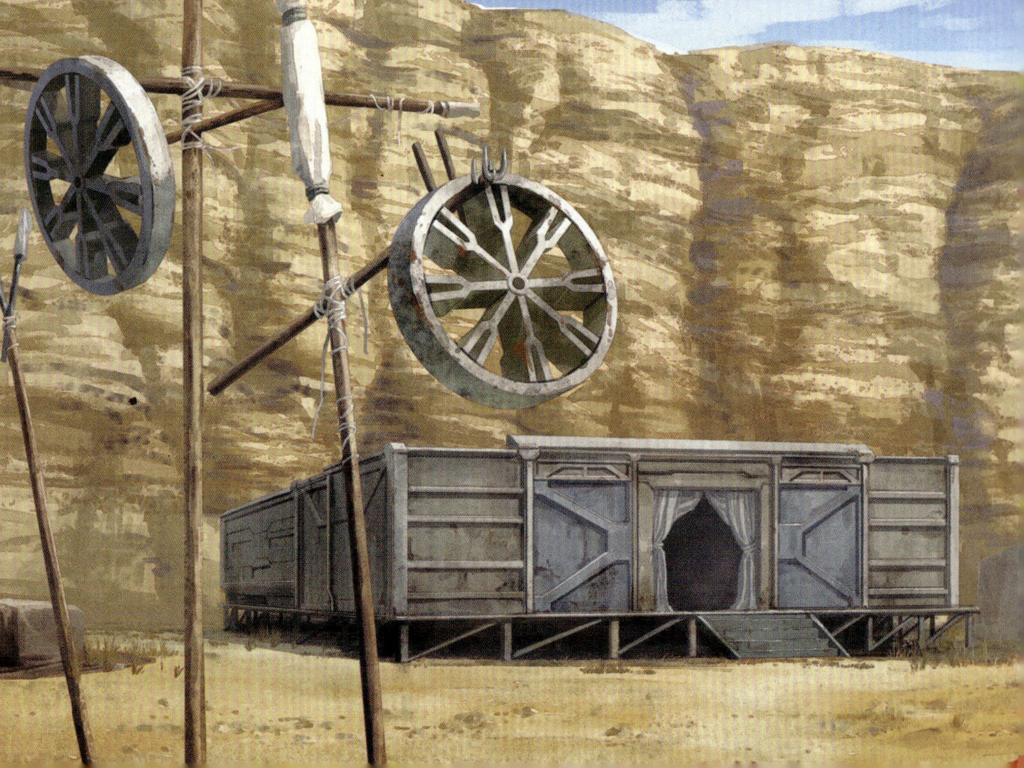

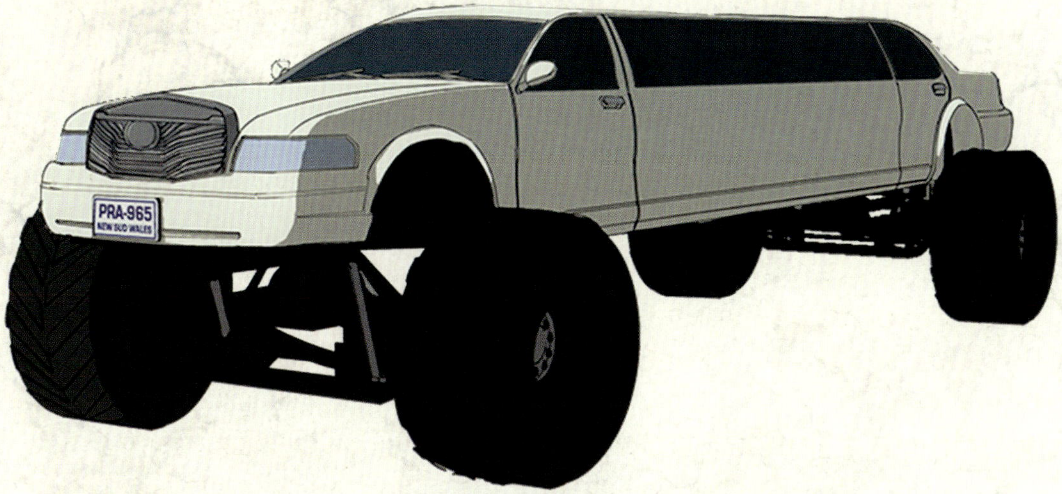

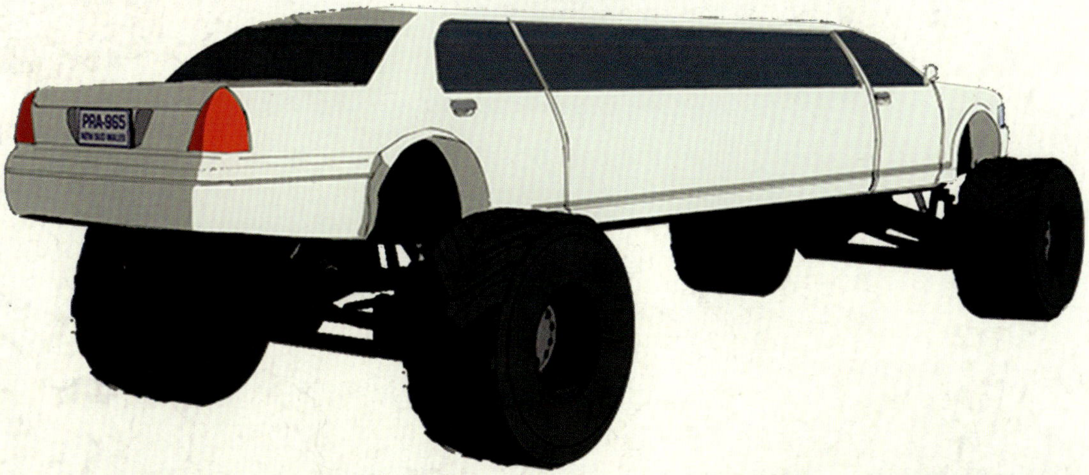

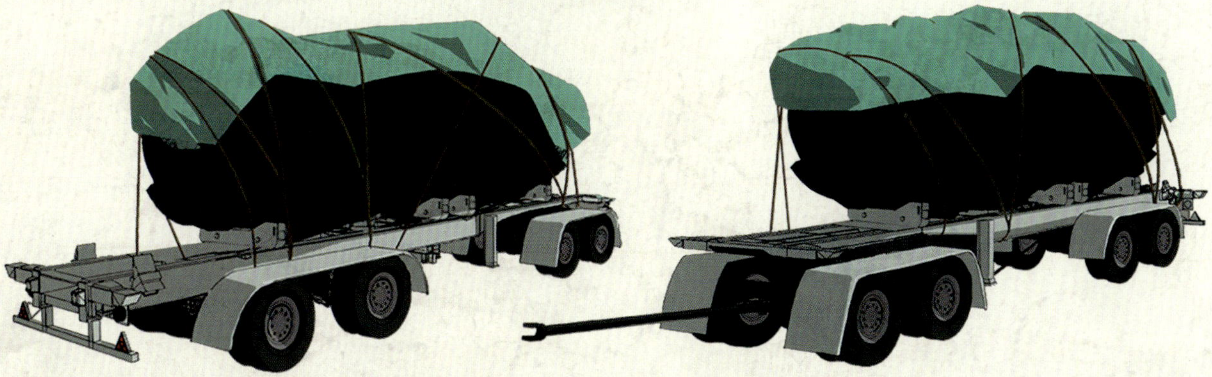

scrounged from PPDC vehicles. Greg Johnson points out that after five years in the outback, what would become of the machinery and technology used to fight the Kaiju, all the hardware left behind by the army? "It would be pieced out, adapted, and used in ways never intended," Johnson says.

Mei and Rickter's home base is named Bogan. The word is Australian slang for someone who's seen as being rough and unsophisticated; it can be used as an insult, or as a self-identifying badge of honor. Bogan's leader, and Mei's superior, is an older man called Shane, who greets the youngsters as they arrive. Arguably, Shane is the true main enemy in the first season, even more monstrous than the giant Copperhead.

At the same time, he looks cool and strong, even if he's much older than most characters in animated series. With his grey hair streaked with white, Shane looks like an old lion. "My main focus for Shane was subtlety," says Kim. "He is a leader who doesn't express his feelings and thoughts.

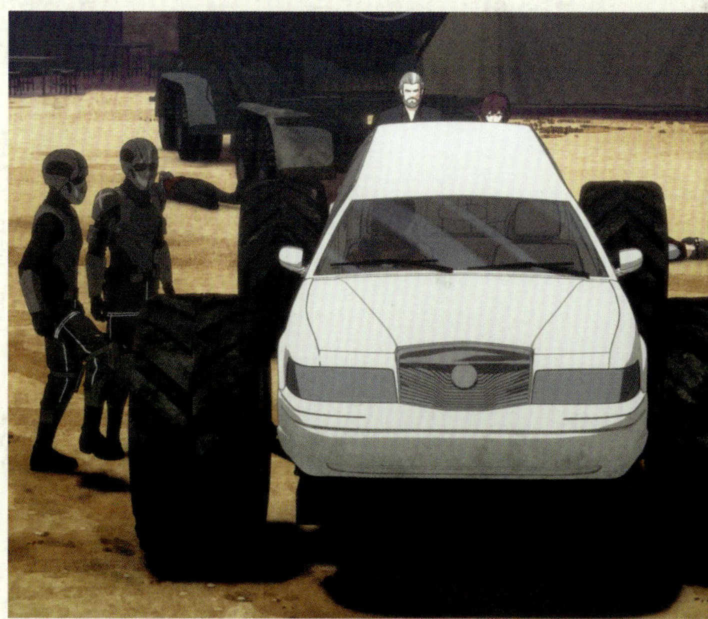

Above // The overbuilt limousine is 'funny and silly,' but also suggests how hardware is cannibalized in this world.

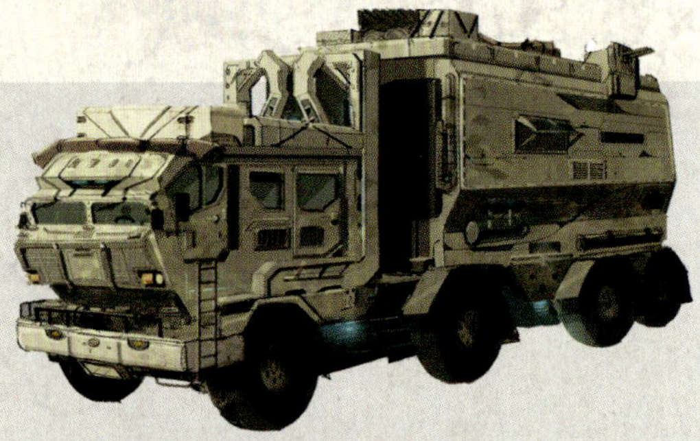

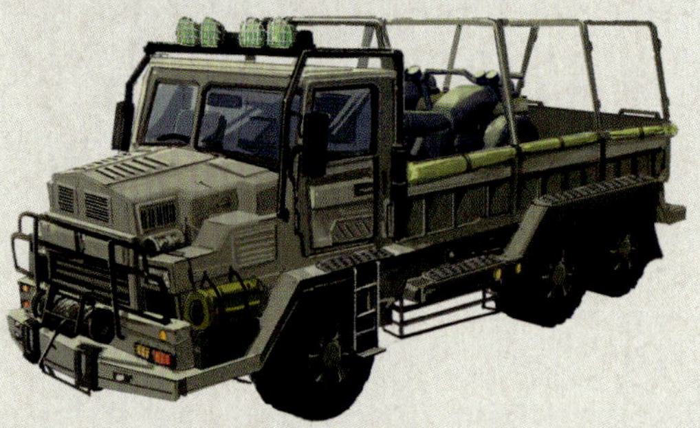

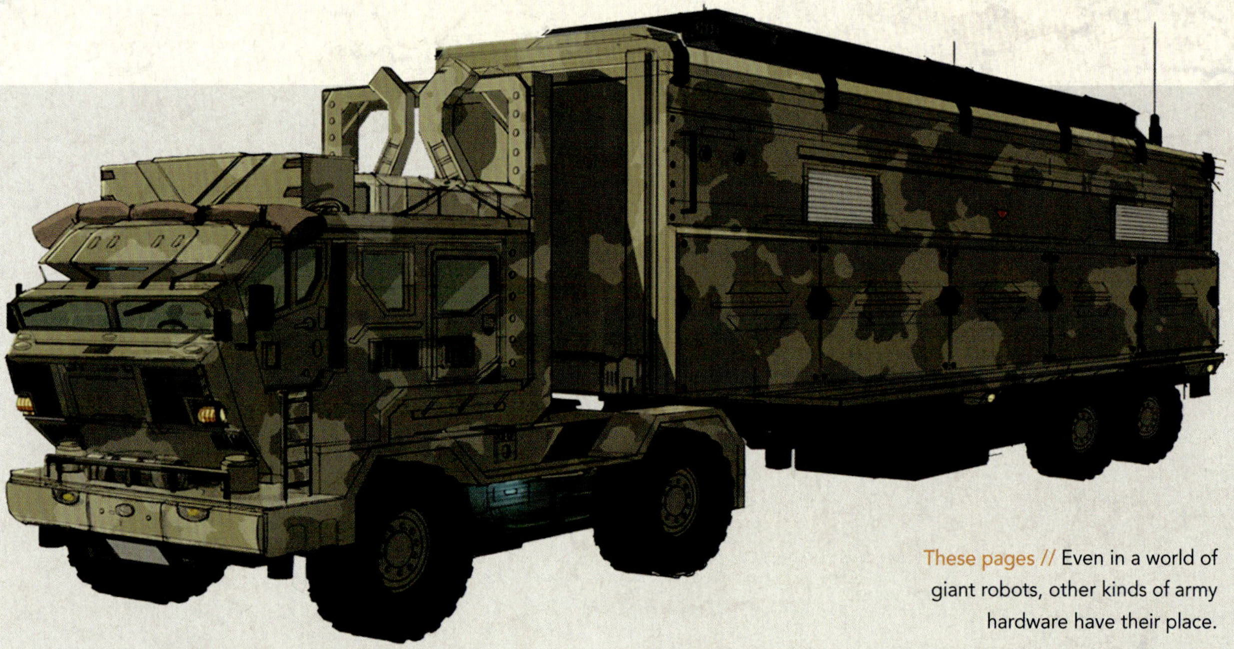

These pages // Even in a world of giant robots, other kinds of army hardware have their place.

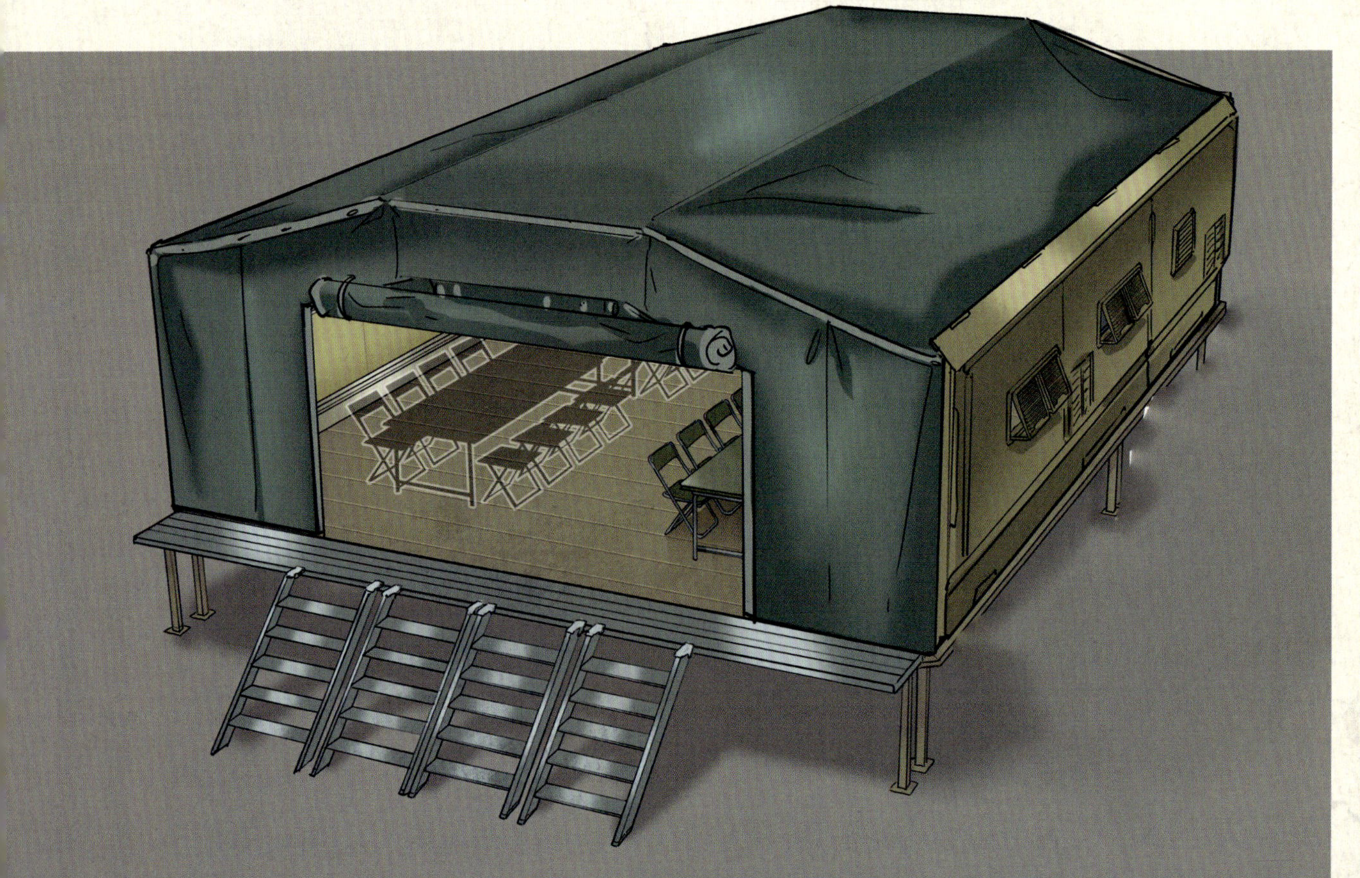

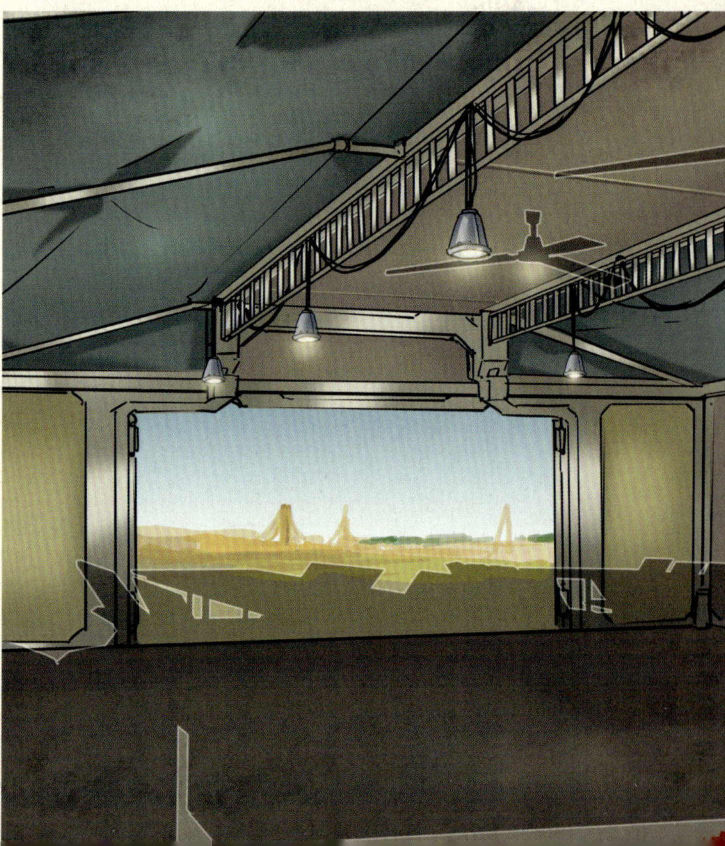

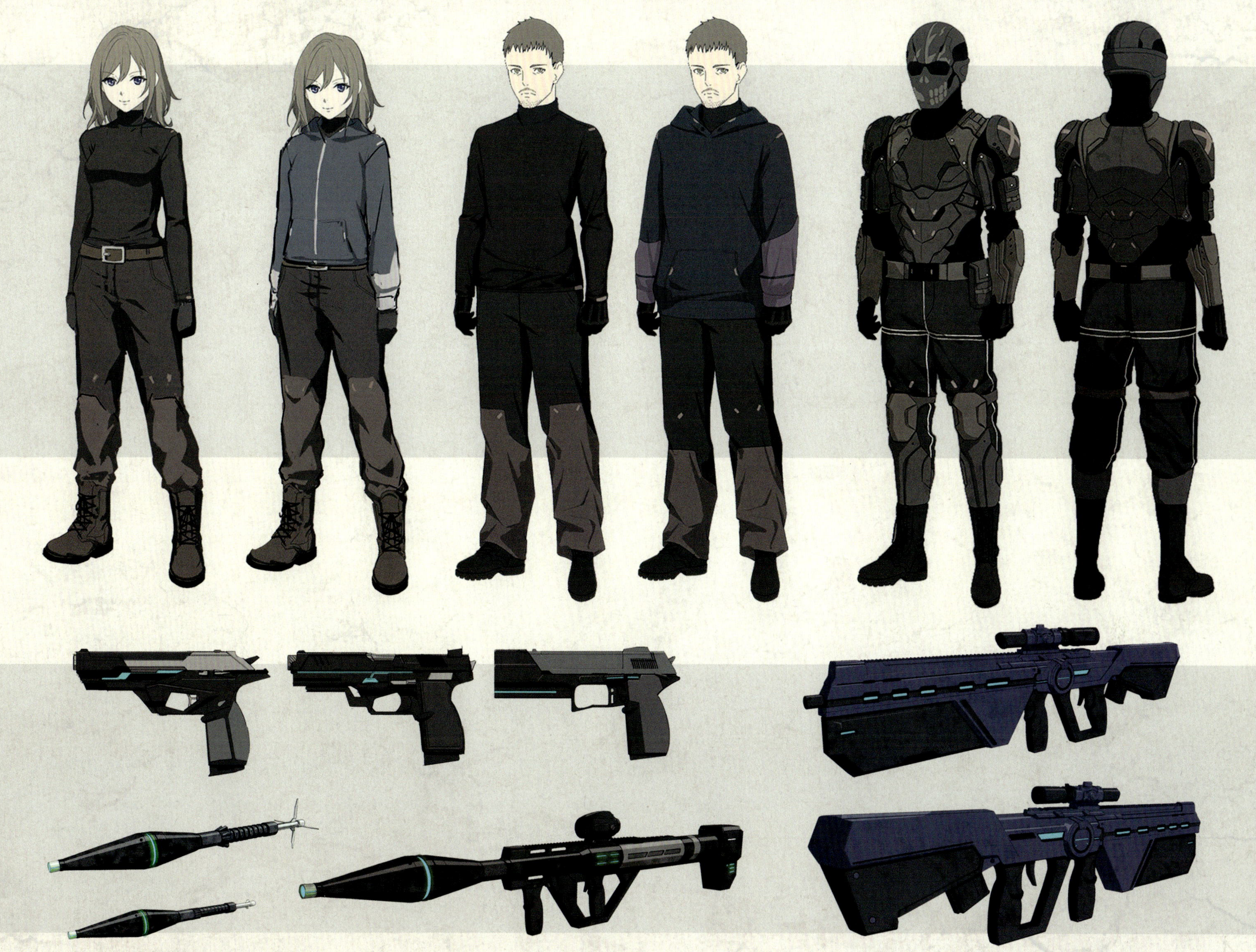

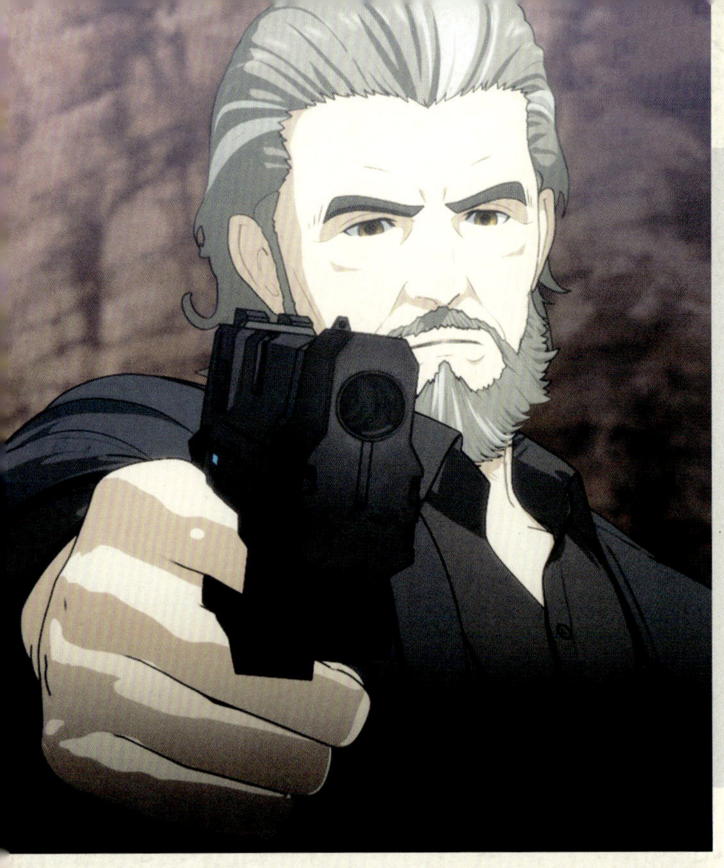

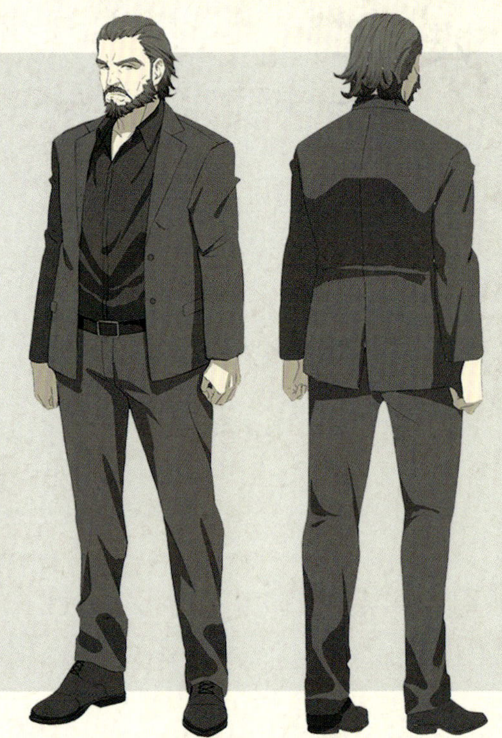

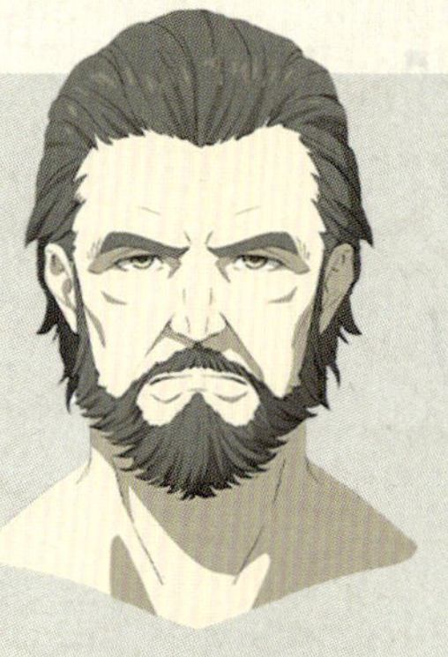

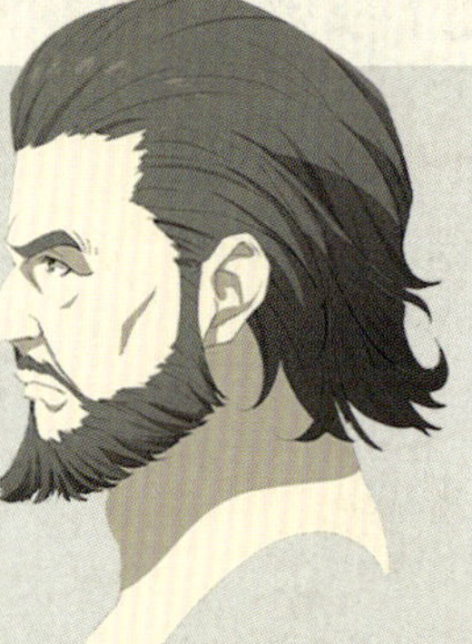

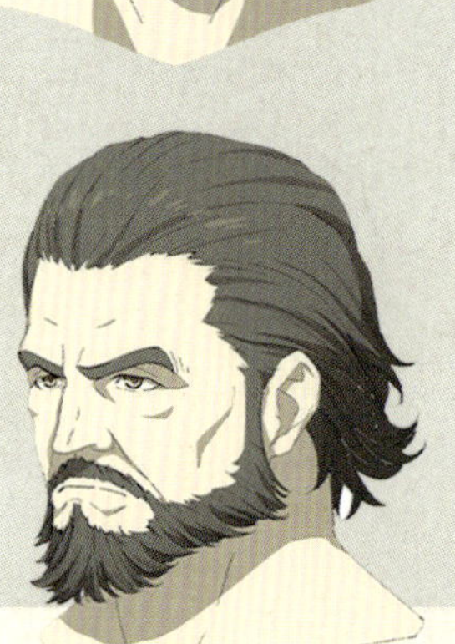

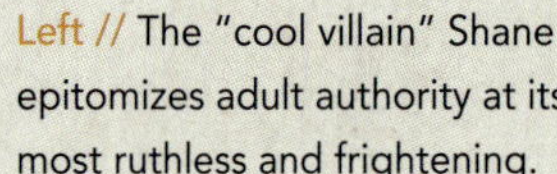

Left // The "cool villain" Shane epitomizes adult authority at its most ruthless and frightening.

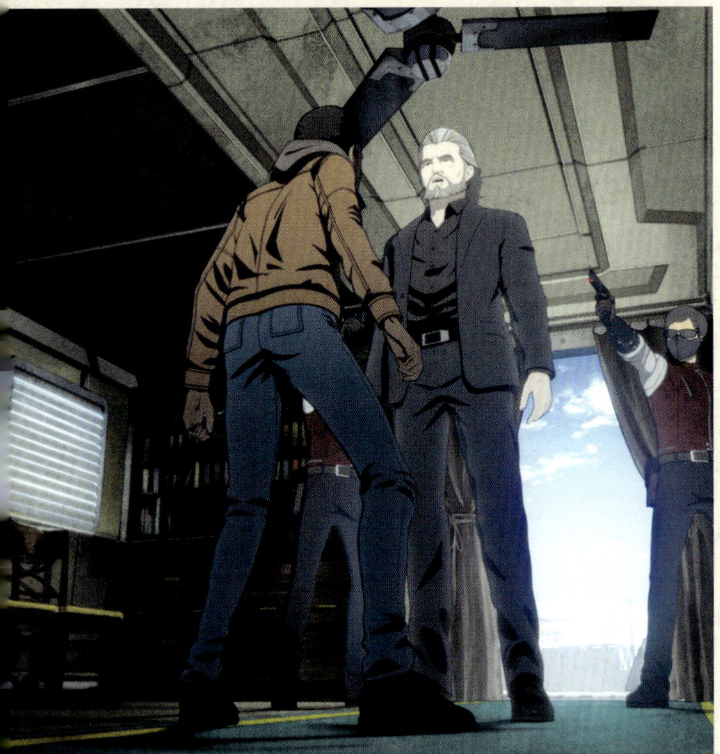

He's a man behind a mask. I knew how his animation needed to be handled from the beginning, and I couldn't wait to see him come alive! I had so many notes for his acting and expressions."

Hiroyuki Hayashi says of Shane, "He's the main adult in the show, and I think that cuts to the core of his role. He's an enemy; he's a stern adult figure who is also the biggest obstacle to the main characters, who are teenagers trying to grow up and expand and move on, quite literally, from their childhood. He's stronger than them, he has more resources, he's smarter, so they're faced with this huge obstacle of this older person trying to keep this younger generation down. Which is something we can maybe say about today's society as well."

Hayashi continues, "Part of the drama is how these kids have to overcome this person, who has an organisation and all these resources they don't, but they still fight against him. He is a villain, but he's also a kind of cool character, he's like a level above every other character in the show."

Yuki Moriyama adds, "Going back to the fact Shane is this archetypal big bad adult figure, that played into his design as well. In a certain way, Taylor and Hayley and the other young characters are looking up at him; he's above them in a lot of ways, in age and status and power.

"But it's not like a comforting kind of 'looking up'," Moriyama continues. "He's not a father figure that you would look up to. You look up there and it's scary. Little details in his design, like the bags under his eyes are constantly dark, and the way his face and his eyes are designed. Even if Shane's just looking neutrally down at Taylor, for example, it looks like he's glaring because he's just got that etched into his face."

Shane reflects the series' wider themes, explains Johnson. "In building the world within The Black"—Shane and other characters use the name to refer to post-blackout Australia—"it would be naive to believe the Kaiju would remain the only threat, and that all of the stranded humans would still have only one goal: defeating that threat. Once

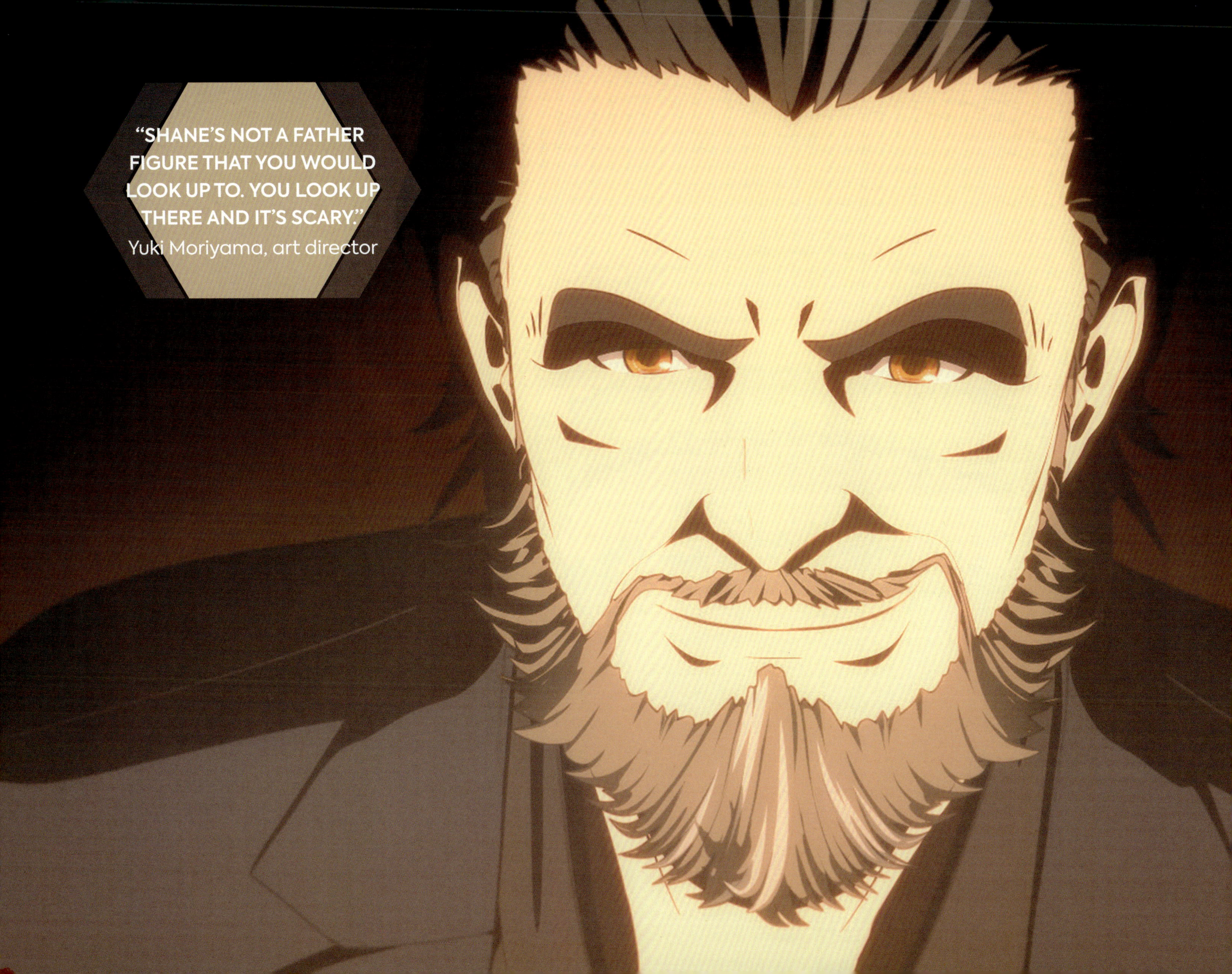

> "SHANE'S NOT A FATHER FIGURE THAT YOU WOULD LOOK UP TO. YOU LOOK UP THERE AND IT'S SCARY."
>
> Yuki Moriyama, art director

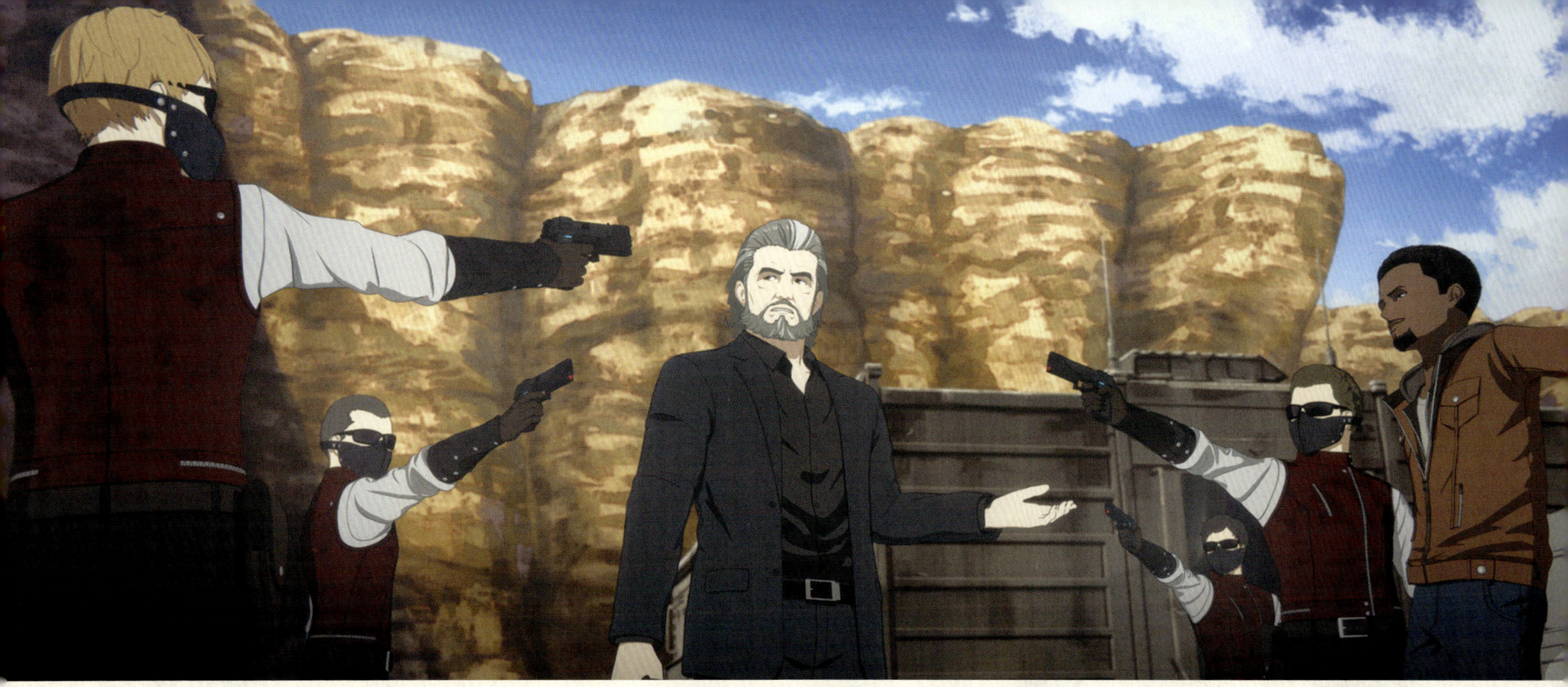

survival becomes the objective, such an approach can take many forms. Like Shane, who becomes a dominant force by gathering together those who have something to offer the collective. Years of life-and-death stakes then forge a new code of conduct, until you become as dangerous as the giant monsters."

After the seemingly benign Shane greets the children, they see him negotiate with emissaries from a different group (one arrives in the overbuilt limousine). Shane trades the Eel eggs for Jaeger power cells—exactly what the children are seeking! The meeting turns tense, and the kids try to sneak away—only to be stopped by Rickter, who makes it clear they're prisoners. Hayley kicks Rickter and his gun goes off, causing the negotiators to panic and start a shoot-out. Yet again, the kids' actions unintentionally result in people being killed.

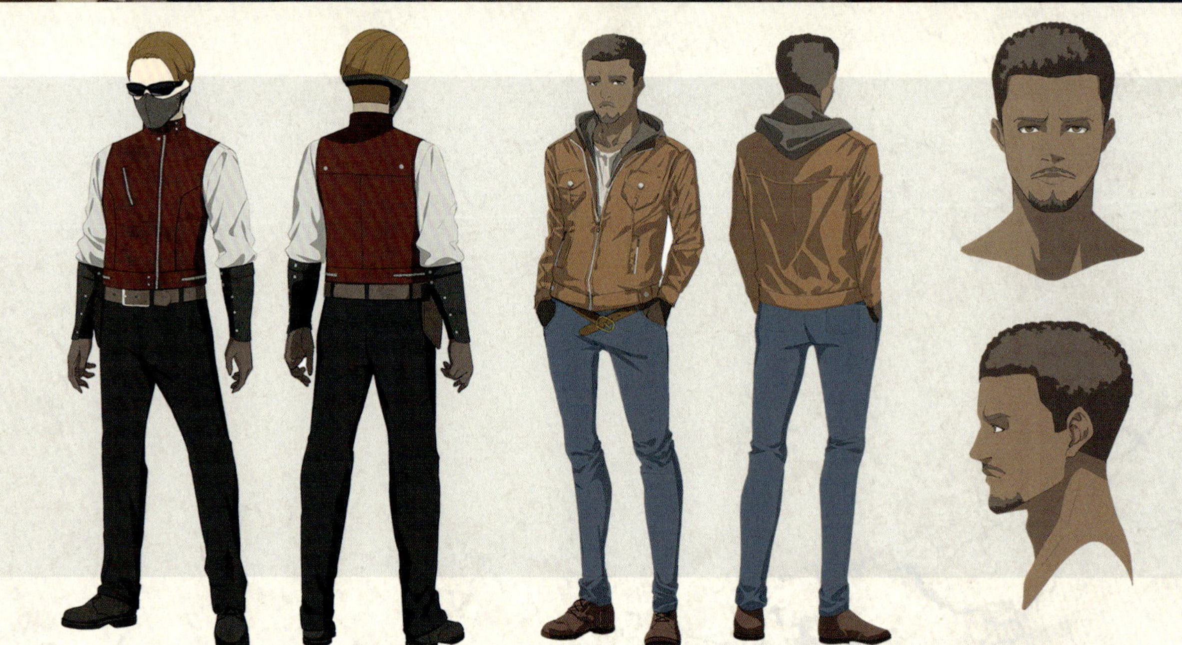

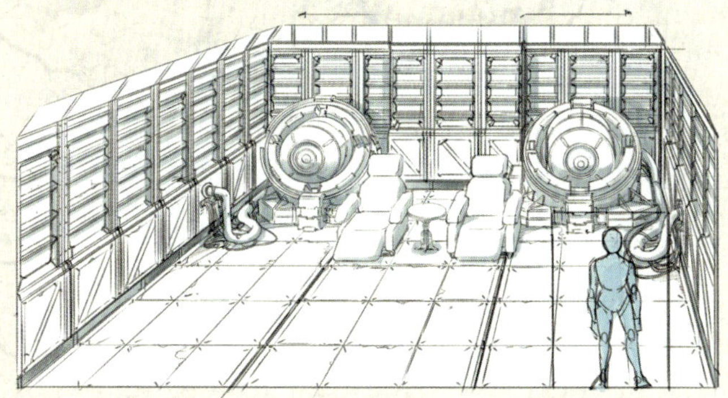

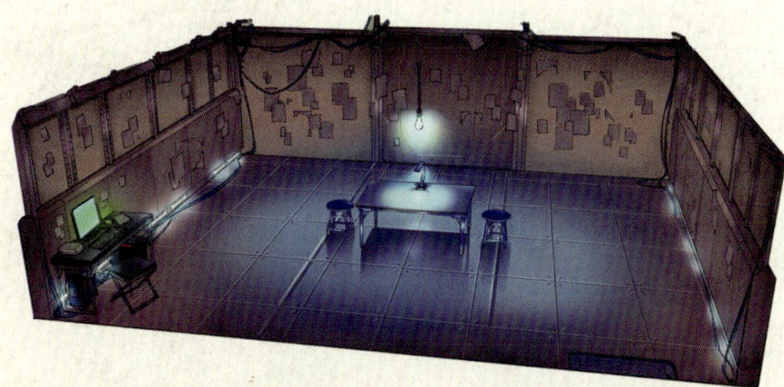

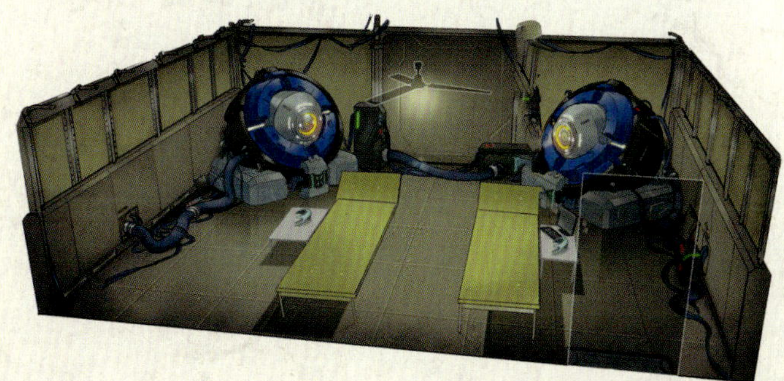

Most of the emissaries are shot dead, though Shane scornfully spares the main negotiator. He destroys the Eel eggs, though, and makes a cryptic reference to "Sisters" who will sort the situation out. Then he interrogates Taylor in a dark room, determined to get some answers from these kids who've caused him so much trouble.

As Shane fires questions, it becomes clear he has Drift abilities and a Jaeger helmet—more detritus from the PPDC—which he's using to get into Taylor's mind. Notably, we don't see the helmet until a last-minute reveal at the end of the episode. It hints that Shane's so good at Drifting that he can make Taylor forget he's wearing the helmet; and as we'll see later, he can manipulate people far more than that.

Greg Johnson was fascinated by the story potential of the Drift. "There is the idea that these neural sessions could be recorded, scrubbed of any mentally scarring emotions, and then played back through the mind of a new cadet in a training session." (We'll see that being demonstrated later, only without the scrubbing.) "Or, as Shane does, move through someone's memories and alter them or even remove them. Someone adept at this could create a new persona for someone. I feel like we've barely scratched the surface of what is possible with this technology—both good and bad."

After strolling through Taylor's memories, Shane emerges triumphant from the interrogation room and tells Mei they have a Jaeger.

"YEARS OF LIFE-AND-DEATH STAKES FORGE A NEW CODE OF CONDUCT, UNTIL YOU BECOME AS DANGEROUS AS THE MONSTERS."

Greg Johnson, showrunner

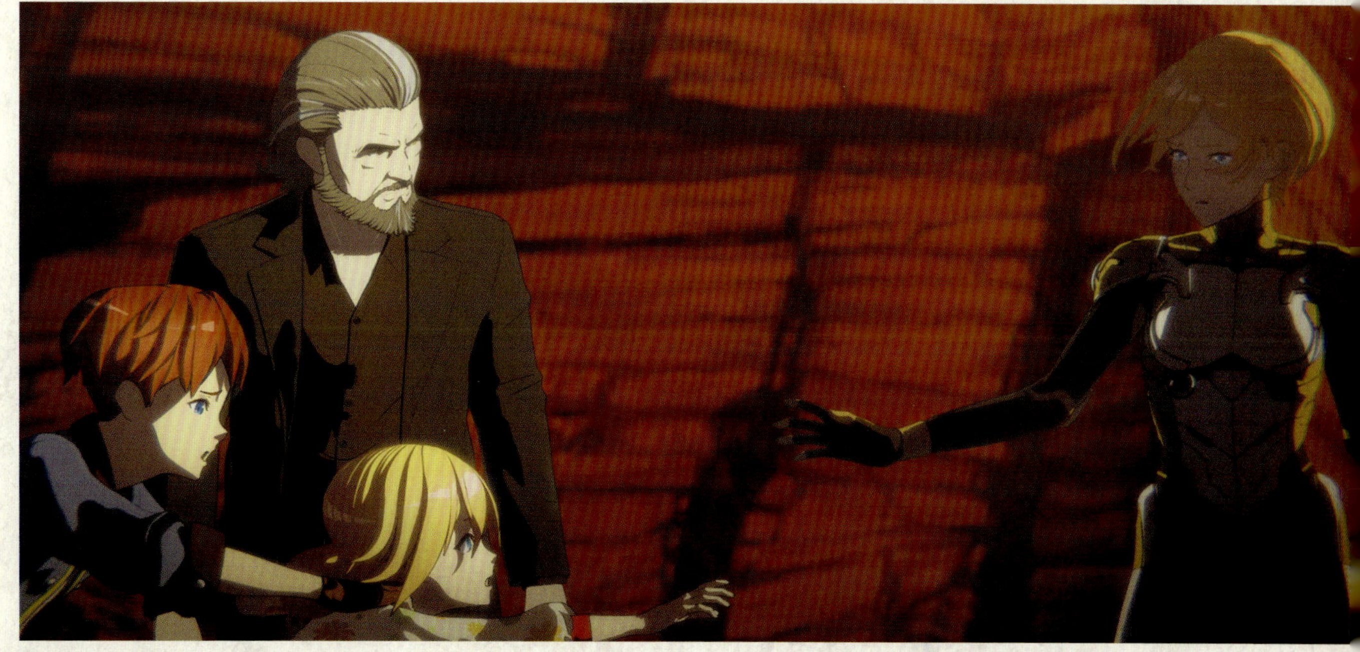

Right // Shane strolls with terrifying ease through Taylor's memories.

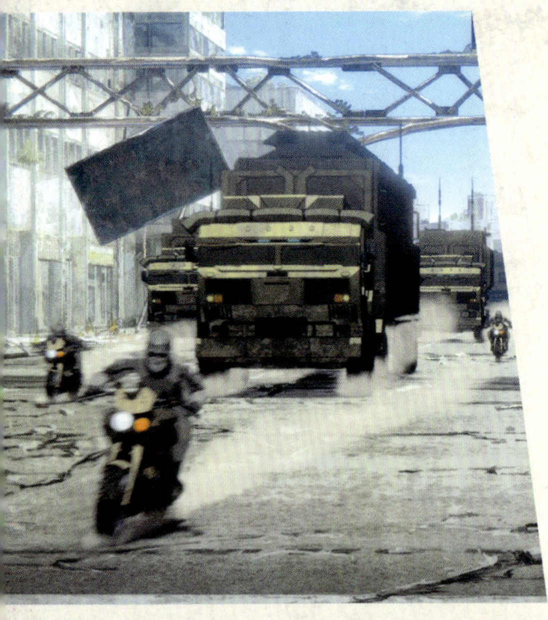

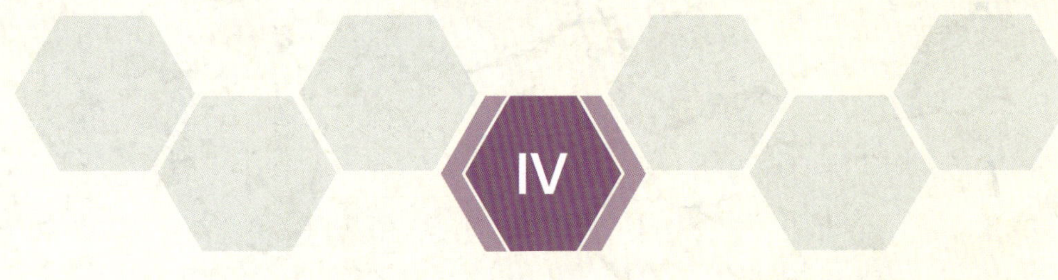

CHAPTER FOUR
COPPERHEAD RETURNS

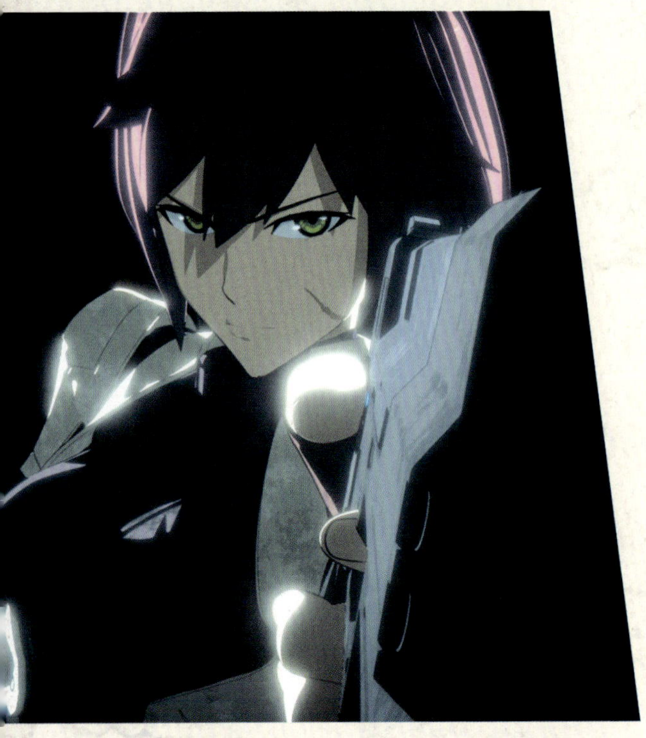

Episode Four, "Up and Running," sees Shane and his men travel to claim Atlas Destroyer, taking the children along with them. The task of driving the Jaeger is given to Bogan's oft-inebriated Drift technician, Joel. It's mentioned that Joel was once a former employee of PPDC (late of Brisbane Shatterdome). Viewers may be reminded of the sometimes erratic scientists in the live-action *Pacific Rim* films.

Joel is responsible for tuning up Shane's "neural bridge", which is why Shane's so powerful in the Drift himself. Viewers may wonder why Shane never tries piloting the Jaeger. The answer seems to be it would involve opening up all his secrets to someone else, and Shane could never do that.

Joel revives Atlas Destroyer with one of the power cells from the previous episode, but piloting the Jaeger is another matter. The technician can Drift himself, but none of Shane's men ('Riders') are capable. The process turns their brains to mush, while the multiple Drifts do terrible things to Joel's own mind.

When one Drift attempt goes especially badly, the Jaeger's alarm starts blaring—and we know what that means. Copperhead hears the sound in the desert, and starts bounding towards the Jaeger at top speed. Hearing the news, Shane reluctantly lets Taylor operate the robot with Mei; he orders them to take the Jaeger to safety.

The neural handshake between the pilots is difficult, as Mei tries to shut off her memories from Taylor. When she's forced to reveal them, Taylor is shocked by her past; Shane trained her as a killer from childhood, claiming her as his possession.

Jae-Hong Kim enthuses about Mei. "I think that Mei is a true main character in *Pacific Rim: The Black*. She's a survivor of this crazy chaotic continent who can live in this kind of world. She's armed with skills and a very interesting backstory. Taylor and Hayley are searching through the continent for their parents, but at the same time, Mei is on the same level: how she was manipulated by Shane, how she was raised up as an assassin. She was a really interesting character to develop."

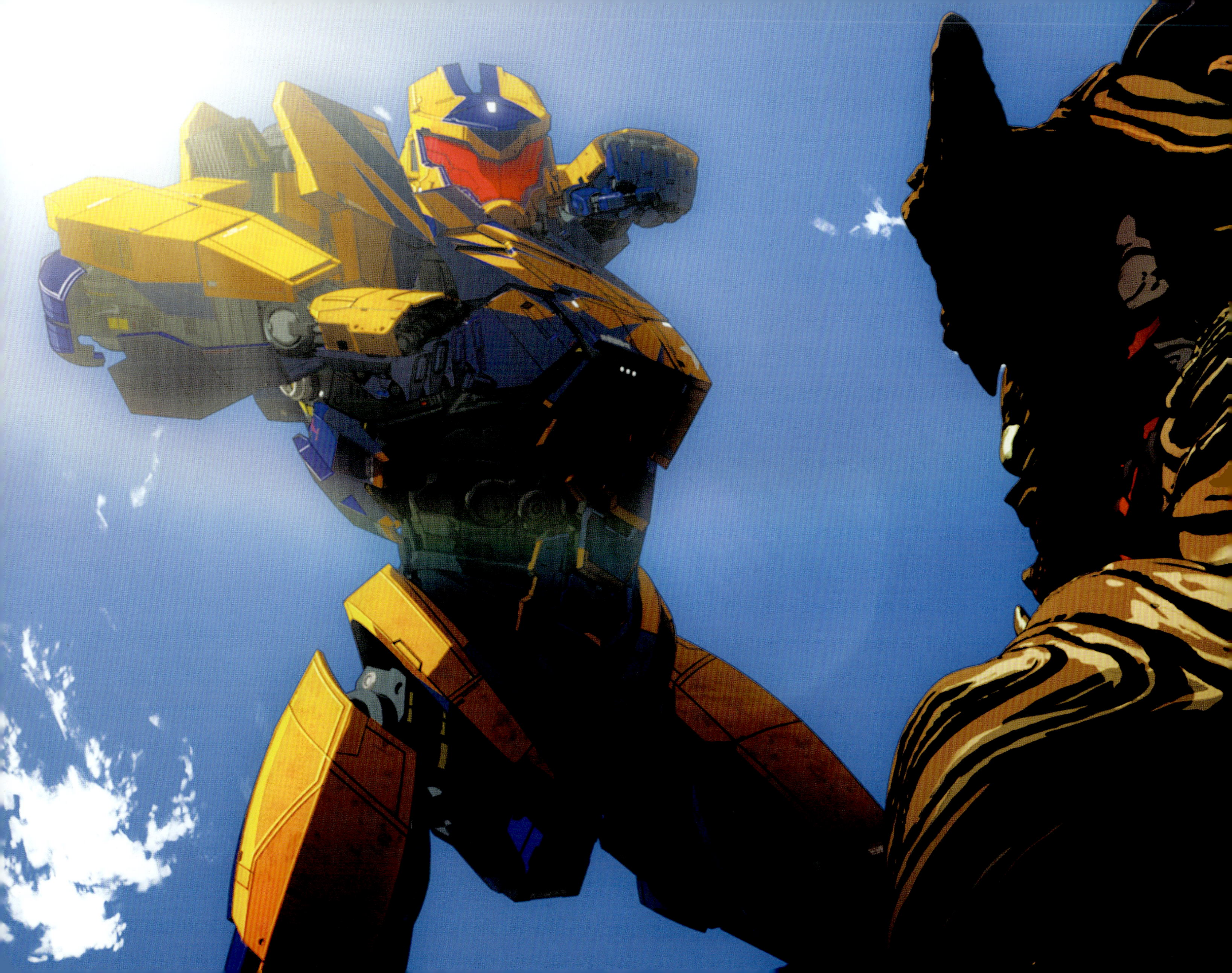

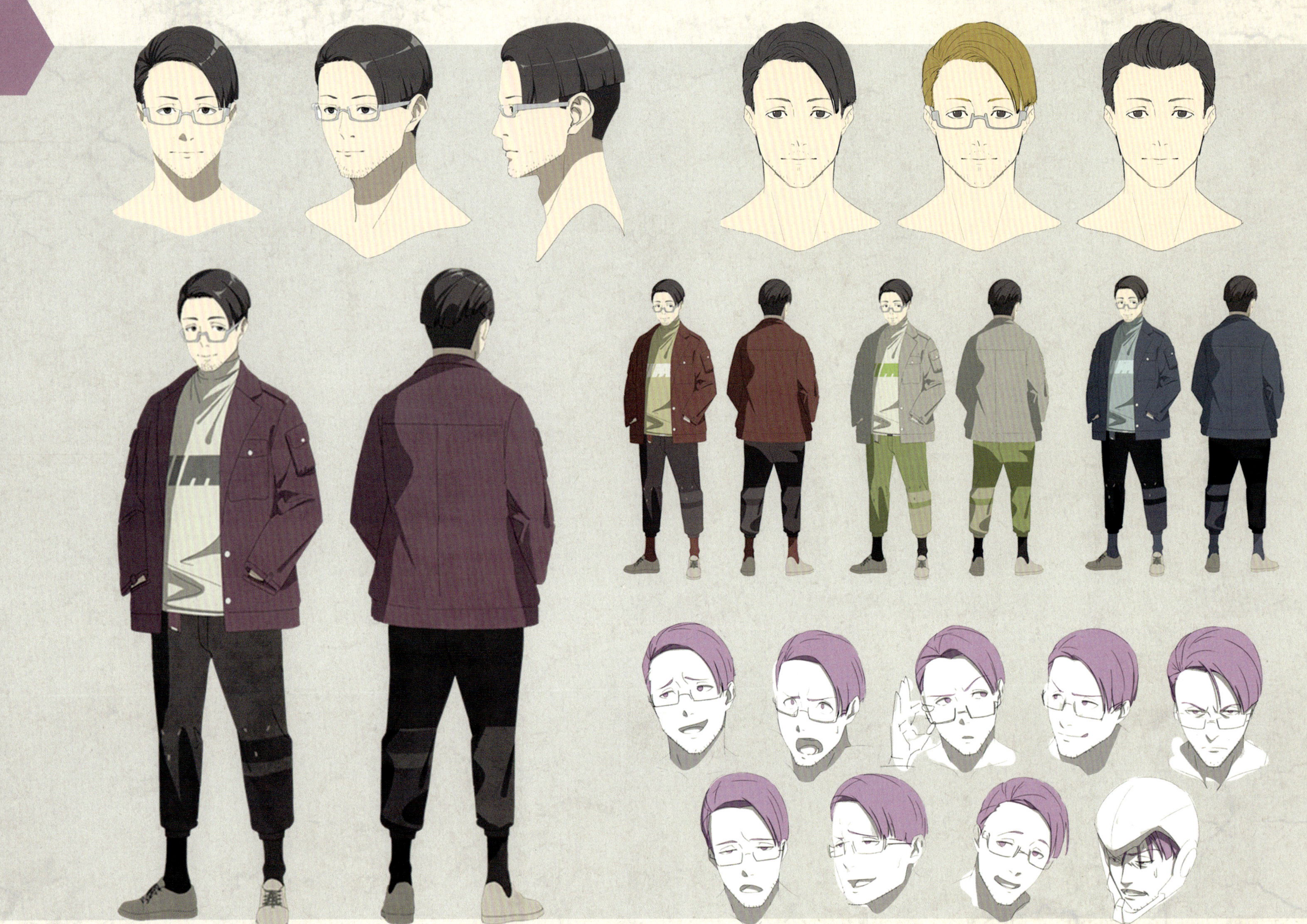

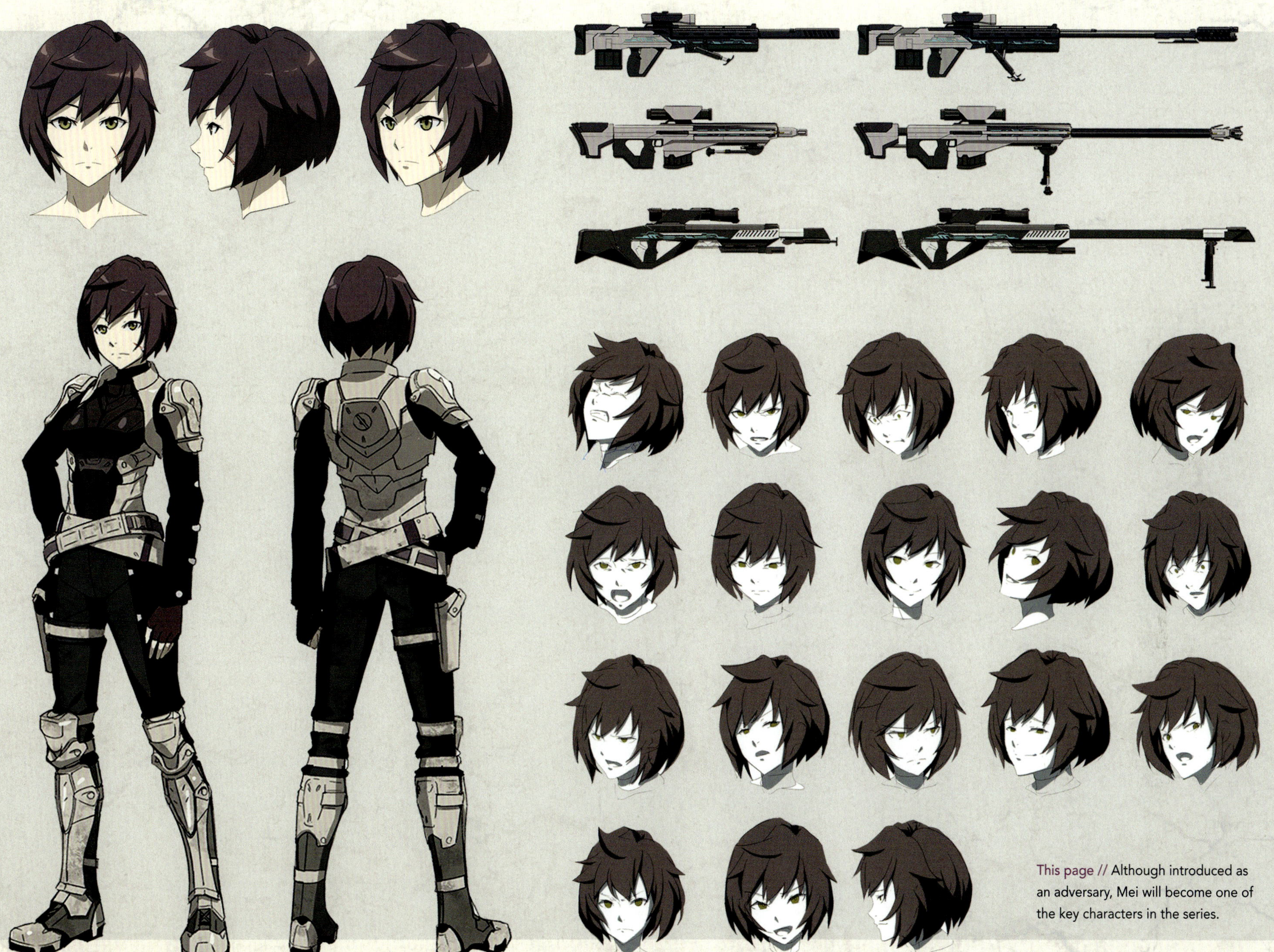

This page // Although introduced as an adversary, Mei will become one of the key characters in the series.

Kim adds that beside Mei, "The rest of the characters all look very simple, apart from their heads; they have normal, casual costume designs. But Mei is like Special Forces, Special Ops, so we had a lot of fun with her. For me, Mei was the most fun to create!"

Some of Mei's combat instincts seep into Taylor, who forces Mei to engage Atlas Destroyer in hand-to-hand combat with Copperhead. Apart from the brief fights in Episode One, this is the first full-on battle in the series between a Kaiju and a Jaeger.

When it comes to animating the Jaegers, Kim says, "One of the most important things I emphasize is the weight of a Jaeger. It's a building-sized robot, but it's very hard to express the weight in CG animation, which shouldn't be compared to multi-billion-dollar live-action movies. You need to feel the weight of every step, swing and punch.

"It was hard to precisely calculate the Jaegers' timing and movement," Kim says. "Quite often when you watch robot animation, you barely feel the weight because it's

"ONE OF THE MOST IMPORTANT THINGS I EMPHASIZE IS THE WEIGHT OF THE JAEGER."

Jae-Hong Kim, director

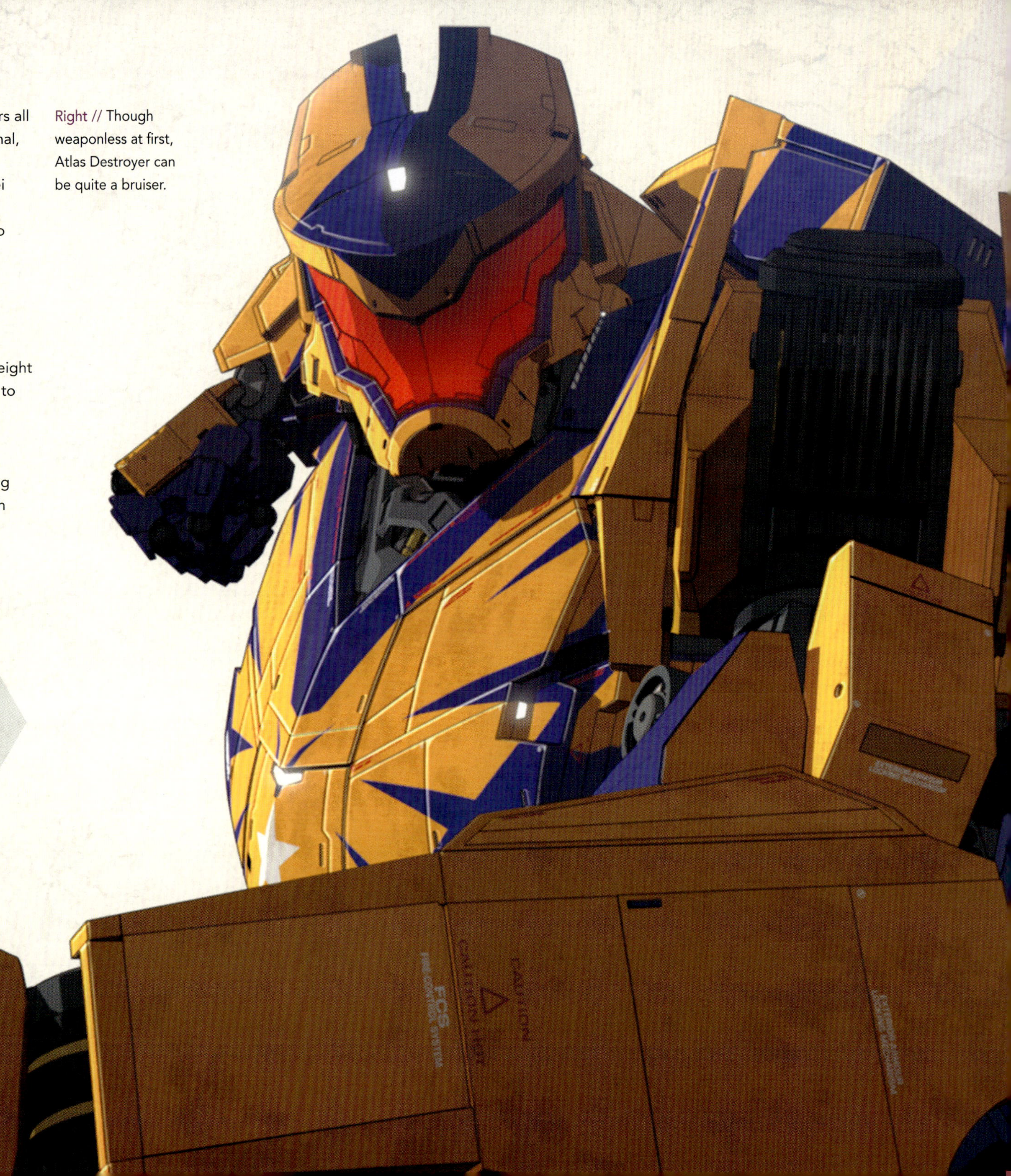

Right // Though weaponless at first, Atlas Destroyer can be quite a bruiser.

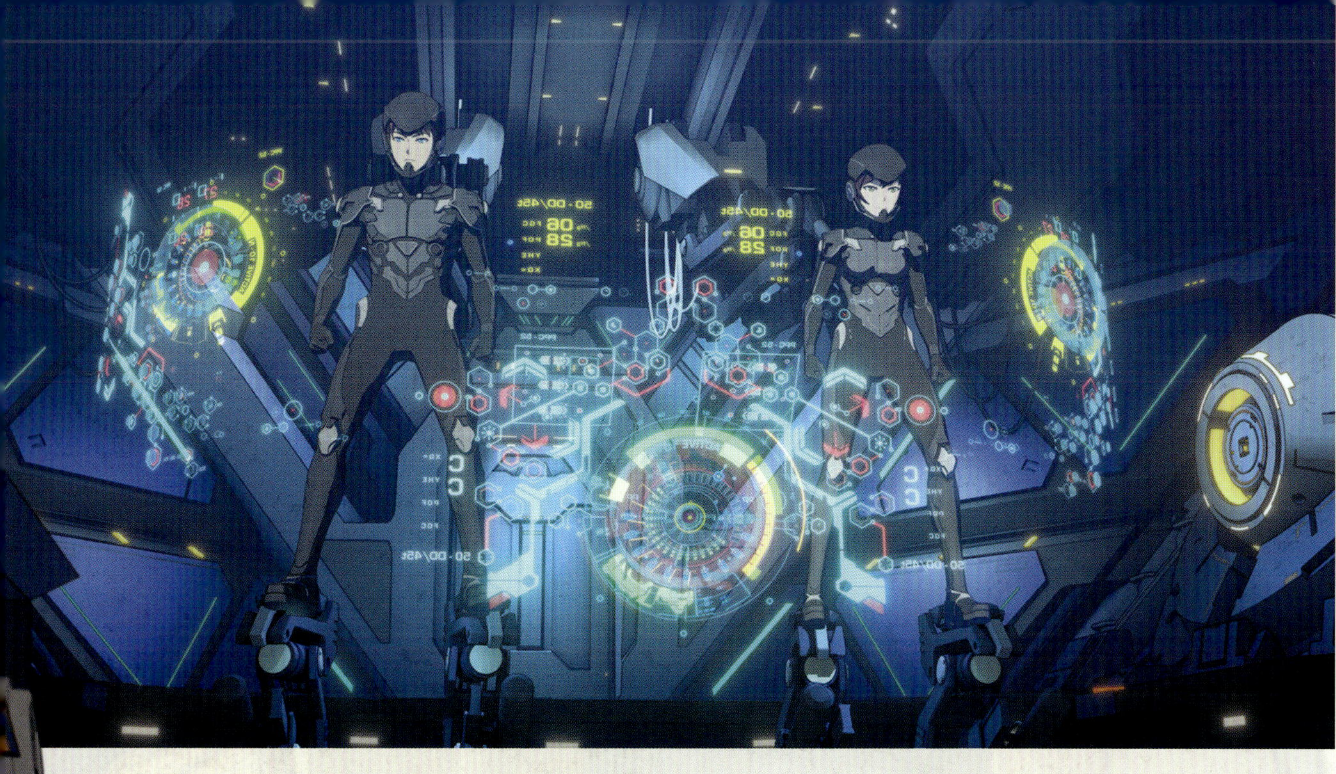

really hard to nail that in animation. Not just when the Jaegers are walking but when they're moving, their parts swinging, I need to feel they're giant but also that they're metal. So,"—Kim imitates a robot's mechanical movement—"you have to play with the timing of the animation. You have to know when to stop, when to hold… Those things are very subtle, but they need to be executed in the shot. We chatted a lot about those kinds of things."

Hiroyuki Hayashi reflects, "For this project in particular, we had highly skilled designers who were able to make robot designs that had great individuality and personality and yet were still functional. We made the Jaeger models just as they were designed, and we were able to animate them without too much issue. They were very functional and mechanical in that sense.

"Also," Hayashi says, "the basis of the series was the live-action films. Even if the giant robots in them were CG, they had to look realistic in a live-action setting. There was a high degree of realism there that we needed to reflect to a degree as well. I suppose we prioritised a sense of reality rather than a more anthropomorphic thing."

However, Hayashi says, "Our animators were very skilled, and a skilled animator can take something as mechanical as a giant robot and manage to imbue it with a humanity and an emotional aspect just through the animation. Even with the human-shaped robots that exist in the real world, people tend to identify with them. They're clearly robots, but they move like humans, they're designed like humans, and so we tend to project humanity onto them. That's part of the balance as well."

Yuki Moriyama adds, "Rather than just typical anime, we have the gigantic influence of the *Pacific Rim* films, which had a huge cultural impact and a very unique kind of design for the giant robots, which is a little different from most giant robot anime. Our designer wanted to keep that unique Jaeger feel as intact as possible."

Moriyama points out one interesting thing about the Jaegers is their heavy armor.

Above // Infected by Mei's combat instincts, Taylor takes Atlas Destroyer into its first full-on battle.

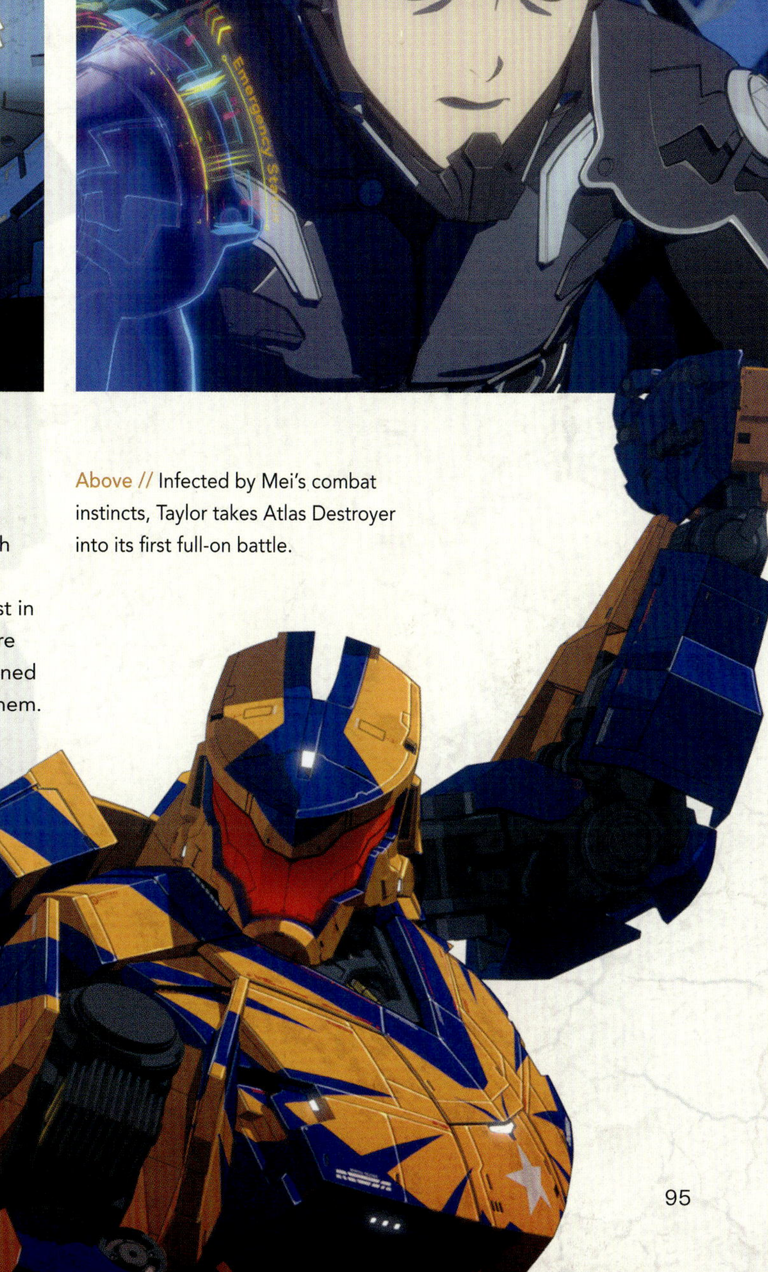

"The Jaegers have armor that moves independently of the inner parts to a certain degree. That is very challenging, but it's also a very unique form of motion and construction. All the way from design to rigged animation, that's something we paid particular attention to. We wanted to keep that unique aspect of the Jaeger intact because it helps contrast the Jaegers from the Kaiju, which have a much more organic motion."

"I loved the grittiness of *Pacific Rim*'s tech," adds Greg Johnson. "If we were to actually build giant robots or bolt together massive walls, that's how it would look. The first *Pacific Rim* film really captured the 'blue collar' aspect, as well as the advanced technology."

During the fight between Copperhead and Atlas Destroyer, Copperhead eats one of the Jaeger's arms. For Jae-Hong Kim, there were crucial details needed when the arm comes off. "If there's nothing coming out from that amputated part… Even with a robot, we need to 'feel' sparks, or oil spitting out, so the audience will feel 'Oooh!' I want the audience to feel like Atlas Destroyer."

Finally, the damaged Atlas Destroyer lures Copperhead onto a minefield set up by Shane's team. The final detonation is one of the biggest spectacles of the series. Copperhead collapses, but it's only stunned.

At the Bogan crew's new camp, Shane rages at Mei for fighting Copperhead against his orders, and the damage to the Jaeger. When Taylor says he was responsible, Shane is ready to shoot him, and Hayley and bOy as well. Unexpectedly, Mei shields Taylor saying she'll leave Shane if he kills the children. Shane seems prepared to let the youngsters go; after all, he has Atlas Destroyer now. But he's lying…

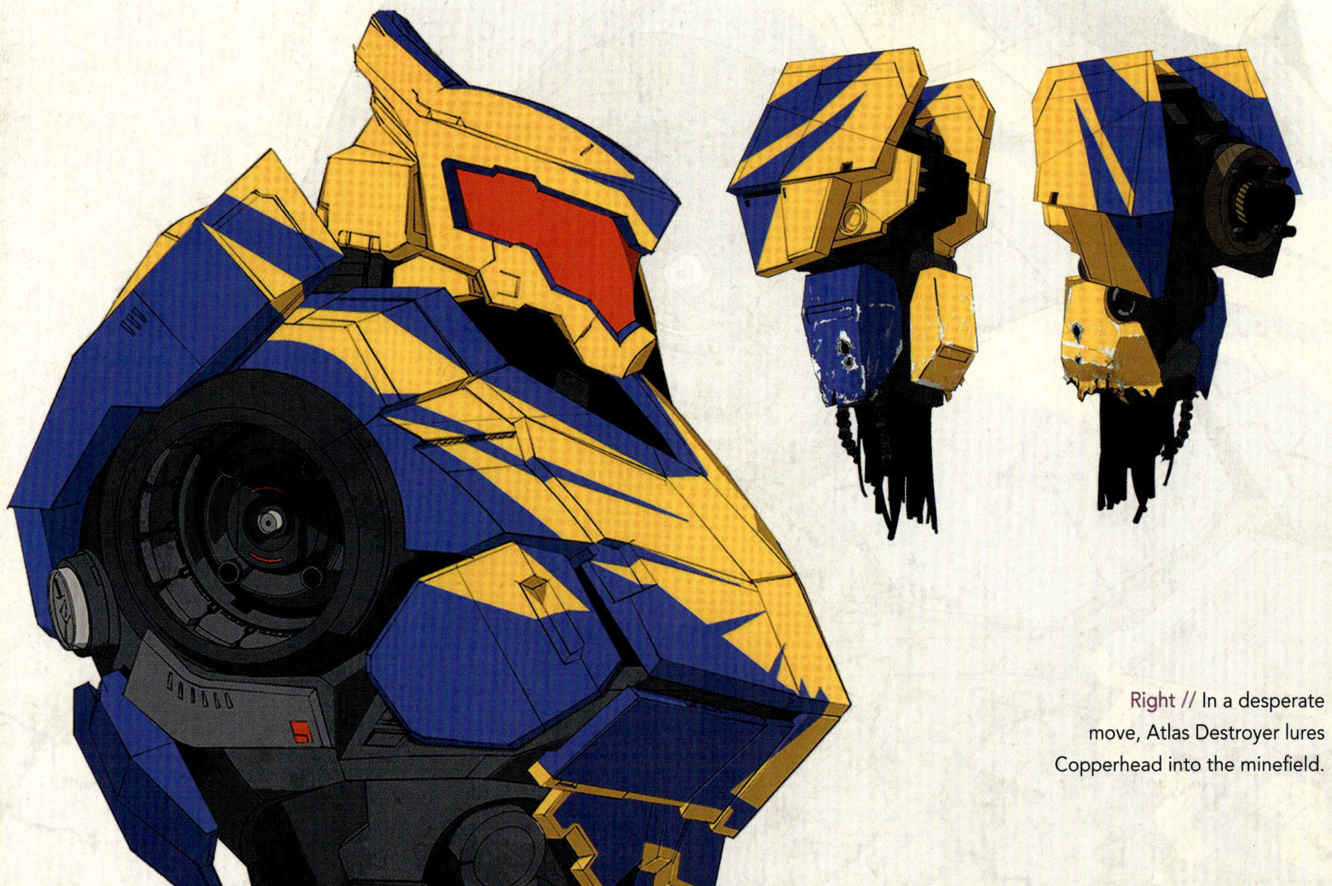

Right // In a desperate move, Atlas Destroyer lures Copperhead into the minefield.

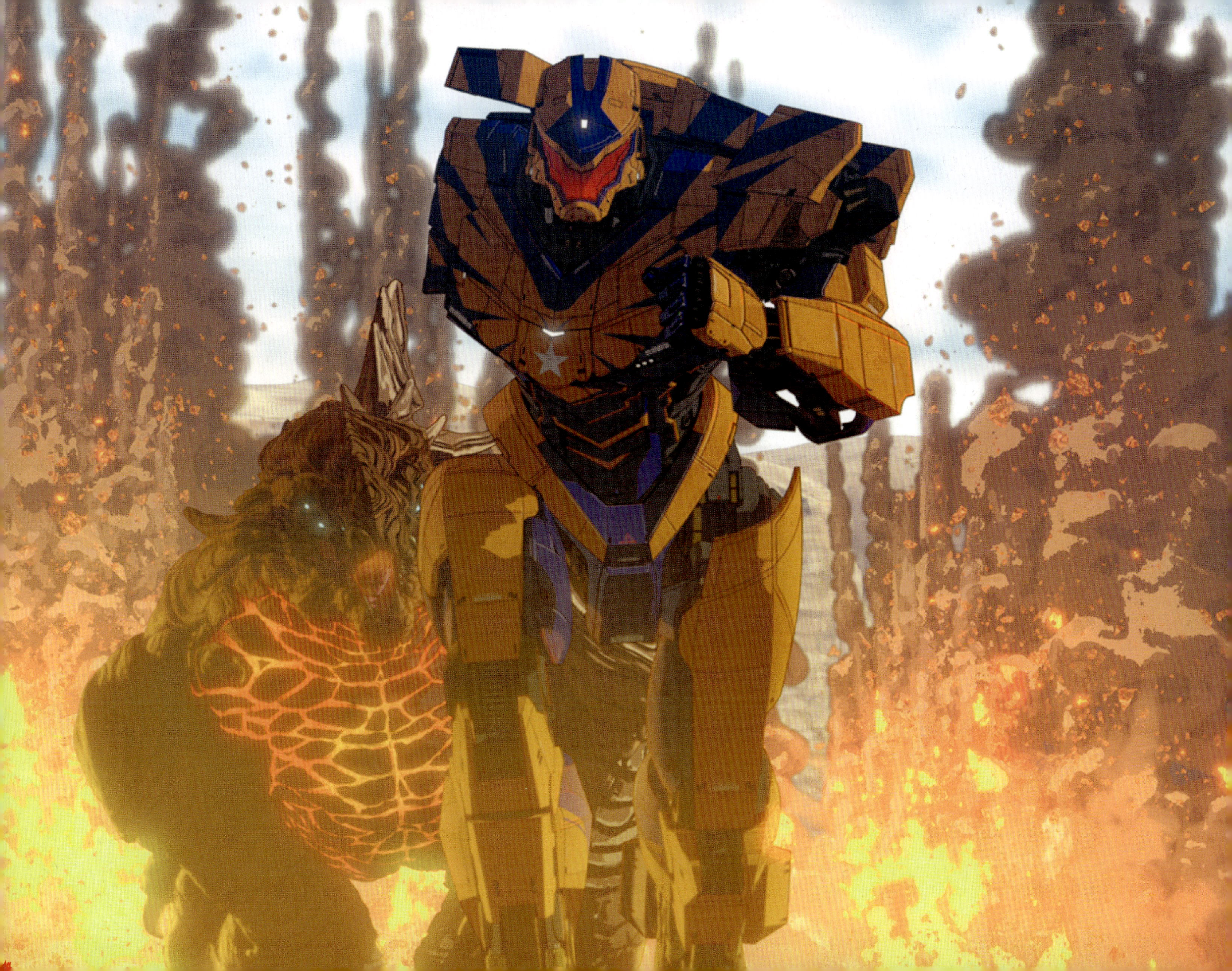

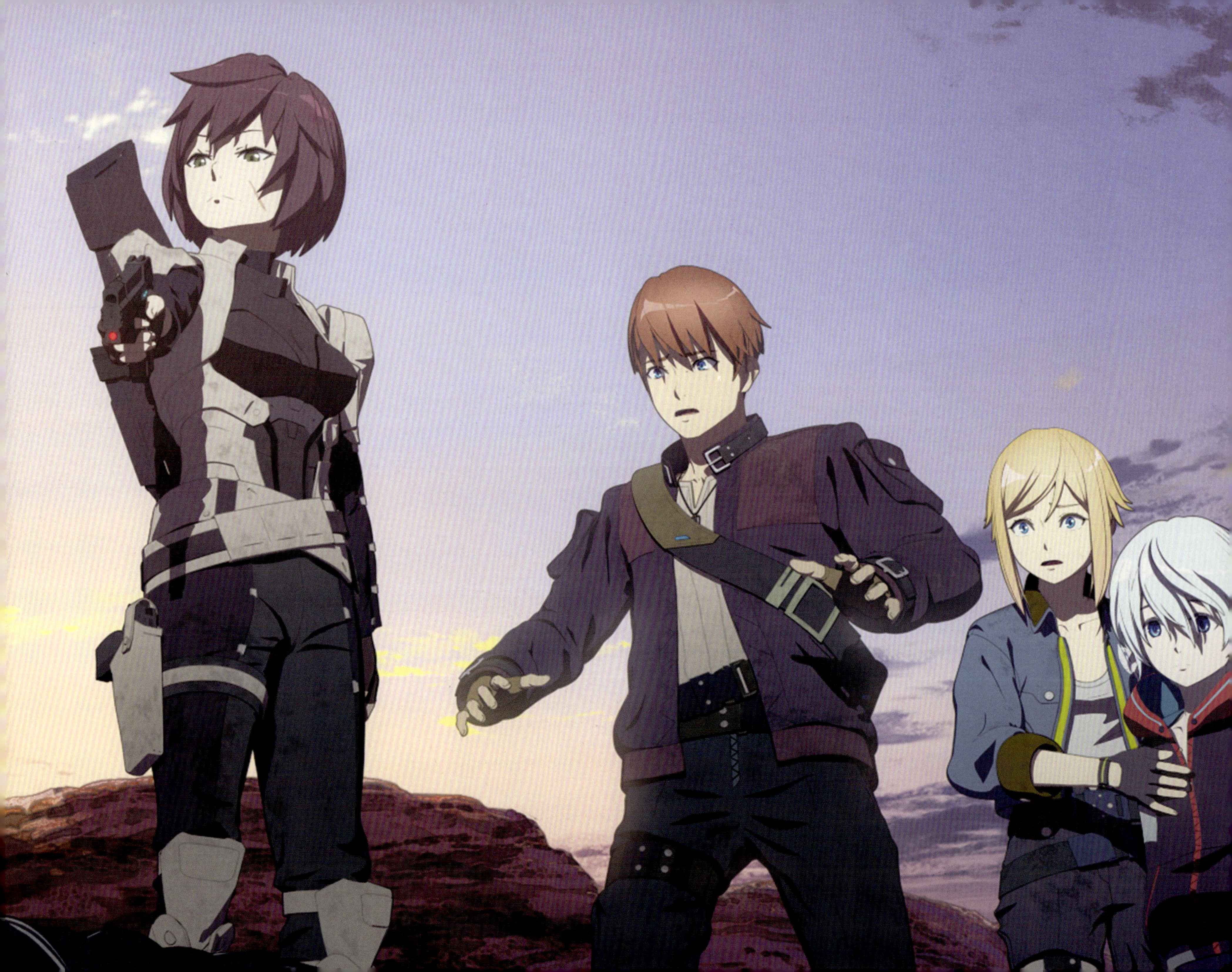

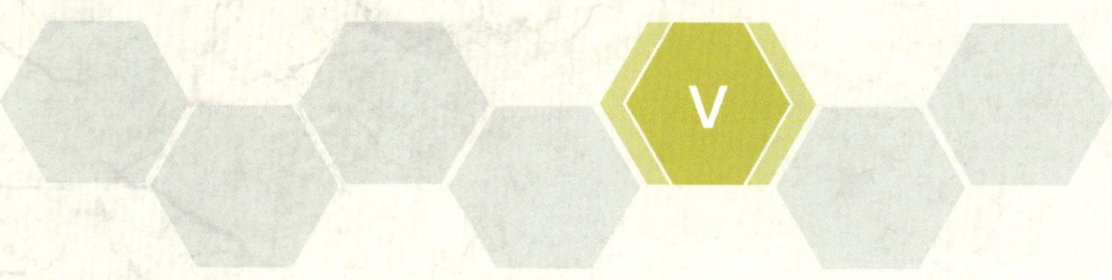

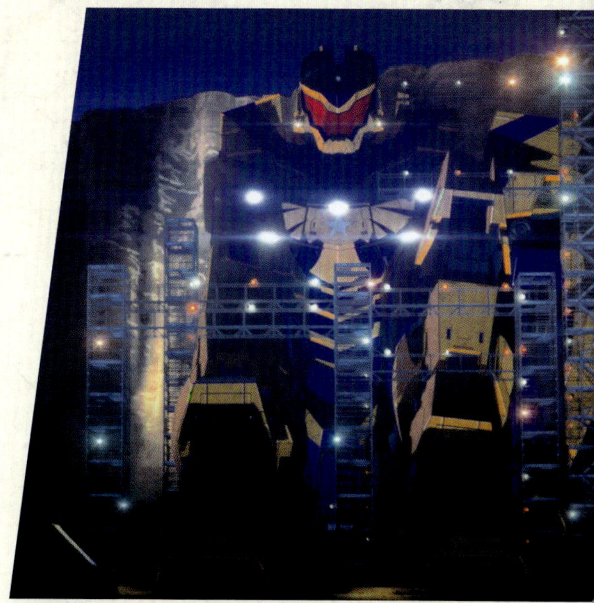

CHAPTER FIVE

KILL YOUR DARLINGS

Episode Five of the series, "Escaping Bogan", doesn't include any battling giants, but its ending still packs a heck of a punch.

Taylor, Hayley and bOy leave the camp at dawn, but Shane sends his henchman Rickter after them. Catching up with his prey in the desert, Rickter gleefully shoots bOy in the chest. He turns to the other two… only for bOy to knock him out, as somehow the bullet didn't harm him. Taylor aims the gun at Rickter, but can't shoot. Unfortunately for Rickter, Mei shows up, with no scruples about killing. Exit Rickter (at least we assume at the time). However, Mei draws the line at killing kids, and the incident breaks her loyalty to Shane.

Joel's trying to fix the damaged Atlas Destroyer, but his mind has been addled by his failed Drifts. He's startled by the appearance of Mei and Taylor. Mei says Taylor will fix Atlas Destroyer, Joel can take the credit, and the children will steal the Jaeger later.

In return, Joel discloses a devastating secret. Shane has been manipulating Mei for years, using Drift technology and other people's memories to keep her loyalty. Not only is Shane's supposed past a lie, but Joel claims Mei's past, her memories, were faked by Shane too. All to deceive a child snatched from a loving family…

Amid these revelations, there's an Easter Egg connection to the *Pacific Rim* films. To get the Jaeger moving, and without any co-pilots available, Taylor is instructed by Loa in 'ghost piloting'—Drifting solo, boosted by the recorded memories of a pilot from the past. The pilot Loa chooses is the Australian hero Hercules 'Herc' Hansen.

Taylor gets to relive Hansen's last stand—a fight we've glimpsed already, in the first moments of Episode One. Afterwards, Taylor can pilot the Jaeger solo, picking up Hayley, bOy and Mei under a hail of fire.

Far away, the group stops to rest. Joel will clearly be an important addition to the team. He's lost his technical skills, but he's picked up new skills from those brain-mushed Riders, from juggling to darts. They'll surely be useful in future episodes.

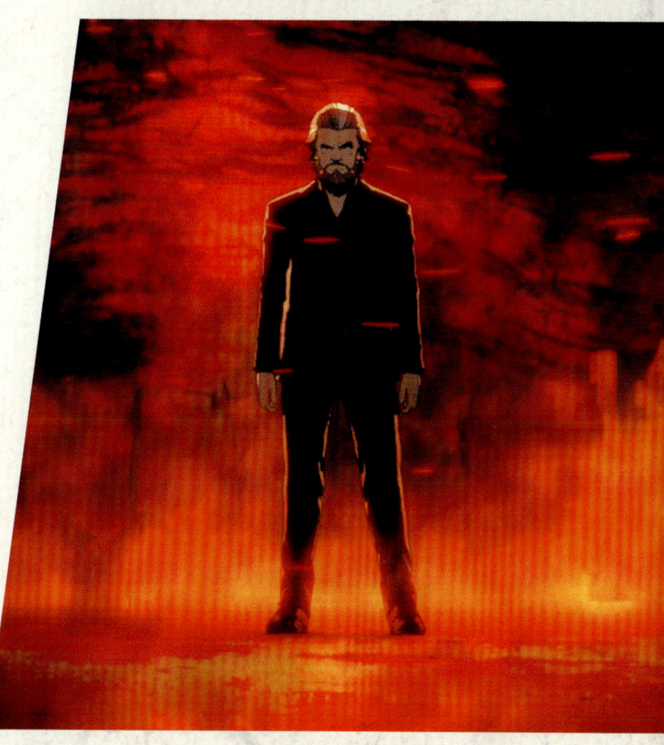

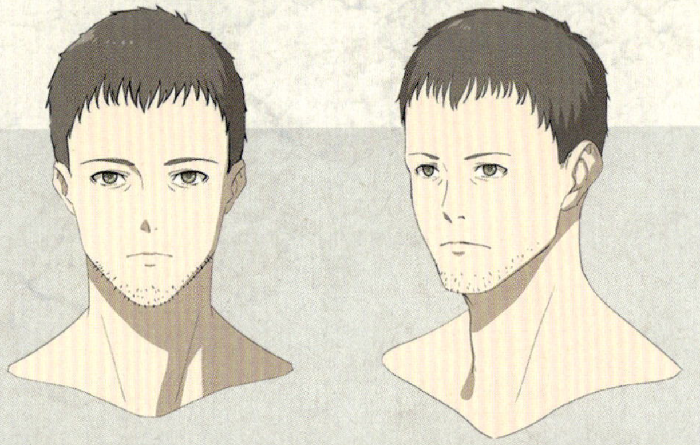

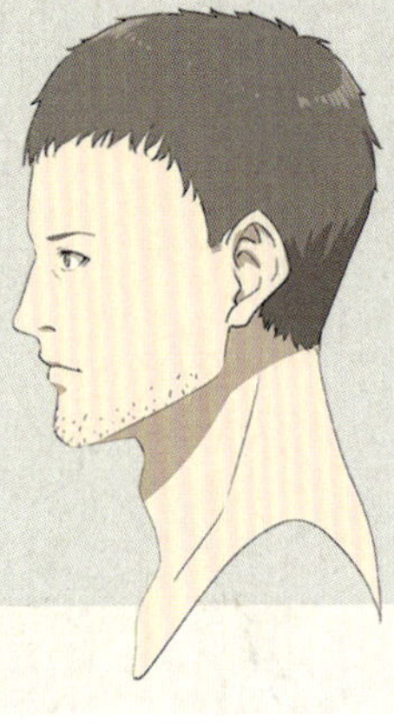

Above and right // Unlike Mei, Shane's henchman Rickter has no compunction about carrying out the most brutal orders.

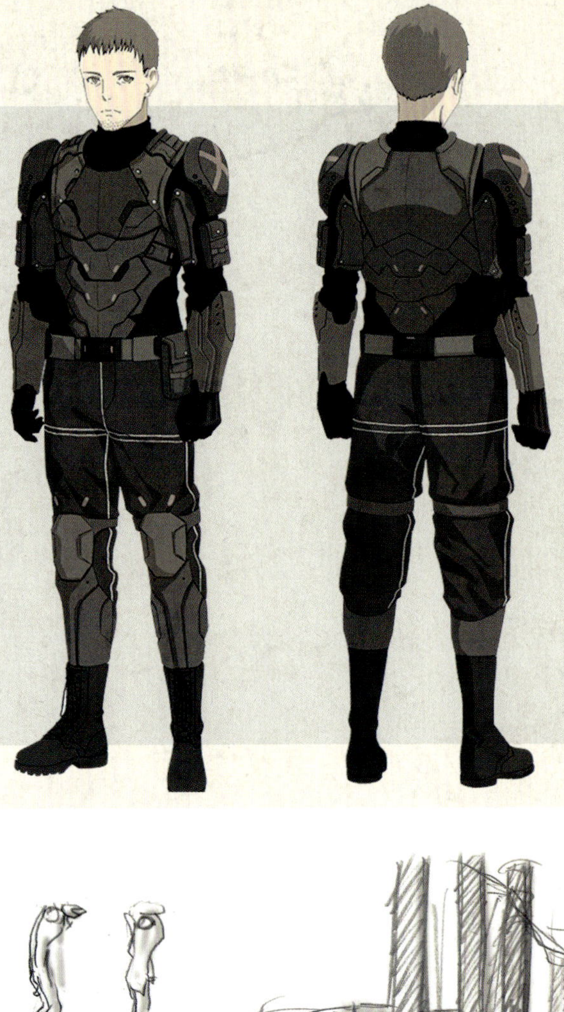

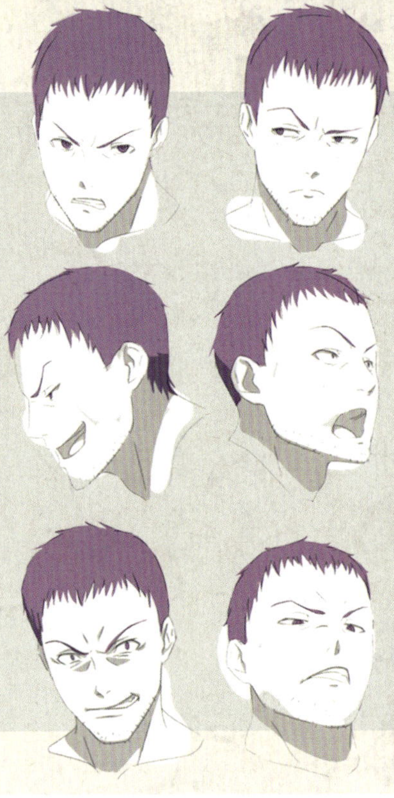

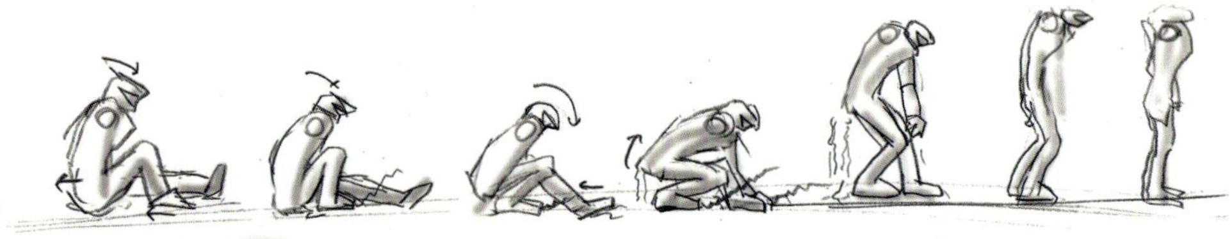

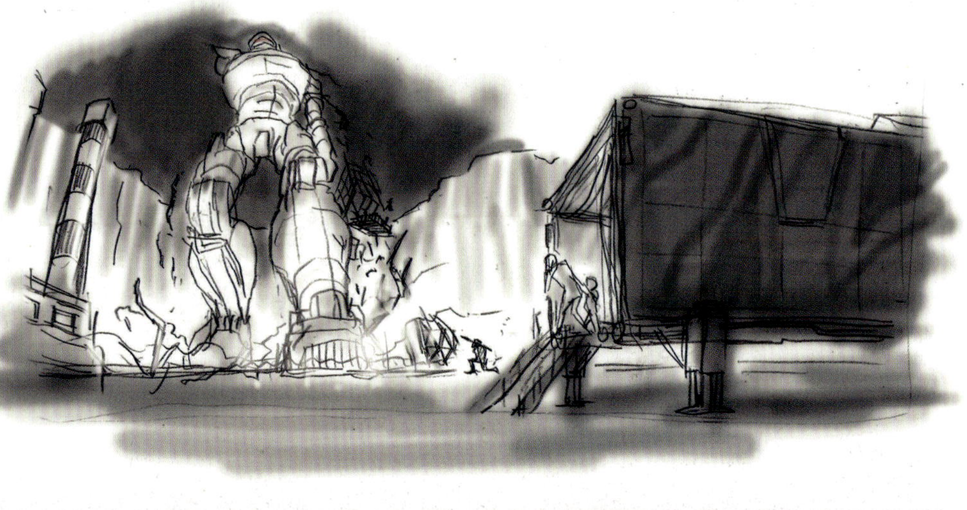

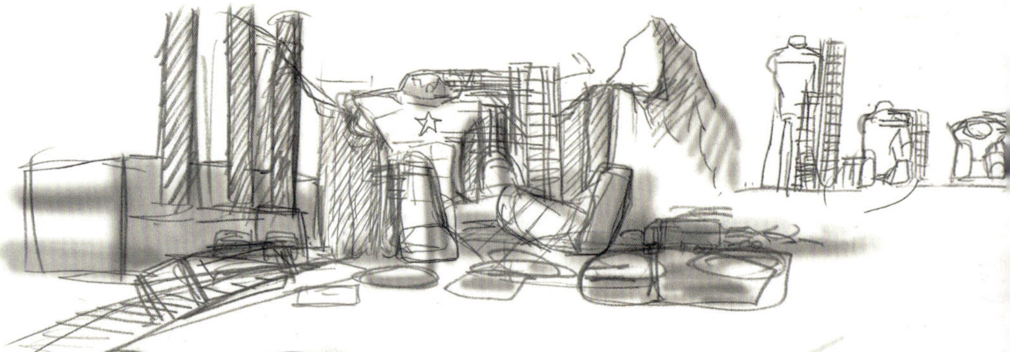

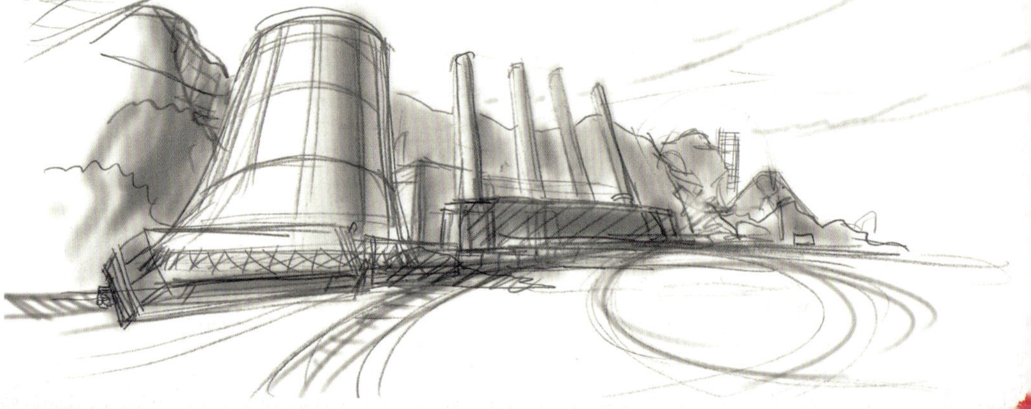

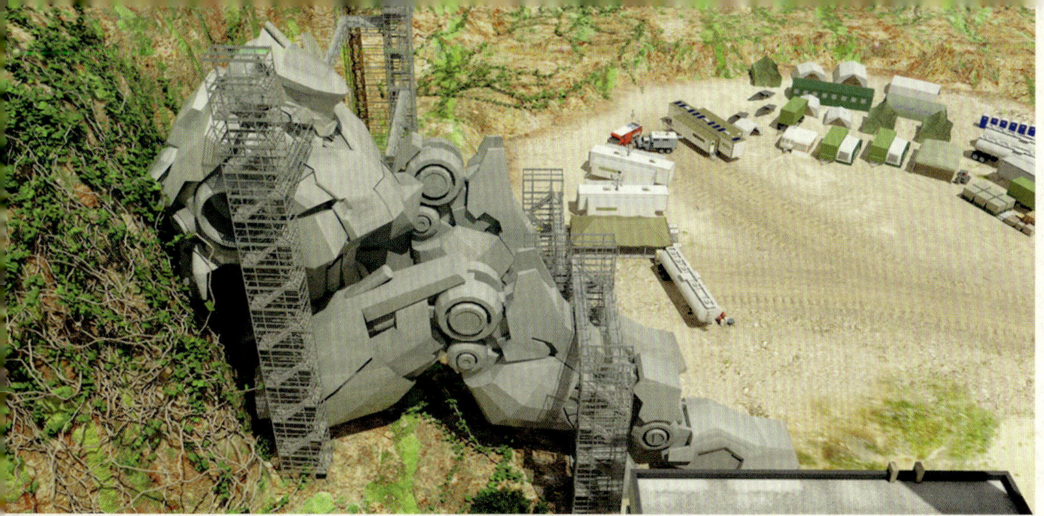
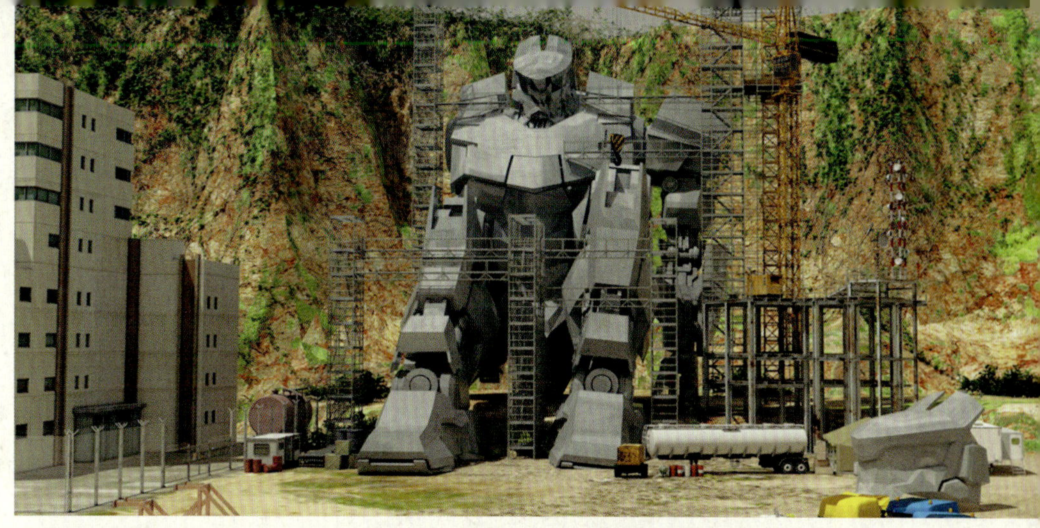
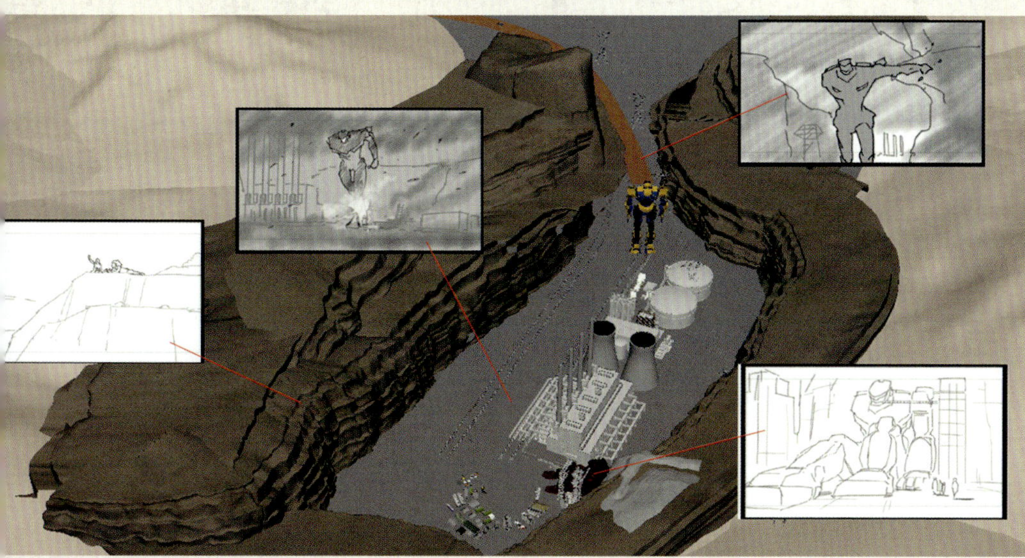
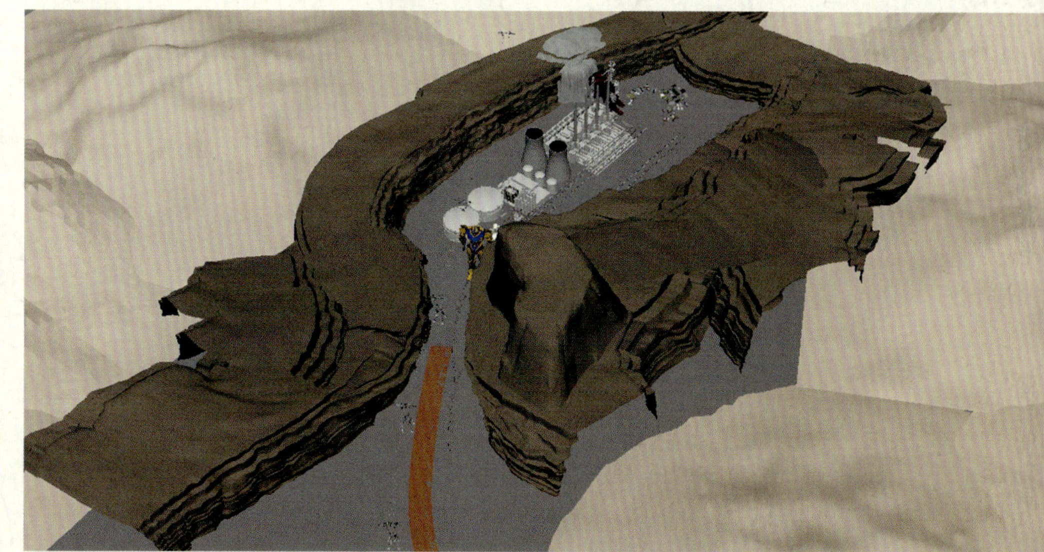
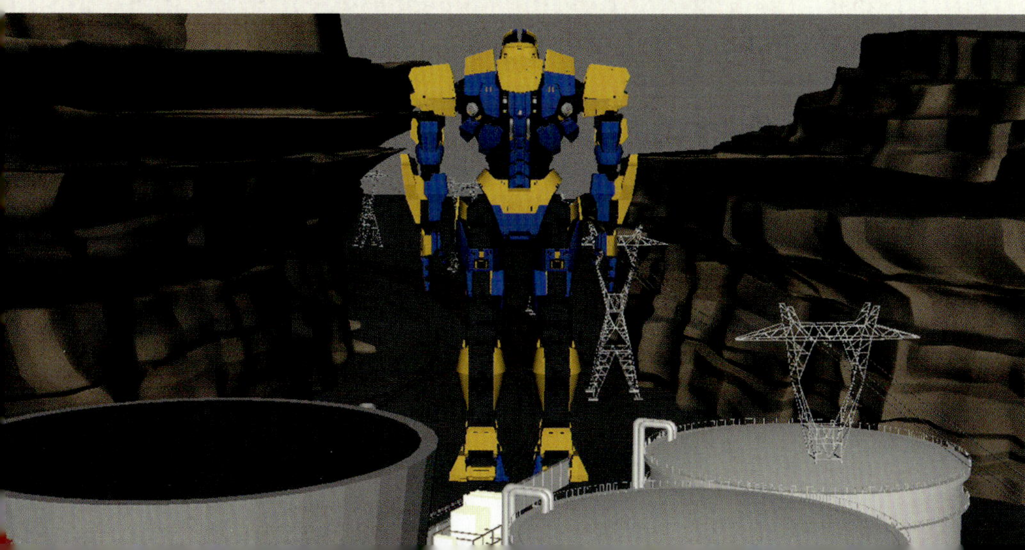
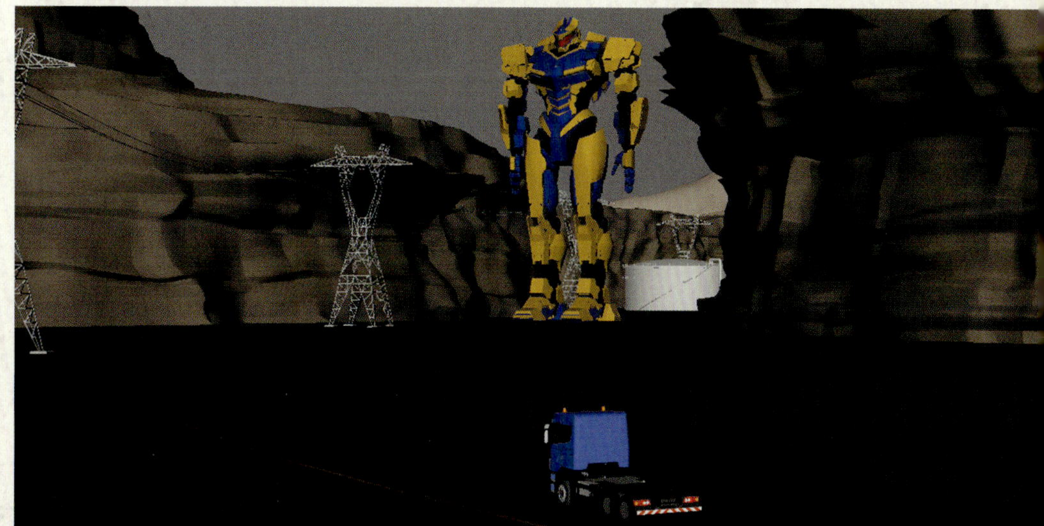

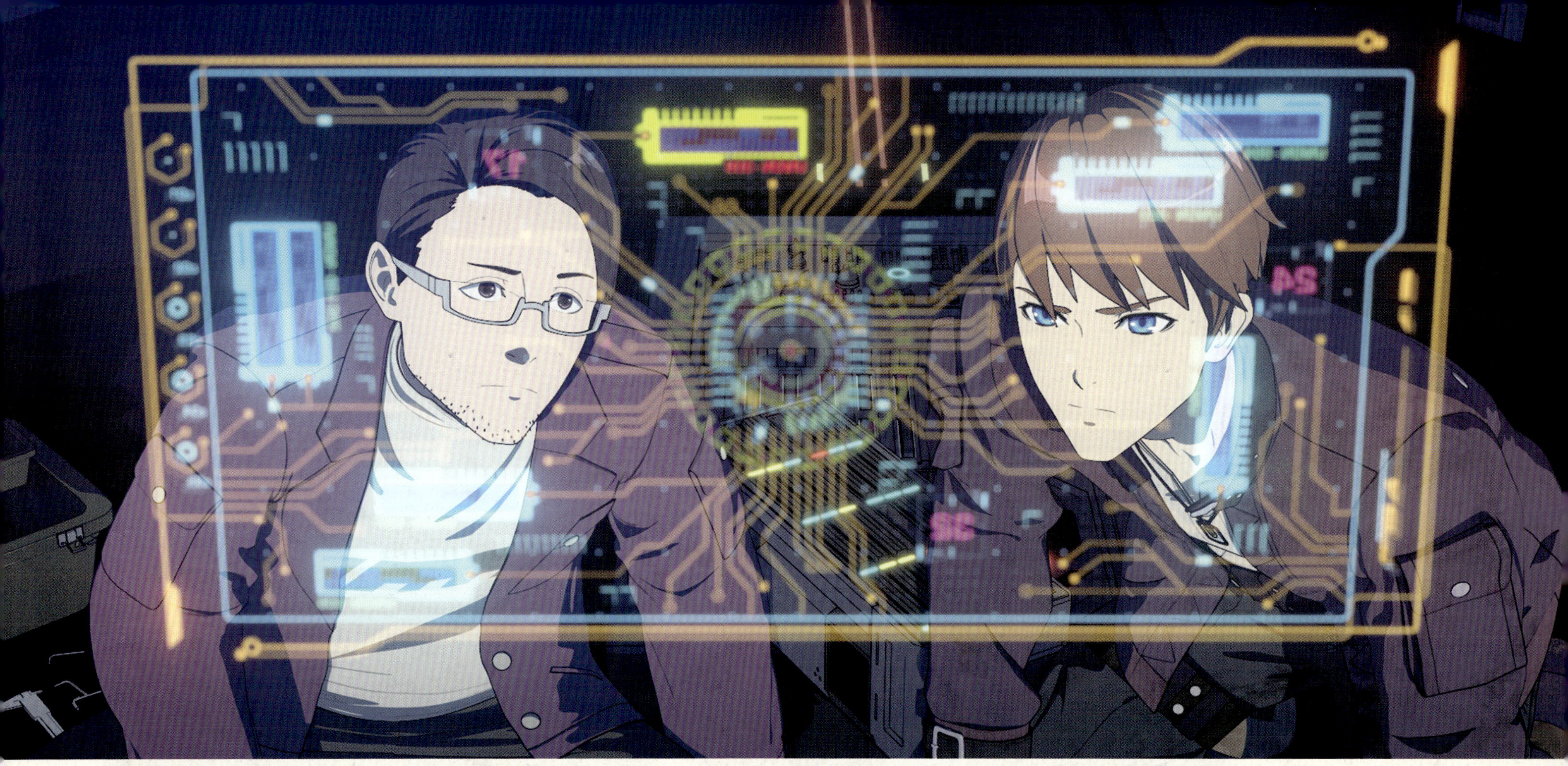

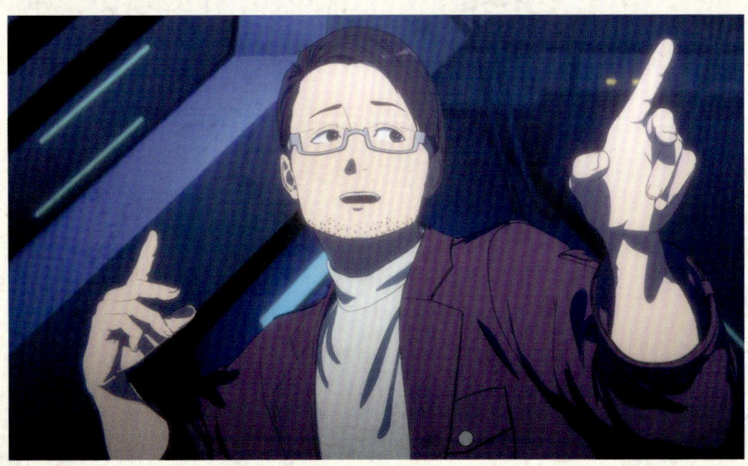

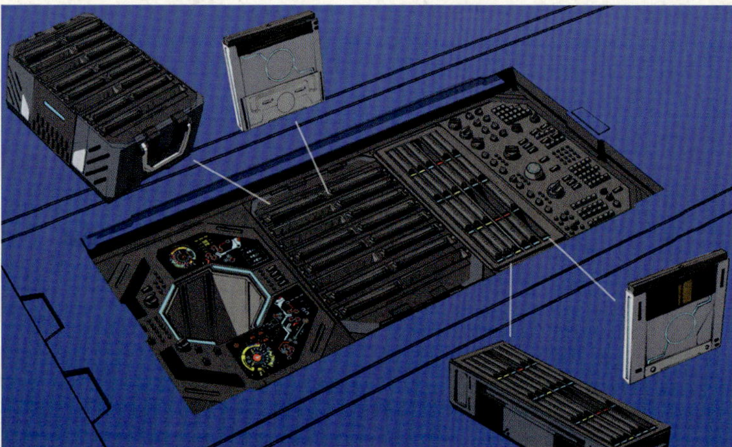

Above and left // Erratic but likable, Joel will be a welcome addition to the show's regular cast… or so we're led to think.

But then Shane calls Mei's walkie-talkie. She's not inclined to answer, and Joel picks up the device to speak to Shane instead. Shane tells him to pass Mei a message—then he detonates the device remotely, blowing Joel's head off.

"Boom!" laughs Jae-Hong Kim. "Even when I read the script, I asked Greg, 'Are we really killing him?' That was basically 'his' episode!" The episode indeed seems designed to set up Joel as a regular character. "But we killed him at the end, and I was going, 'Wha…' I had to double-check with Greg, but he was like, 'Yeah, I'm killing him,' and I was like, 'Wow!' It was very unexpected, but I figured it would be very impactful for the storytelling."

Kim adds, "Usually in animation, you don't really kill characters. Look at *GI Joe*, nobody dies!" Characters do often die in anime, but *Pacific Rim: The Black* was plainly made with the Western market in mind. "But luckily, Legendary Pictures and Netflix agreed it was okay to kill the characters," Kim says. "We were like 'Really?' and they said 'Yes.'" Joel will be far from the last character to die…

Greg Johnson himself says Joel's fate was planned from the start. "Making everyone think this guy would join this new family seemed to make perfect sense… and then when you see his exit, you realize nobody is safe in The Black. The thing about Joel, though, is when we created his arc, we hadn't cast the role yet. Then the actor Vincent Piazza (Lucky Luciano in *Boardwalk Empire*) came in, and his performance absolutely made us fall in love with the character. We could have probably changed the end of that episode in order to bring him back, but Craig and I really liked going out on that surprise. So, adios Joel."

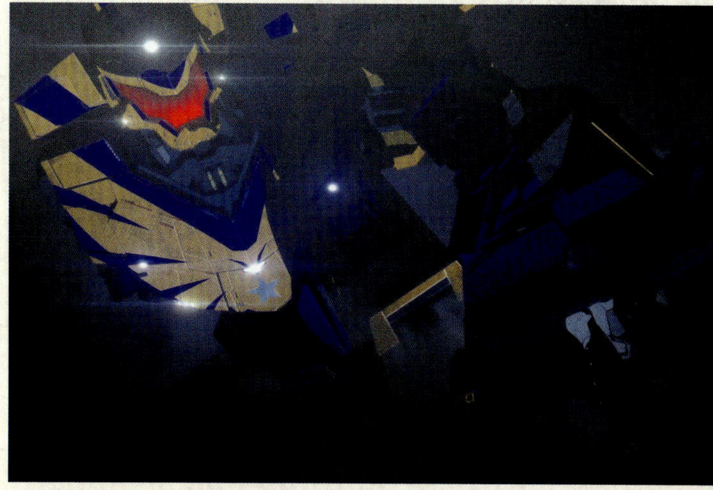

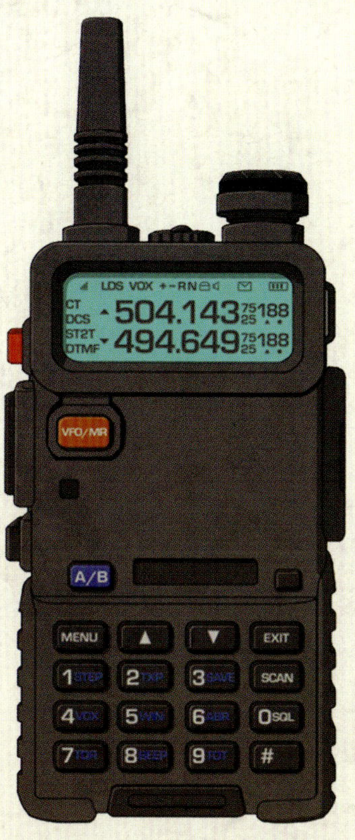

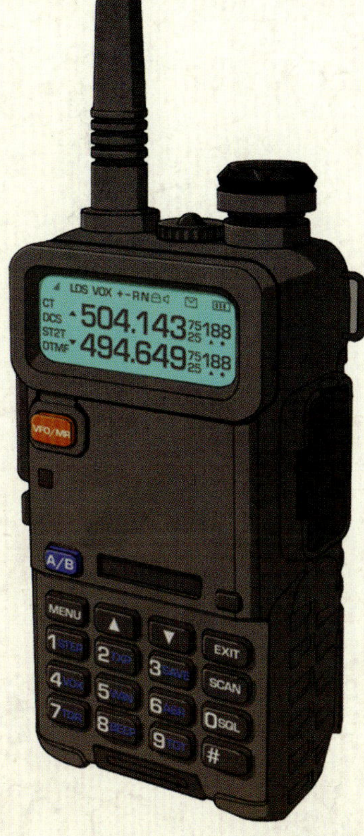

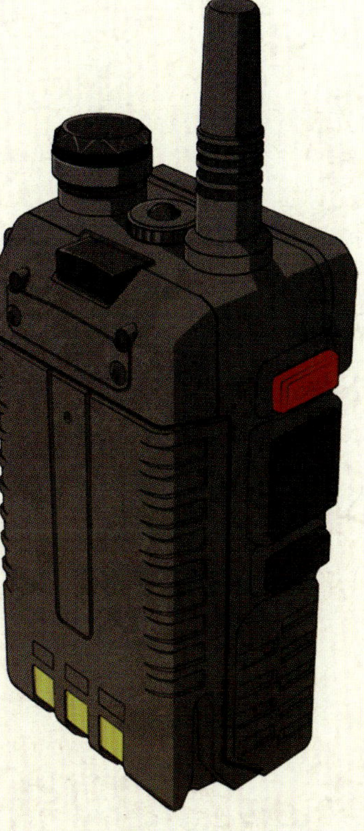

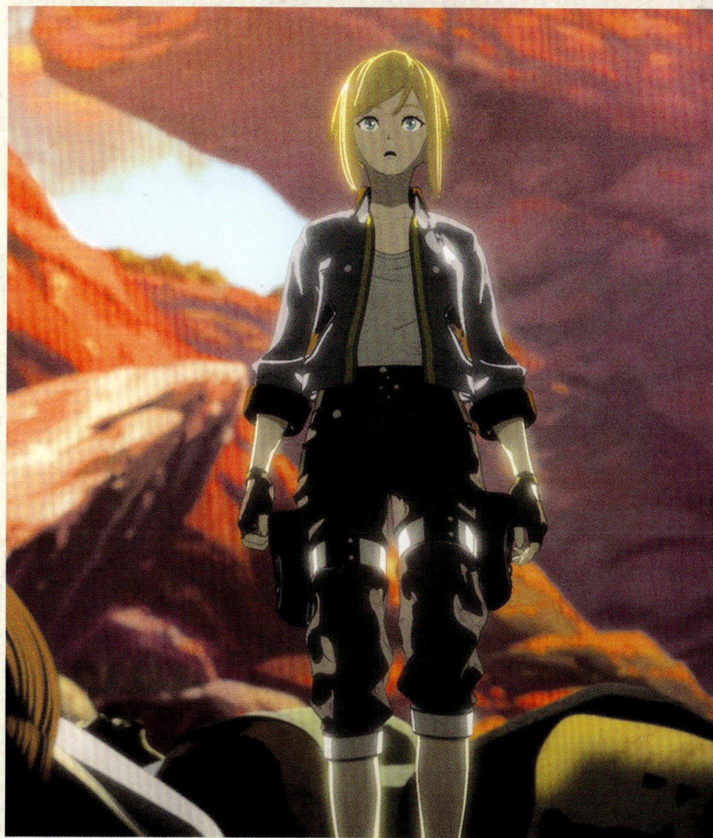

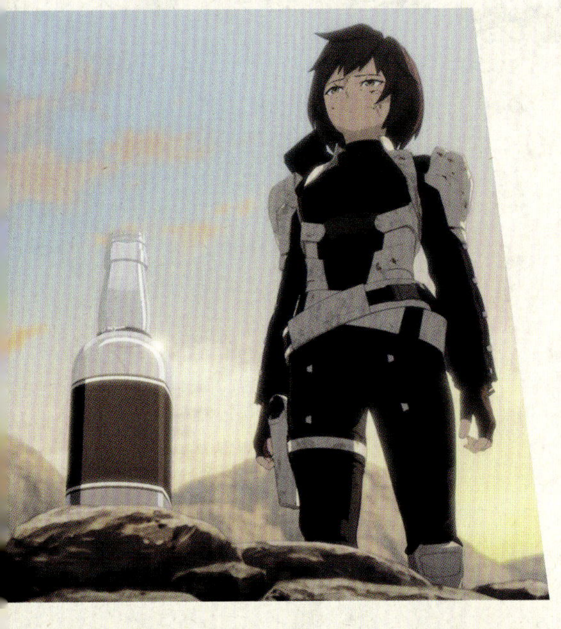

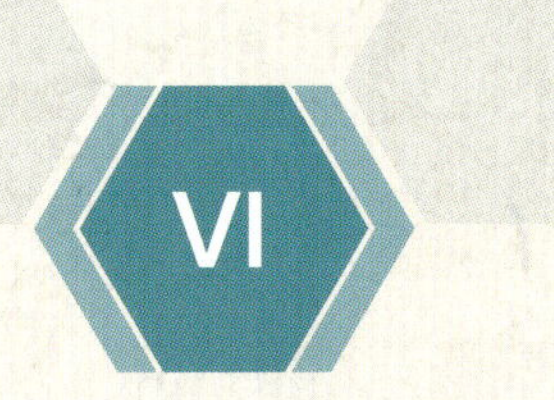

CHAPTER SIX
THE DRONE IN THE BONEYARD

Episode Six, "Boneyard", sees the family that seemed to be growing reduced back to the trio of Taylor, Hayley and bOy. After burying Joel—whose death affects her deeply—Mei walks out on the others, shunning Hayley's offer of friendship.

An eruption of fiery light appears in the distance, and bOy runs off towards it. It's a new breach, which means a new entry point for Kaiju. The siblings' pursuit of bOy leads them to a shallow, shadowy depression in the desert, with the breach forming in the middle of it.

Also in the depression is a bizarre 'graveyard', with the massed remains of Kaiju and Jaegers together. Loa identifies three of the Jaegers as November Ajax, Valor Omega and Titan Redeemer, all previously seen in *Pacific Rim: Uprising.*

bOy stands calmly at the brink of the iridescent new breach. Before Atlas Destroyer can reach him, a Kaiju climbs from the chasm—an Acidquill monster, like those from the first episode. Ignoring bOy, the Kaiju attacks the Jaeger, which is terribly hampered by having only one arm. The monster pins the Jaeger and is about to deliver the death blow, but a new combatant grabs the Acidquill by the tail, swings it around and brings it crashing to the ground!

This newcomer is the mystery giant from Episode Two. Now it's revealed; a gigantic biped that's metallic like the Jaegers, with a maw full of massive steel teeth.

It's called Apex, and like the 'dead' Jaegers in the graveyard, it first appeared in *Pacific Rim: Uprising.* That film introduced a new kind of giant; Drone Jaegers, ostensibly a new kind of Jaeger built to help beat the Kaiju. But the Drone Jaegers were really a trap; they were Kaiju-Jaeger hybrids, built to fight humanity.

"We did some touch-ups for Apex," says Jae-Hong Kim, "because the writers wanted to connect some storylines from the live-action movies. Since this show is set after the second film, Greg Johnson and Craig Kyle decided to use Drone Jaegers. The Drone was already a hybrid creature, Kaiju and mecha, so we didn't have much trouble re-using it.

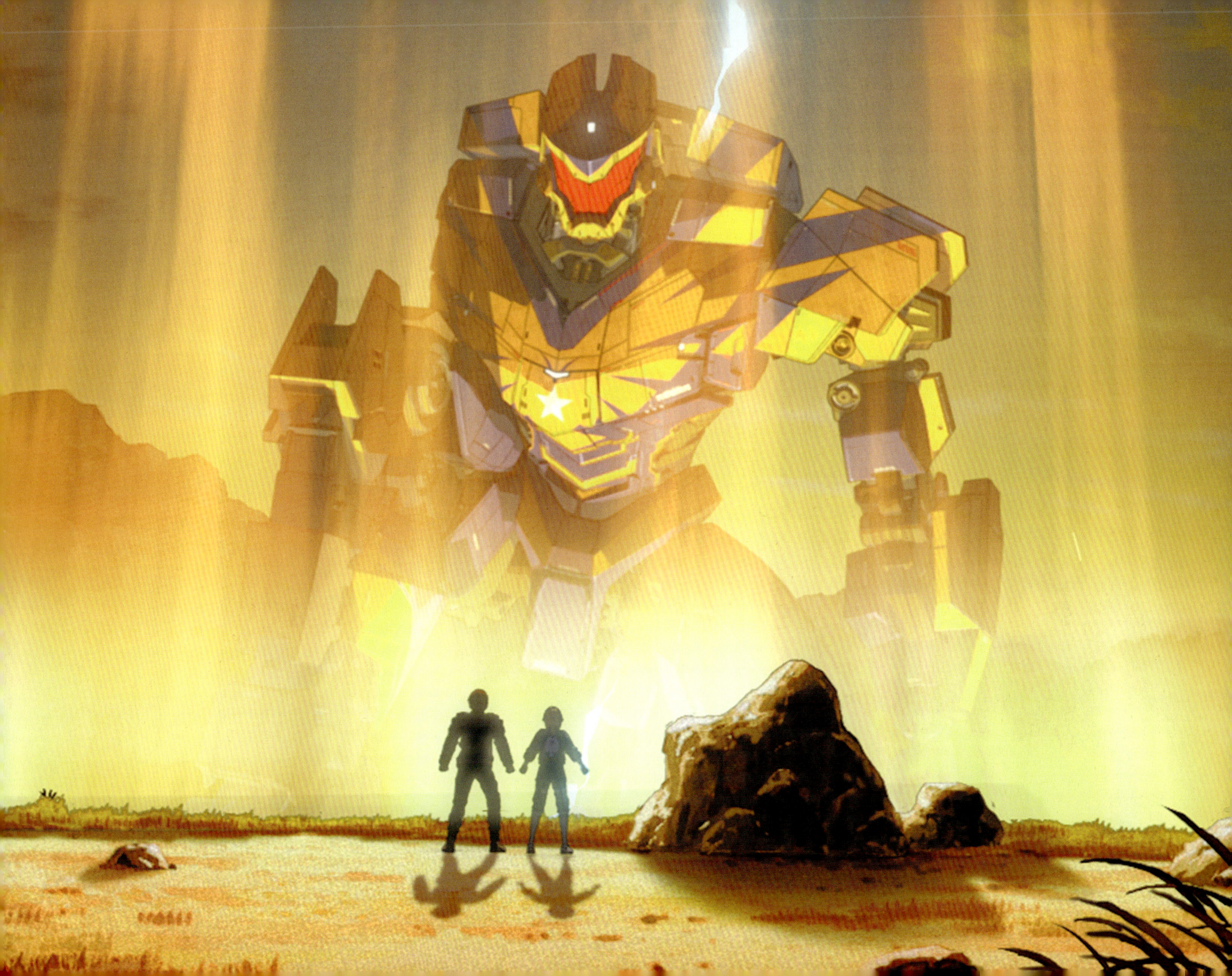

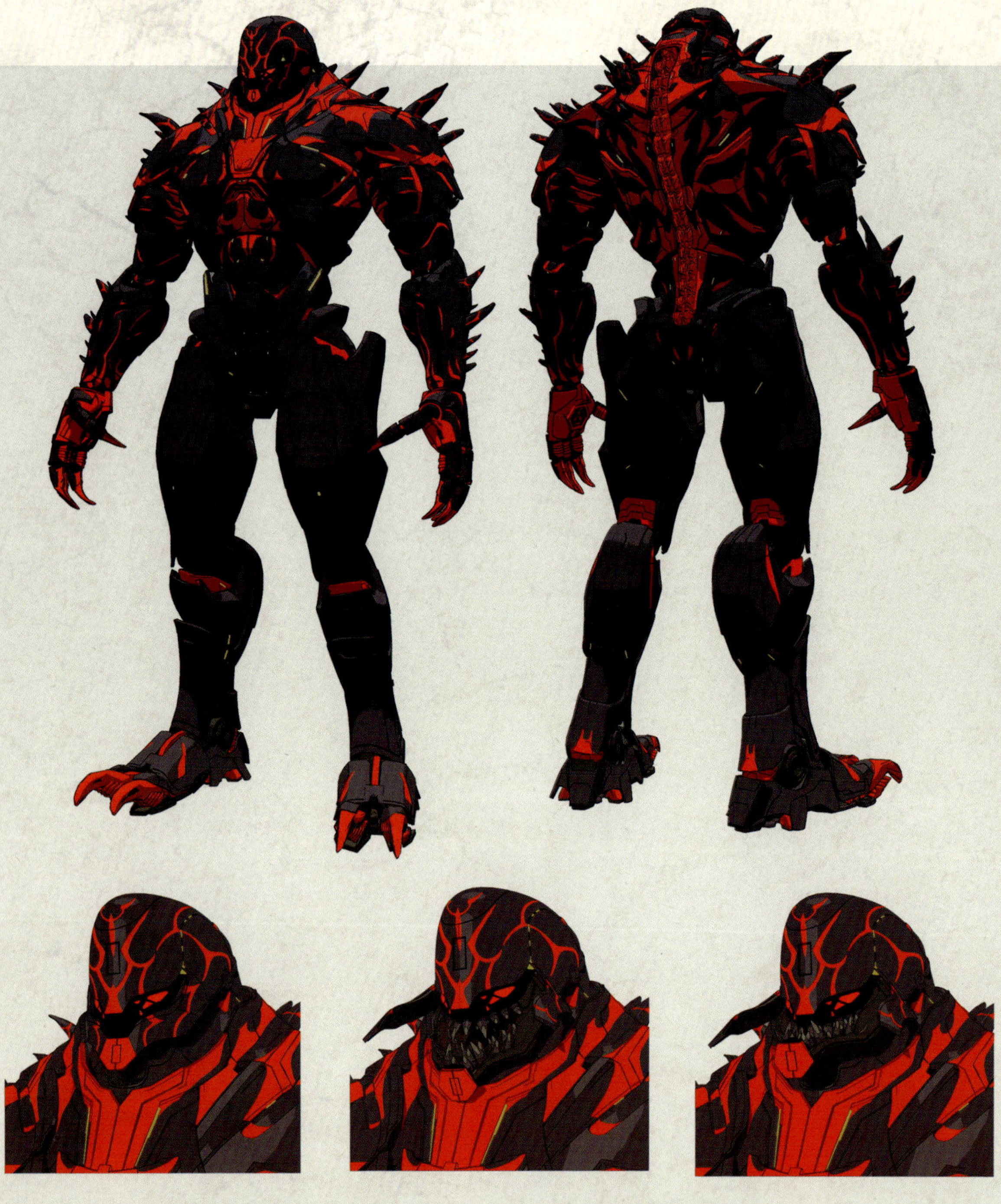

Polygon's design team did a terrific job to augment the look of Apex, adding teeth and thorns!"

Finishing the Acidquill, Apex leaps to smash Atlas Destroyer. But there's a tiny obstacle in its way. bOy is standing on the fallen Jaeger's 'face'. Apex's huge fist smashes down; surely it must pulverise him. Instead, Taylor and Hayley see the impossible— bOy holding Apex away from the Jaeger, the giant's fists stopped by bOy's tiny hands.

Instead of continuing to fight, Apex leans slowly, even respectfully, towards bOy. The giant establishes a neural bridge with bOy; caught in that bridge, Taylor and Hayley see the Apex's memories. After the battle in *Uprising*, Apex evolved from a quasi-Kaiju into a bio-mech being, not aligned with Kaiju or with humans.

Greg Johnson comments: "Both sides of Apex—the Jaeger and the Kaiju—are not only warriors designed for violence, but warriors pitted against one another. Once those sides become mashed together, any semblance of good or bad becomes irrelevant. There is no allegiance to anyone because Apex is the only one of his kind. An 'Only', as we were calling him. That is until he meets bOy, a human and a Kaiju mashed together, and the only one of his kind. Are they monsters? Not to each other. Are they capable of monstrous acts? Absolutely. As we all are."

Before leaving, Apex gives the children a 'present'—the arm of a Jaeger. It's compatible with Atlas Destroyer, and connects to its shoulder in moments. Not only does the Jaeger have two good arms again, but now it has a weapon: a projectile saber chain. That's good, because Copperhead is near...

Left // Streaked with crimson, Apex may look like a demon, but he's really one of a kind.

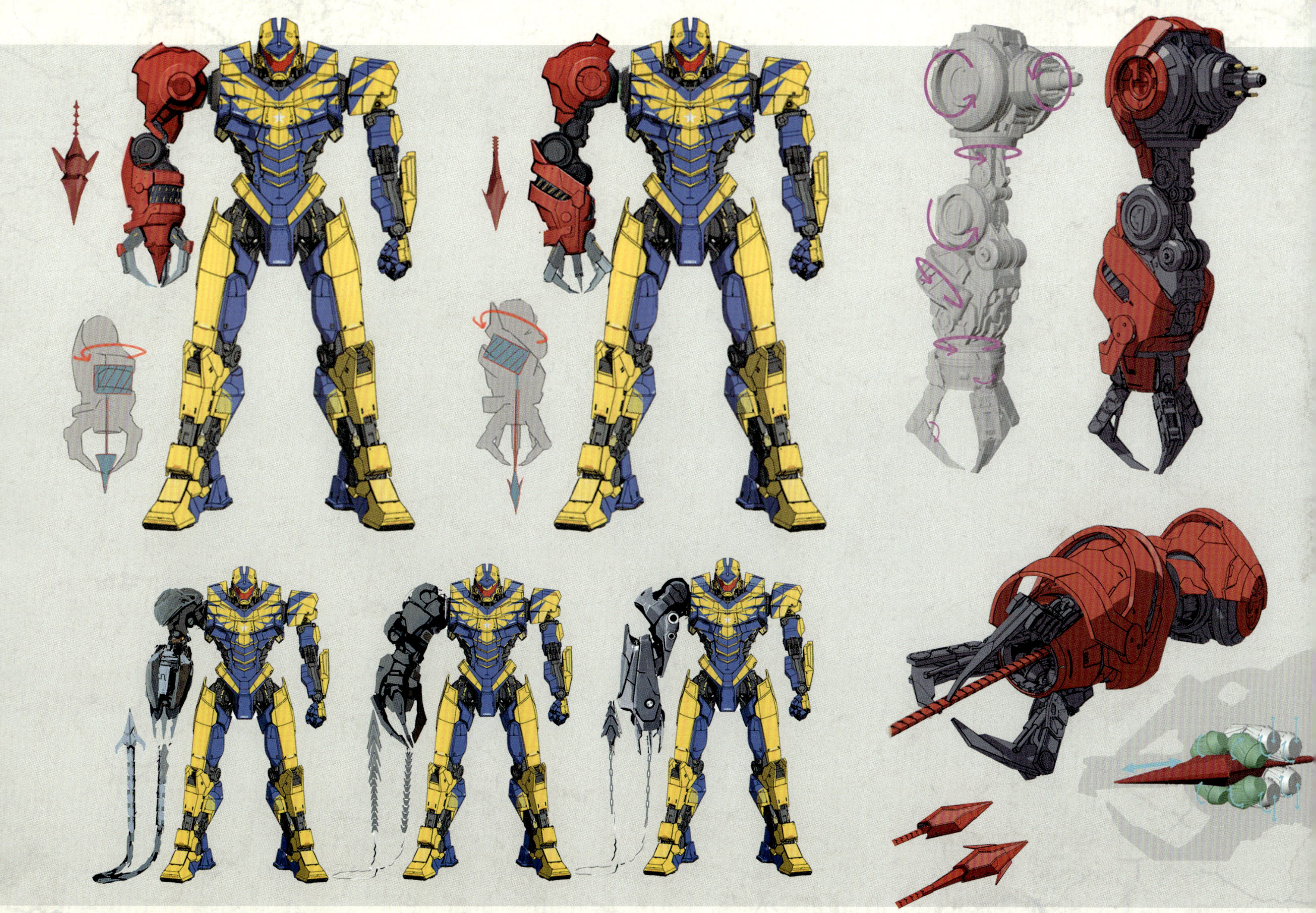

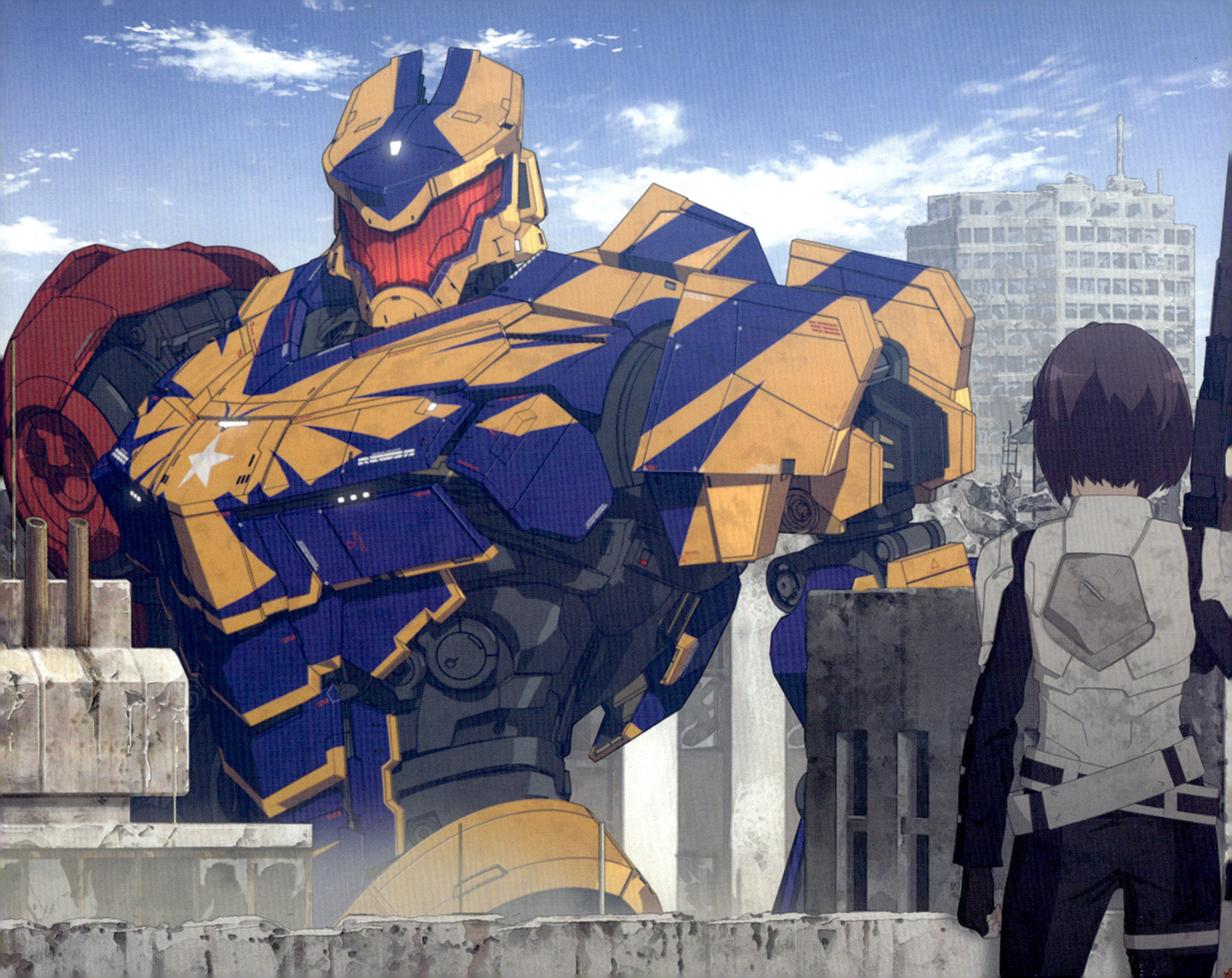

CHAPTER SEVEN

THE BOY AND THE BEAST

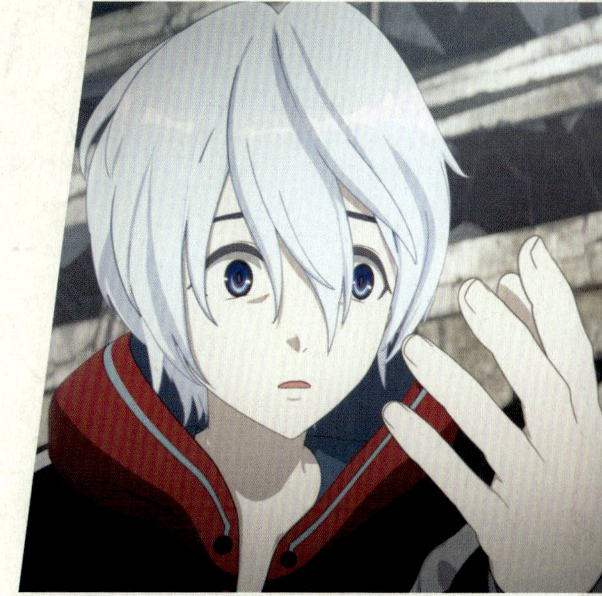

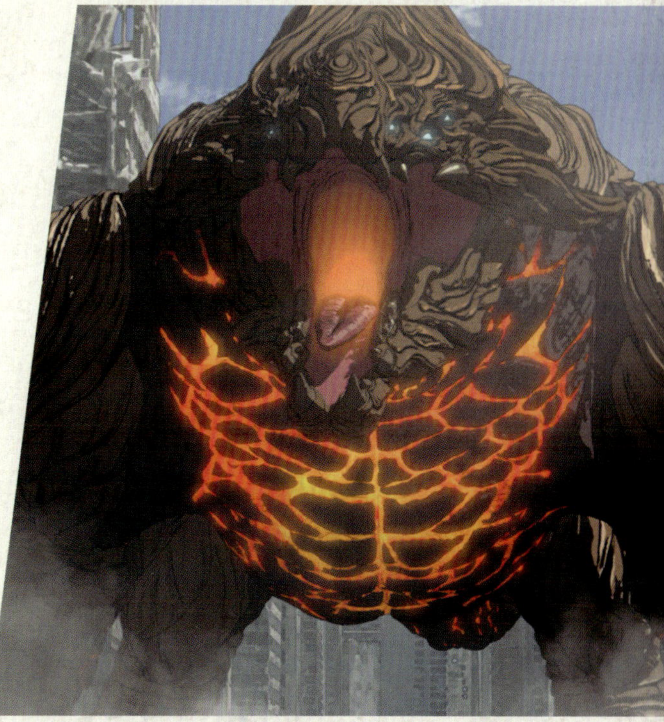

In "Showdown", the last episode of Season One, Loa detects an unknown Jaeger in the nearby Clayton City. There, the children find Mei in a derelict Chinese restaurant. She's angry to see them, yet Hayley and bOy's innocence somehow touches her. For once, the blackout didn't knock out all the city's power grids, and Mei offers them hot chocolate.

The children dance boisterously to the café jukebox. Remarkably, even Mei is pulled into the scene and enjoys herself. But she sees herself in a reflection and has traumatic memories of Shane. Snapping back to her usual cold personality, she orders the others out.

The children find the Jaeger that Loa detected. It's Hunter Vertigo, the Jaeger piloted by Taylor and Hayley's parents, but now it's collapsed and empty. All the siblings find inside is a recorded message, showing Ford and Brina abandoning the battered Jaeger during an attack. The couple's fate is unrecorded, leaving Taylor and Hayley in anguish.

Before they can return to Atlas Destroyer, Copperhead pounces. The youngsters can only run; bOy sees Hayley knocked out. bOy looks at the advancing Copperhead, and he roars. Hayley awakes in time to see bOy transform… into a Kaiju!

The bOy-Kaiju looks tough, but very nimble and fast, even more than Copperhead. Of all the Kaiju in the series, this creature seems closest to human. "We needed a different type of Kaiju mix-up, with human and Kaiju," says Kim. "The fight style had to be different. Instead of big and powerful, this Kaiju is small compared with other Kaiju, and fast. Agility and speed are his weapons. The face was the hard part. He shouldn't be too cute, but not too monstrous... It was hard to nail down."

"This is something that we struggled with," says Hiroyuki Hayashi. "We really thought about how to make the transformation from bOy's human form to a Kaiju, and what kind of Kaiju we wanted to make him into, and how to express that transformation. We discussed it a great deal

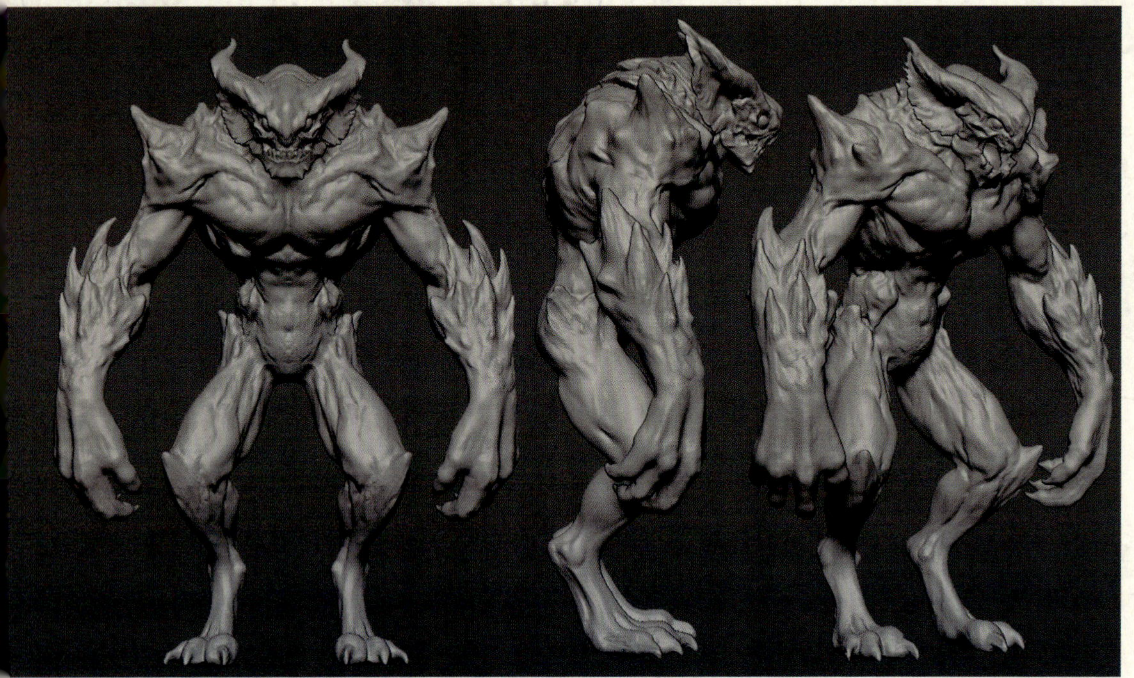

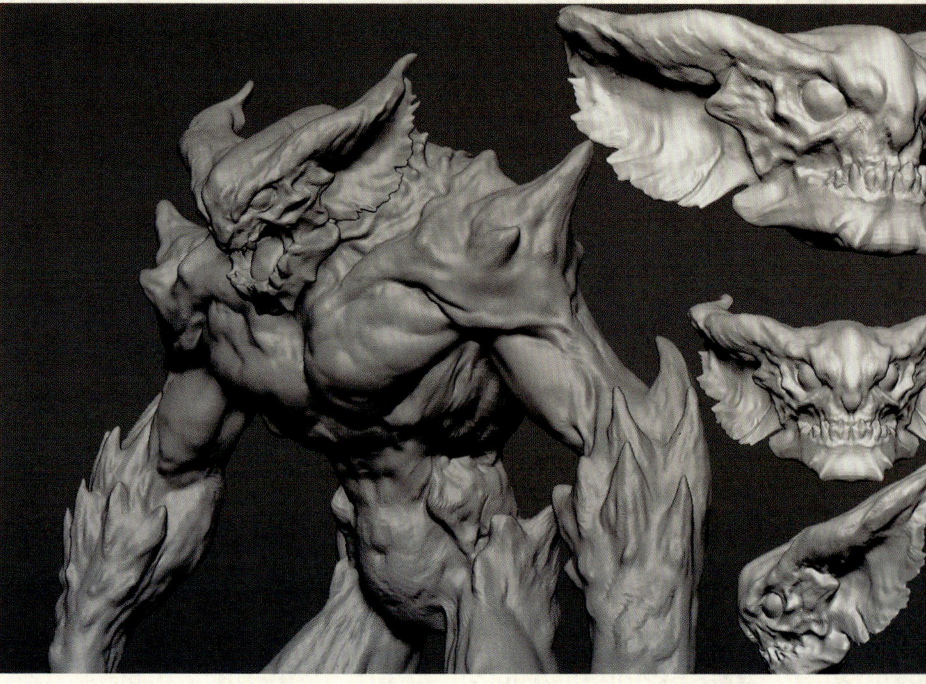

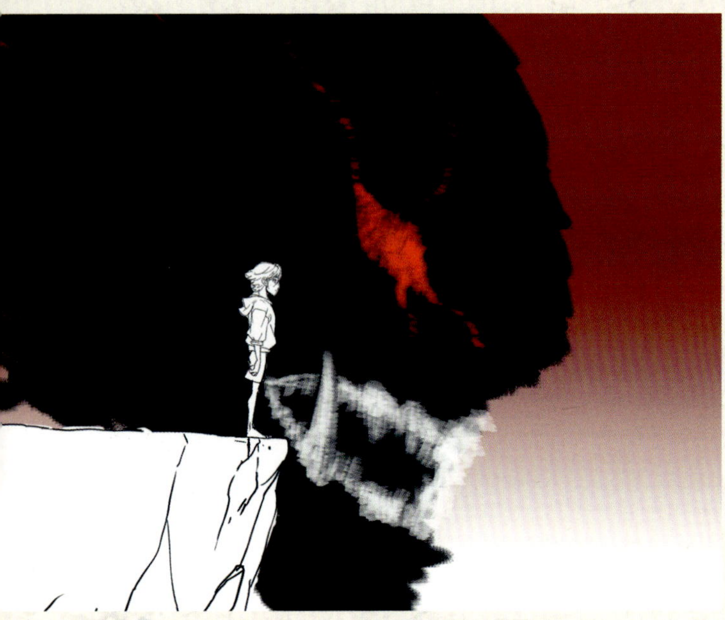

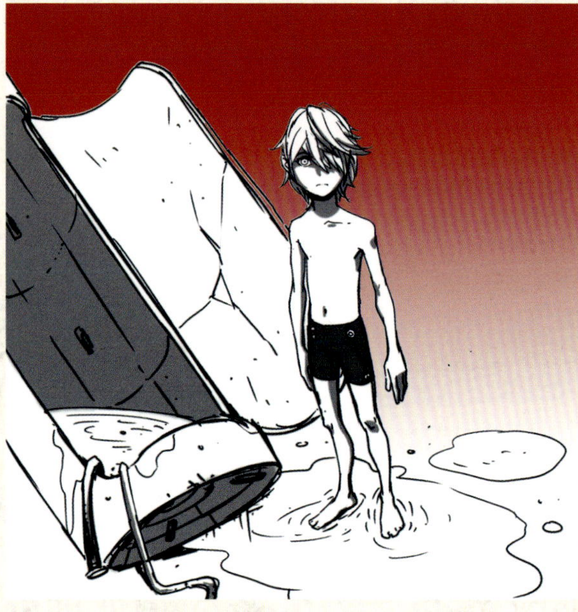

with the showrunner, and there was a lot of back and forth. Ultimately, the showrunner gave us a design that ended up pretty close to the one we went with at the end."

Yuki Moriyama says, "The biggest difference between the Kaiju version of bOy and all the other Kaiju, from a simple design perspective, is the fact he's the only Kaiju with a set of facial expressions. So, despite being a Kaiju, he has a sad face, he has a happy face; he has a range of emotions. If you look at him, he's clearly a monster, but he has that element of humanity, that emotional aspect to him as well. You can see it very simply just by the expressions on his face."

For all bOy's fury in his Kaiju form, even he can't take down Copperhead. But salvation arrives—Atlas Destroyer, piloted by Taylor and Mei. The pilots lacerate the Kaiju with

Above and left // There's a beast in this bOy, but also a trace of bOy in the beast...

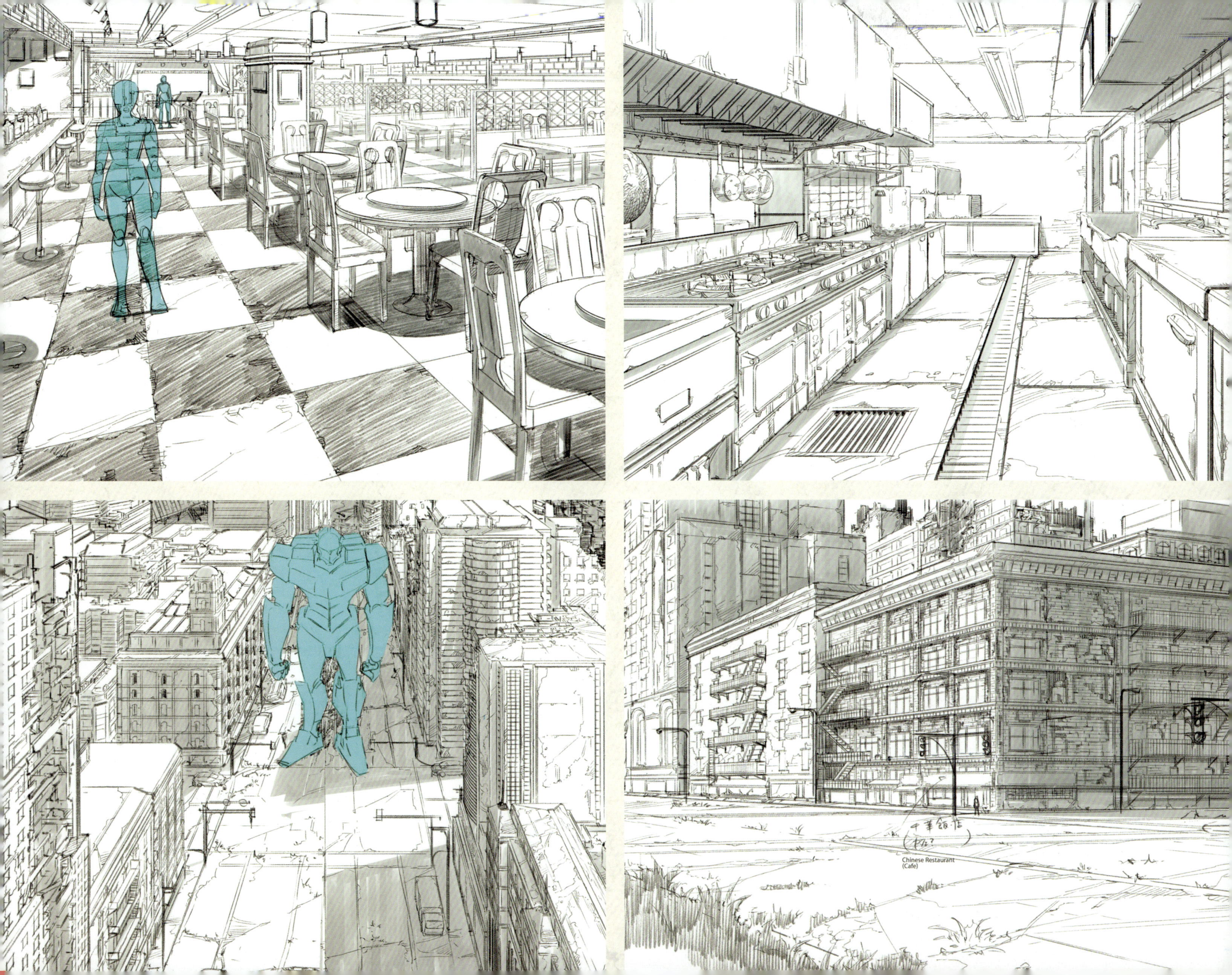
Chinese Restaurant
(Cafe)

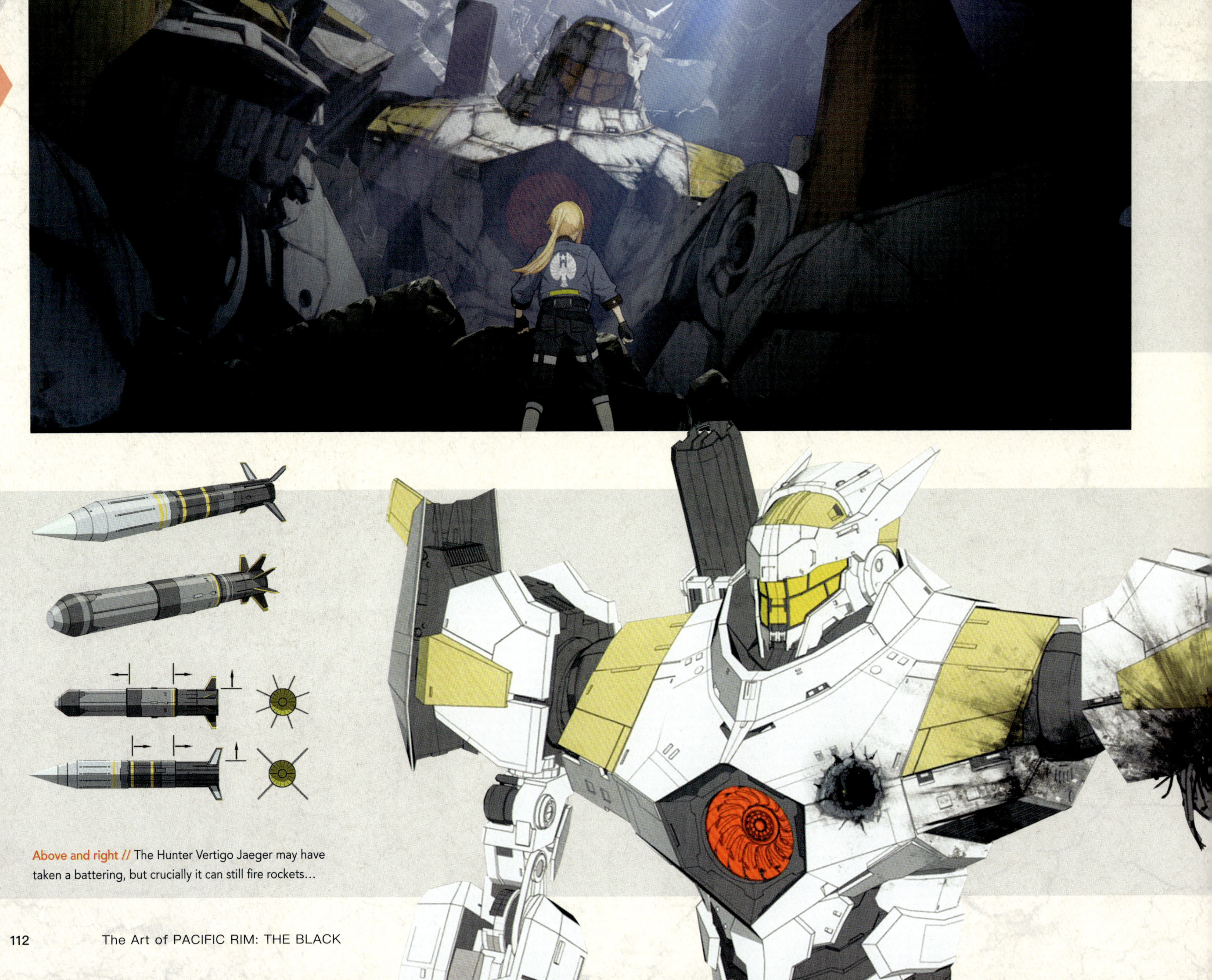

Above and right // The Hunter Vertigo Jaeger may have taken a battering, but crucially it can still fire rockets…

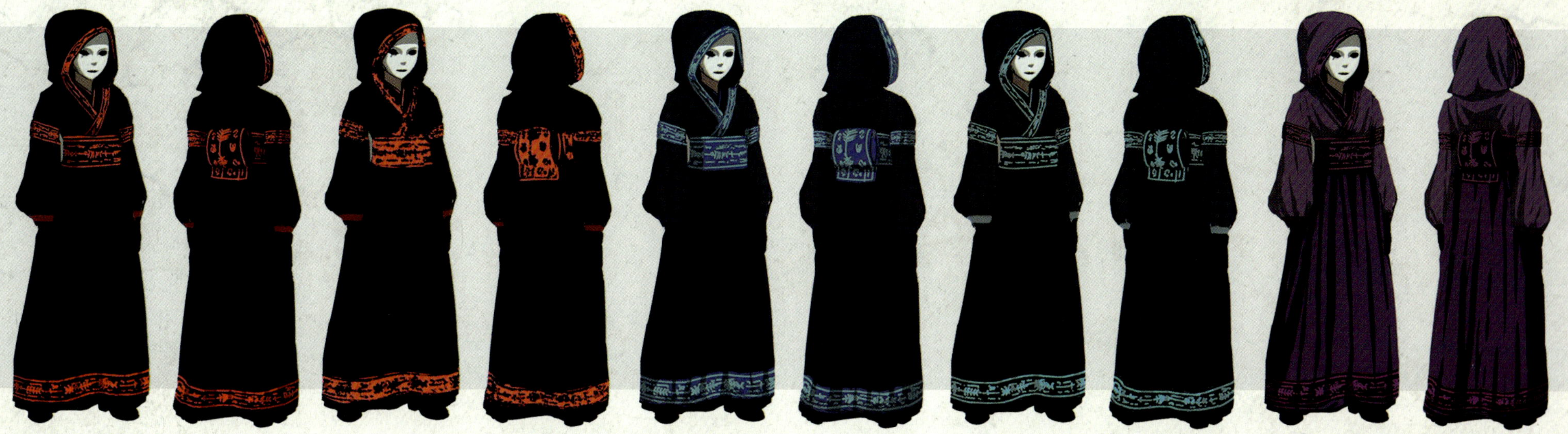

the projectile chain, hit it with an exploding tank truck, and tear off its forepaw—sweet revenge! But the monster still won't go down…

Except that earlier in the episode, the children saw that Hunter Vertigo had a mini-rocket jammed in its firing tube. Climbing onto her parents' Jaeger, Hayley realigns the rocket with a kick, then goes inside, powers up the Jaeger, and fires. A second later, Copperhead is a gooey mess on the streets.

Greg Johnson comments, "In service to the multi-season story arc, we knew our characters would not make it to the coastline in the first season, so we needed a big victory to go out on. Taking down Copperhead gave us that, allowing Taylor and Hayley to finally start healing from the trauma that launched them into [the] unknown."

Hayley tries to calm the monstrous bOy, still trapped in rubble. Above on a rooftop, we see Rippers looking down, only these Rippers have masters. They're commanded by human figures; these strangers wear dark cloaks with ornate patterns that seem to glow. Their faces are covered by impassive white masks.

Back in Episode Three, Shane had made an offhand reference to the "Sisters". Here they are, proclaiming the coming of the Kaiju Messiah as Season One ends.

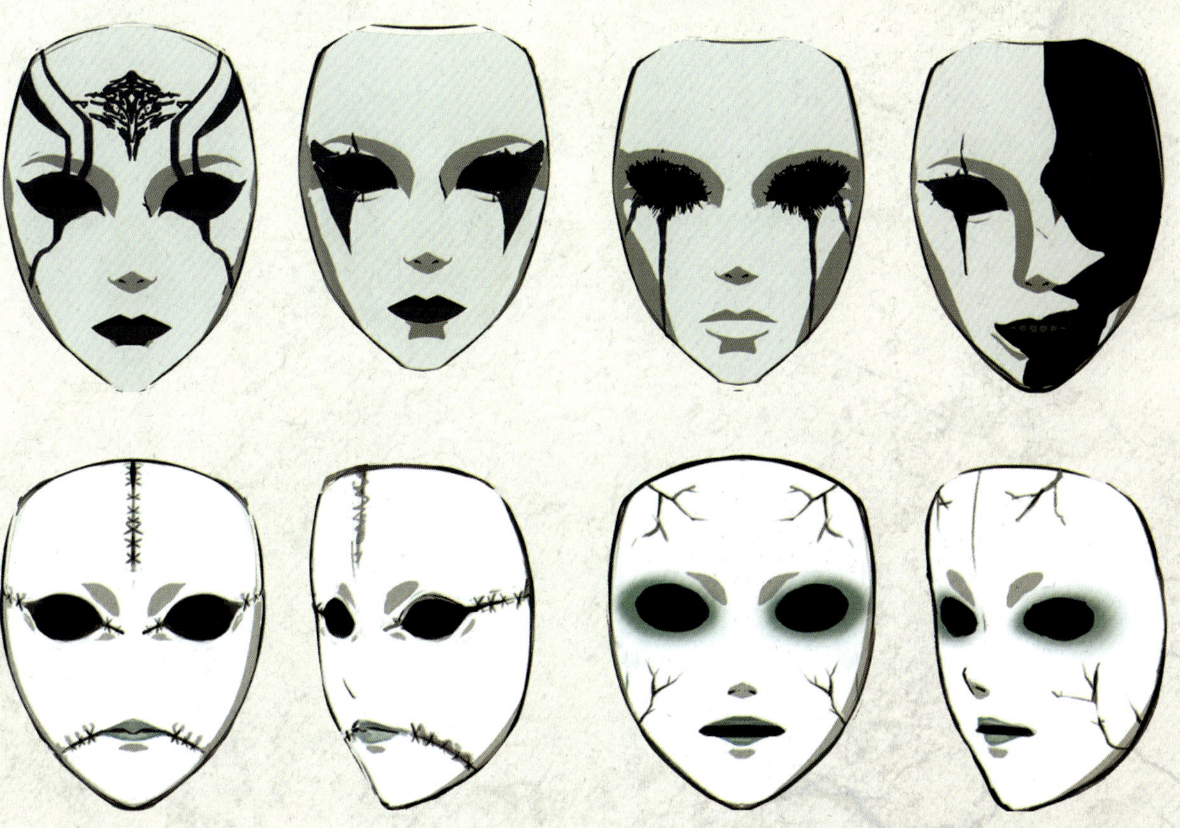

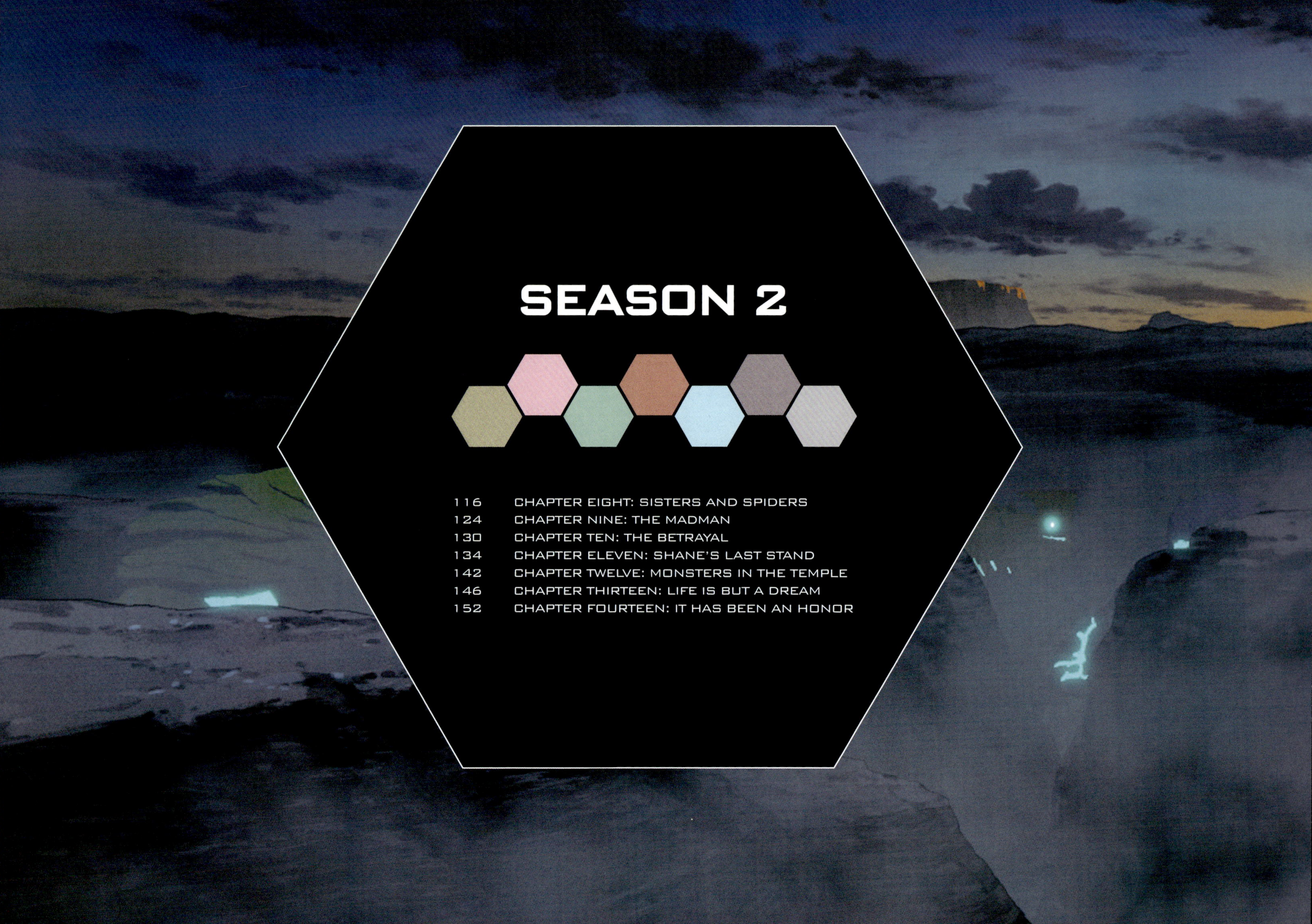

SEASON 2

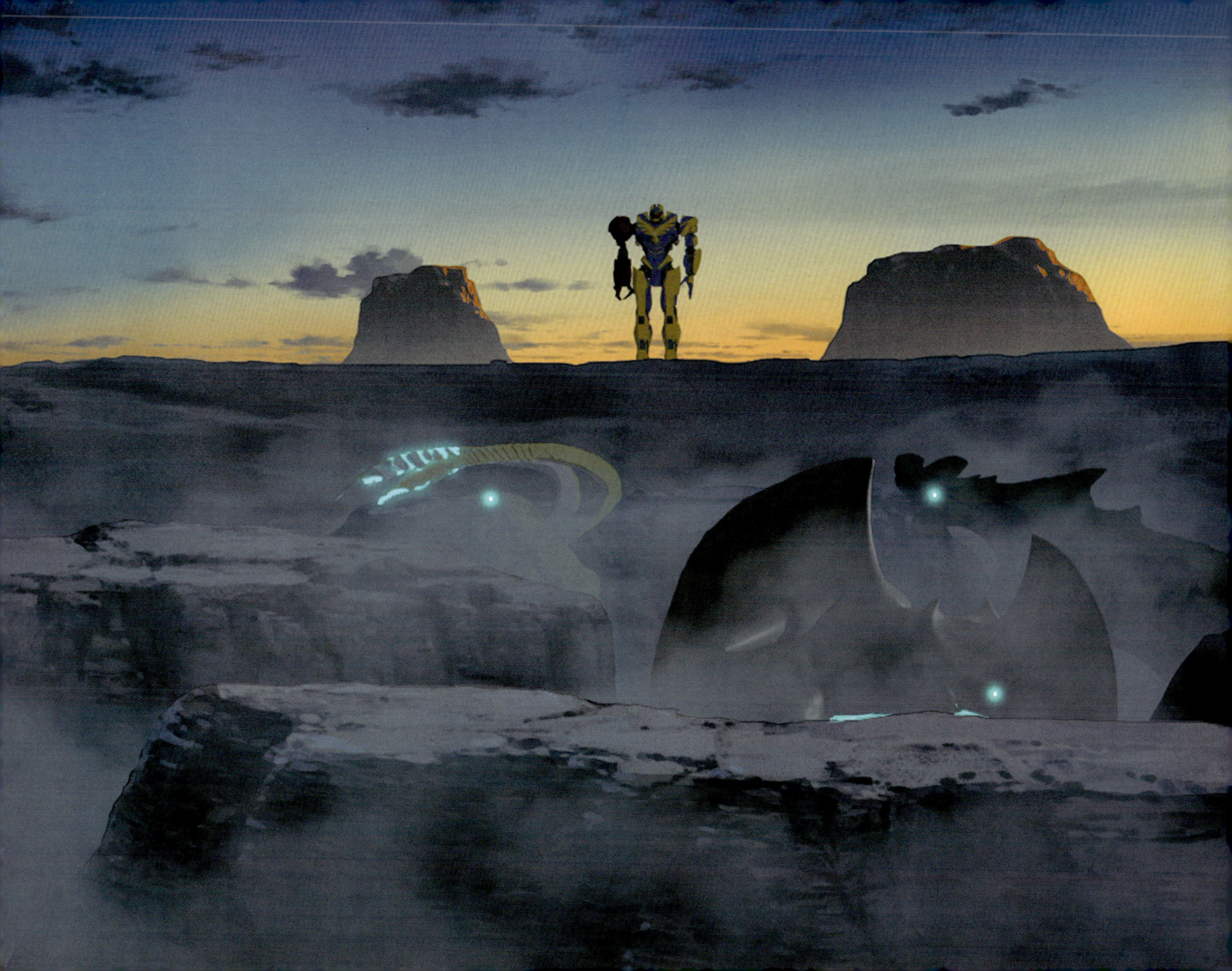

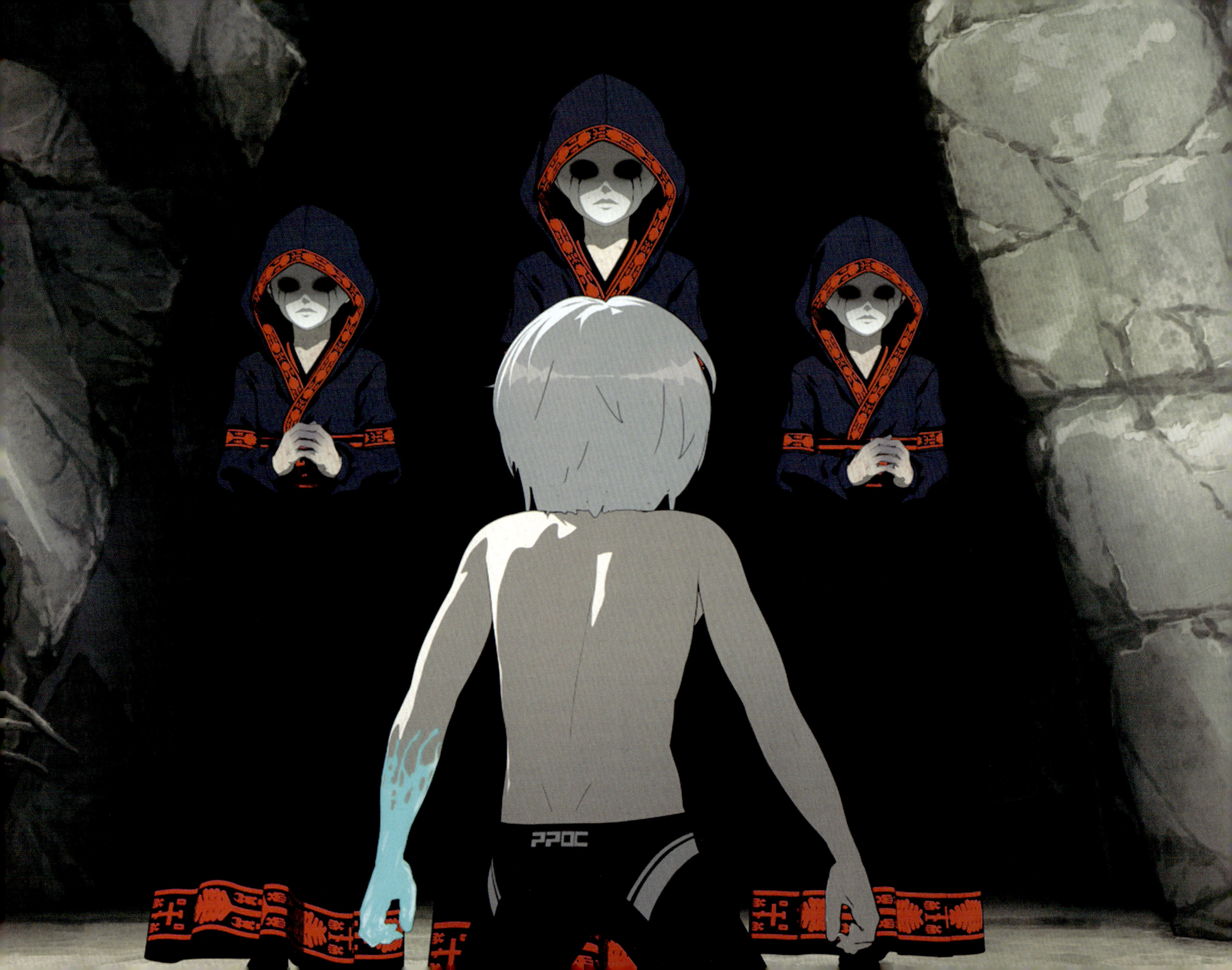

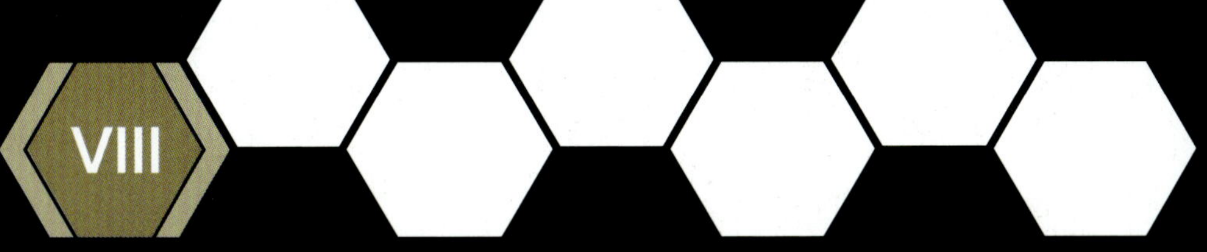

CHAPTER EIGHT

SISTERS AND SPIDERS

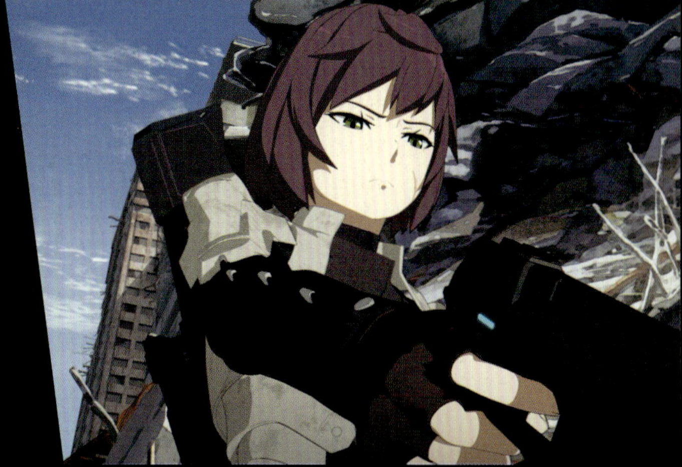

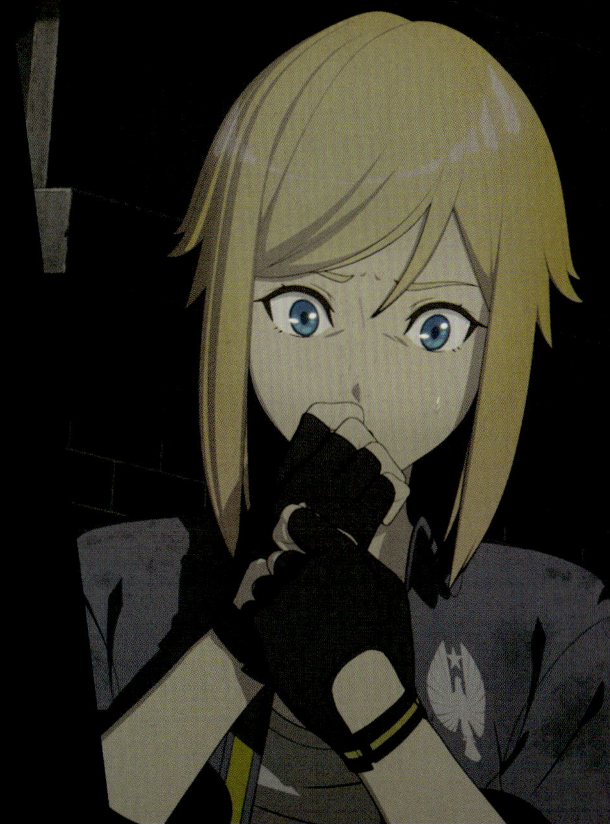

Most people would assume making the second season of a series like *Pacific Rim: The Black* would be more straightforward than starting the first. The creators confirm that was the case, at least to an extent.

According to Duer, "By the time we were deep into Season One and starting to prep Season Two, we knew certain things weren't working and some things worked well. By the end of Season One, both the American and Japanese sides started to understand each other in terms of creative 'likes' and 'dislikes', the personality of each character, the dynamics of relationships amongst the cast, and what needed to stay within *Pacific Rim* mythology. We also changed certain production workflows and pipeline arrangements so we could stay on schedule and budget. Production means always evolving and making adjustments as we go."

Speaking about Polygon, Kim says, "They are fast learners, and smart. We had some adjustment time at the beginning, but in the second season it was a smooth ride. There were fewer notes from our side, and they had a lot more involvement than in the first season. They suggested more ideas and set designs, and we were glad to accept their ideas because that's the spirit of working as a team!"

Earlier, Duer stressed the importance of reusing CG assets. Was it possible to reuse assets from the first season in the second in ways that made it cheaper? "Yes, theoretically the cost per episode becomes cheaper if you re-use characters and location assets," Duer confirms. "However, it depends on the type of series and how the story is told. This series is a traveling show, showing the kids' journey from inland Australia to coastal Sydney. Although there are some reused characters and locations, we constantly visited new locations along the way."

Duer continues, "In order not to get crazy with introducing new locations and new characters, the writing had to be well planned in advance to keep the asset count within the budget and schedule. On occasion, we had to go back to the script and cut certain locations and characters, and thus sections had to be re-written."

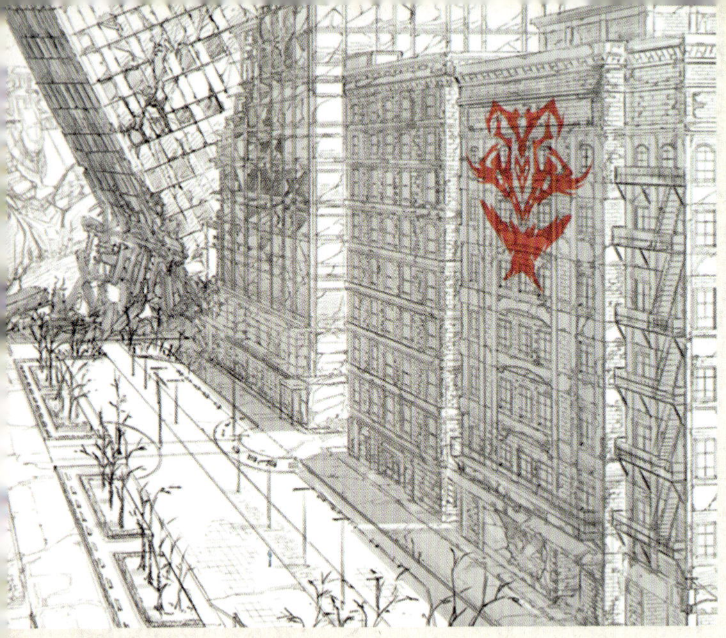

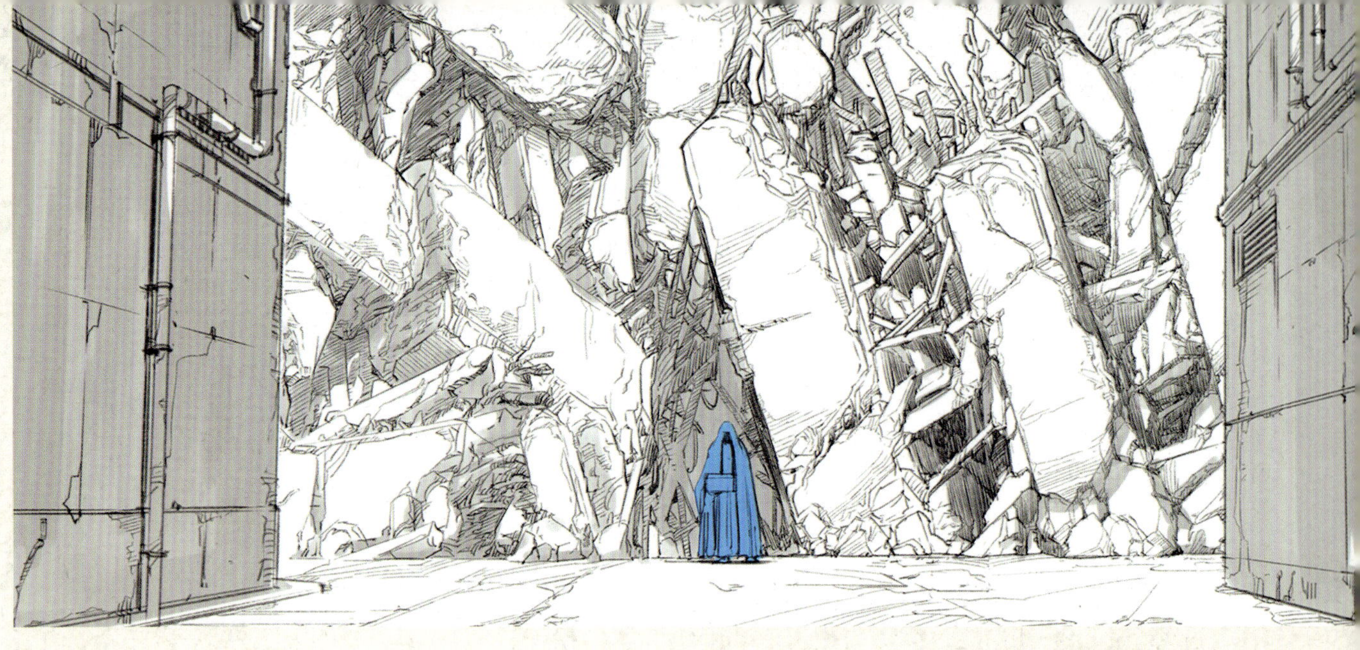

Kim adds, "We already spent (actually 'overed') our asset counts in the previous season, so one of the big tasks for Season Two was to reduce the number of assets. Of course, that would save time and money for production, but at the same time, that should not limit the creativity of the storytelling and animation. Our writers did a great job on that."

Whereas Season One had harsh shocks, such as Joel's fate in Episode Five, Season Two feels even darker, far more than the *Pacific Rim* films. On this trend, Johnson says, "Since *Pacific Rim: The Black* is about enduring the Kaiju occupation and not triumphing over the invasion, there is a natural feeling of darkness that does influence the tone. Watching our characters navigate this while still maintaining hope is what lifts it out of despair."

Johnson continues, "The live-action films also had their darkness: an active black market (in Kaiju organs), a devout Kaiju religion, the psychological wounds of Drifting. In an unchecked Kaiju-dominated landscape, the dark corners become more prevalent. Legendary and Netflix saw the value in telling character-driven stories in this harsher environment, and fully embraced it."

Kim adds, "I've always insisted this show needs weight in every aspect. Color, light, shadow… I didn't want this anime version of *Pacific Rim* to look lightweight. So yes, it was intended and planned out the way you see."

Season Two starts seconds after the first season ended. Many series would use a break between seasons to have time pass 'in story', to give the characters a break. Not *Pacific Rim: The Black*. "We did discuss adding a story break between seasons," says Johnson. "But to justify a pause would require giving the first season more of a wrap-up, to leave our characters in a new normal that would feasibly fill and sustain that gap. Such character gymnastics would have felt too rushed if forced into the end of the previous episode. Especially since Taylor wants to leave bOy behind." This point will be a huge source of conflict in Season Two.

"Also," adds Johnson, "our stories have a momentum, a sense of urgency that would suffer, in my opinion, from a passage of time between seasons."

Episode One of Season Two, "bOy", starts with the siblings at loggerheads again, much as they were a season ago. Hayley is determined to protect the bOy-Kaiju, while Taylor argues that "bOy" doesn't exist anymore. Hayley has come to regard bOy as a family member, a view Taylor can't share. Despite her brother's horrified warnings, Hayley reaches out to comfort the Kaiju… and it shrinks back into human form, a 'boy' once more.

Hayley's fearlessness before bOy, even when he's a monster, may remind viewers of *King Kong*. "Beauty and

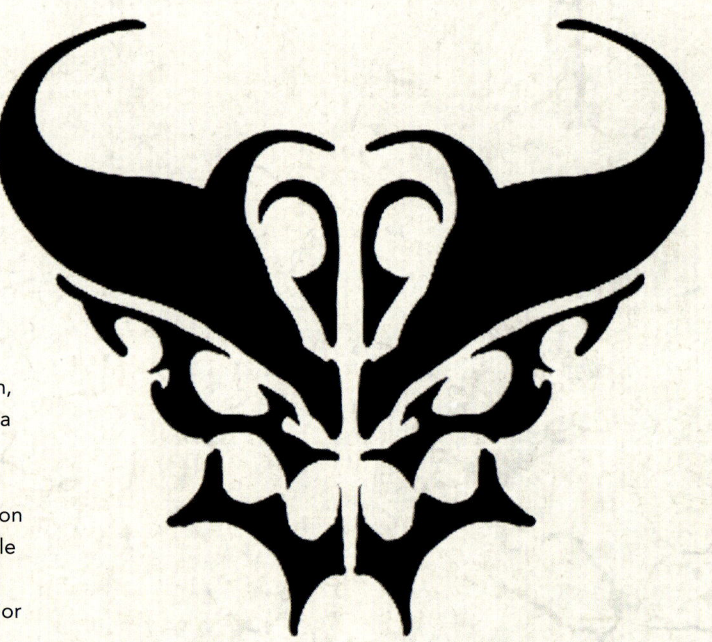

Above // The insignia of the Sisters, who will be the children's greatest foe in Season Two.

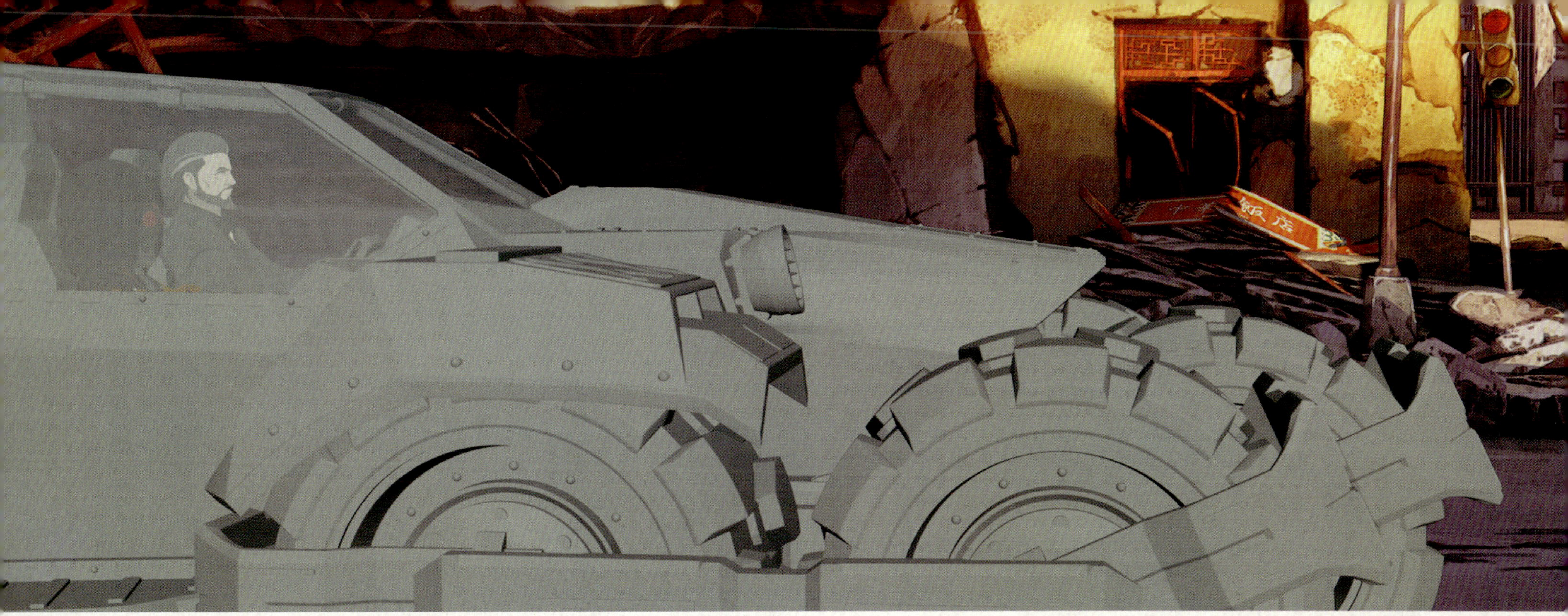

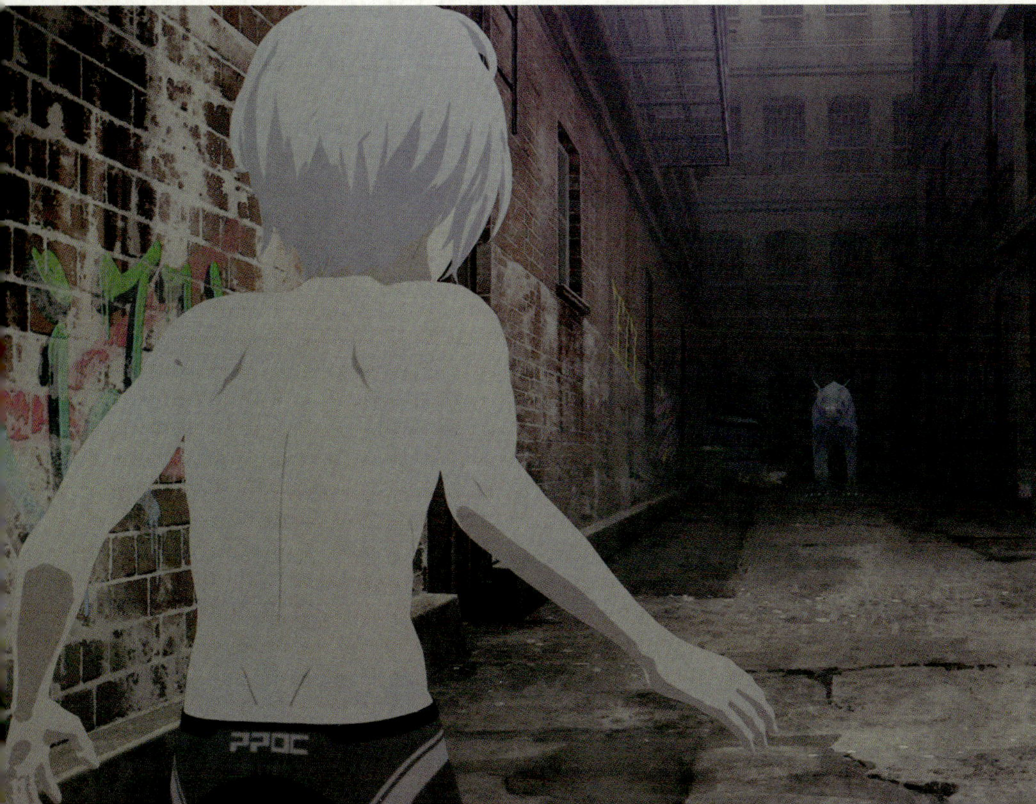

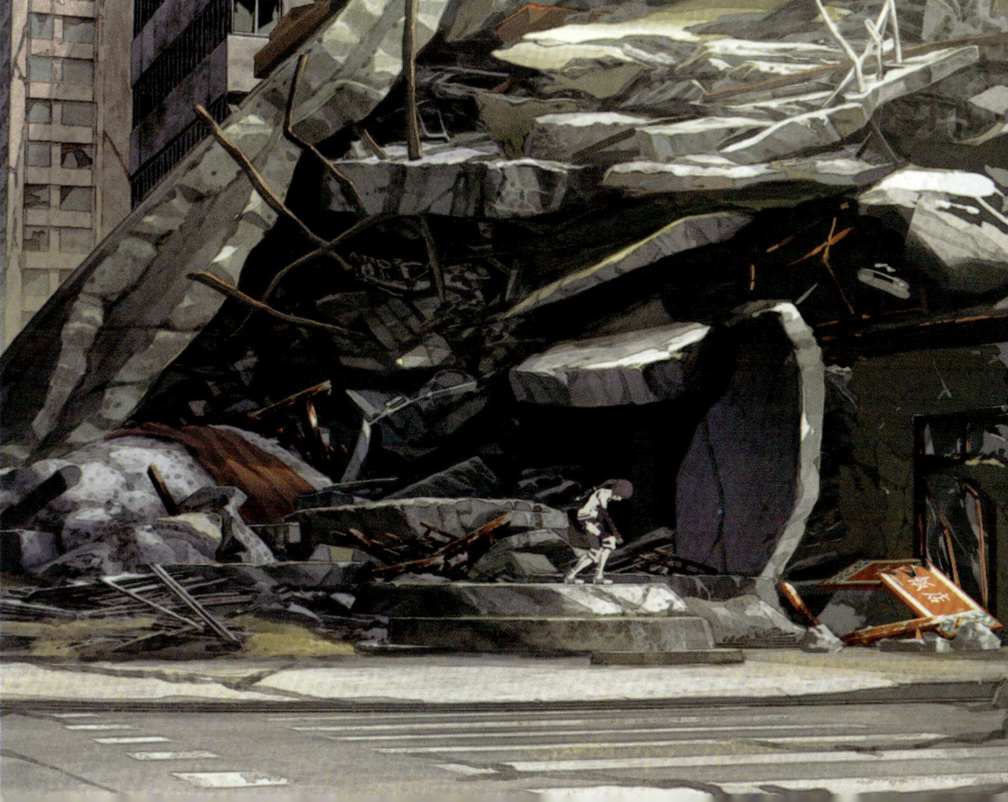

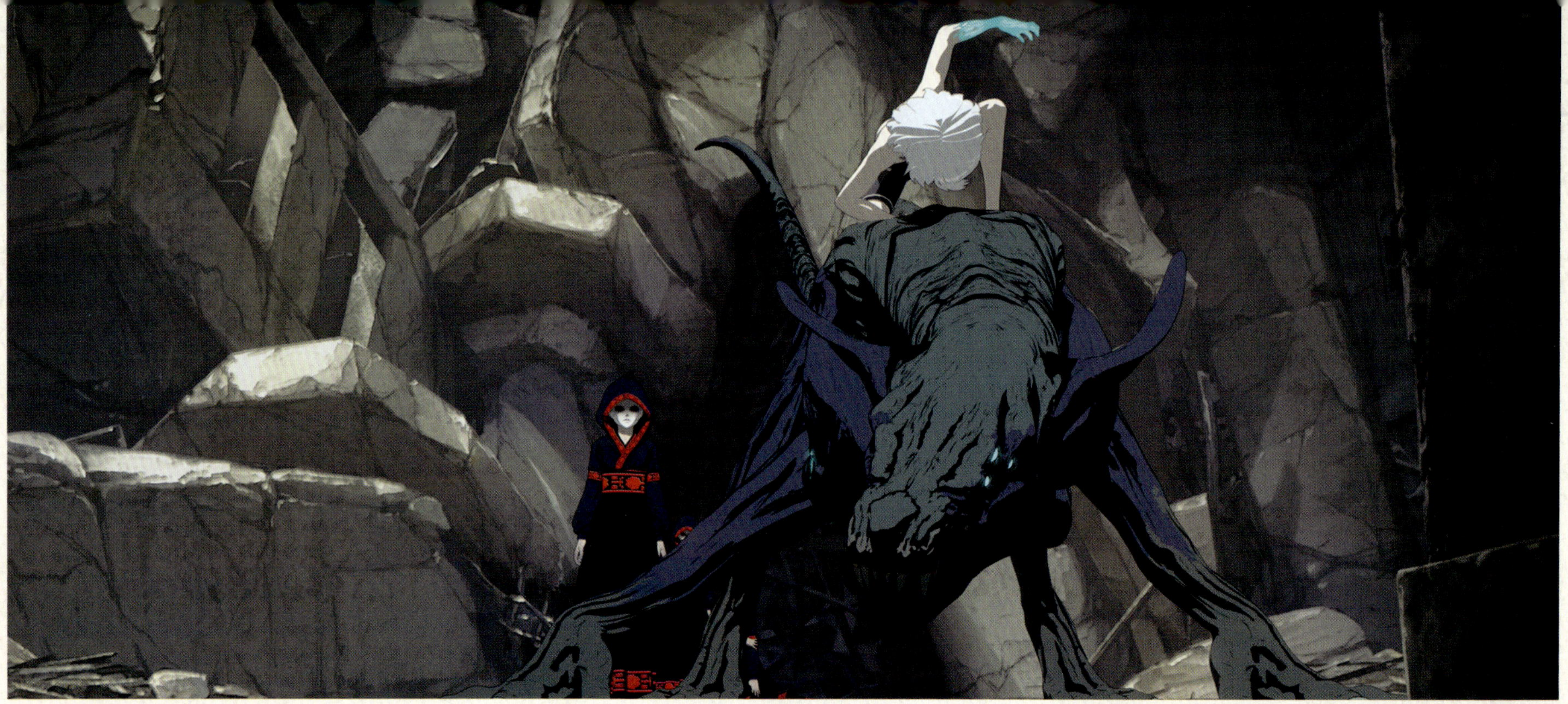

the Beast; a tale as old as time," Johnson says. "We love the idea that 'humanity' can take different forms. It can also be so buried that you're not even sure there's any left. The fact that Hayley can find the vulnerable child within a towering Kaiju says a lot about her. She has taken responsibility for bOy, and that means seeing him through his painful struggles."

Even when he turns back, bOy's not the same. His right eye now has a crimson pupil, and the skin around it is gray and scaly, a reminder of bOy's Kaiju form. Kim and the other staff discussed post-transformation looks for the youngster. "We had some ideas how he would look after he transformed, but we were already over budget," Kim says. "So we had to find a simpler solution, and adding a scar was the easiest way."

A series of unearthly howls break out over the city, and bOy, as always, rushes off to investigate. He quickly encounters Rippers, but kills them in seconds—even in 'human' form, bOy has gained lethal powers. He's pursuing

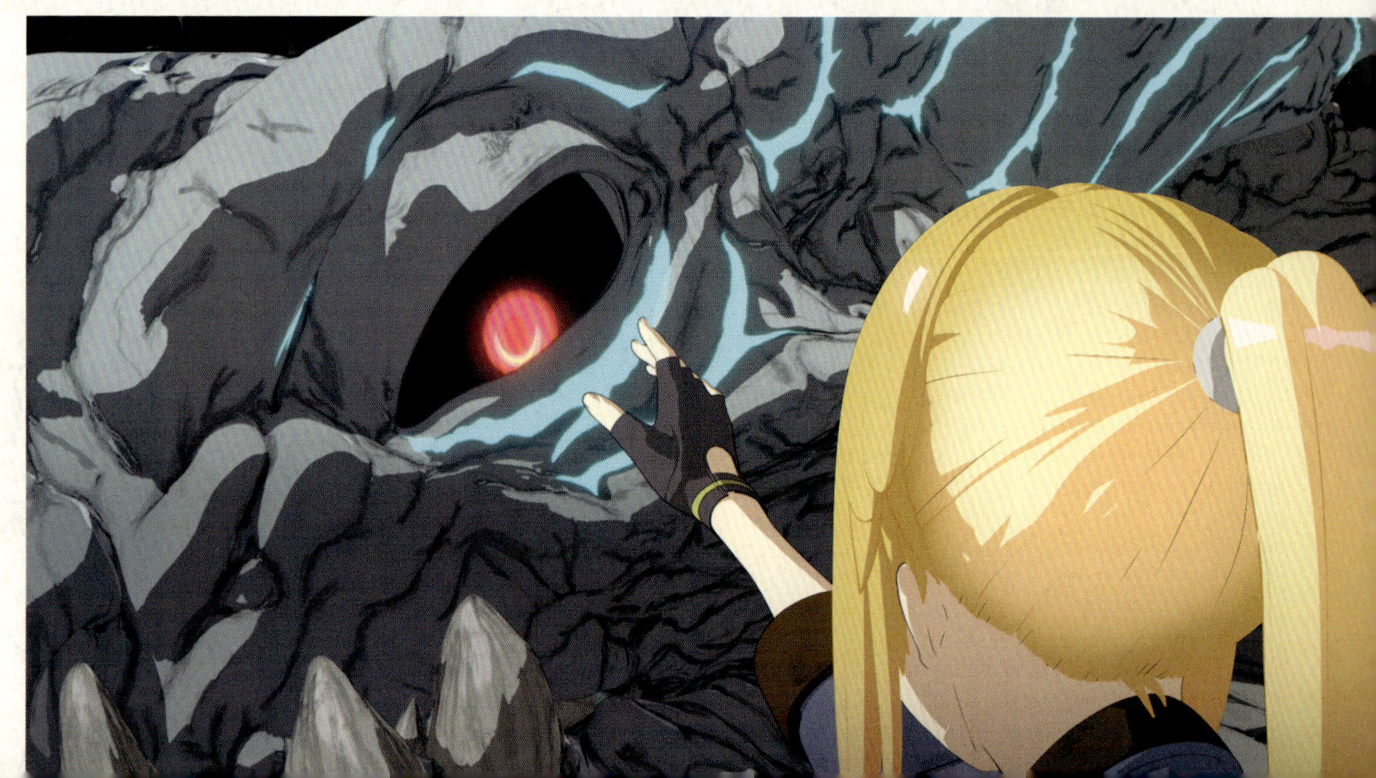

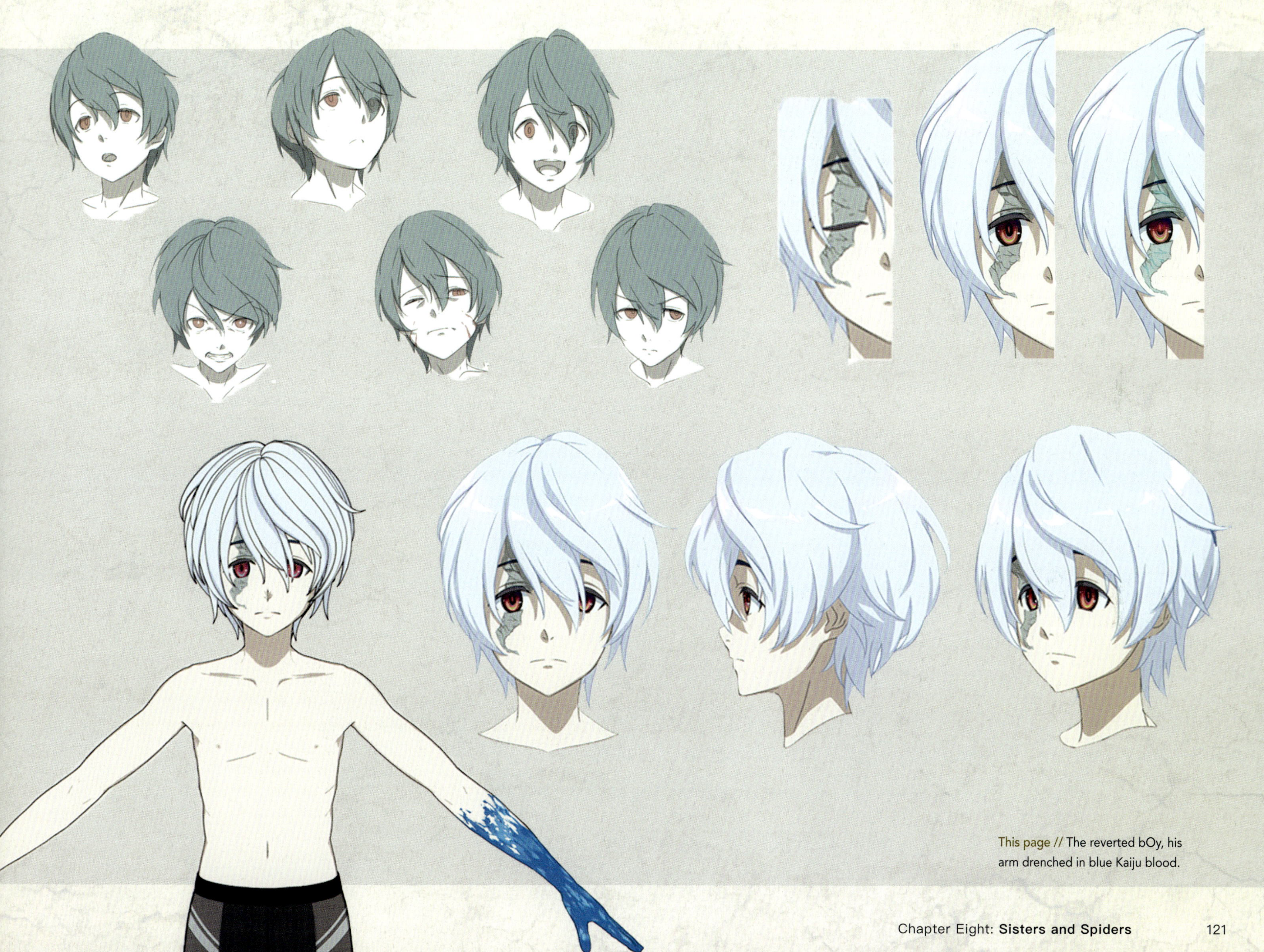

This page // The reverted bOy, his arm drenched in blue Kaiju blood.

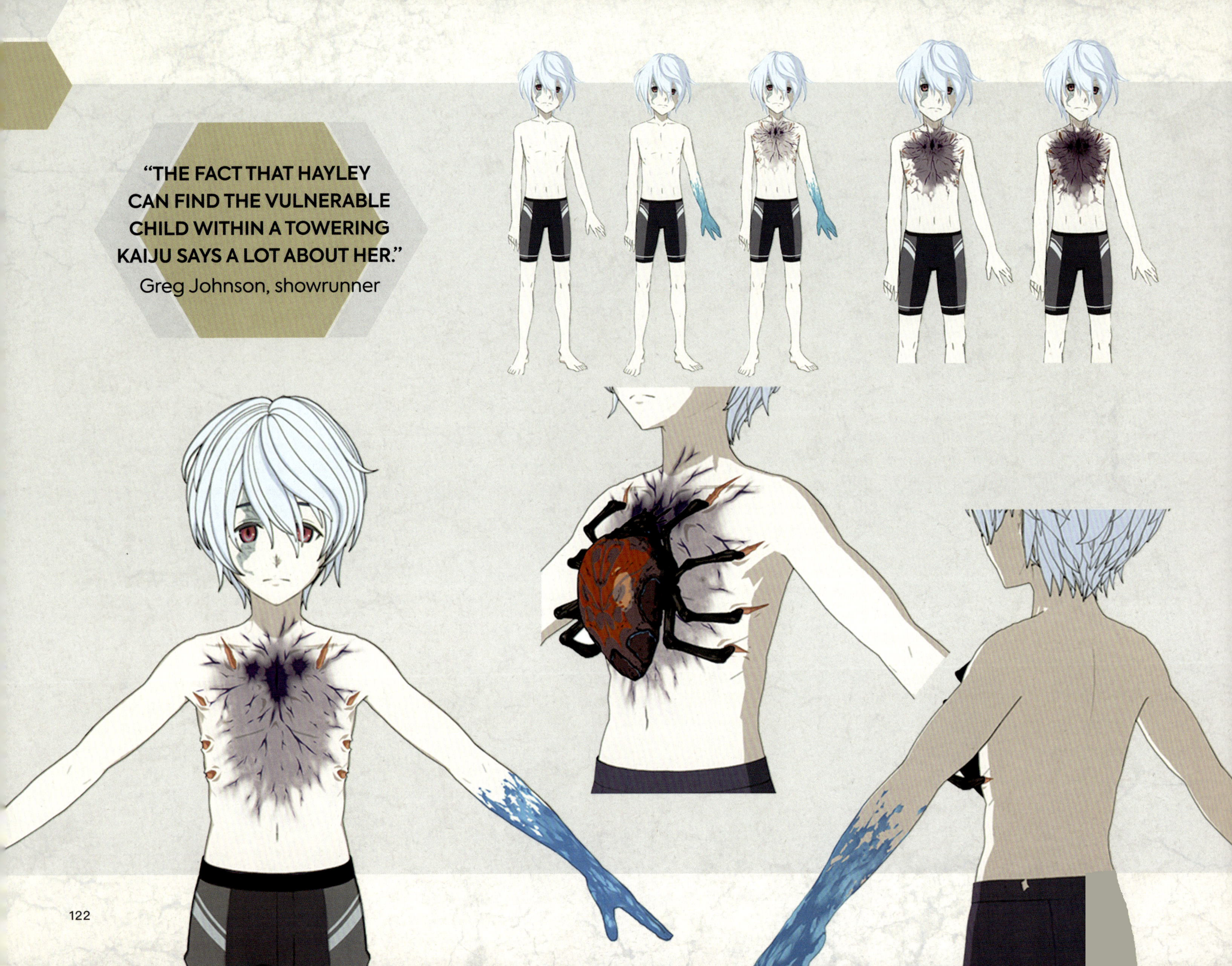

> **"THE FACT THAT HAYLEY CAN FIND THE VULNERABLE CHILD WITHIN A TOWERING KAIJU SAYS A LOT ABOUT HER."**
> Greg Johnson, showrunner

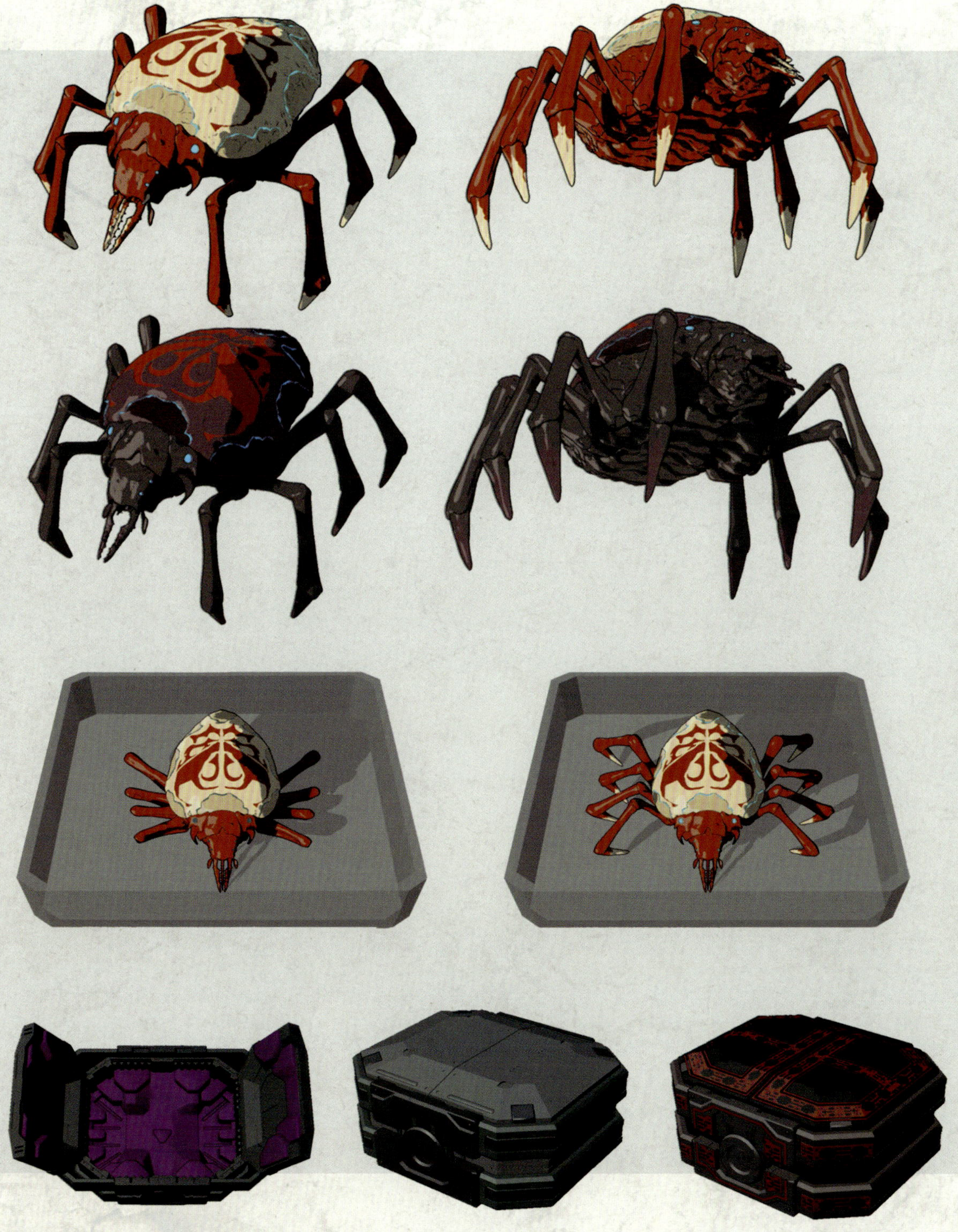

other Rippers through alleys when he runs into their controllers, the Sisters, who see him as the Kaiju Messiah.

Johnson explains the Sisters aren't new to the mythology. "The Sisters of the Kaiju originated in the films, where you briefly see the nun-like religious followers in front of their temple. They also show up in some of the *Pacific Rim* graphic novels." (Specifically, they appear in *Pacific Rim: Aftermath*, a comic book series set between the films.) "They're cultists, who started religious institutions in support of the creatures and viewed the Kaiju as sent by the gods, who were displeased with humankind."

"Greg Johnson had a very clear idea about the Sisters," says Jae-Hong Kim. "Creepy and eerie! He had a certain image in his head, with details about what their masks should look like and the robe length... I started working with a designer to come up with their look. The key for the image was 'Creepy'."

bOy sees the Sisters as another threat, breaking one woman's arm with the same brutality he showed the Rippers. But another sister calmly opens an ornate box. A huge Kaiju spider—actually a "Kaiju tick"—leaps out of it onto bOy's chest, pumping him with venom. The Sisters are distracted by Hayley and Taylor's approach, and melt into the shadows.

Hayley is distraught at bOy's injuries, and begs Mei for help. Mei has been distant since she helped take down Copperhead, but she reluctantly says one person might be able to help bOy—a "crazy drongo" who lives with Kaiju in the desert. Taylor persuades Mei to help pilot Atlas Destroyer—after all, her only alternative is to stay completely alone.

The youngsters travel in the mecha, trying to sort out their differences. Finally, they arrive at the crazy drongo's home, a valley packed with Kaiju...

Left // You'd have to really love arachnids to appreciate this gift of a Kaiju tick.

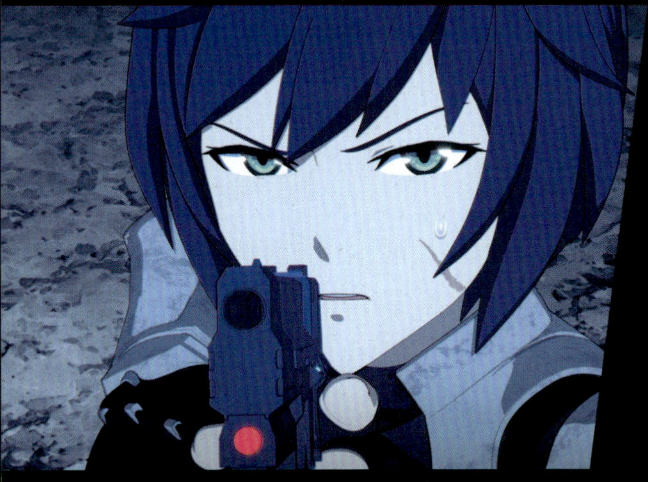

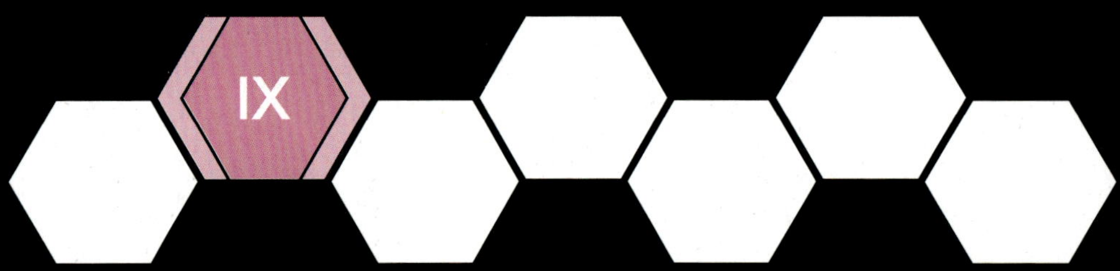

CHAPTER NINE
THE MADMAN

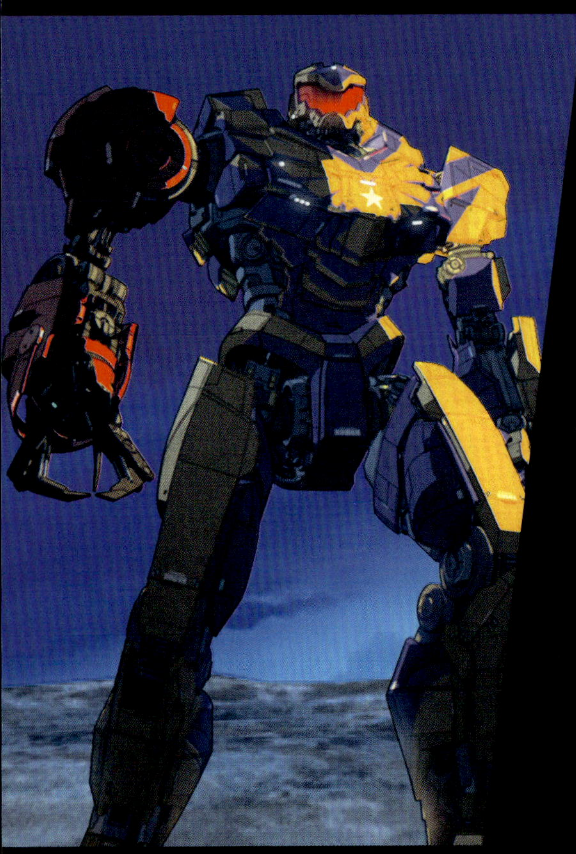

"The Never Never", Episode Two of Season Two, presents arguably the star of the whole series, the Bunyip Man. It's tough to reach him—Taylor and Mei refuse to try, but a stray Acidquill takes their choice away by knocking Atlas Destroyer into the valley. All seems lost, but the Kaiju hordes are distracted by a human figure on a mesa. He drops captive Rippers down the slope, drawing the Kaiju away to feed on the luckless animals.

This is the Bunyip Man, an eccentric seemingly tailor-made for the apocalypse, voiced by New Zealand actor-comedian Rhys Darby. "He was everyone's favorite character," says Kim. "He has a strong character and an odd personality in this hopeless continent. I would say he adapted himself pretty well after The Black. We came up with so many different image designs for him; lunatic-ish but not completely nuts, 'cause he's a survivor! I also requested his acting to be broader than the rest of the characters. His amputated arm was one of the signatures of who he is." (A bunyip, incidentally, is a creature from Australian Aboriginal mythology.)

The missing arm is the result of an unfortunate accident involving the Bunyip Man's favorite Kaiju. This beauty's called Lucy, and she's a Trespasser (seen in the first live-action film), with four eyes and a vast crest on her head like a bone hammer. Despite his lost limb, the Bunyip Man talks to the dino-sized Lucy as if she's a pet poodle.

Johnson says, "Bunyip Man came out of discussions about how humans left behind in The Black would adapt to sharing the land with these giant monsters. Especially once recognizing that the Kaiju are evolving, becoming more 'creatures of the land' and less 'weapons with a singular purpose'. As such, the idea of a lone, slightly crazy Kaiju Whisperer started taking shape."

We get to enjoy the Bunyip Man's patter for several minutes, as he examines bOy at Hayley's request. "Bunyip Man's dialogue developed through the research of word usage in Australia and New Zealand," says Johnson, "filtered through the minds of myself and episode writer Paul Giacoppo. Rhys Darby brought so much personality to the role that our odd little recluse really came to life."

Sad to say, the Bunyip Man isn't around for long. He prepares to inject bOy with anti-venom, but he's distracted by his enemies, the Sister cult, who kill off his captive Rippers. Lucy looms up at that moment, expecting a live meal. The Bunyip Man tries to placate the Trespasser, patting Lucy's massive teeth… and Lucy gobbles him up.

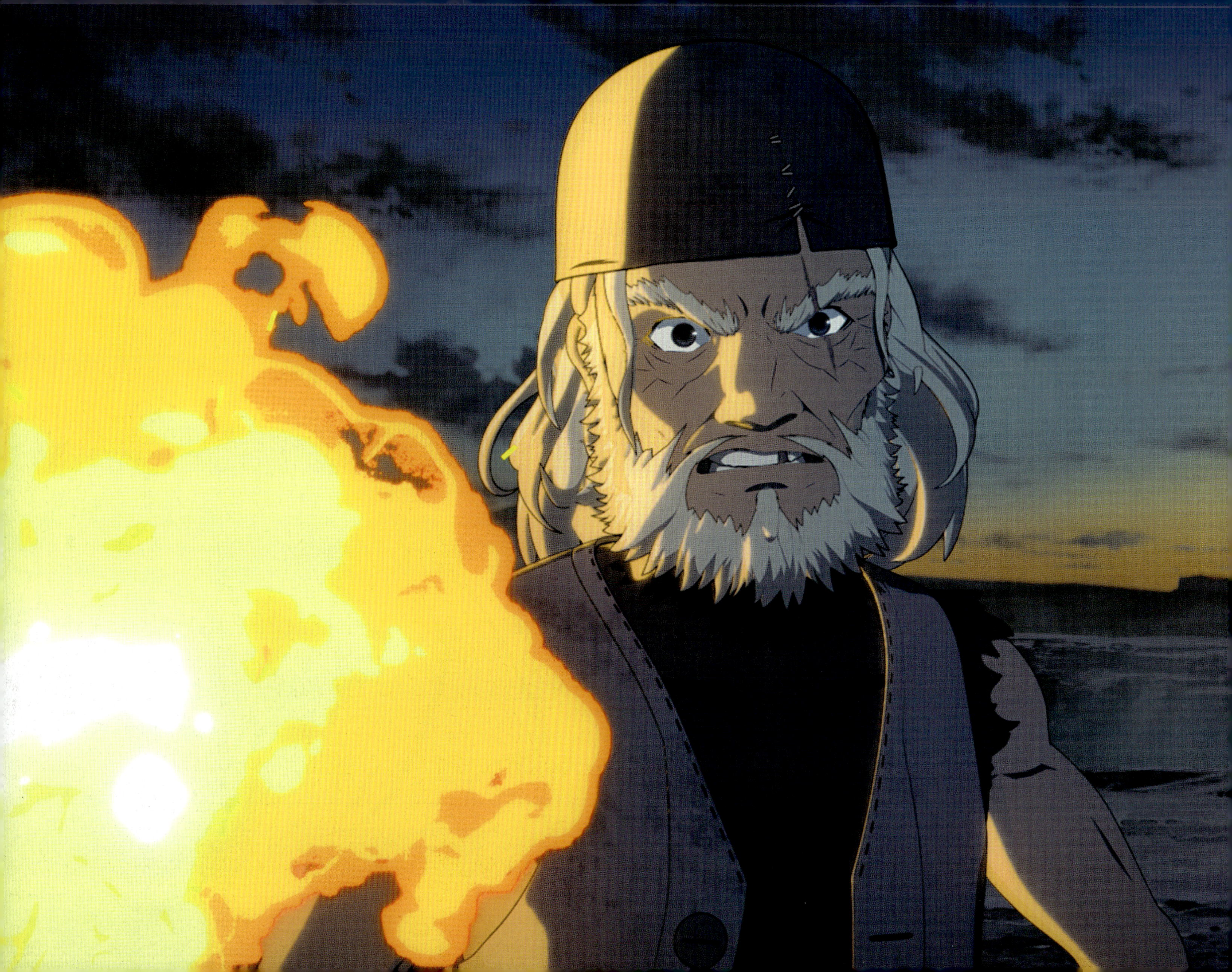

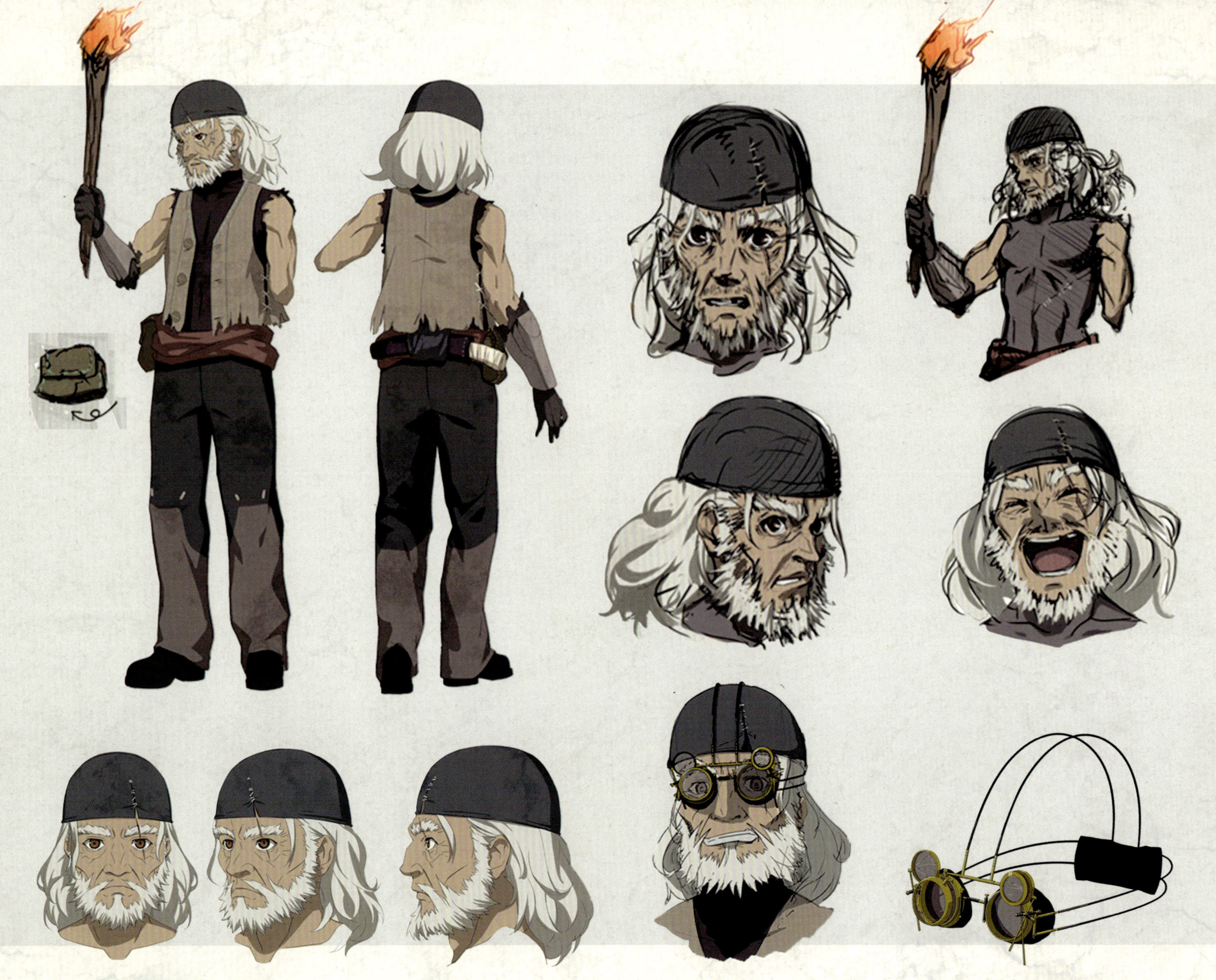

"As for his fate," says Johnson, "we were inspired by a true story about a man who wholeheartedly believed he'd had a loving relationship with wild predators, only to be killed and eaten by them as soon as they were hungry enough." Johnson may be referring to the bear lover Timothy Treadwell, whose life and death was the subject of Werner Herzog's documentary, *Grizzly Man*. The Bunyip Man's end can also be seen as a blackly comic counterpoint to Hayley's trust of the bOy-Kaiju in the previous episode.

"His ending was ...Yes, it was shocking—but I liked it," says Kim. "No one would expect how he ended in that way! Greg aimed for that, I guess, and I believe most audiences would have wide-open mouths at the moment!"

A frantic chase follows; Hayley shows unthinking heroism, saving Mei's life at great risk to her own when Mei falls from a cliff. With the anti-venom lost, the youngsters can only get back to Atlas Destroyer and flee the Kaiju hordes, finally ducking into a narrow canyon. Strangely, the Kaiju don't follow, and when the characters see wrecked Jaegers ahead, they know why. They've entered the territory of the Sisters...

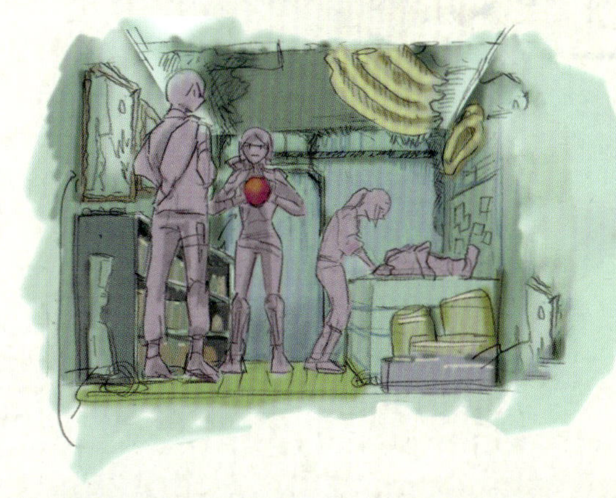

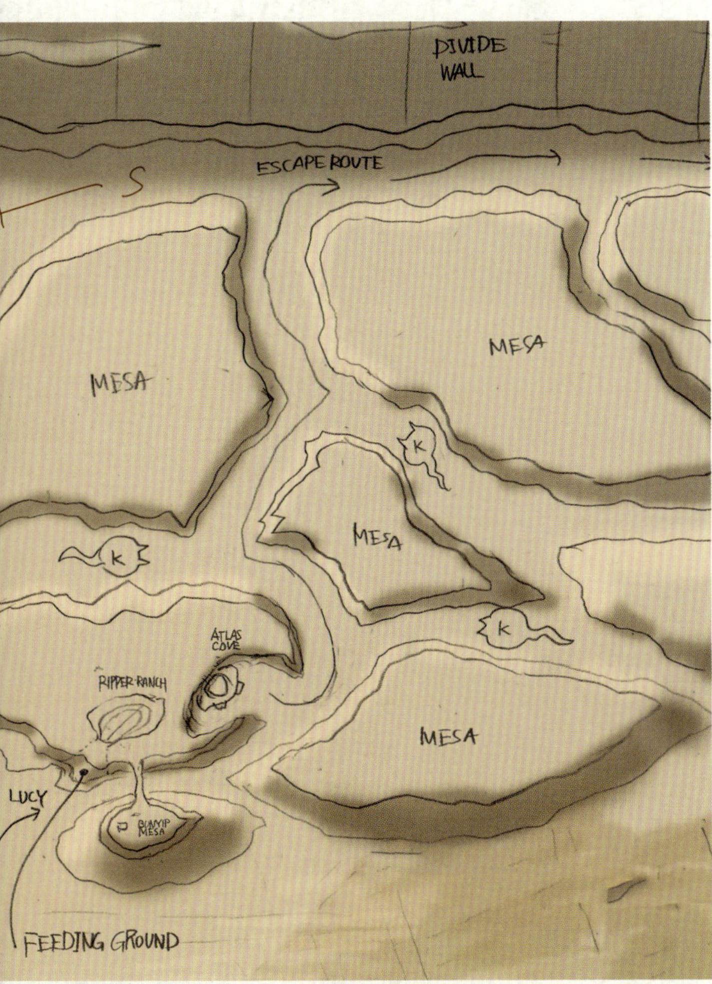

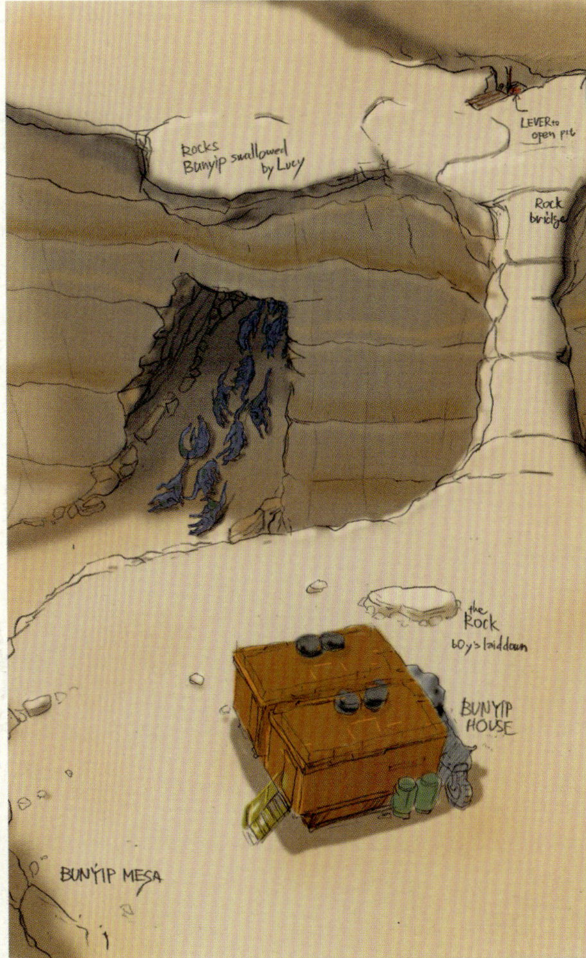

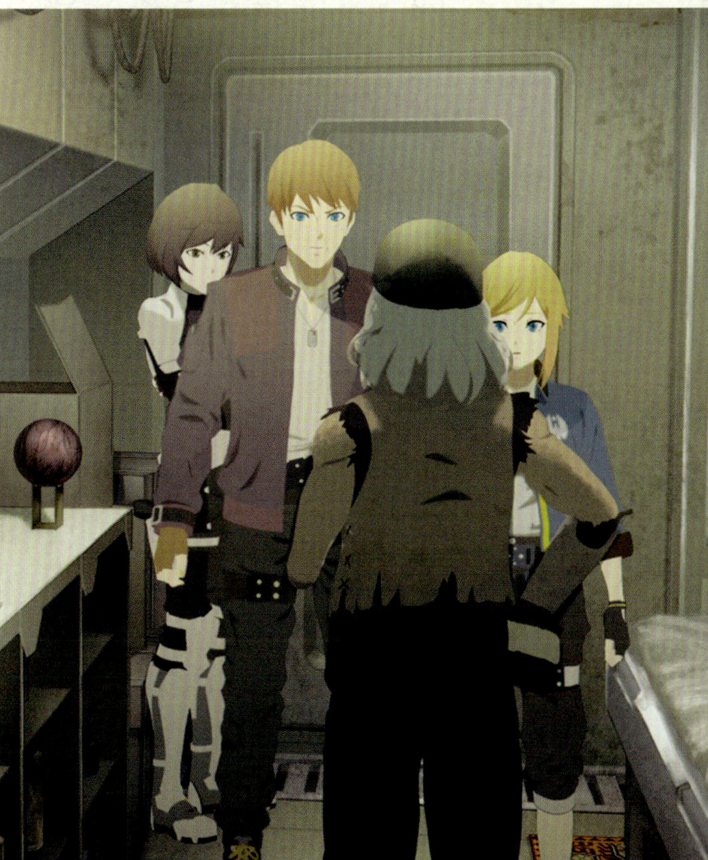

Above // For Taylor and Hayley, the Bunyip Man is only a brief encounter, but he's a memorable one.

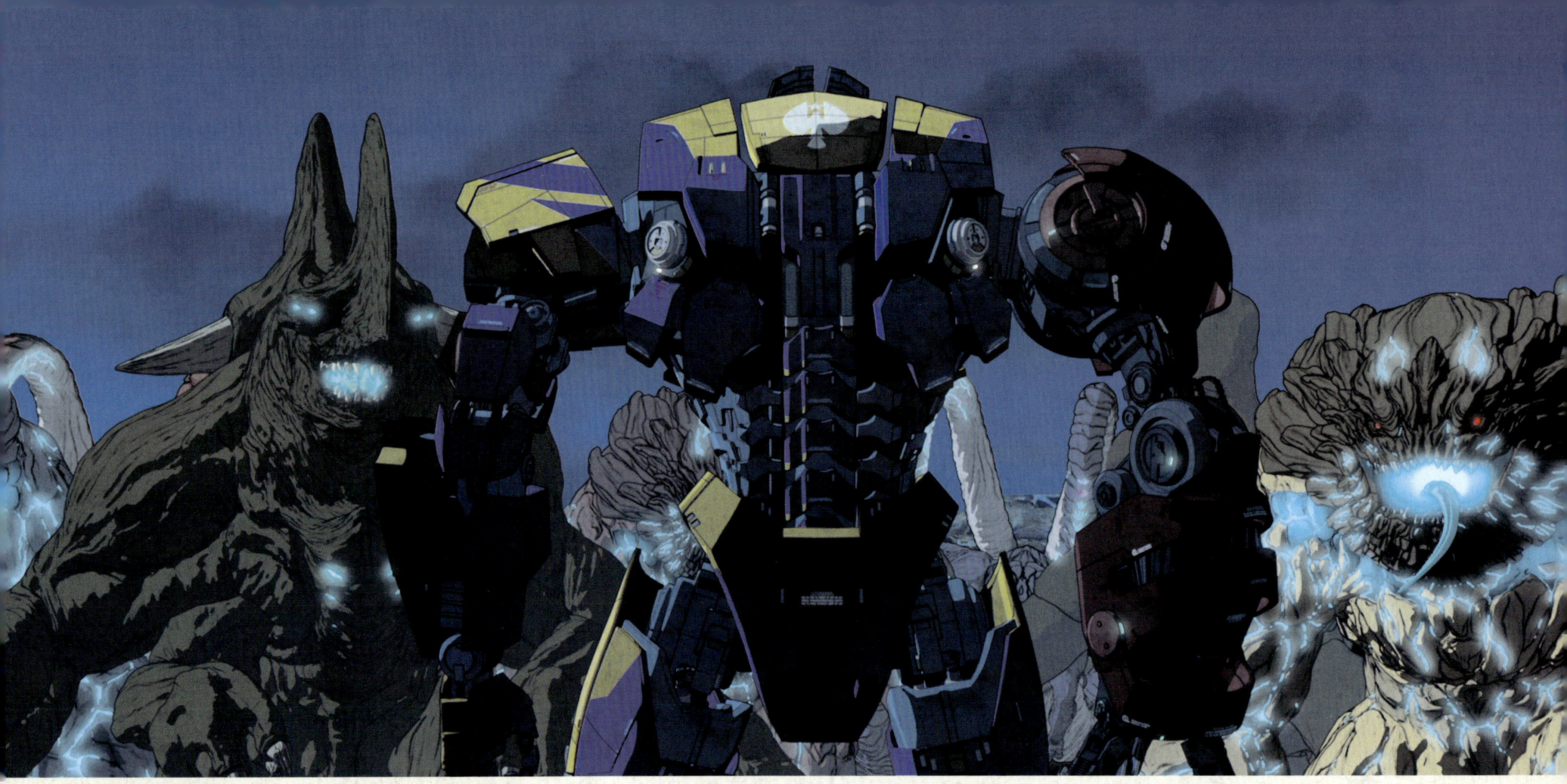

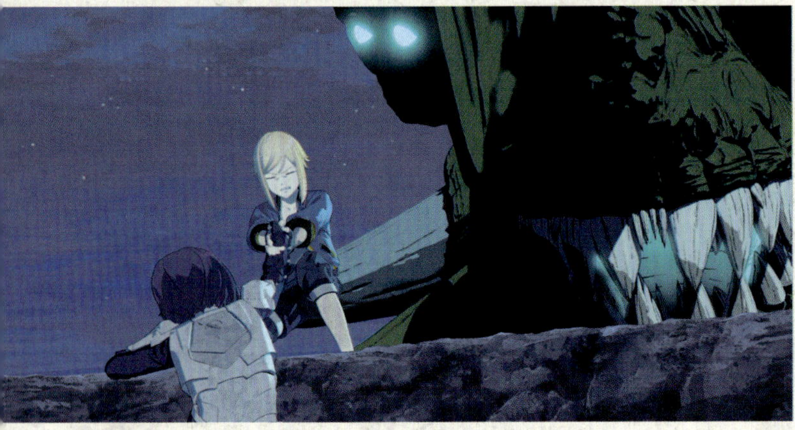

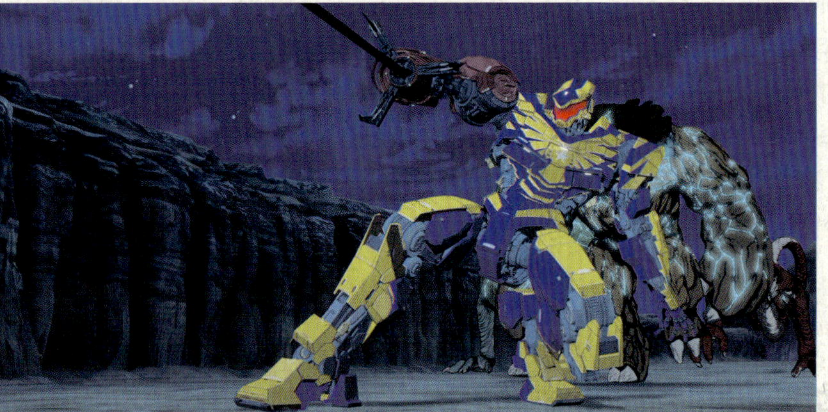

This page // The youngsters need all their courage in the valley of the monsters.

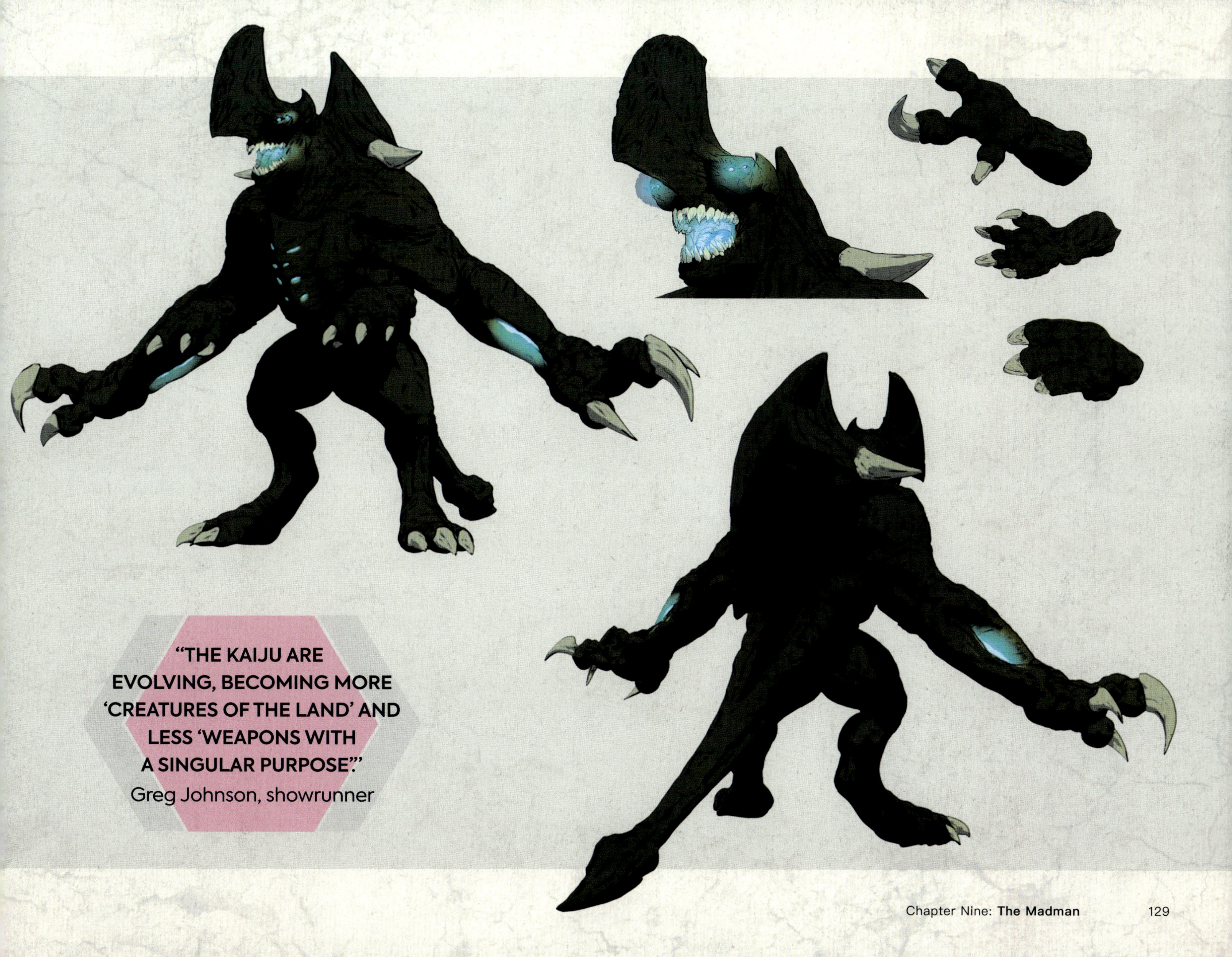

"THE KAIJU ARE EVOLVING, BECOMING MORE 'CREATURES OF THE LAND' AND LESS 'WEAPONS WITH A SINGULAR PURPOSE.'"
Greg Johnson, showrunner

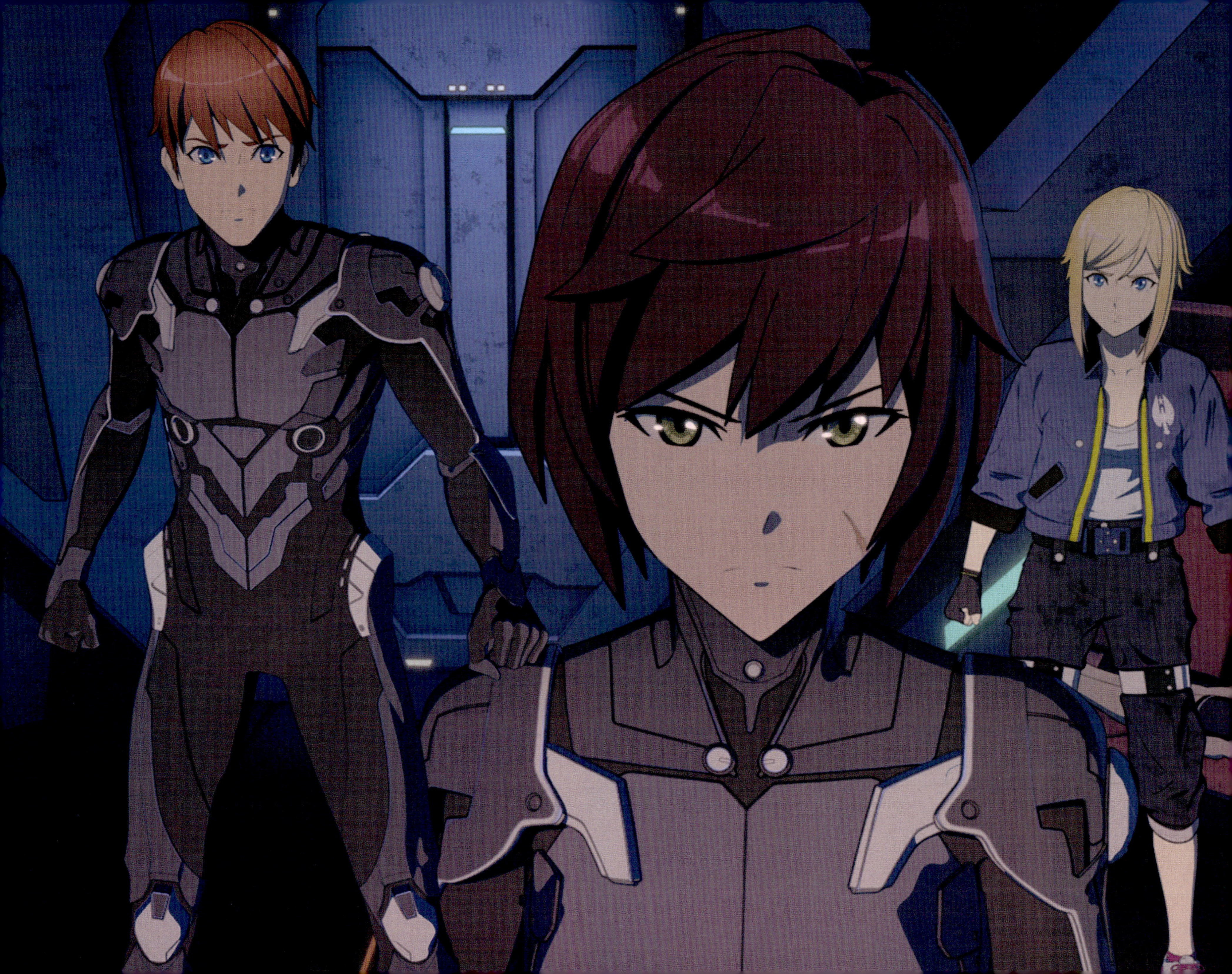

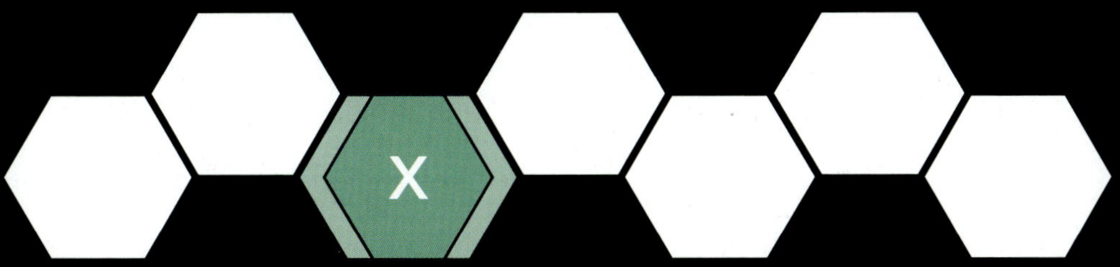

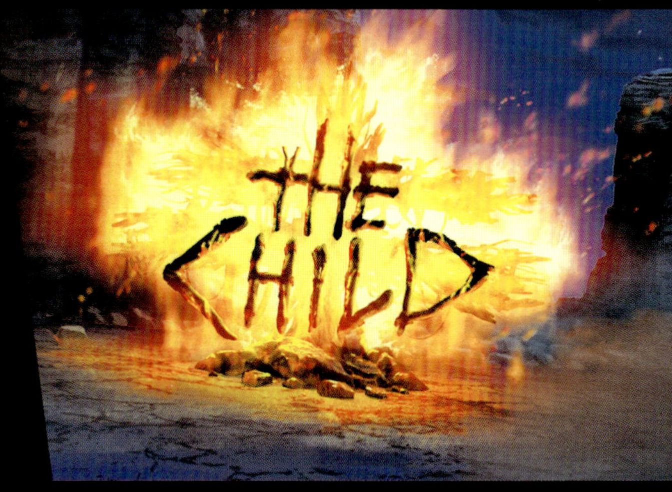

CHAPTER TEN

THE BETRAYAL

In Season Two, Episode Three, "Divide", the youngsters learn what the Sisters want from them, courtesy of a blazing sign in the canyon reading 'THE CHILD'. Mei realizes the Sisters know bOy is a Kaiju, and that the cult has been maneuvering them to their lair since Clayton City. For Mei, the answer's obvious; they must hand bOy over to the Sisters.

A row erupts, with Hayley adamant that they can't abandon bOy, while Taylor insists the only thing that matters is getting himself and Hayley to Sydney. After Sisters board the outside of the Jaeger and damage its mechanisms, Mei pulls her gun on Hayley. Taylor acts as peacemaker, saying Hayley and Mei should rest while he repairs the damage.

Outside, Taylor sees three Sisters waiting in the dark, and makes his decision. While Hayley is sleeping, he carries bOy outside, and leaves the child there for the Sisters.

The first season had Hayley getting her friends killed and then having to live with it. In Season Two, it's her brother who's put through a moral wringer. "The impetus of Taylor's motivation springs from one pivotal moment in the series; his promise to keep Hayley safe," says Johnson. "To basically hold together what's left of their family until they're all united. It's what smothers their relationship back at Shadow Basin, and what drives his decisions moving forward. bOy represents a threat to that promise. In keeping true to Taylor's character, it makes perfect sense he'd choose the option to remove that threat from their lives."

Johnson reveals Taylor's decision wasn't always planned. "Taylor handing bOy over to the Sisters is the result of letting the characters inspire the plot points. We talked early on about having the Sisters perform more of a raid on Atlas in order to abduct bOy, but it's much more powerful if Taylor takes the responsibility of that decision onto himself."

At dawn, Hayley is devastated to learn what Taylor's done. Mei is furious for a different reason; she wanted to hold onto bOy for longer as a bargaining chip. Two 'hybrid' Kaiju appear, bonded telepathically with the three Sisters who took bOy. This time, Atlas Destroyer can't avoid a fight.

The hybrids are bipeds, unlike the quadruped Copperhead and the Acidquills that plagued the youngsters in Season One. "The storyboard had to be crafted carefully so the animators can understand how the fighting style had to be changed," says Kim. "That was another task for me to stylize in each fight. Atlas Destroyer doesn't have many weapons, and can't repeat the brawl style of fighting. I had to come up with different styles or ways of fighting for the

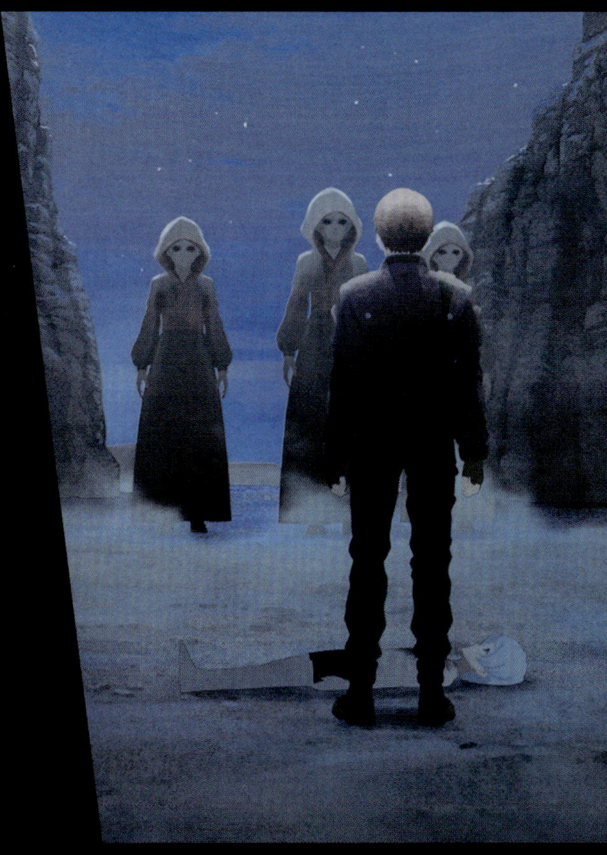

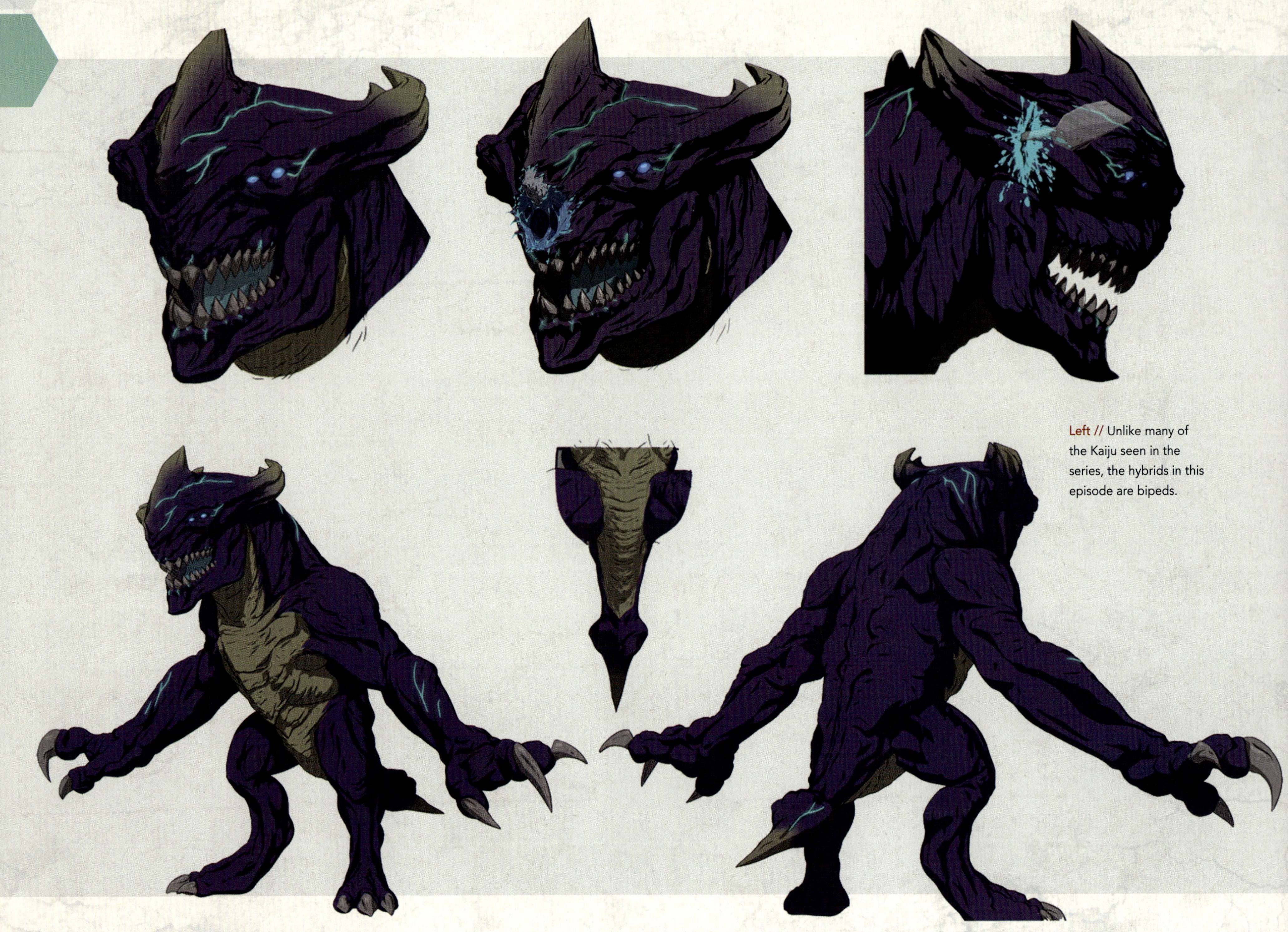

Left // Unlike many of the Kaiju seen in the series, the hybrids in this episode are bipeds.

battle sequences. Coming up with different choreographies for the fights was a hard challenge."

Steered by Taylor and Mei, Atlas kills one hybrid with the saber chain, and impales the other on a rock pinnacle. Above, the three Sisters send more Kaiju after the Jaeger… but two Sisters are stabbed from behind. The killer is Shane, still ostensibly pursuing Atlas Destroyer, though even his underlings know he's really after Mei.

Out in the desert, the youngsters confront Shane. Mei is adamant that she'll never come back with him; she's not forgotten what happened to Joel. In response, Shane pushes forward his captive, the surviving Sister, and strips off her hood. Underneath is the face of Brina Travis, long-lost mother of Hayley and Taylor. But she's horribly transformed…

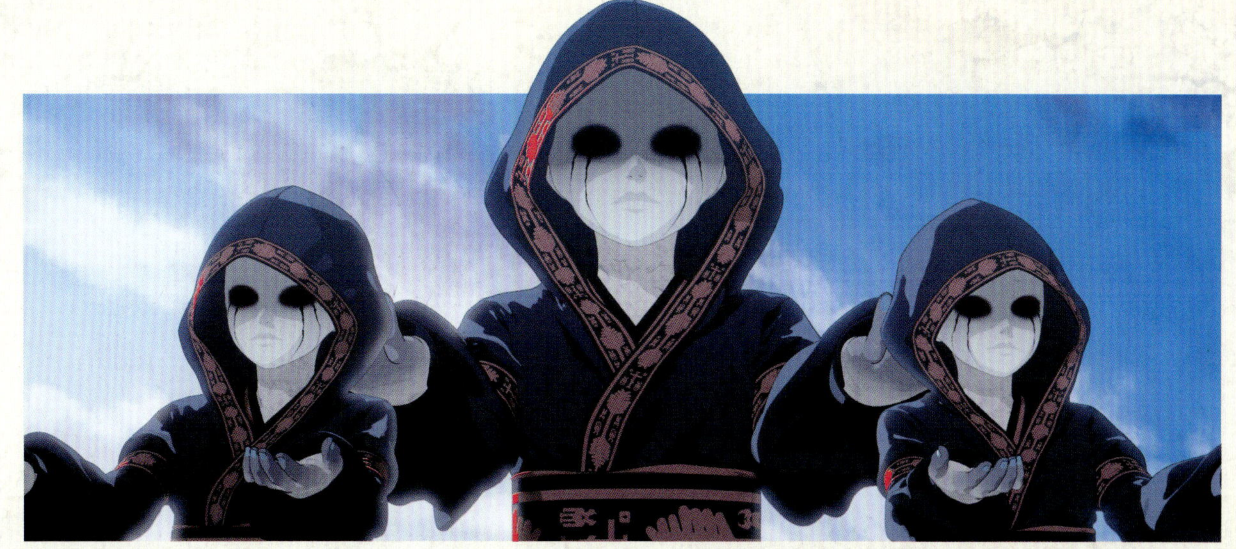

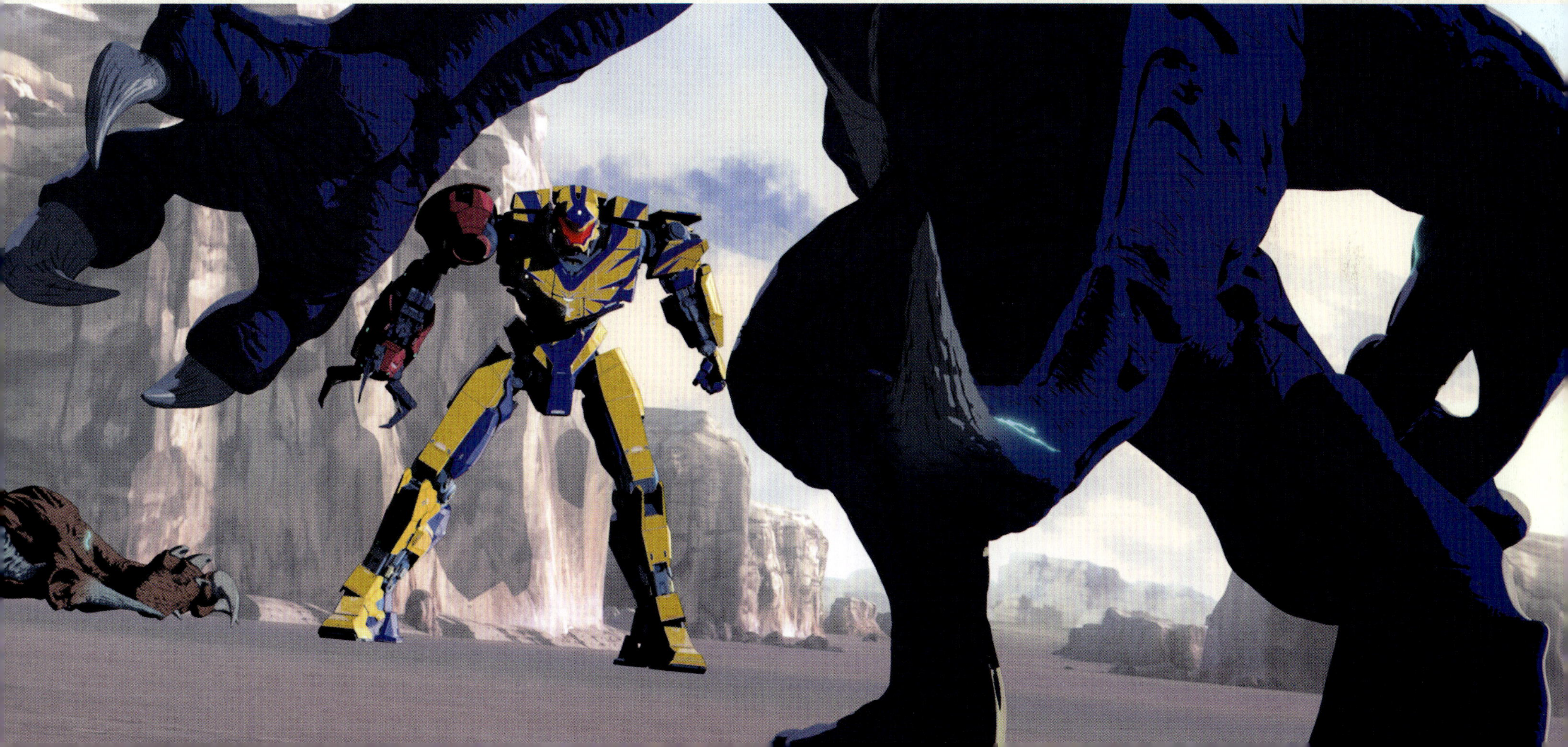

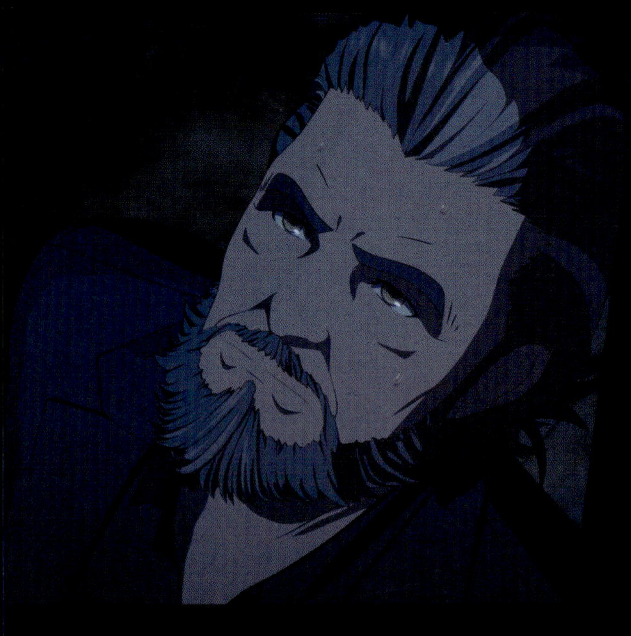

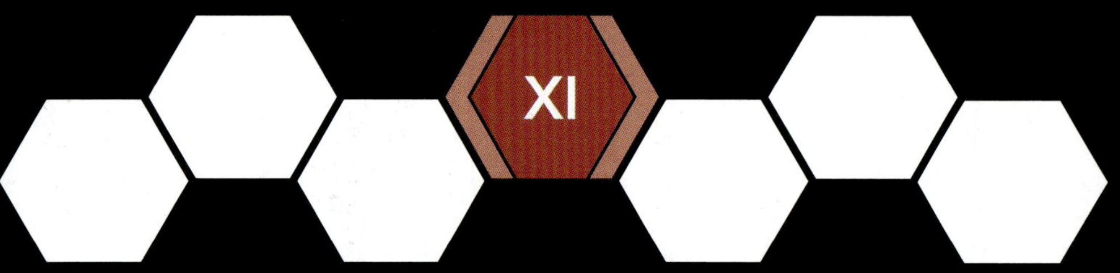

CHAPTER ELEVEN

SHANE'S LAST STAND

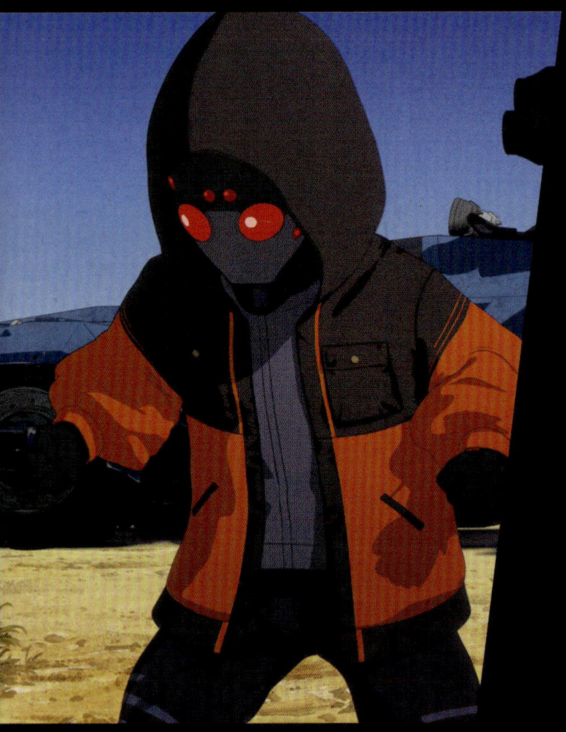

Episode Four of Season Two, "Sisters of the Kaiju", shows us what the Sisters look like under the hood. "Greg Johnson's request about the Sisters' faces was clear," Kim says. "Pale, and veins revealed through skin like a vampire. Actually, I brought up the word 'zombiefied' to Greg and he was like, 'They're not zombies,' but I thought that was the closest word to describe the look of the Sisters' faces. Also, it was hard to add veins to the face skin in '2D-looking' animation because they could look like just lines on the skin, not veins."

Kim adds, "Another task was that Brina should not look too gross and hideous when her face was revealed. She should be clearly identifiable. That's why she has her hair remaining and the same look on her face."

In other ways, Brina might as well be a zombie. She shows no sign of recognising her children, and snarls at them bestially. The Sisters have got into Brina's mind and filled it with something else.

Shane makes a surprise offer—he can use the Jaeger's neural bridge to connect with Brina, and free her mind from the Sisters' hold. In return, he wants the Jaeger and Mei. Mei is furious, but Shane's unusually mild, simply repeating that Mei belongs with him. Afterwards, Shane's assistant, called Spyder, tells Mei that Shane is sincere.

Spyder was sometimes seen working for Shane in Season One, but he plays a larger role now. Watching him, it's hard not to think of a certain desert-dwelling *Star Wars* species. "It was very clear from the beginning that Spyder has a short stature and is masked," says Kim. "Also, we had to make sure he should not look like a child," Kim adds. The character is voiced by a little-person actor, Martin Klebba, who played Marty in all five *Pirates of the Caribbean* films.

The episode shifts to bOy, in the hands of the Sisters in their cavernous desert temple. He's stretched out on a stone altar, recalling shades of vintage horror films about Satanic cults. "Originally, we were just going to give the Sisters unintelligible whispers," Johnson says. "But writer Nicole Dubuc wrote actual chants in her script that really elevated the scenes. The Sisters are a ghastly bunch, and the fact that

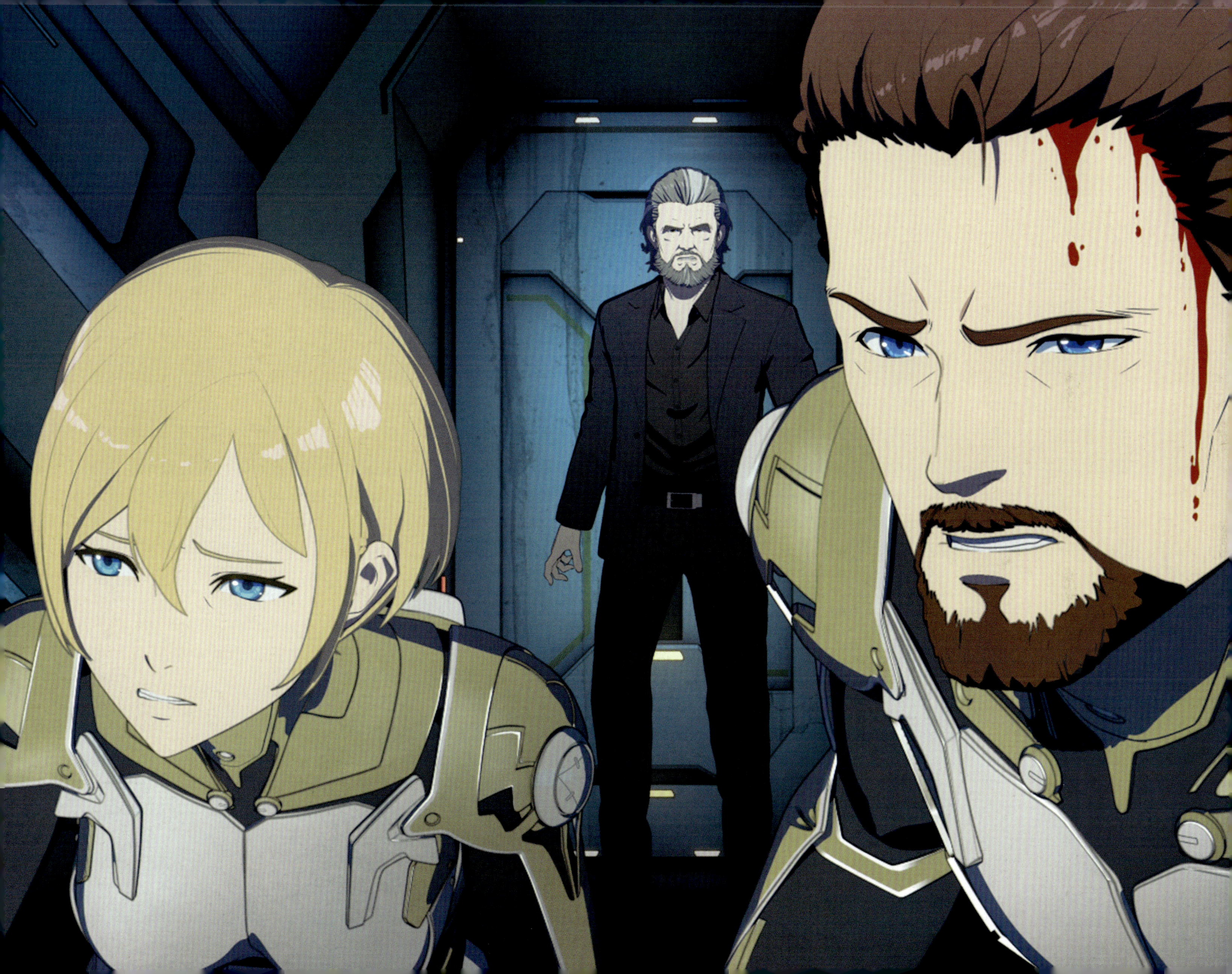

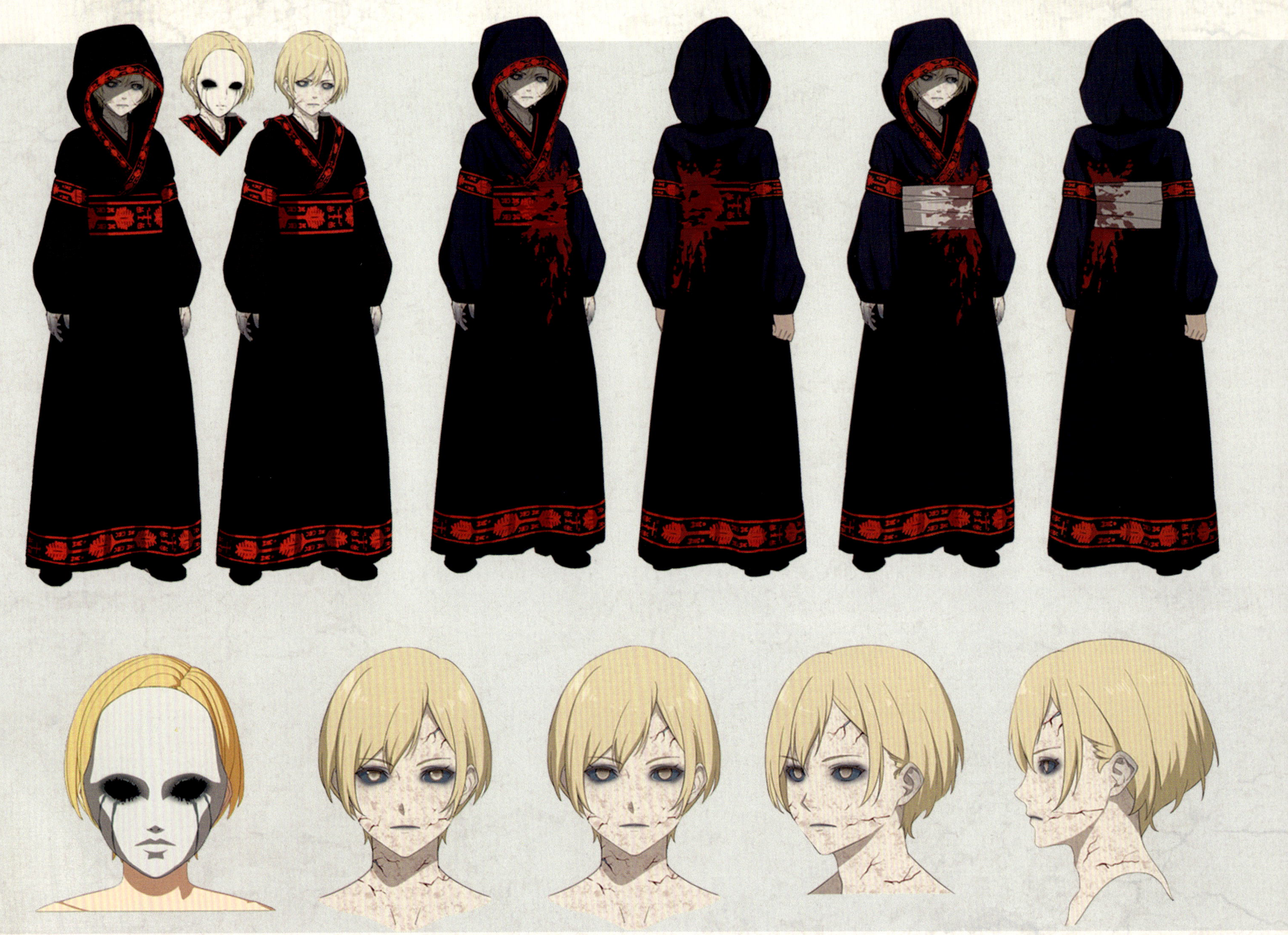

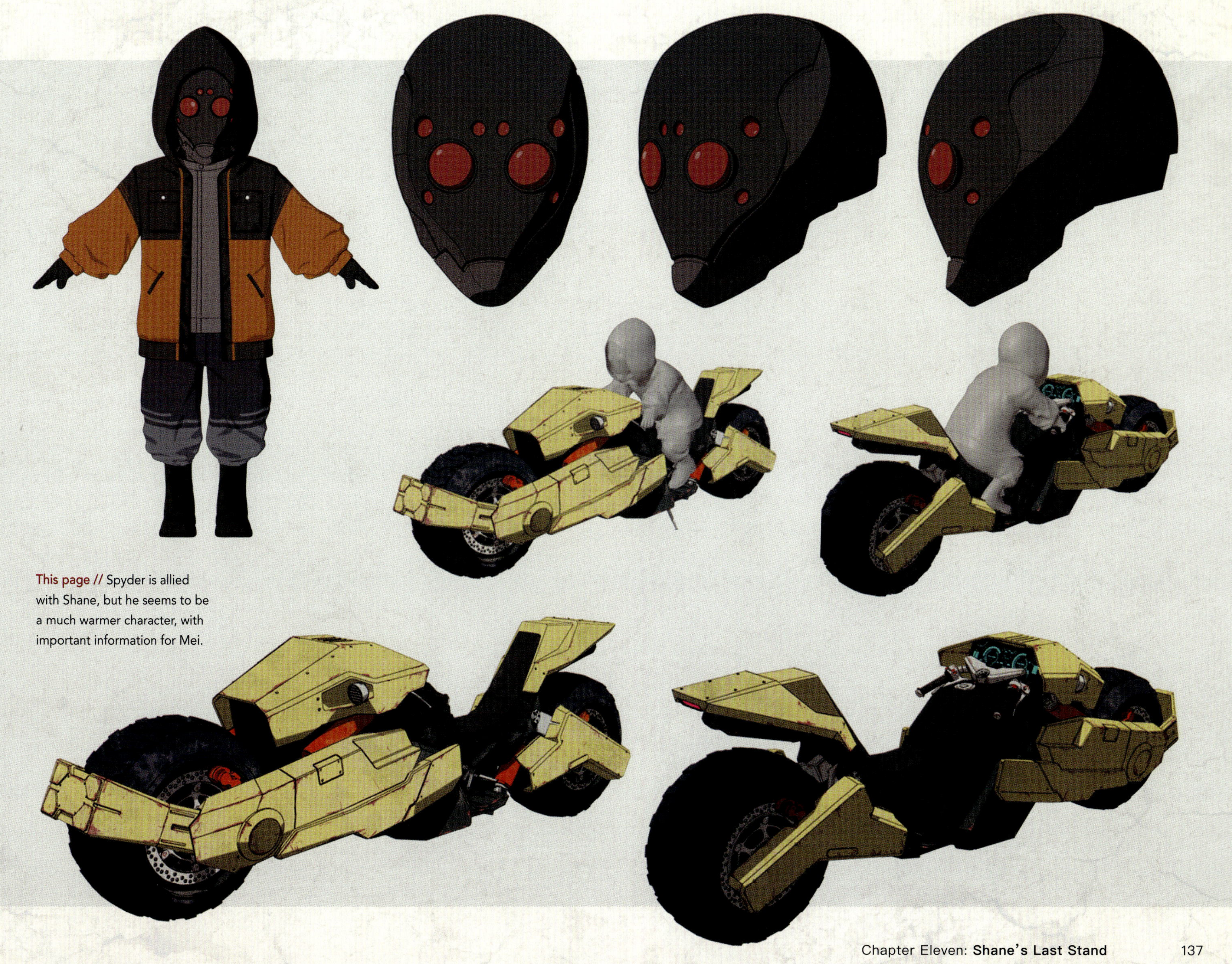

This page // Spyder is allied with Shane, but he seems to be a much warmer character, with important information for Mei.

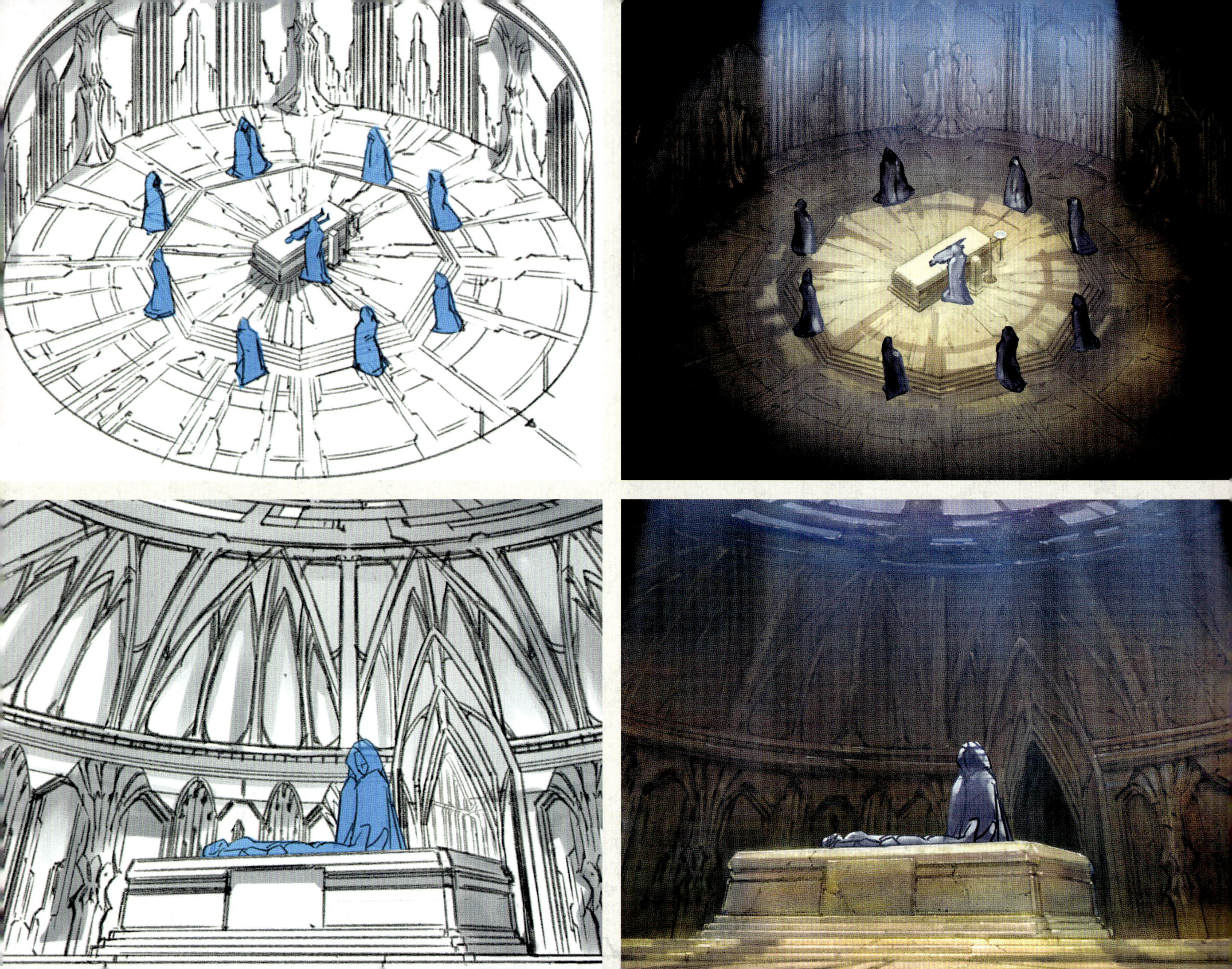

eerie chants echo throughout their temple just gives them another level of creepiness."

The helpless bOy is greeted by the Sisters' leader, the white-robed High Priestess. While the other chanting Sisters suggest a hive mind, the High Priestess has her own powerful voice. She's played by the Hawaiian actor Leilani Jones Wilmore, who gamers may know as the Voodoo Lady in the *Monkey Island* series.

However, that wasn't why she was chosen for the part. "Wilmore was chosen as the High Priestess based simply on her outstanding audition," says Johnson. "In my head, I always heard the voice as Australian. But then I listened to Leilani's take, where she used a mixture of accents, and it really resonated. I sent her audition, and a few others, to various members of the team for their votes, and they all agreed her interpretation was the one."

This episode, though, belongs to Shane. He uses the Drift helmet in Atlas Destroyer to link with the possessed Brina, despite Loa's warnings of the danger. As when Shane linked with Taylor in Season One, we see him passing through the subject's memories, but this time it's very different. Shane isn't in control; he's gone into a mind infested with the Sisters' consciousness, and it's out to crush him.

The imagery of the sequence came from one of Greg Johnson's personal dislikes. "Once the story brought us to the point where a character would Drift with the poisoned mind of a Sister, we wanted a way to visually represent that poison. I personally find mold so disgusting that I can hardly look at it. The thought that the Sisters' darkness would spread like mold through each and every memory, mutating and perverting them, really felt like an applicable metaphor. Mold ruins what it embraces, as does the Sisterhood."

Shane's journey takes him further and further backwards in time, but he finds that each memory of Brina is controlled by the Sisters, as their 'mold' draws ever closer. Finally, Shane gains access to a single deep memory, sealed from the rest, the last trace of the real Brina. The memory is of Brina introducing young Taylor to his newborn sister Hayley. "Brina hides one precious memory of her children that the Sisters can't get at," says Johnson, "and that memory is the lifeline Shane uses to rescue her. Her children are her salvation."

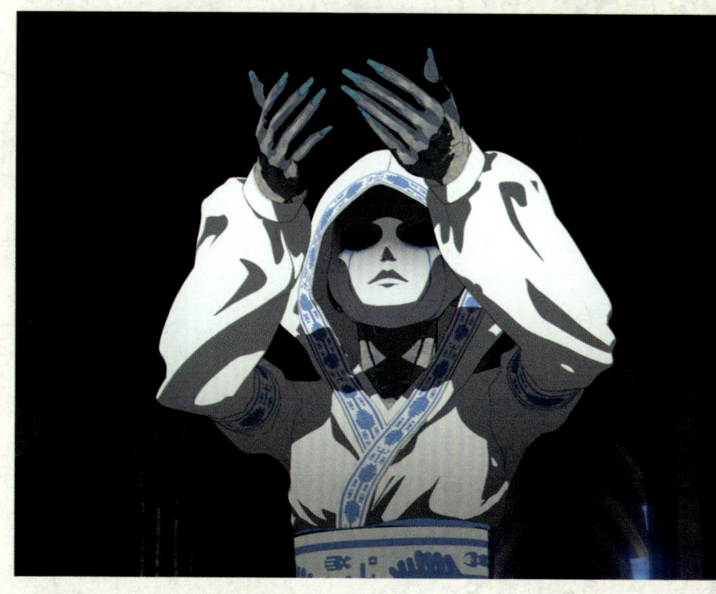

This page // The mysterious High Priestess of the Sisters, voiced commandingly by Leilani Jones Wilmore.

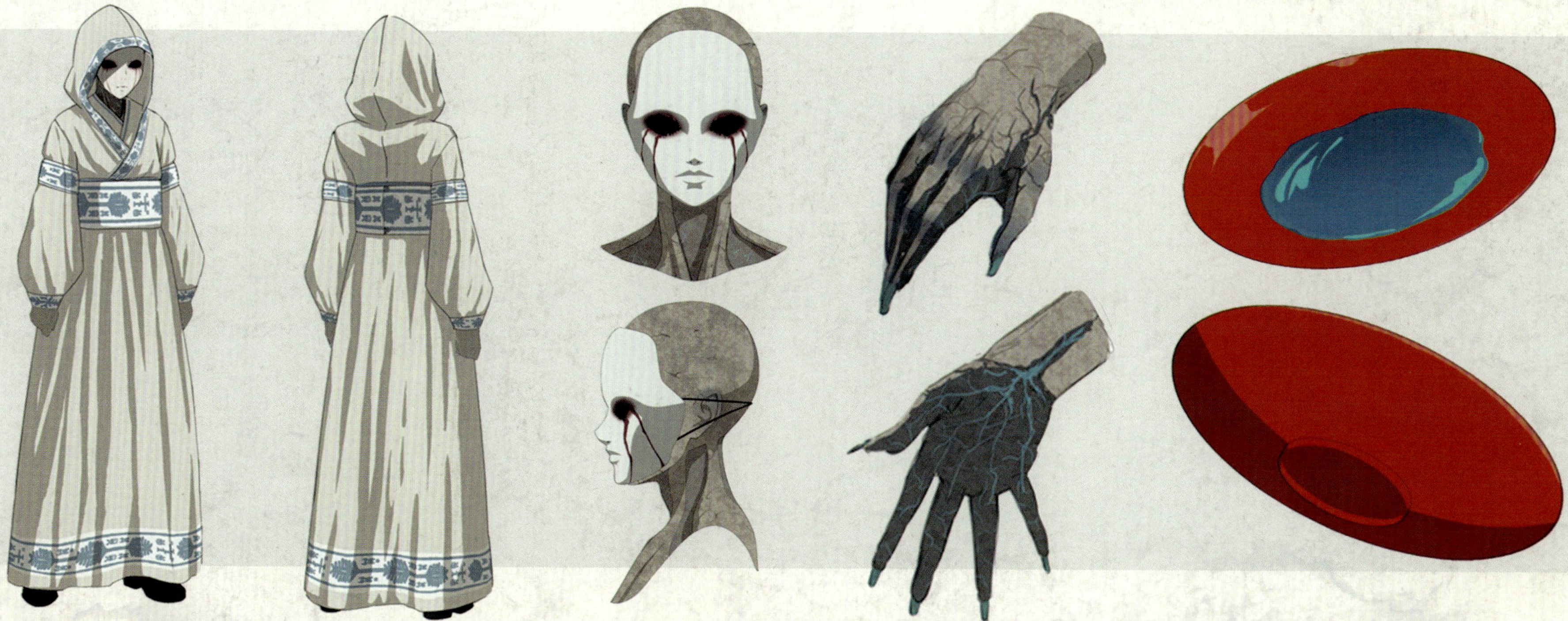

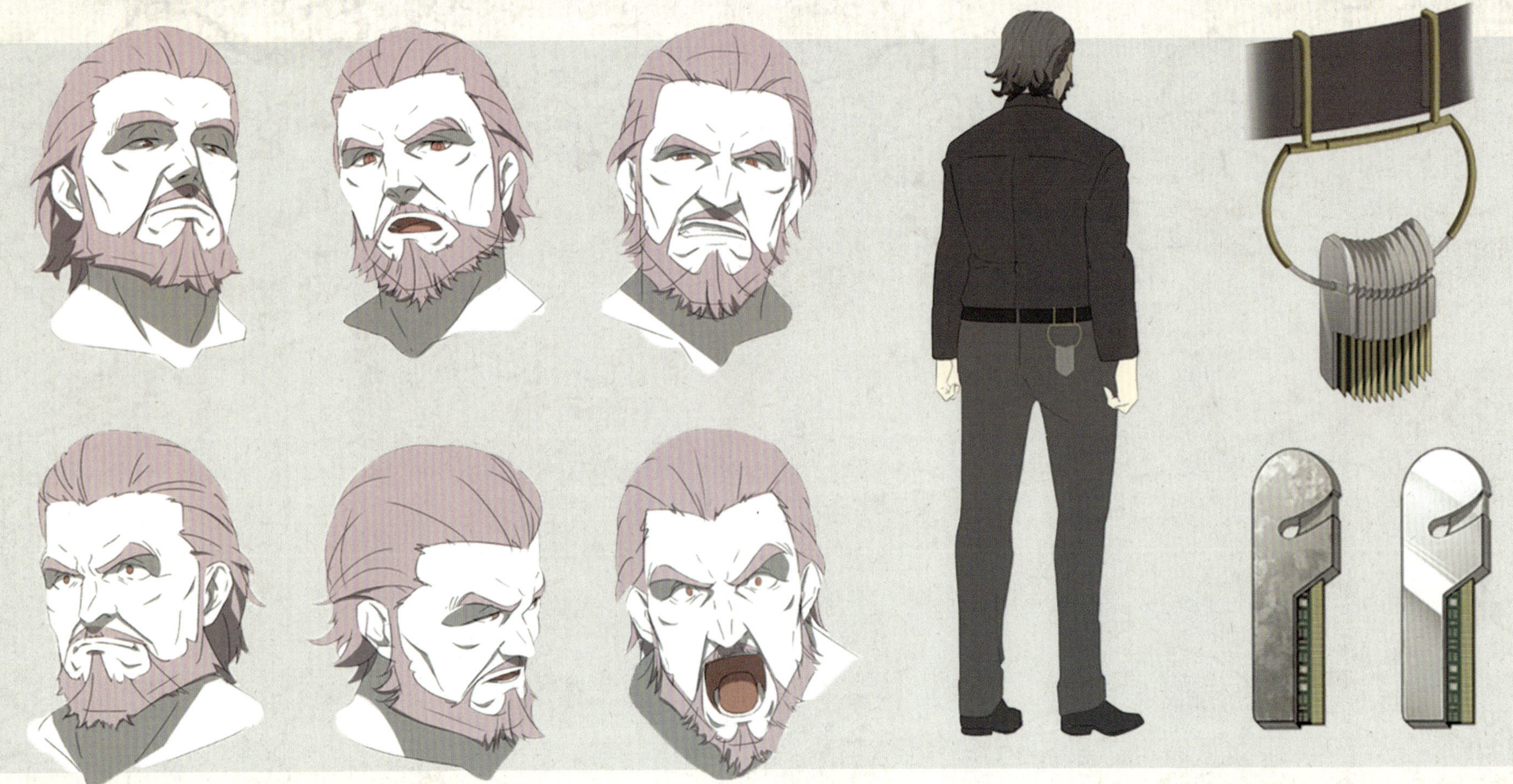

But while Shane saves Brina, he can't save himself from the 'mold'. Moreover, he sees it as an acceptable sacrifice—not made for Brina, but as atonement for the 'daughter' Shane's lost already. In Atlas Destroyer, Brina awakes to her children's embrace, while Mei finds Shane dead. For all her bitter rejection of him, she sobs for a lost father.

Outside, Spyder's equally devastated when Mei tells him what happens; he realizes Shane knew he probably wouldn't come back. He'd left something with Spyder—a data key that holds all of Mei's original memories, her true identity.

The episode clarifies one scene from the first season. In the memorable shock ending to Episode Five, viewers might presume that if Mei had taken the walkie-talkie instead of Joel, Shane would have killed her instead. Johnson confirms that's not the case. "Shane would not have detonated the walkie-talkie if Mei was the one holding it; he would have asked to speak to Joel. Hopefully his efforts to restore his relationship with Mei, or at least prove to her that she meant the world to him, will be enough to prove he was never out to harm her."

Right // Shane's journey through Brina's memories proves to be his last.

"THE SISTERS' DARKNESS WOULD SPREAD LIKE MOLD THROUGH EACH AND EVERY MEMORY, MUTATING AND PERVERTING THEM."

Greg Johnson, showrunner

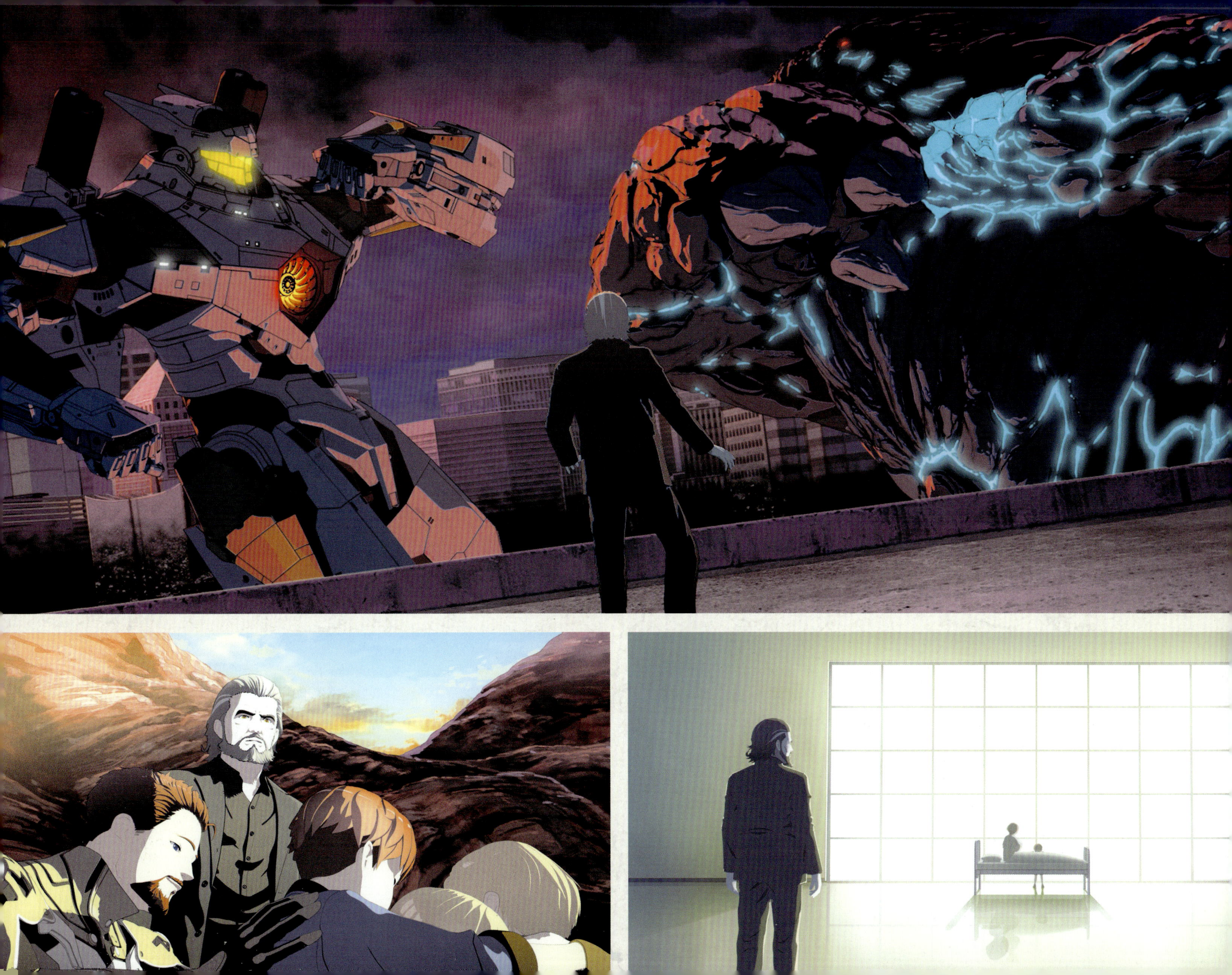

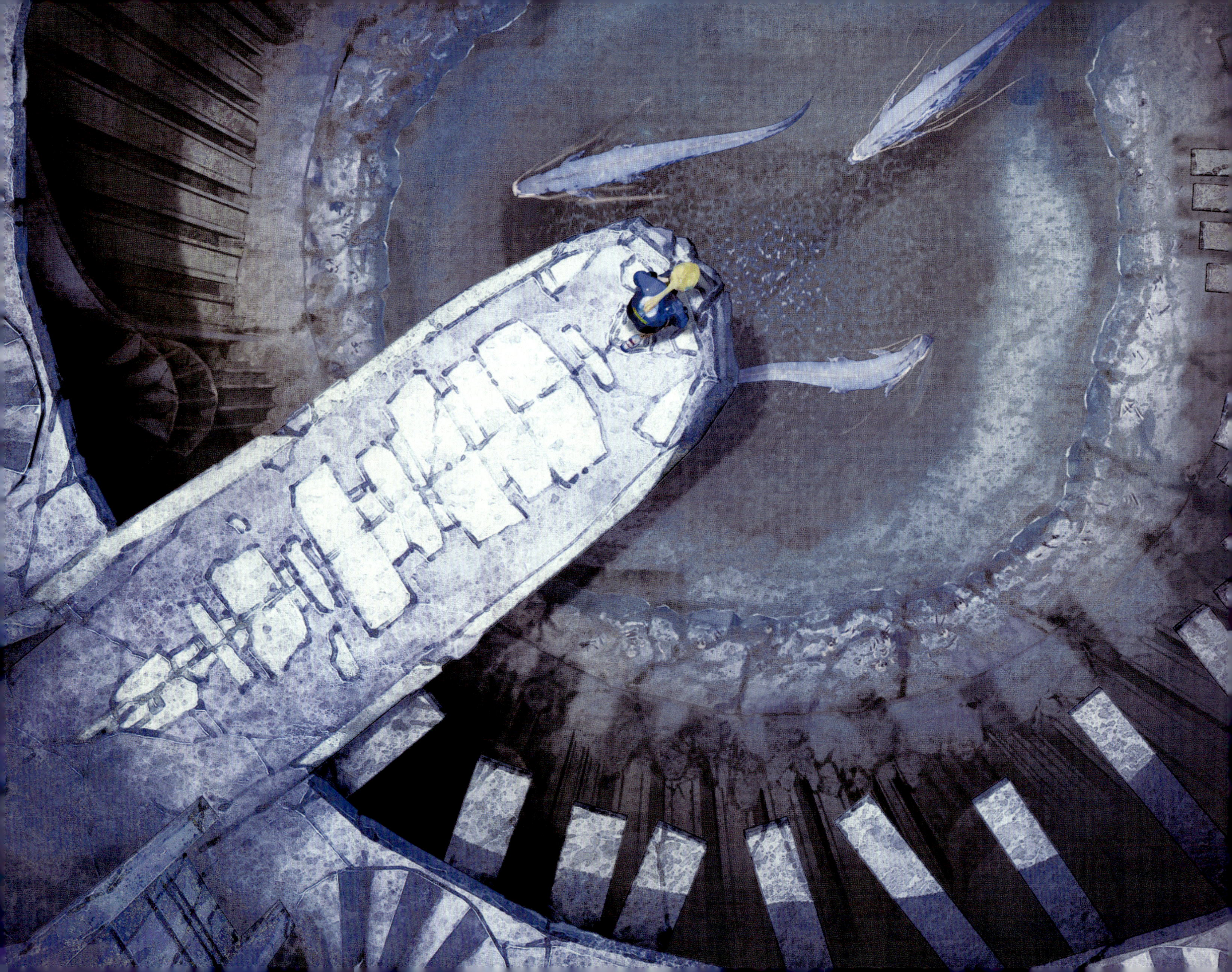

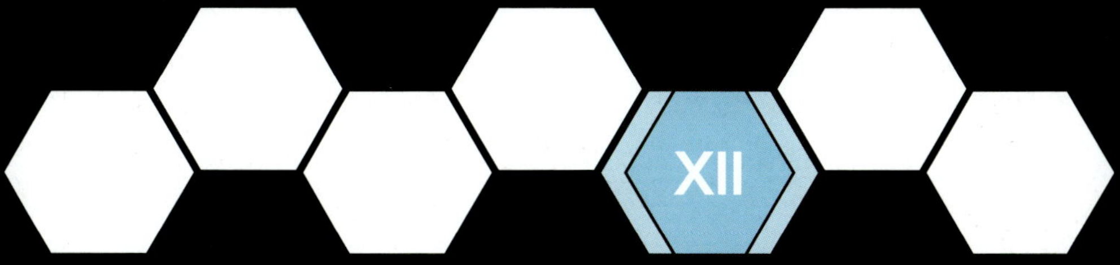

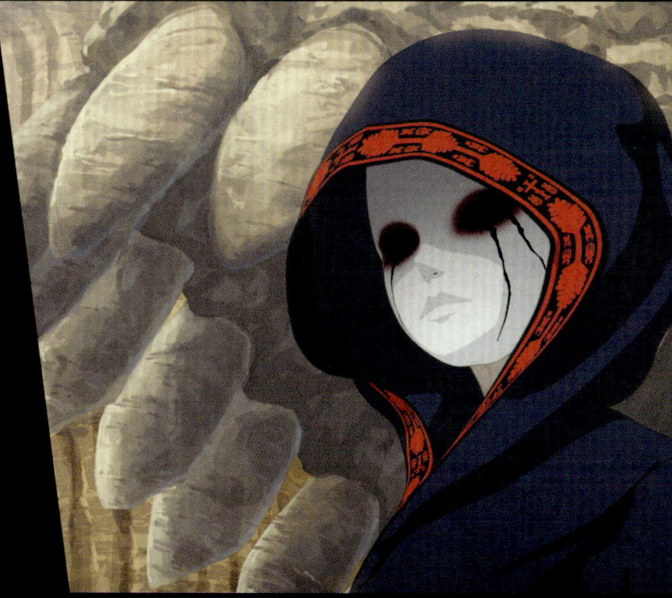

CHAPTER TWELVE

MONSTERS IN THE TEMPLE

Episode Five of Season Two, "Mind, Body, Soul", is a character-heavy episode. Spyder offers to take Mei to search for her real family, but she opts to stay with Taylor, Hayley and Brina. By now, no-one believes Mei's insistence that she's being pragmatic.

Meanwhile, the children connect with their long-lost mother. Despite her joy at having Brina back, Hayley refuses to abandon bOy, especially when Brina confirms the Sisters will use Kaiju transfusions to purge the humanity in him. Finally, Hayley brings up the unsayable—how her parents hurt her by leaving her at Shadow Basin, and how she has a wider family now, one that includes bOy and Mei. (Mei is shocked at this comment, but doesn't argue.) Brina finally agrees Hayley is right; they can't abandon bOy.

Meanwhile, a giant figure marches over the desert—the Apex from Season One, which is still telepathically linked to bOy and has been drawn by his calls for help. His progress is witnessed by Shane's former underlings in the Bogan group. They're led by Rickter—it turns out his gunshot wounds courtesy of Mei were not fatal. Until now, we've rarely seen the Apex in daylight, except for a flashback in Season One. Its livid crimson streaks make the giant look even more demonic.

Brina uses her Sister clothes to infiltrate the cult's skull-paved temple, and enters its altar room as bOy's ceremony nears its climax. However, the presence of the High Priestess is too powerful for Brina, who falls under her sway again. Taylor and Hayley also enter the temple, but Brina corners them in a chamber that looks like something from an Edgar Rice Burroughs story, with a stone ledge over a huge pool containing ravening water monsters.

"The visual representation of that pit came from the creative geniuses at Polygon," says Johnson. "I originally wrote it as a chamber with a simple pool of water in the floor since I was trying not to overburden the asset count for Polygon. But Hiroyuki Hayashi inspired his artists to create something quite stunning."

Johnson explains that this chamber pays off a story point from Season One, way back in Episode Three. "The

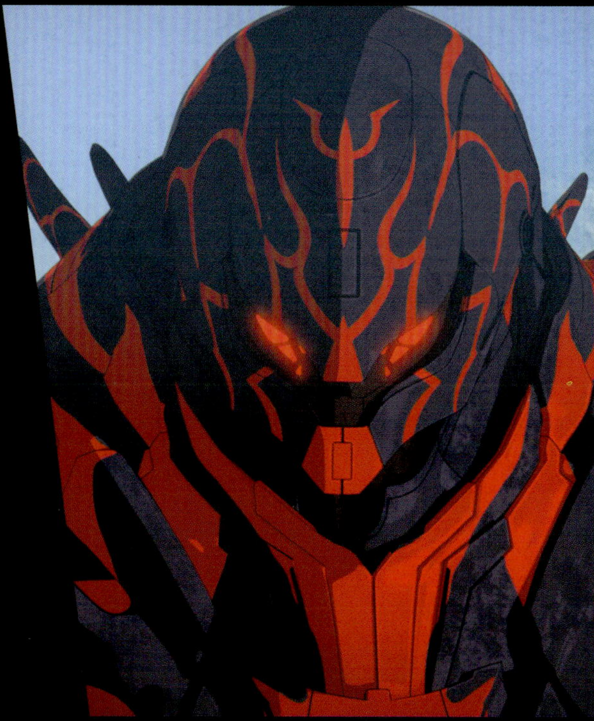

creatures in the water are young Kaiju Eels, hatched from the eggs that were gathered by Shane's people, then traded to Ferno, who traded them to the Sisters." (Ferno was the unseen leader of the group that visited Shane in Season One, Episode Three.) "Our idea is that the Eels would strip the flesh from anyone thrown into the pool, essentially leaving only their skeletons, the skulls of which are used to pave the temple floor."

Luckily, Mei has stolen a Sister's cloak and infiltrates the altar room, literally snatching bOy from under the High Priestess' nose. Meanwhile, the possessed Brina tries to stab Taylor, but can't do it; the emotional conflict snaps her back to her senses. They all race for the temple entrance, but Brina holds back to deal with the Sisters' Rippers. She kills one, but is badly mauled by a second Ripper before she manages to dispatch it, showing a level of savagery comparable to bOy's.

Brina staggers to the entrance, and her children help her into Atlas Destroyer. They've rescued bOy, but has the Sisters' ceremony already turned him into a monster?

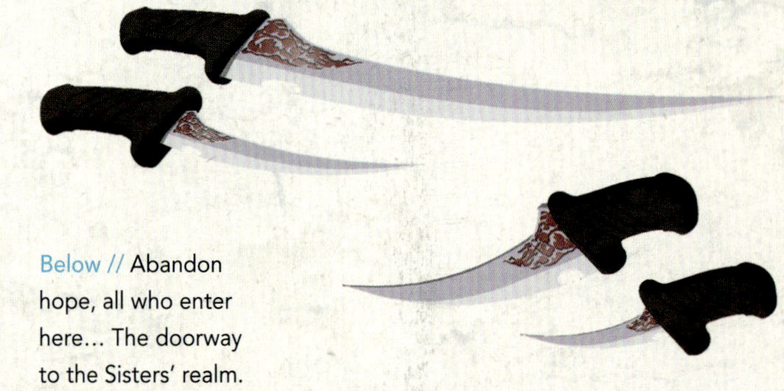

Below // Abandon hope, all who enter here... The doorway to the Sisters' realm.

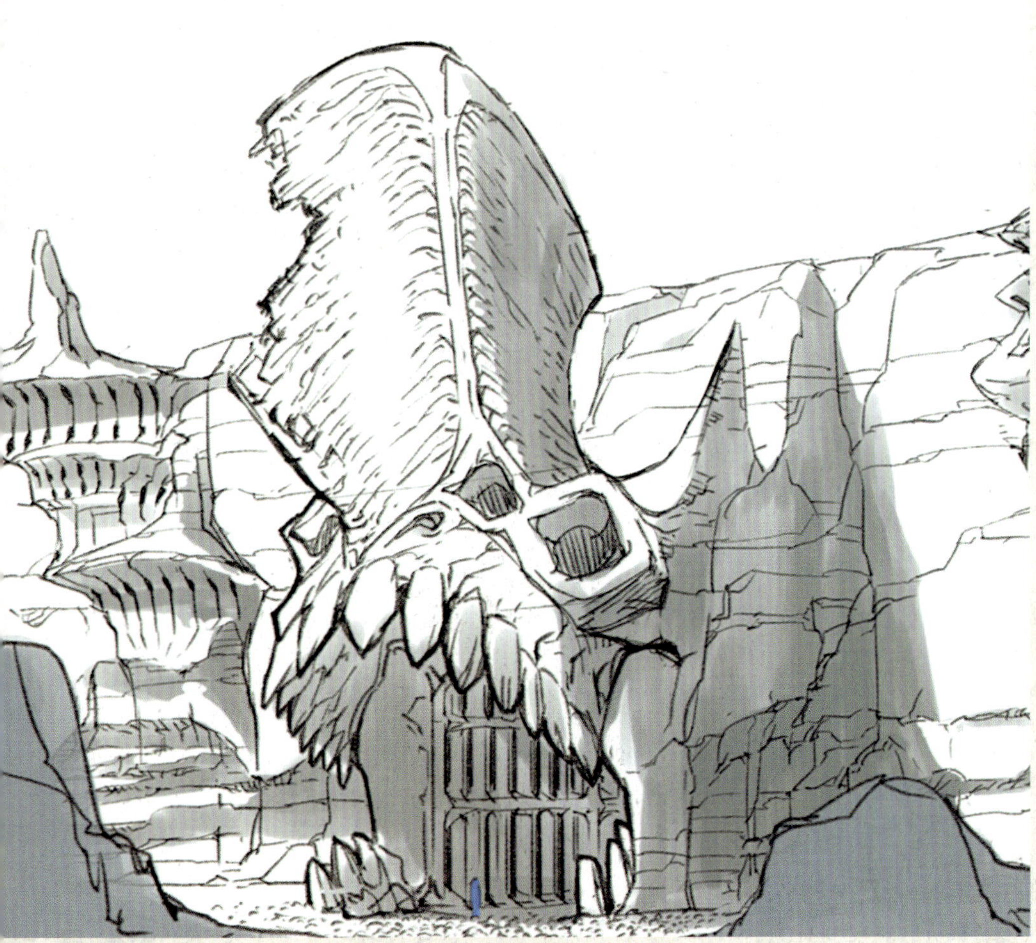

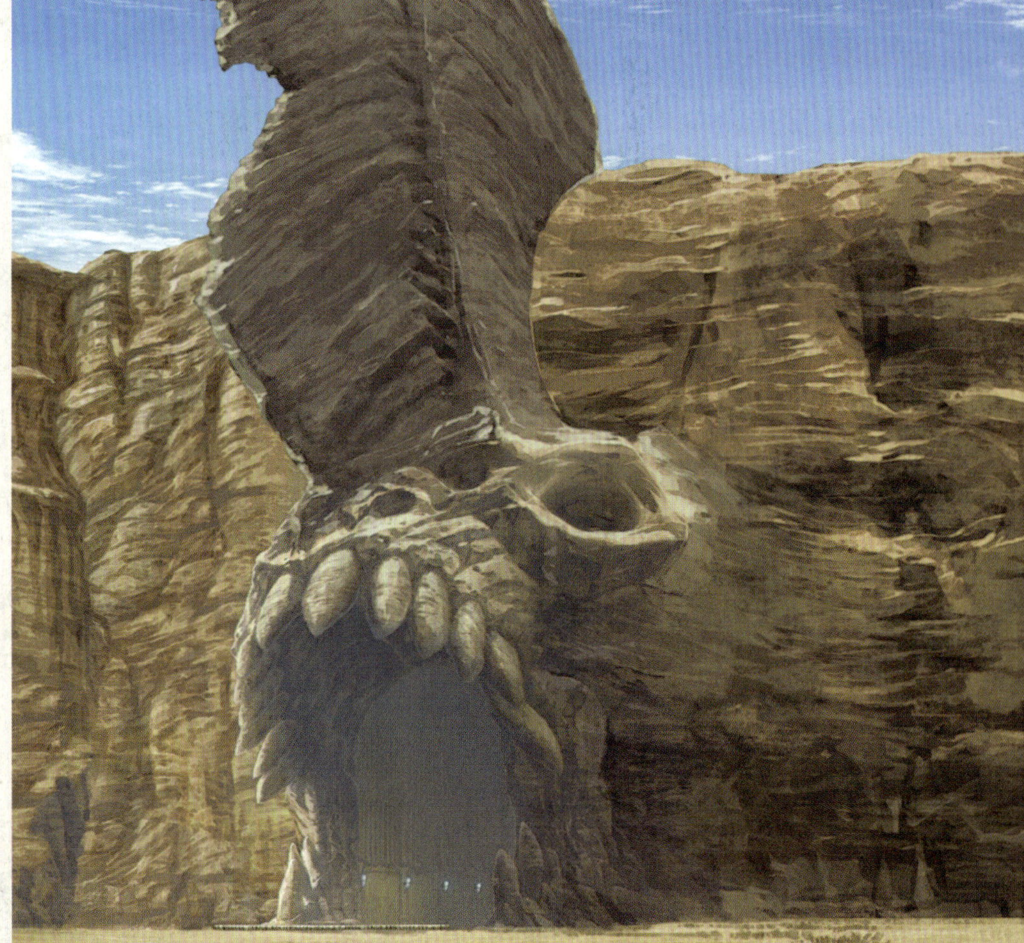

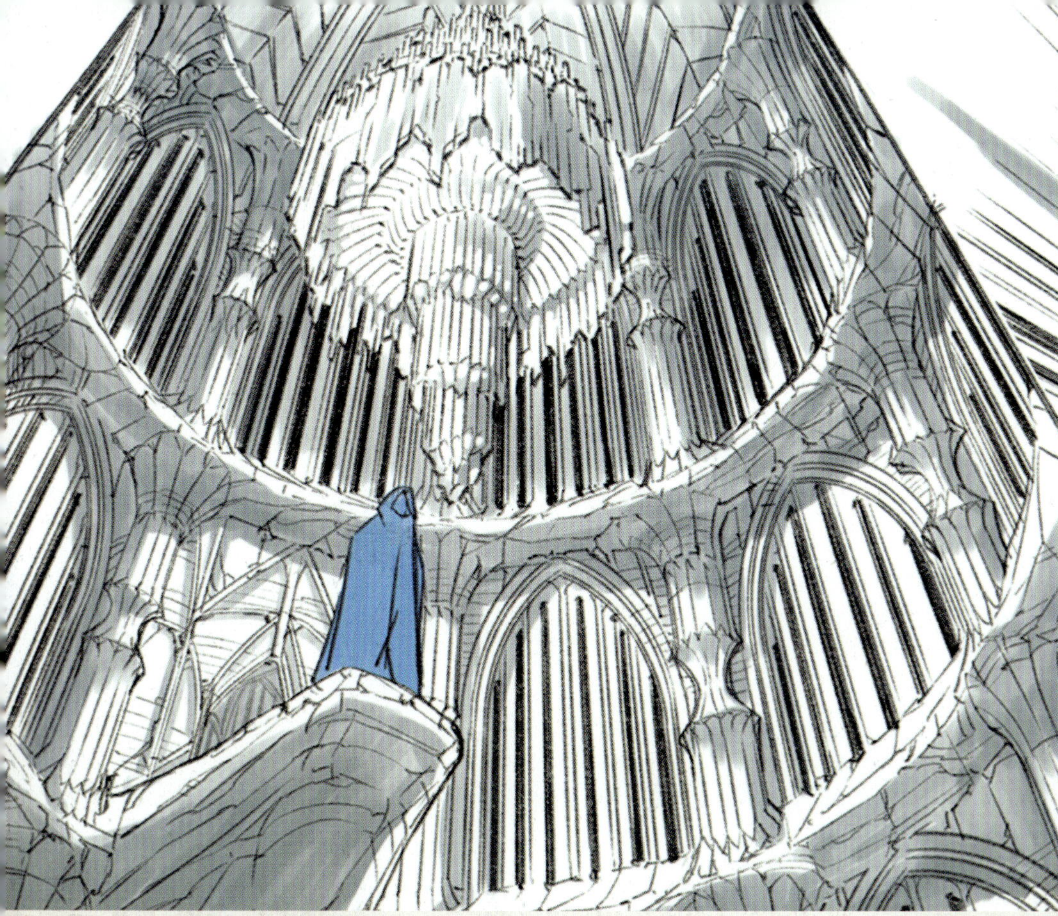

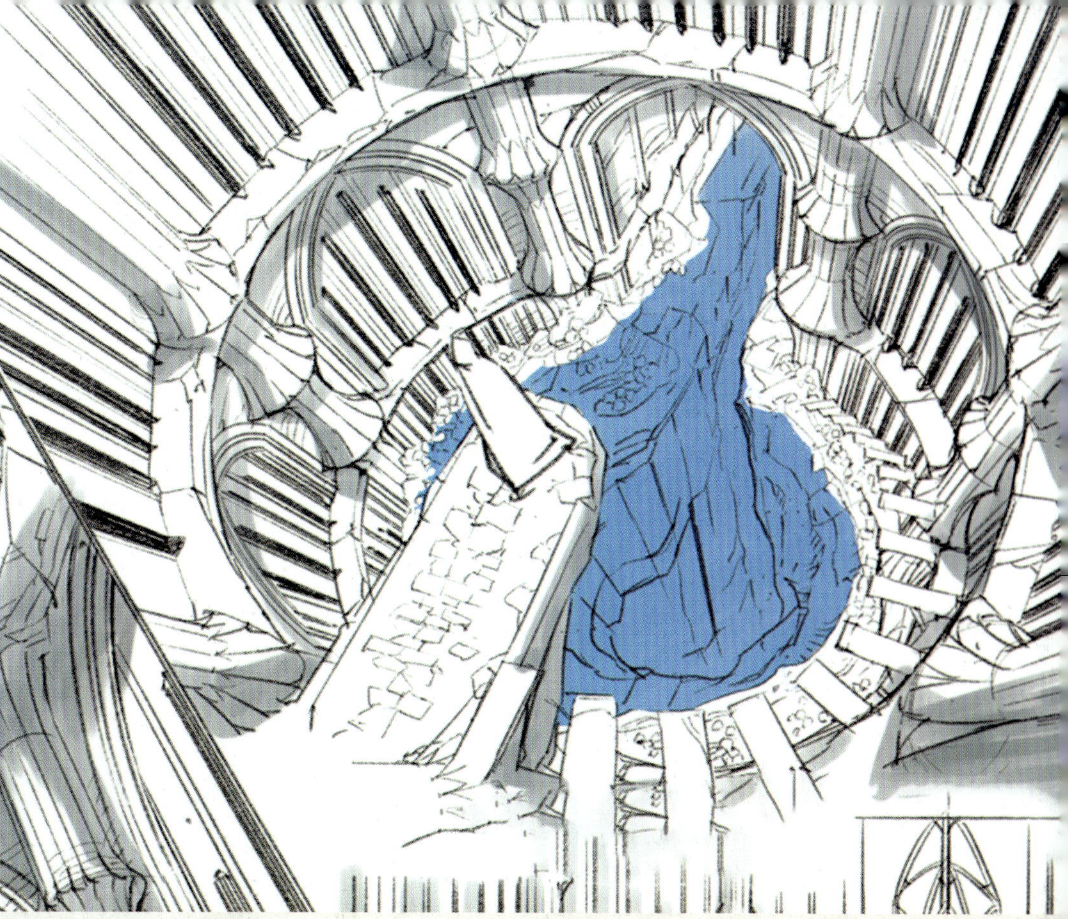

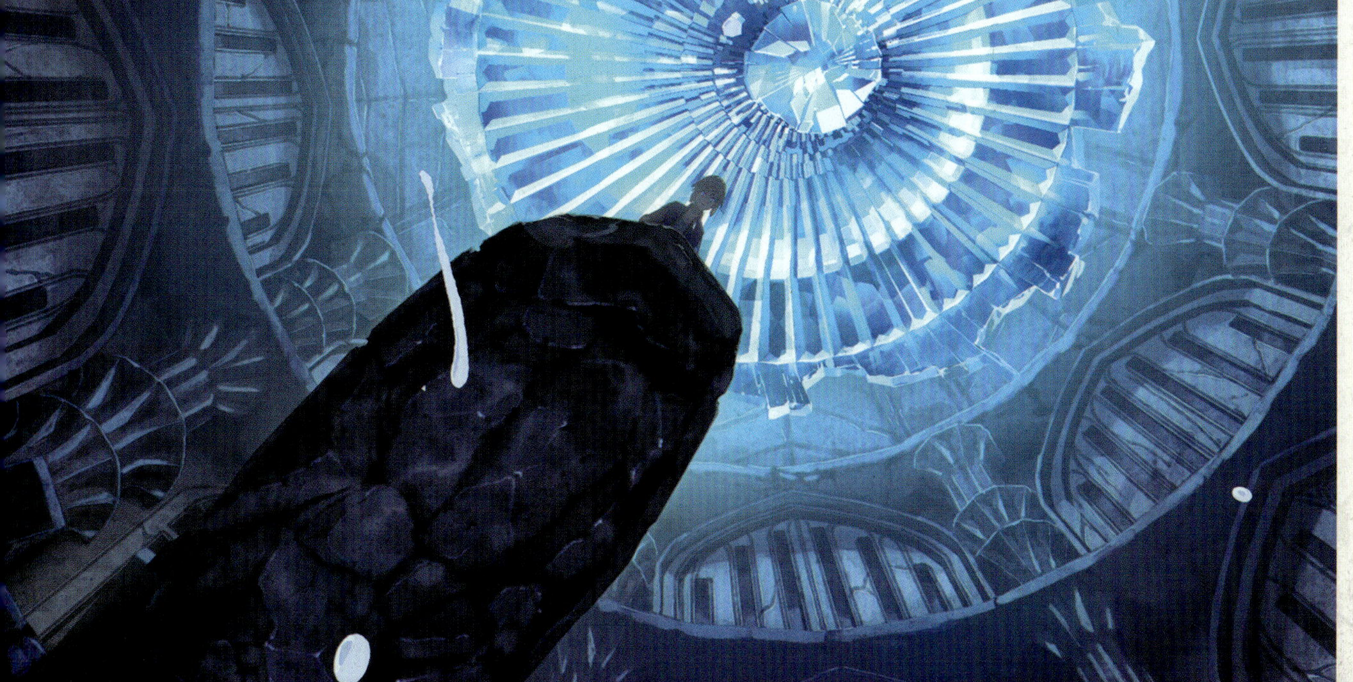

Above and left // Inside, the domain of the Sisters feels like an evil cathedral.

"THE VISUAL REPRESENTATION OF THE PIT CAME FROM THE CREATIVE GENIUSES AT POLYGON."

Greg Johnson, showrunner

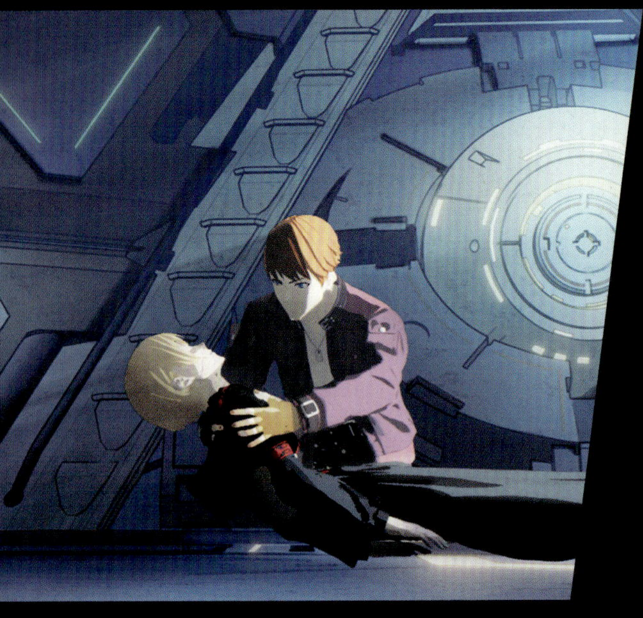

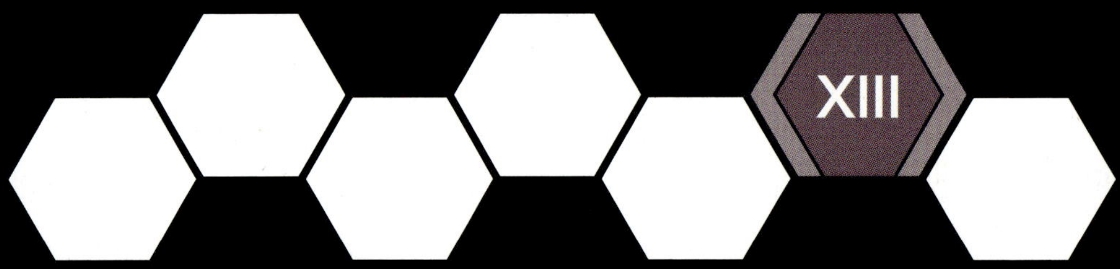

CHAPTER THIRTEEN

LIFE IS BUT A DREAM

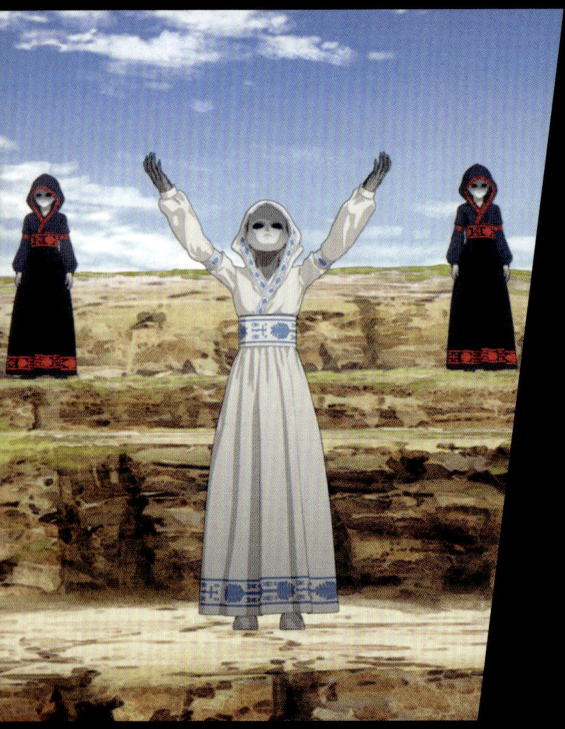

After so many painful trials, Episode Six of Season Two, "The Twilight Run", sees the characters catch something almost never seen in the show—a lucky break. Atlas Destroyer fights through the Kaiju sent by the Sisters, and escapes the cult's territory. Meanwhile, Brina heals from her injuries, and bOy awakes as his old self—the Sisters' ceremony to 'turn' him failed after all.

Then something even more remarkable happens. Atlas Destroyer marches on and on, heading determinedly towards the Sydney base… and it actually gets there. Loa opens communications, and for the first time in five years, the characters hear the voices of the PPDC. In what seems like seconds, the characters are suddenly at the base, emerging from the Jaeger to be faced with yet another miracle. Rushing up to them is Ford Travis, who somehow survived the Sisters' attack in Clayton. Unbelieving, Brina falls into her husband's arms, her family finally united beyond all hope.

If only it was true.

We've already seen a line of shock deaths in the series: Taylor and Hayley's friends in Shadow Basin, Joel, the Bunyip Man, Shane… Now Brina, who was reunited with her children for such a brief time, succumbs. She's not in her husband's arms. She's not even in Sydney. Instead, her last moments are in the Conn-pod of Atlas Destroyer, linked to a Jaeger helmet, still in the Sisters' heartland. Brina never recovered from the wounds inflicted by the Ripper in the temple. Everything since then has been a gift from Loa—a synthetically created dream of family bliss, created by the A.I. to comfort Brina as she dies.

"Just as Taylor and Hayley were Brina's salvation, Brina is theirs," says Johnson. "Craig and I wanted a powerful conclusion to Brina's story, one that fully represents the fierce love and sacrifice of a mother. With everything she has to give, Brina delivers her children from the Sisters. Parents pouring everything into their children is often reciprocated when they're older, and the children ease their transition out of this world. That's what happens here.

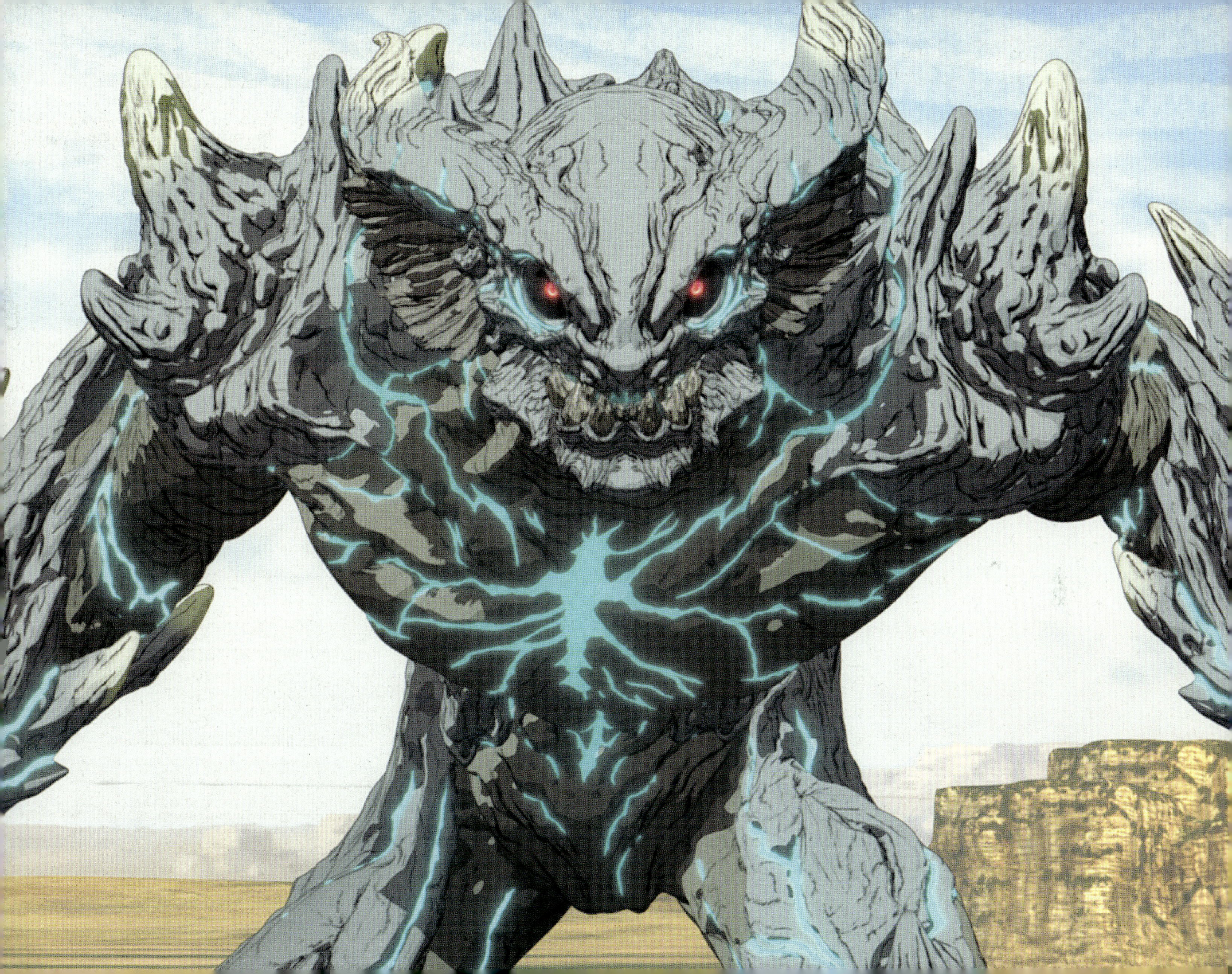

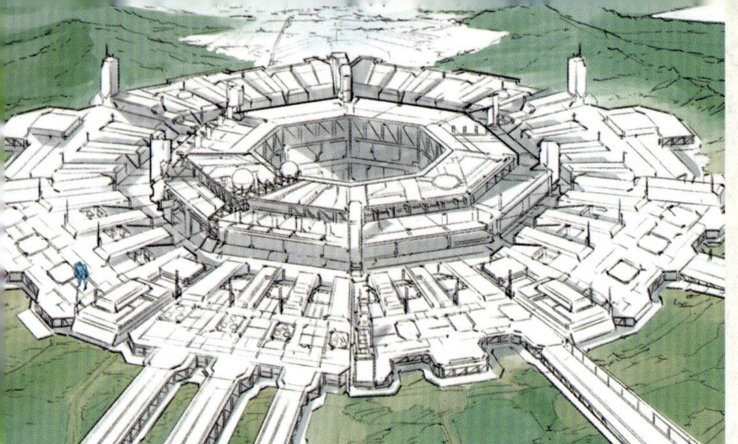

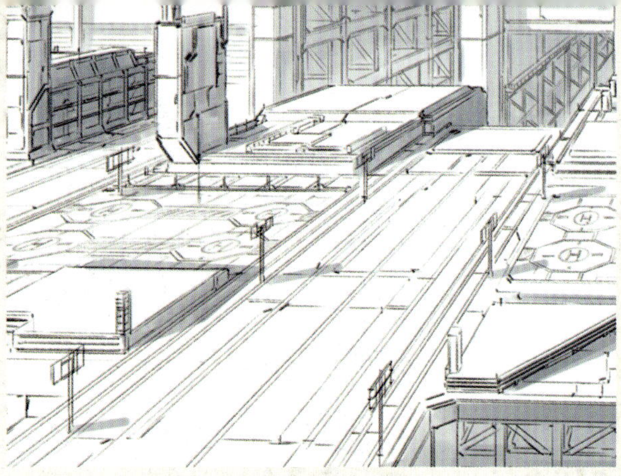

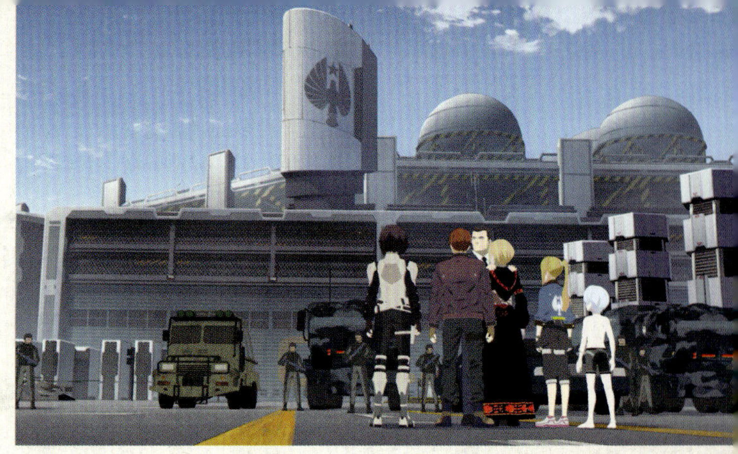

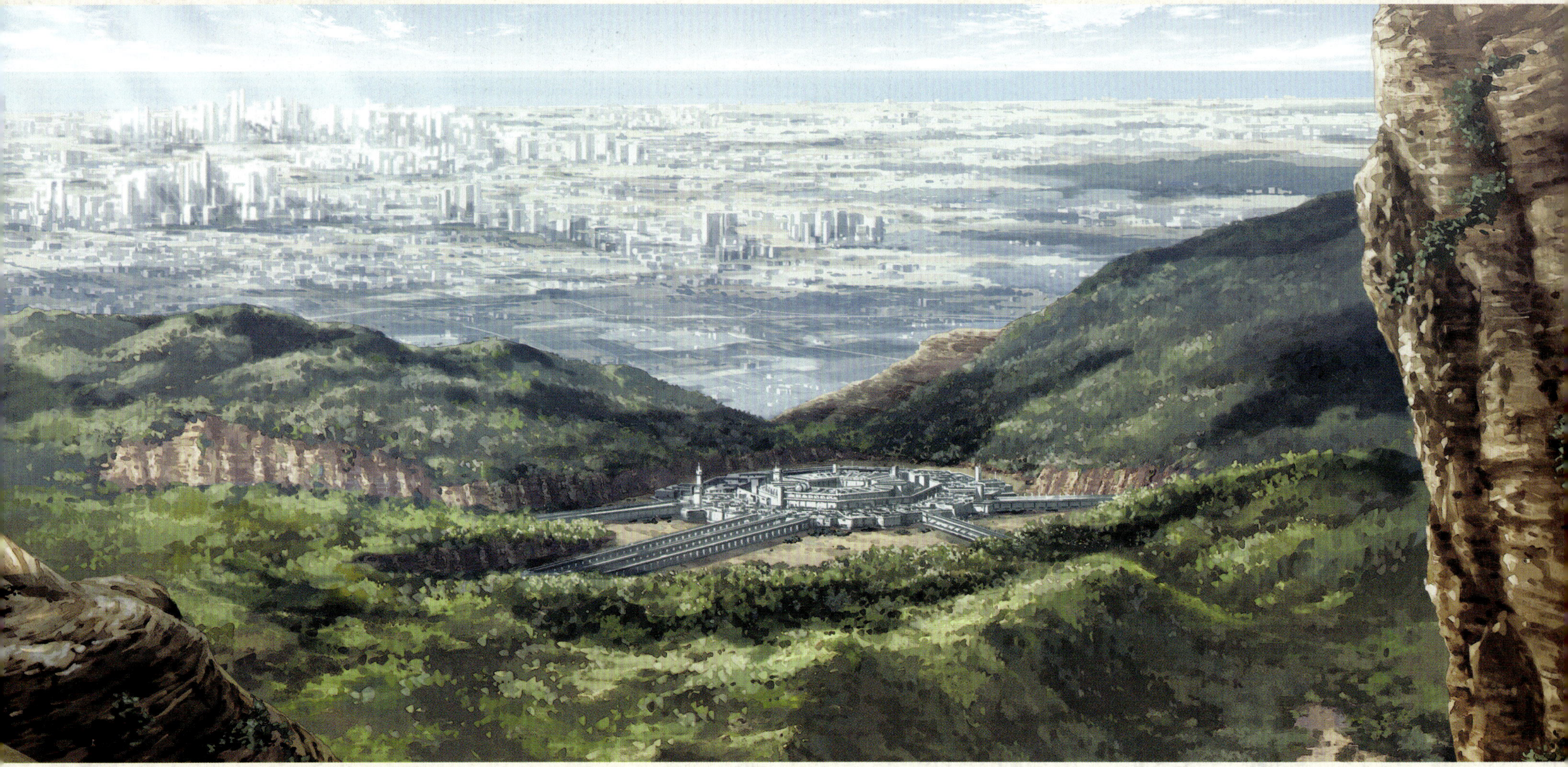

Taylor and Hayley gave their mother the happy ending we all hope for."

The next scenes show that Hayley was right when she talked about a wider family, though she may have overlooked one of its members. On the Jaeger's exterior, she sits quietly with Mei, who's dealing with her own bereavement but doesn't object when Hayley calls her "sister".

In the Jaeger, Taylor pours out his shame and guilt to Loa, saying bitterly that the A.I. can't know what guilt is. Loa corrects him—she was programmed with emotions, and her anxiety for a previous set of Jaeger pilots may have caused their deaths. This pays off a mystery from Season One, when Loa reacted strangely to one of the wrecked Jaegers in the Boneyard.

A new crisis erupts. bOy wakes with the Sisters' chants ringing in his head; he rushes outside the Jaeger and changes into his monster shape. At first he's torn, but the Sisters and their High Priestess have assembled in the desert, and their chanting is too much for him. Roaring, the bOy-Kaiju launches a frenzied attack on the Jaeger. One combatant must destroy the other...

Until a new party shows up: Apex. Holding the struggling Kaiju, it projects a scanning beam at bOy, struggling to recreate their neural bridge from the Boneyard. The Sisters fight back; bOy attacks Apex with all his savagery, plus Kaiju strength. The result is the goriest battle in the series, even if Apex, like the Kaiju, bleeds blue. But in the end, Atlas Destroyer holds bOy long enough for Apex to complete the bridge and restore bOy's mind, though bOy stays in Kaiju form.

Its task finished, Apex sinks to its knees, eyes dimming, and the Drone Jaeger seemingly dies. bOy roars in tribute to his soulmate. Knowing the Sisters will send more Kaiju, the youngsters resolve to race to Sydney at top speed...

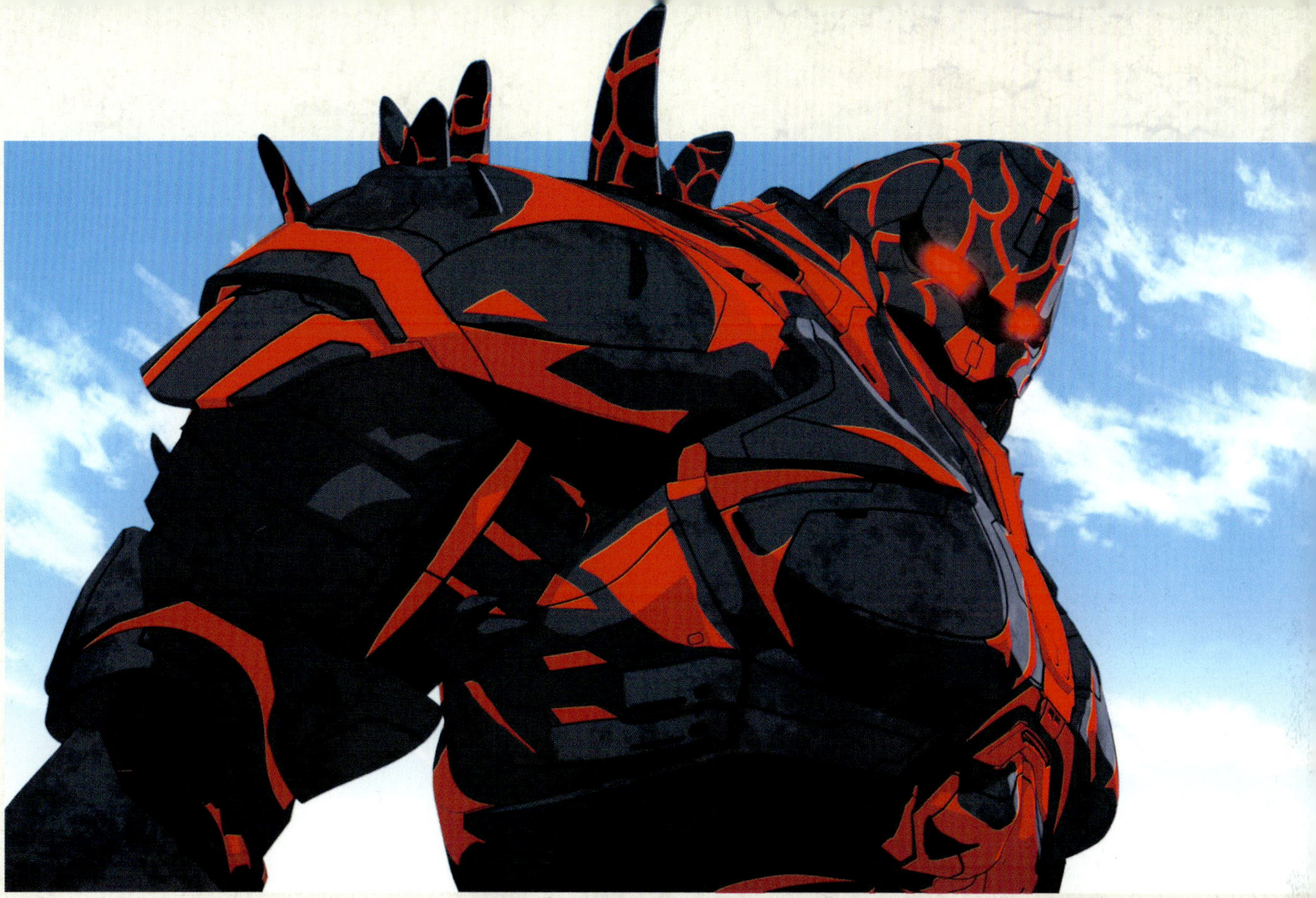

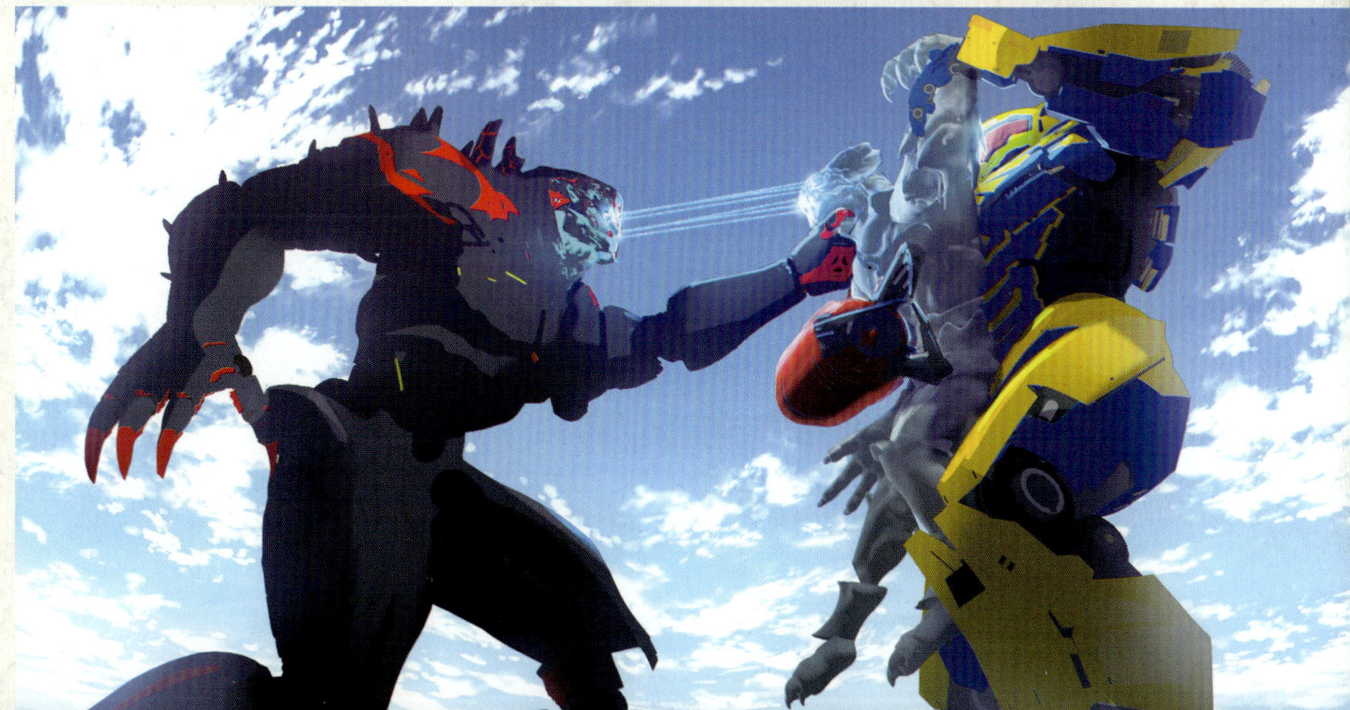

Right // Apex arrives to rescue bOy, its only friend in the entire world, and seemingly giving its life in the process.

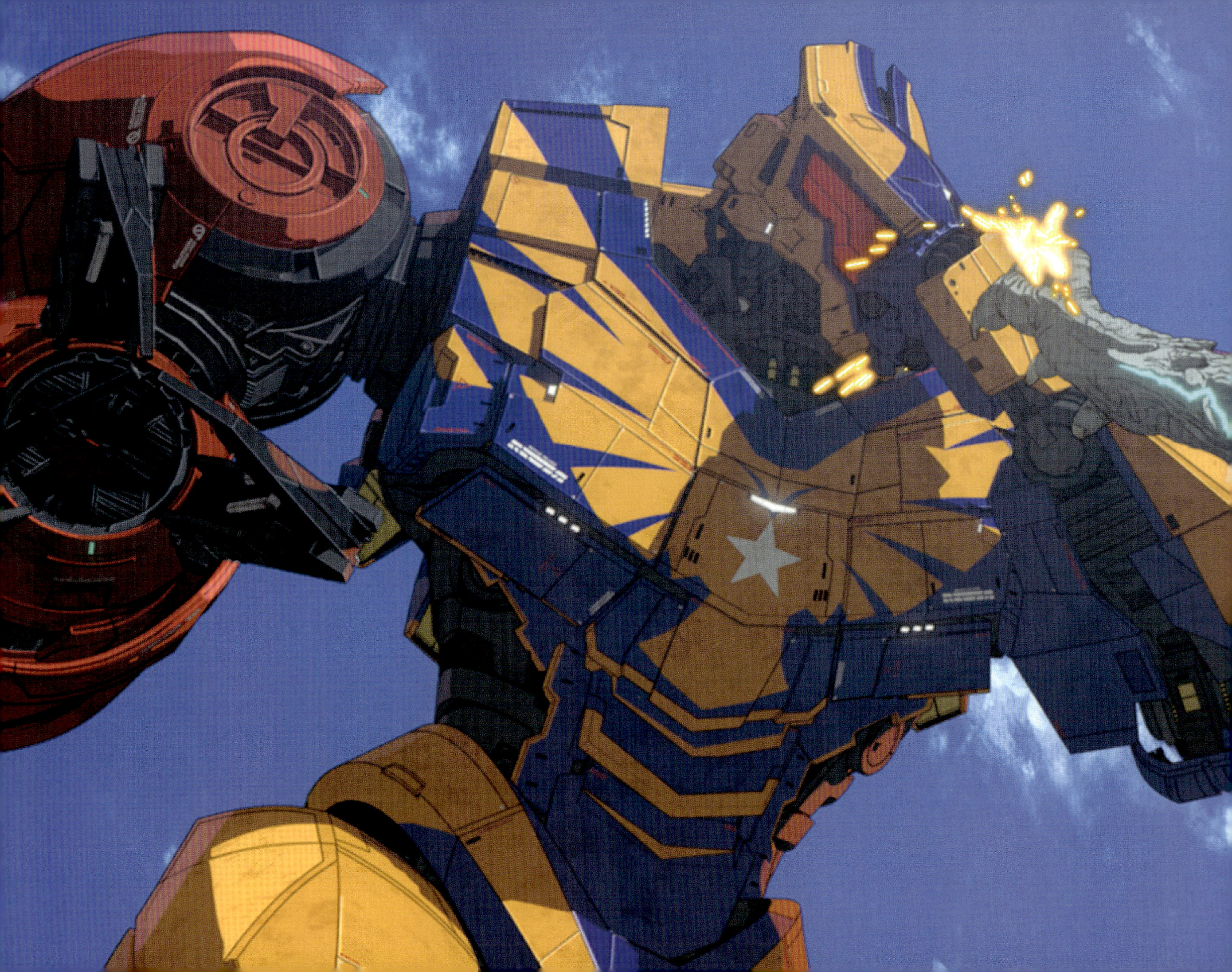

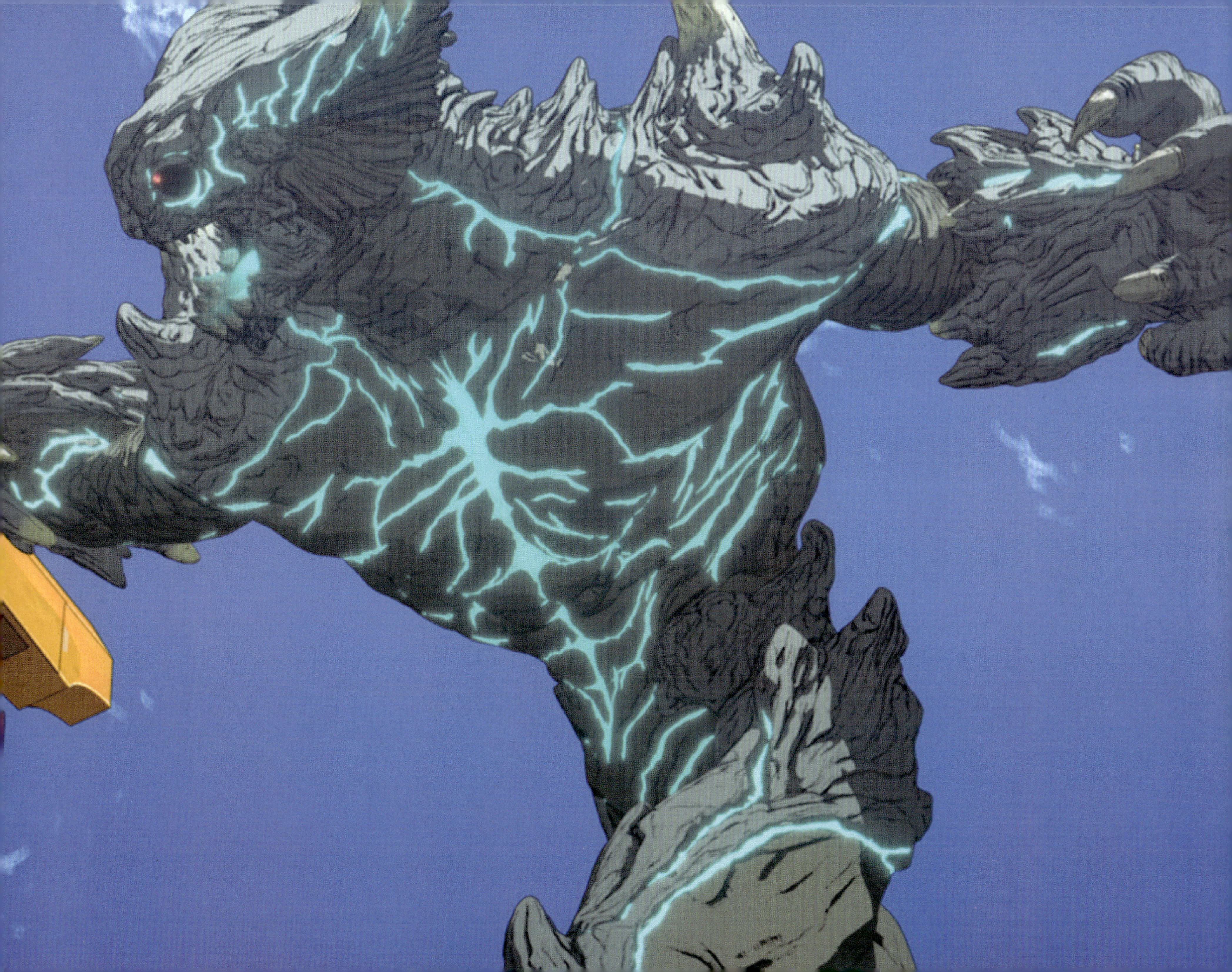

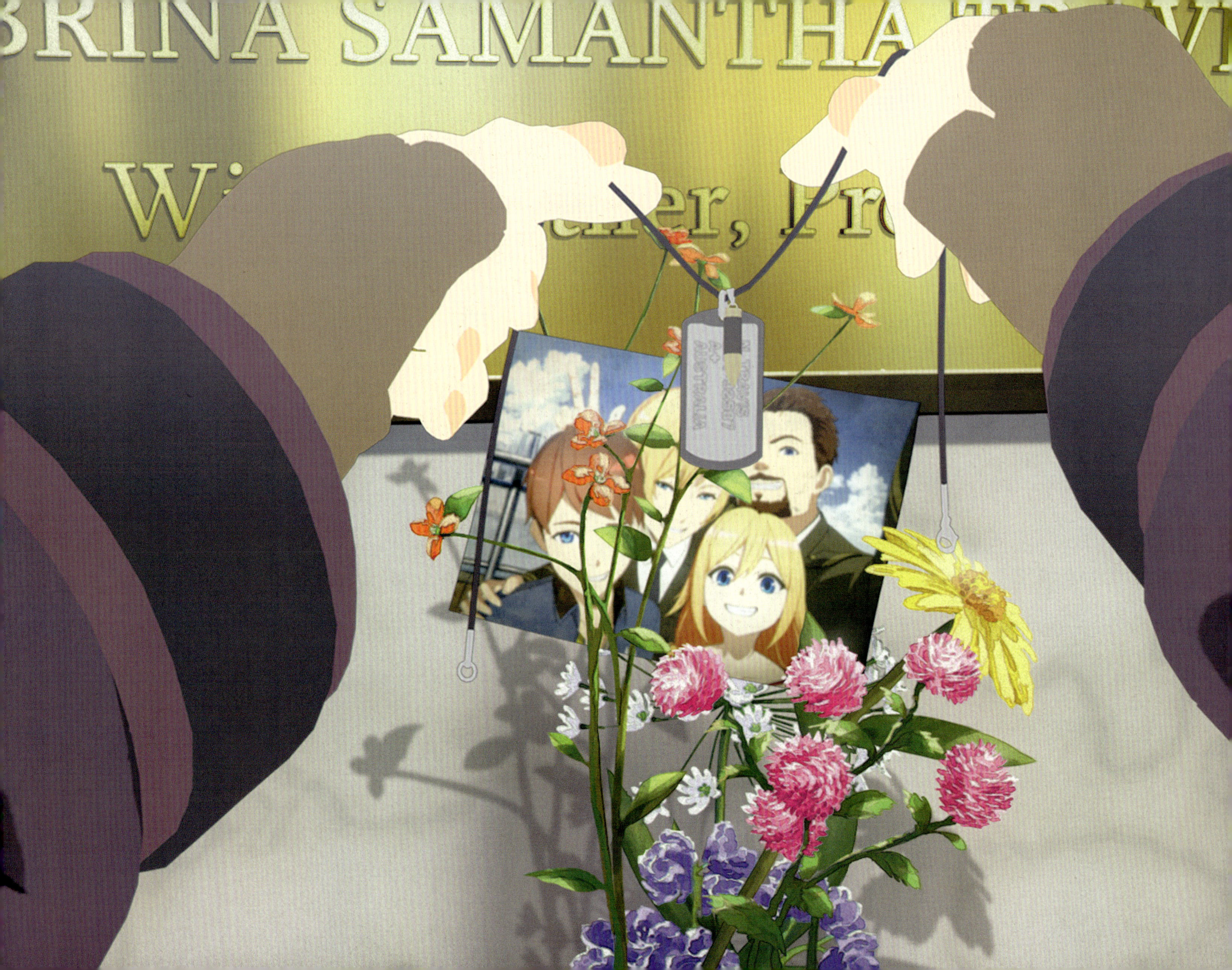
BRINA SAMANTHA

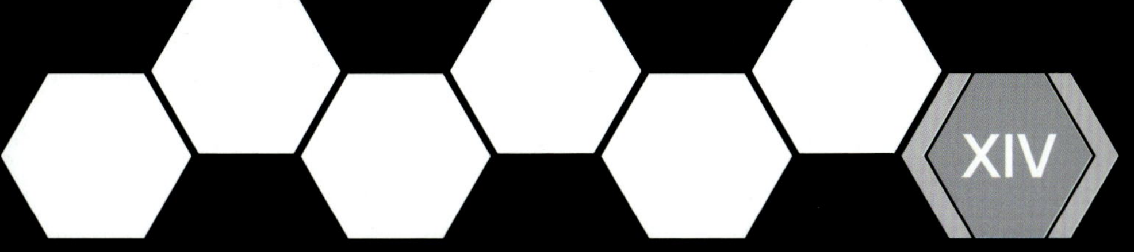

CHAPTER FOURTEEN
IT HAS BEEN AN HONOR

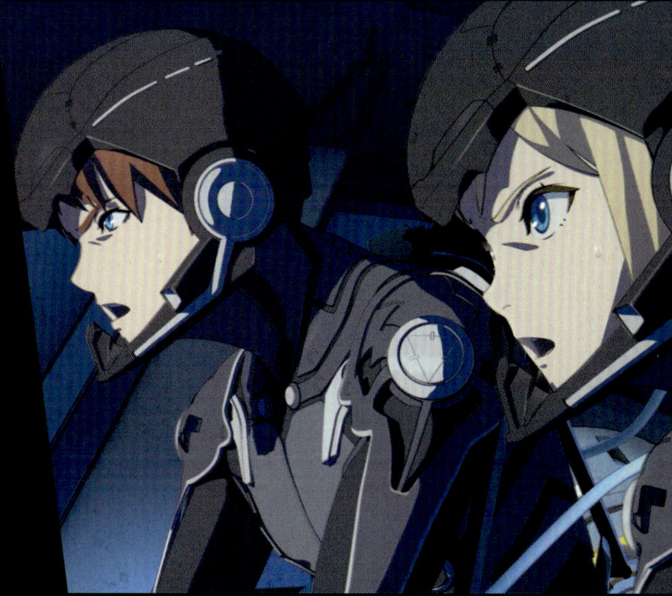

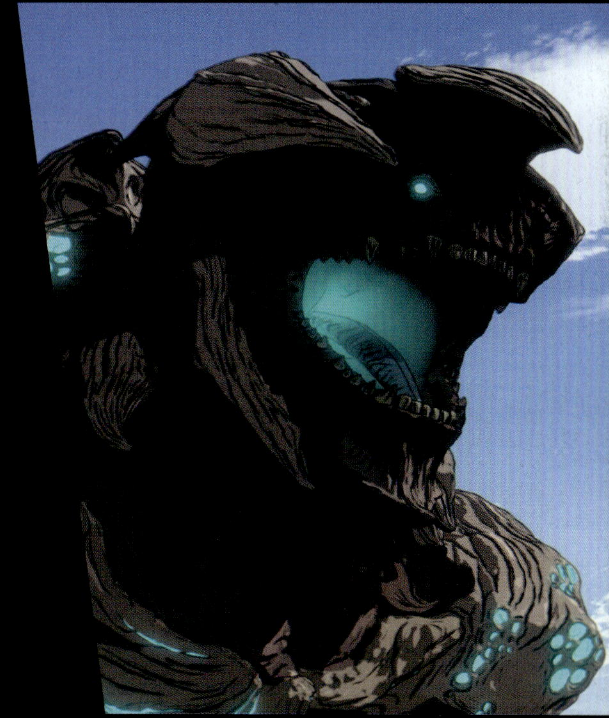

"Final Approach", Season Two's finale, sees a strange group in the desert: Hayley and Taylor in Atlas Destroyer, the Kaiju version of bOy racing along outside, and Mei in an overbuilt buggy left by Shane—the Jaeger's scanner was damaged, so Mei must look out for monsters.

Despite the crisis, there are still family moments. Hayley visits bOy outside the Jaeger, assuring him he will turn back from monster form again—and if he doesn't, she still loves him. Meanwhile, Loa surprises Taylor by declaring he will indeed reach Sydney, a place that doesn't seem real to the boy anymore. The youngsters' hope has infected the A.I.

Unwelcome old friends crash the scene—two full-grown Kaiju Eels, like the one in Season One. Taylor and Hayley do a professional job of killing one, Drifting like veterans, but they're floored by how quickly bOy dispatches his Eel. Even Mei concedes that bOy is worth keeping around, while Taylor acknowledges to Hayley that she was right about bOy all along. "Whoever made him, whatever the plans were for him, you changed it all."

Then everything ramps up…

As the Jaeger nears Sydney, the Sisters summon their biggest beast, a towering biped called a Breacher. It doesn't look so different from bOy, but it's much, much bigger. "Copperhead was the main villain from Season One," says Kim, "and we need something bigger and stronger for the final battle with Atlas because this is a robot anime, right? The Breacher is the last Kaiju to battle with Atlas. We went through early Kaiju designs provided by Polygon and found one, but bulked up the size so it could damage Atlas right."

As the Breacher approaches, Atlas Destroyer comes into communication range with Sydney base. We've already seen the building and staff in the simulation Loa made for Brina, including base commander Rask (voiced by Nolan North, who gamers may know as Nathan Drake in the *Uncharted* series of video games).

Unfortunately, when the Jaeger opens communications, things don't play out as they did in the simulation. As far as

Sydney Base is concerned, Atlas Destroyer was detonated five years ago, as Loa mentioned in the very first episode. Given the sight of bOy-Kaiju on their scanners, not to mention the Breacher, Sydney Base sends up a storm of missiles.

bOy is stunned by the blast. Undeterred by the missiles, the Breacher catches up with the Jaeger and lays into it like the world's biggest boxer. Many of the Sisters are destroyed in the blast, but the High Priestess survives and unmasks. Beneath, her face is monstrous, more Kaiju than human. "We wanted the Sisters to take their devotion even further by introducing Kaiju DNA into their bodies, which alters them physically," says Johnson.

Kim points out that the High Priestess' reveal is a deliberate contrast to the previous reveal of Brina—for all the changes wrought on her, Brina was identifiable. "The High Priestess was the opposite," Kim says. "The ugliest

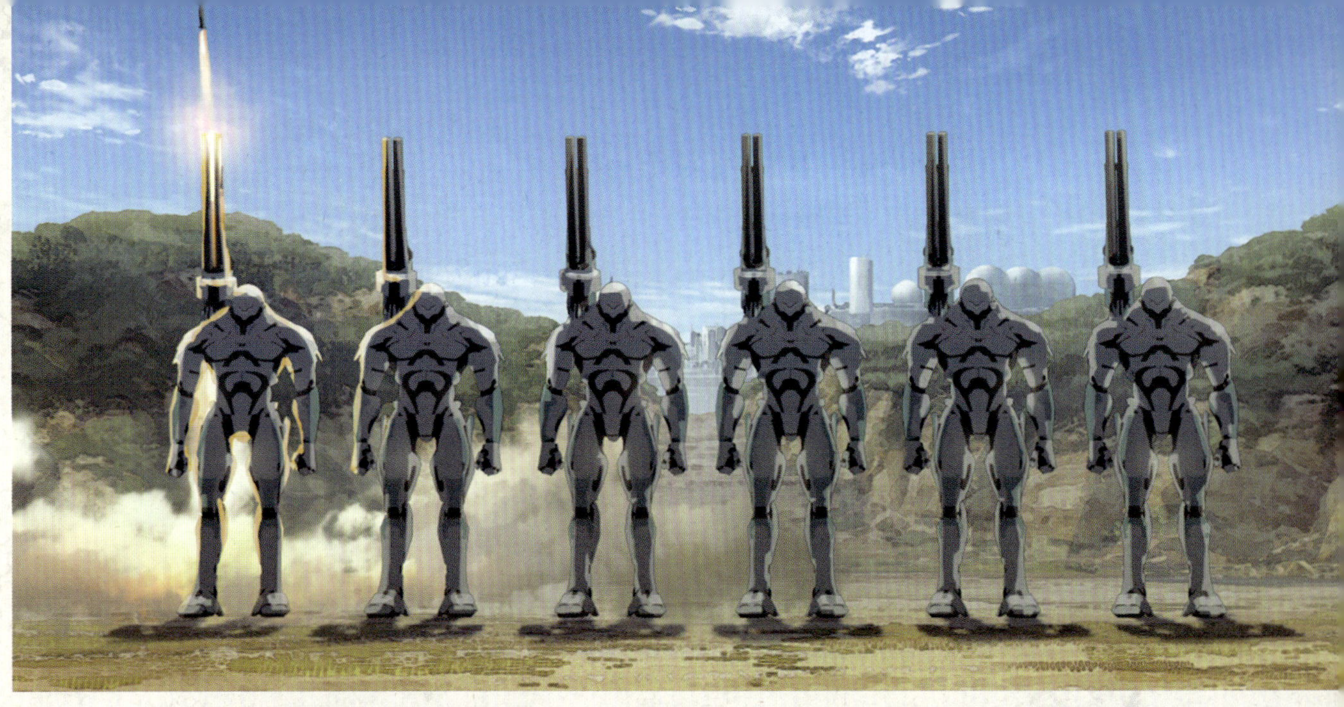

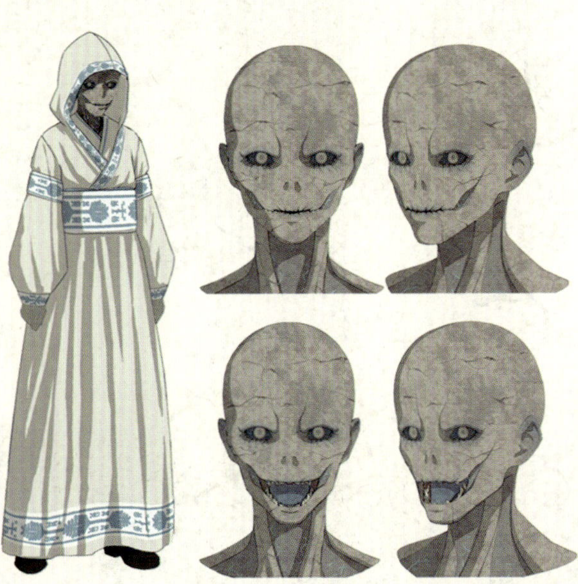

Above // Take heed—if you inject Kaiju DNA into your body, this is how you'll end up.

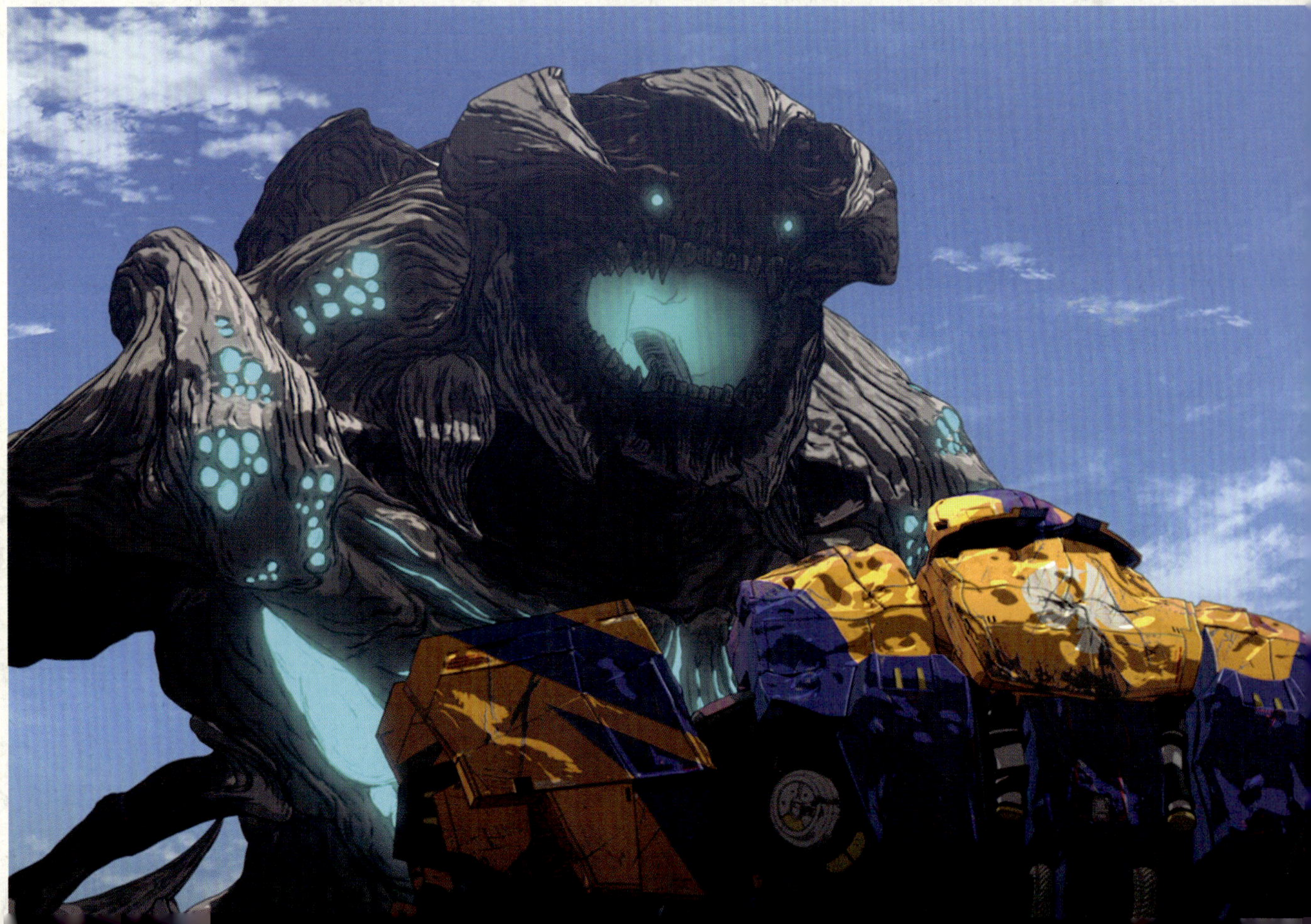

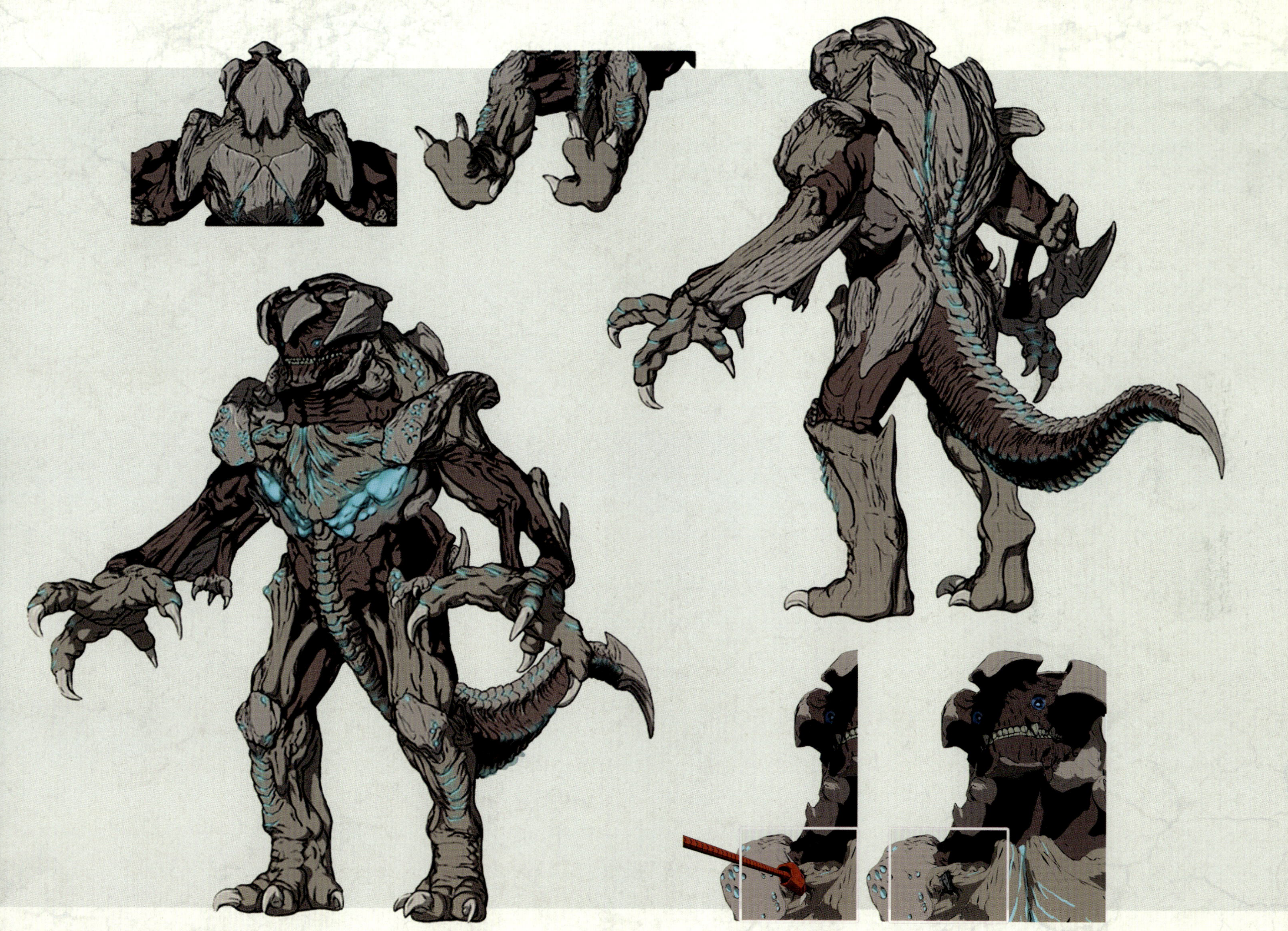

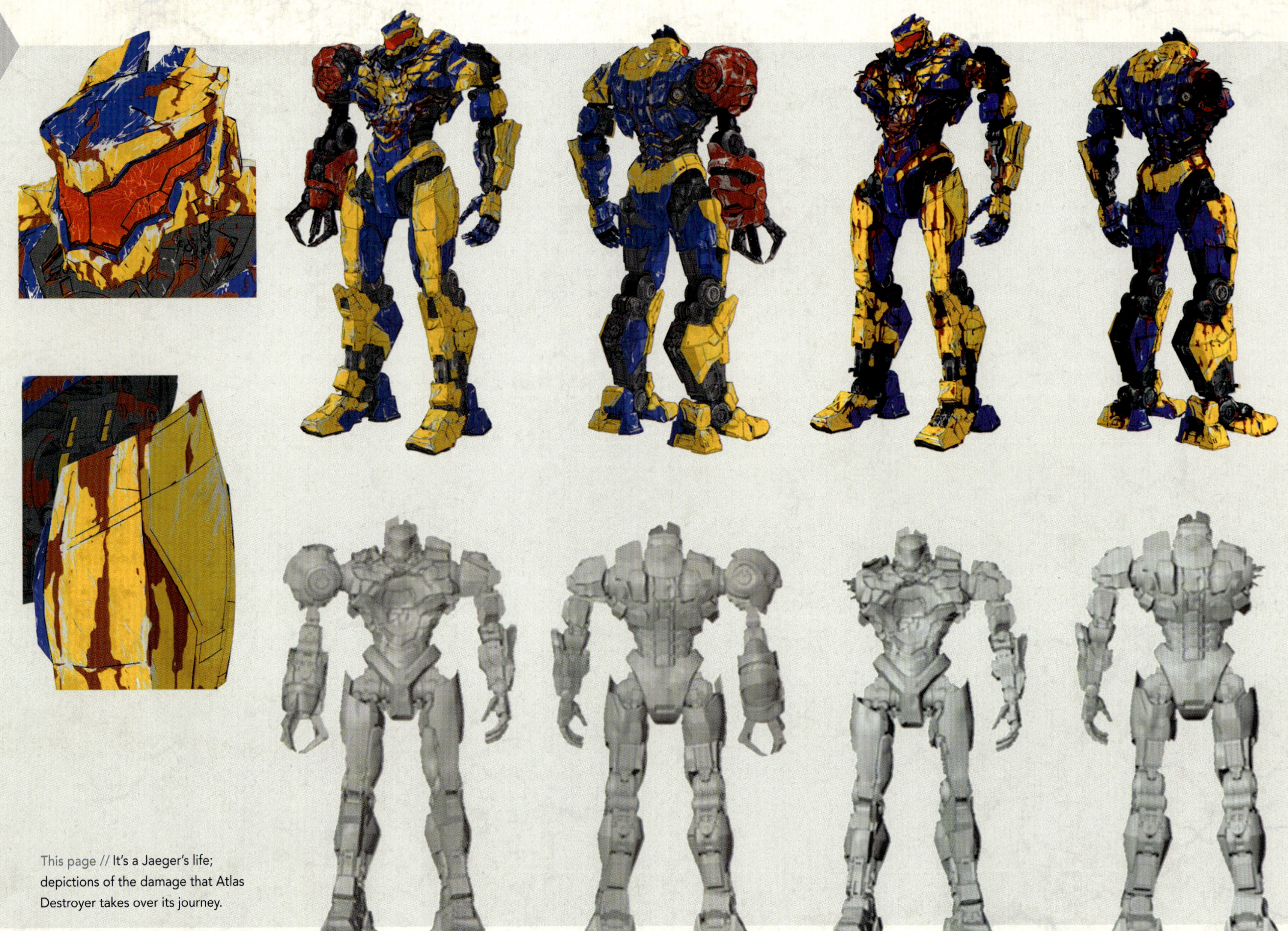

This page // It's a Jaeger's life; depictions of the damage that Atlas Destroyer takes over its journey.

face was requested, and it needed to be more shocking to the audience."

Mei confronts the High Priestess, standing over a seemingly helpless human-sized bOy. The Priestess claims Mei is as ruthless as she always was, and tells her to discard her fake family—exactly what the Priestess was telling bOy all through the season. It doesn't work on Mei, but she's distracted fighting a Ripper, and the Priestess flees with bOy… until he wakes up and runs her through with his hand. At last, his tormentor is finished.

But it seems Hayley and Taylor are too; Atlas Destroyer has taken a lot of damage over the series, but it's nothing compared to what it suffers now, with oil gushing from its chest like blood. For Kim, it's the culmination of all the Jaeger's previous battles, especially the moment when Copperhead ate the Jaeger's arm in Season One.

Kim says, "I really want the audience to feel the same way that Atlas Destroyer feels. It's not just about the pilots, I want the audience to be synched up with the Jaeger as well. I wanted the oil to look similar to blood so the audience can feel the pain, even though Atlas is a robot. I wanted the action shots to look more gory, brutal, like mixed-martial-arts fights. Stripping the Jaeger's plates is like taking the flesh out of Atlas."

For all the siblings' desperate courage, the Breacher batters and tears Atlas Destroyer apart until it's crawling in the dirt. In the darkened Conn-pod, Loa announces action must be taken; her pilots must survive.

Starting the Jaeger's ejection protocol, she bids farewell to her charges: to Hayley, the heart of the journey, and Taylor, who's grown into a true leader. "It has been an honor," she says, forcing them into ejection tubes and sending them hurtling out of the Jaeger, where they land at a safe distance as the protocol counts down to zero. Then… Loa detonates, consuming Jaeger and Breacher in a massive fireball.

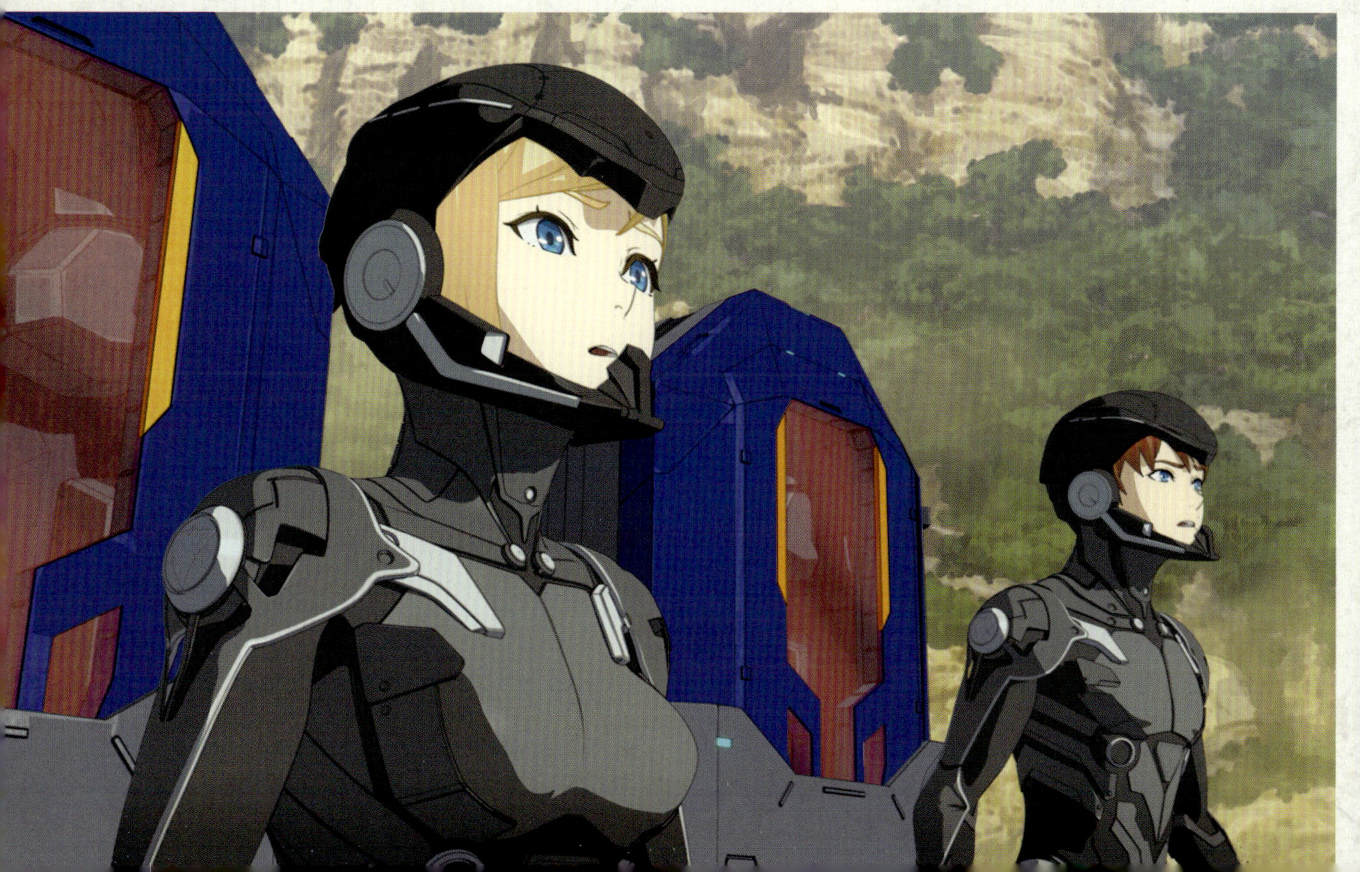

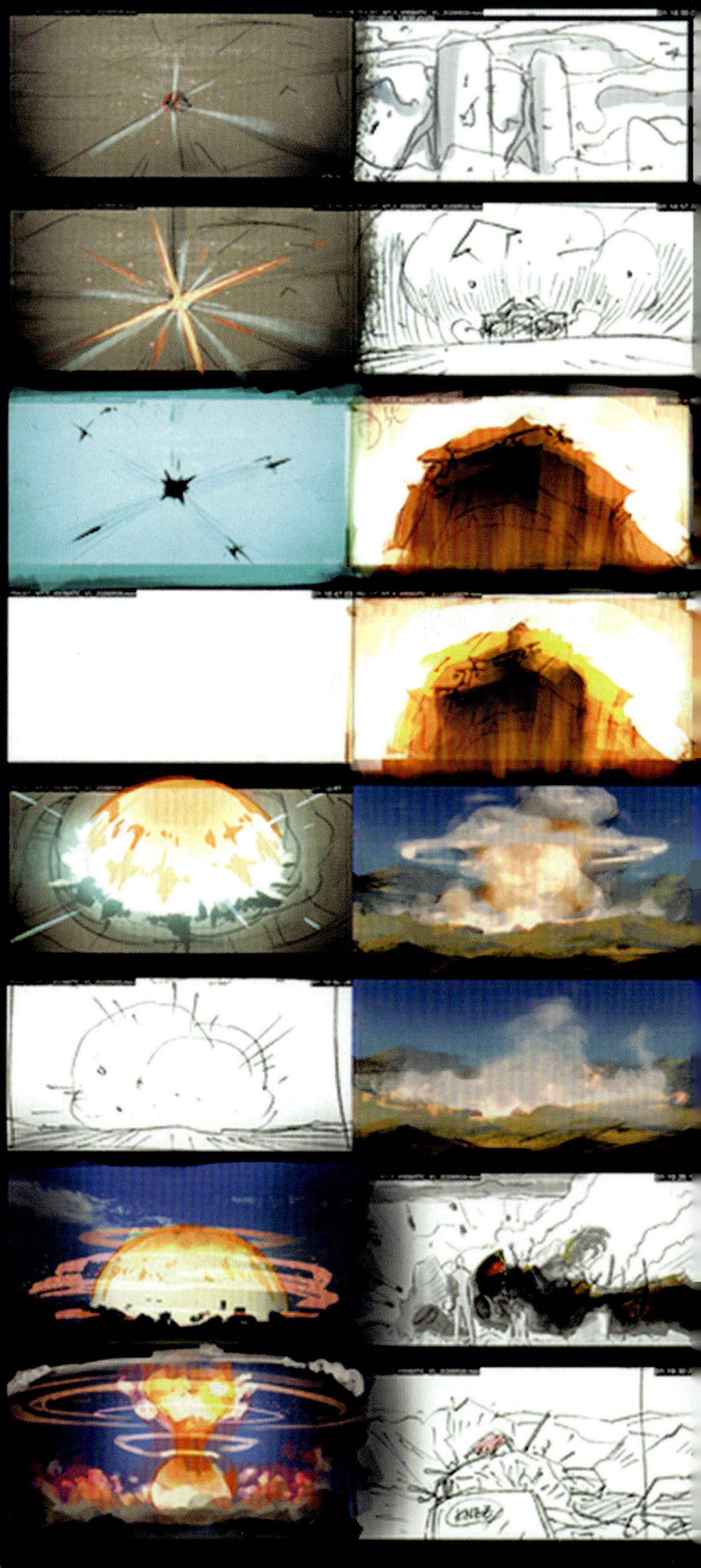

It's an intensely emotional scene, the last sacrifice of the series, and for Hayley and Taylor, the loss of a second mother figure. Or… is it? Some viewers might wonder if Loa is essentially a computer programme, and computer programmes can generally be backed up. Might Loa still be around in some form; for example, on some A.I. equivalent of the Cloud?

While Johnson won't be drawn on details, he says, "I think it's a fair assessment that somewhere Loa still exists."

Atlas Destroyer isn't all gone. Its battered head and one arm lie in the vast crater that marks its last stand. Mei and bOy hurry up to the scene; a sobbing Hayley embraces her white-haired, human-sized, half-Kaiju brother. Taylor and Mei smile at each other wearily, then turn at the sound of aircraft arriving from Sydney Base.

And so the journey ends, perhaps. The last minutes of the series are full of memories—we see a family photo that Shane walked through previously in the Drift, and flash back to Brina's farewell to a young Taylor at Shadow Basin. As Hayley and Taylor pay their respects to Brina's memorial in Sydney Base, they know their past will be with them always. As for their future…

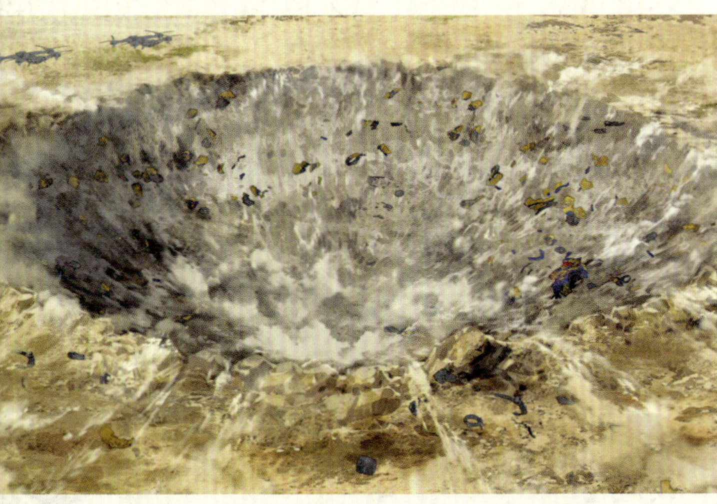

Above // The final resting place of the heroic Atlas Destroyer.

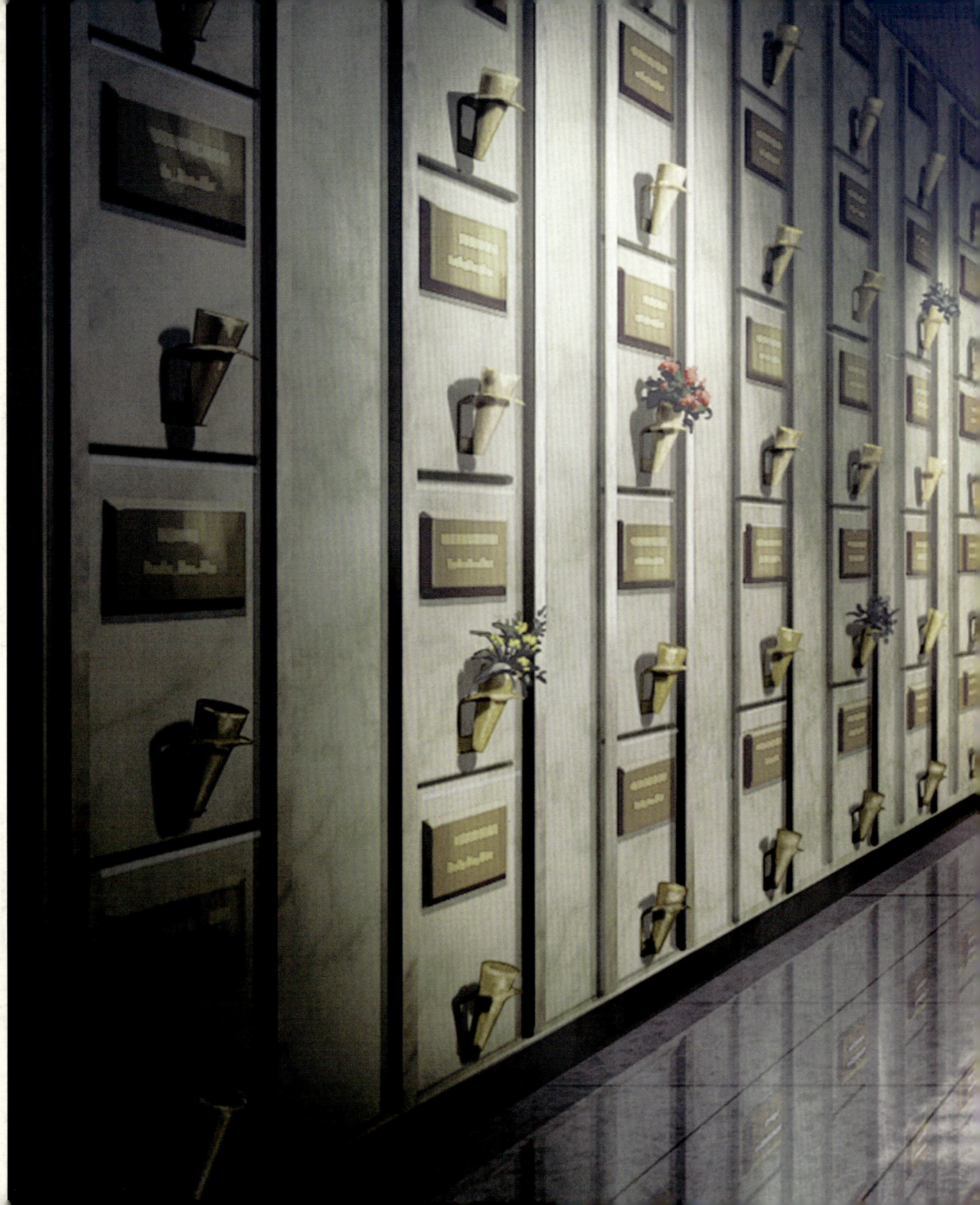

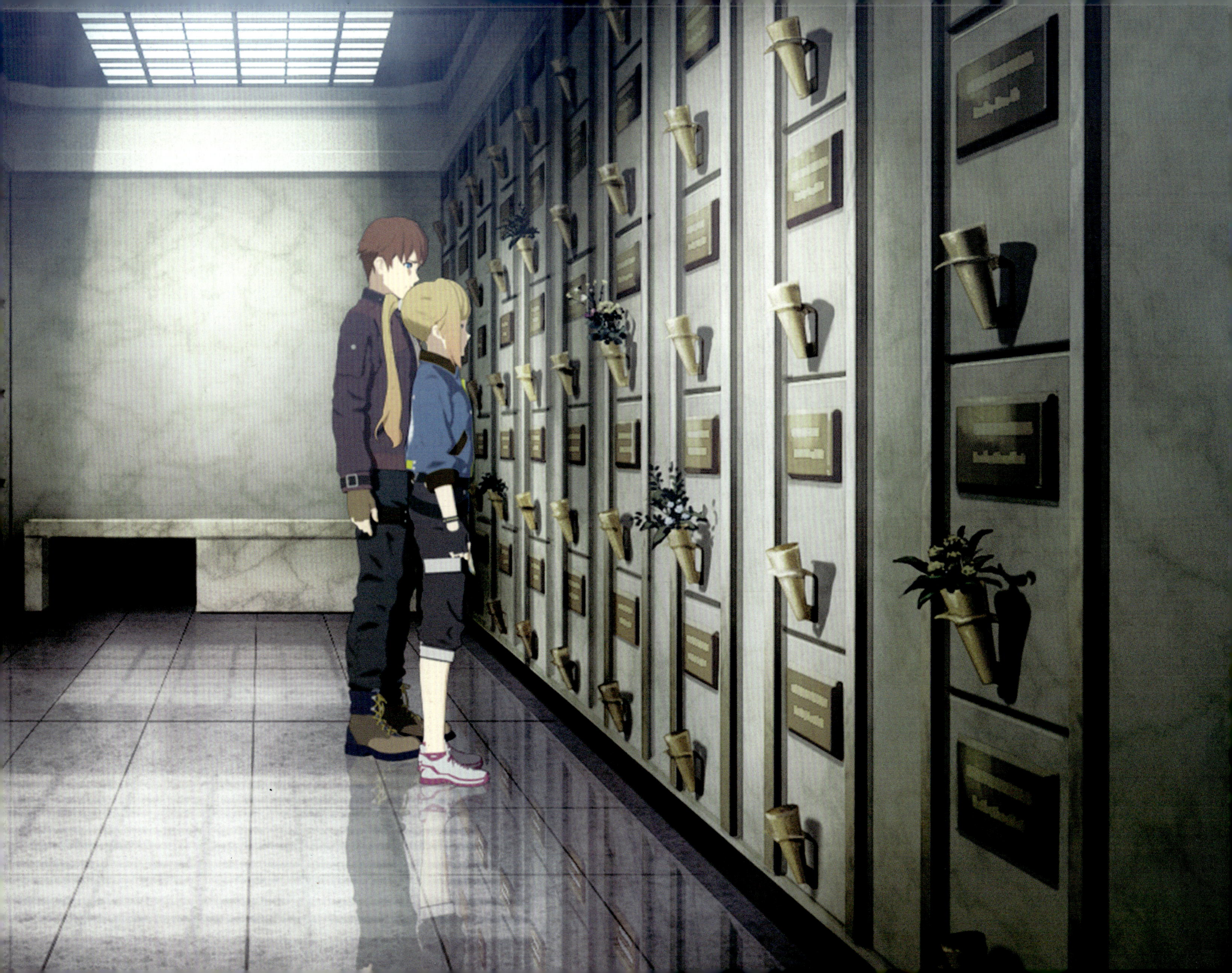

ACKNOWLEDGMENTS

My thanks to all the interviewees in this book for so generously giving up their time to answer my questions; to Robert Napton at Legendary for acting as a fantastic intermediary; and to Andy Jones at Titan for inviting me to write this book in the first place.

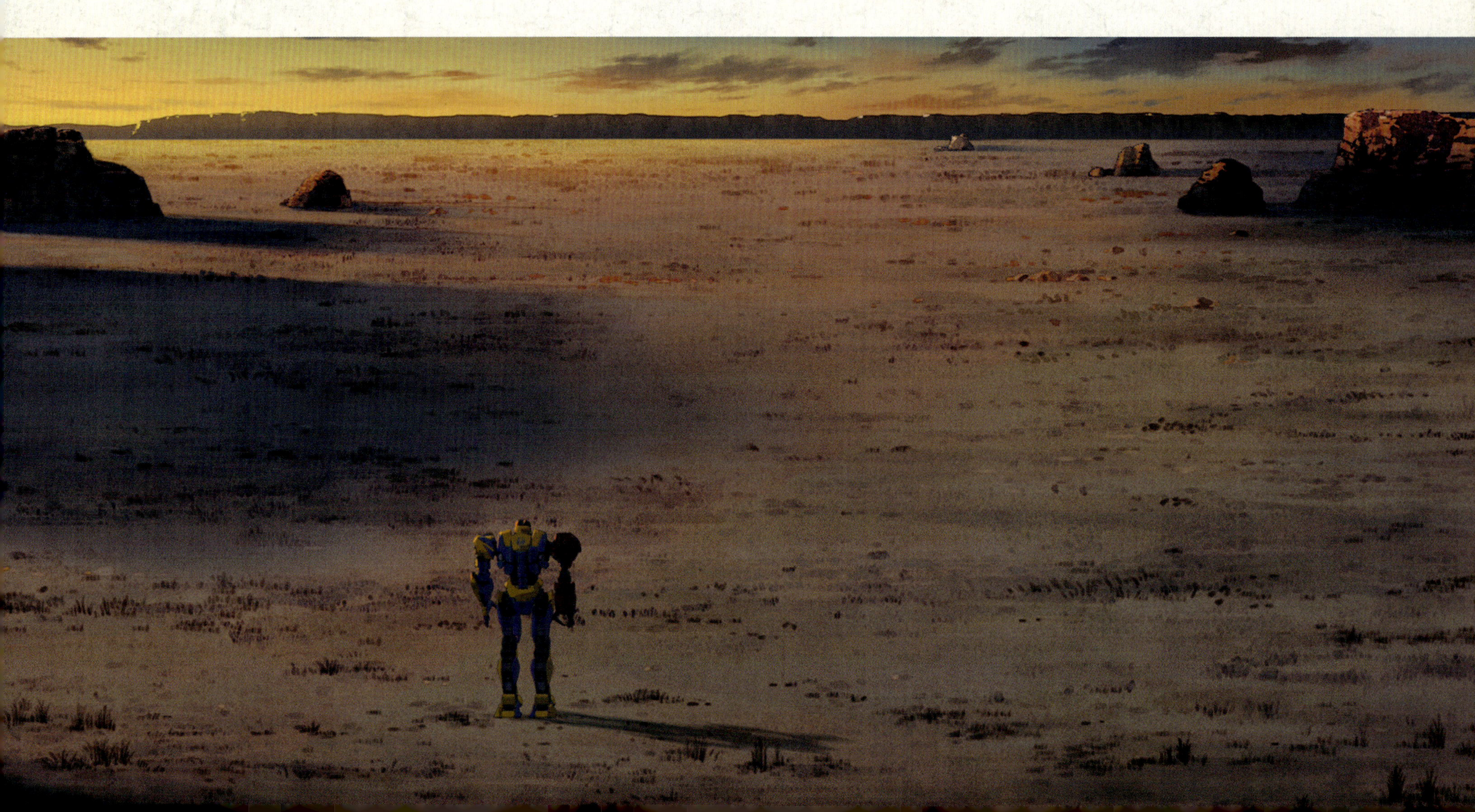

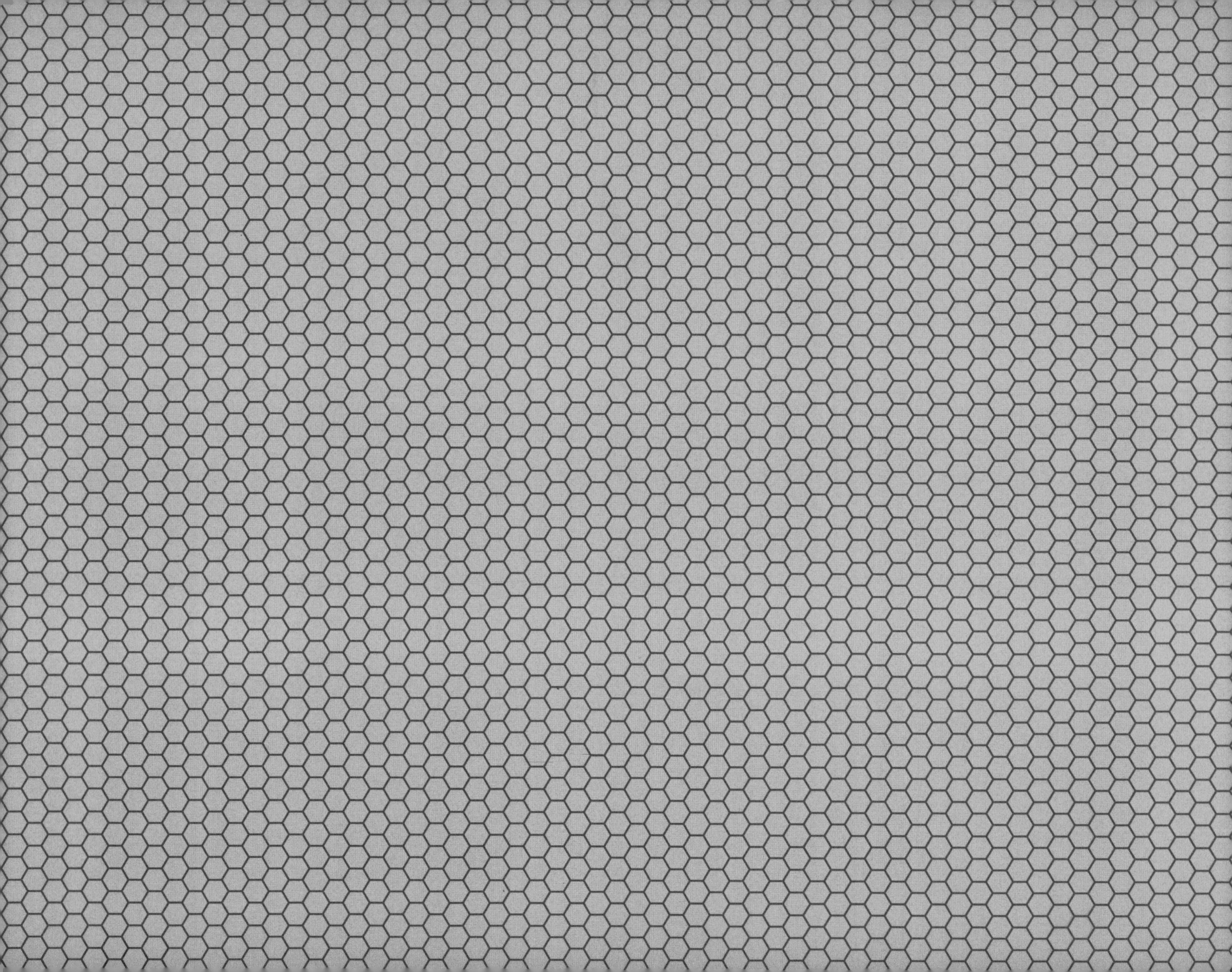